Warfare and Society in Europe, 1792–1914

D0082658

Warfare and History
General Editor
Jeremy Black
Professor of History, University of Exeter

Warfare and Society in Europe, 1792–1914

Geoffrey Wawro

Routledge
Taylor & Francis Group

LONDON AND NEW YORK

First published 2000
by Routledge
2 Park Square, Milton Park, Abingdon, Oxon, OX14 4RN

Simultaneously published in the USA and Canada
by Routledge
270 Madison Ave, New York, NY 10016

Reprinted 2002, 2003 (twice), 2004, 2005, 2006

Routledge is an imprint of the Taylor & Francis Group

© 2000 Geoffrey Wawro

Typeset in Bembo by Taylor & Francis Books Ltd
Printed and bound in Great Britain by
T.J. International, Padstow, Cornwall

All rights reserved. No part of this book may be reprinted or
reproduced or utilized in any form or by any electronic,
mechanical, or other means, now known or hereafter invented,
including photocopying and recording, or in any information
storage or retrieval system, without permission in
writing from the publishers.

British Library Cataloguing in Publication Data
A catalogue record for this book is available from the British Library

Library of Congress Cataloging-in-Publication Data
Wawro, Geoffrey.
Warfare and society in Europe, 1792–1914 / Geoffrey Wawro.
p. cm. – (Warfare and history)
Includes bibliographical references and index.
1. Europe–History, Military–19th century. 2. Europe–History,
Military–20th century. I. Title. II. Series.
D361.W38 2000   99-41813
355′.0094′–dc21   CIP

ISBN 0–415–21444–0 (hb)
ISBN 0–415–21445–9 (pb)

For Cecilia

Contents

Maps

Preface

As a historian, I have been fortunate to come of age in the time of the 'new military history', a genre that does not skimp on technology, generalship or battles, but takes care to place war in its larger social, political, economic and cultural context. This has been an important evolution, for wars have decisively shaped the history, borders and culture of Europe and the world, and warfare itself is never the product of military planning and technology alone; it is the reflection of society. Thus this book inclines to the conclusion that rational, rich, unified and technologically adept states have generally succeeded at war. Mar or subtract any one of these variables and the trouble begins: Napoleonic or Wilhelmine irrationality, Austro-Hungarian disunity, Italian poverty, Russian backwardness, and so on. It is, in short, impossible to understand the waning of France, the convulsions of Germany, the decline and fall of Austria-Hungary, the growing pains of Italy, or the smash-up of the Russian Empire – all functions of war – without probing the society and politics of each of these creatures. A book on this scale naturally limits the enterprise, but I have probed as deeply as 100,000 words permit.

In military and political terms, the period covered by this book was Europe's finest hour. The entire century between the French Revolution and the outbreak of World War I witnessed a steady growth in European wealth, population, power and influence. When the Great War broke out in 1914, there were more Europeans (460 million) as a percentage of the world's population (20 per cent) than ever before or since. Europeans drove the 'second industrial revolution' in steel, chemicals, electrical machinery and automobiles, and controlled 84 per cent of the earth's surface through their overseas empires. In retrospect, it is dismaying to see how little the Europeans made of this dominance; indeed, they frittered it away in a sequence of wars, some described in this volume, some in volumes to come. Perhaps this is the real impetus for European union today: the realization that inter-state conflict destroyed Europe's preeminence.

The structure of this book is largely chronological. There are a number of recurrent themes, including the interconnection of war and politics, the social dimensions of strategy, civil–military relations, and the power and lethality of military technology intelligently applied. One important lesson obtrudes: revolutions in military affairs like those launched by the French in the 1790s and the Prussians in the 1860s lose their punch once other states adopt them. Napoleon ran roughshod over his adversaries only until they copied the French style of war. Once the Prussians, Austrians and Russians recast themselves as French model armies, Napoleon lost his key advantage and was beaten. Similiarly, Moltke's military revolution flattened the Austrians in 1866 and the French in 1870, permitting Prussia to annex Germany and make itself the first power of Europe. Moltke's successors foolishly believed that the master's key innovations – rapid movement and fire-intensive tactics – could be made to work again and again. Hence the Schlieffen Plan and the desperate German invasion of France and Russia in 1914. What Schlieffen and his acolytes failed to grasp was that the French, Russians and British had effectively 'Prussianized' their armies in the decades after 1870, making the German struggle for control of Europe in 1914 as ultimately futile as Napoleon's 100 years earlier.

My wife Cecilia and I had two sons during the writing of this book, lusty, happy boys whose beaming contrast with the horrors recounted in these pages has continually reminded me of the human cost of war. That is not the least of their contributions; Cecilia – to whom this book is dedicated – has juggled career and family to facilitate my work; my boys – Winslow and Matías – have been a ready source of love and amusement. I have other debts: to Paul Kennedy, my doctoral advisor at Yale University, whose ecumenical method infuses this analysis; to Ronald Finucane, chairman of the History Department at Oakland University, who has supported my research and writing in all manner of ways; to George Baer, chairman of the Strategy and Policy Department at the US Naval War College, who engaged me as a visiting professor for two halcyon years. At Newport I read the naval theorists for the first time, lived and worked among professional soldiers, sailors, airmen and marines, and absorbed exciting new ways to analyse and interpret war. Thanks are also due to the series editor, Jeremy Black, who kindly invited me to write this book and gave it a close, critical reading. Finally, my thanks to the history editor at Routledge, Heather McCallum, who has pushed the book through all of the usual bottlenecks with efficiency and vim.

Rochester Hills, Michigan
June 1999

CHAPTER ONE

Napoleon and the road to Waterloo

Napoleon Bonaparte cudgelled modern war into existence. The greatest general of revolutionary France, he overthrew the French republic that had raised him from obscurity and crowned himself 'Emperor of the French' in 1804 at the age of thirty-five. Napoleon's reign lasted ten years, until 1815. In this single decade of war and statecraft, he subjugated most of Europe and perfected the military innovations of the French Revolution in continual campaigns against Britain, Austria, Prussia and Russia. He nearly beat them all, but was finally overwhelmed by attrition, British sea power, and a vast European coalition that slowly adopted Bonaparte's method of war, and then combined in an invincible anti-French alliance.

Though an undoubted genius, Napoleon benefited from military reforms begun in the last years of France's ancien regime. In the 1770s, French army reformers had increased the army's complement of artillery and had reorganized the cumbersome old regimental army into manoeuvrable all-arms 'divisions' that united infantry, cavalry and artillery in stand-alone units. This French divisional system − a product of the Enlightenment − permitted armies to grow. With his force riven into divisions, a field commander could control and direct a much larger army. General staffs were needed to coordinate the new divisions, and this too was discussed by the eighteenth-century reformers. In 1775, Pierre Bourcet stressed the importance of maps, march tables and painstaking preparation for war. Jean de Gribeauval, a colleague of Bourcet, called for a great expansion of the French artillery. The *philosophes* of the Enlightenment were fascinated by technology and machines, and France's military *philosophes* were no different. In artillery, the French discerned a 'force multiplier', a machine that could wreak as much havoc as 100 men; they eagerly embraced it earlier than other armies, and Gribeauval laid the groundwork for Bonaparte's success by standardizing the calibre and ammunition of French cannon and grouping them in highly mobile, fire-intensive six- and eight-gun batteries (Black 1994: 153–4). Another French reformer, Jacques de Guibert, anticipated what was perhaps the most striking change in war inaugurated by the French Revolution and Empire. In his *Essai General de Tactique* of 1772, Guibert insisted that modern war be conducted pitilessly and made

1

to pay for itself. Armies needed to jettison their burdensome supply wagons and live instead 'at enemy expense', plundering peasants along the march routes and 'pursuing the enemy with flame and steel'(Best 1982: 56–9). In short, France's eighteenth-century reformers aimed to make the French army flexible, responsive, and frightful. They dreamed of a day when the French army would plan operationally, not tactically, coordinating multiple blows by multiple units on a broad front to envelop hostile armies and penetrate swiftly and smoothly into enemy territory.

At first, few credited the dream. In the eighteenth century, war remained a small, lumbering affair dedicated to the capture and appropriation of enemy resources, not their destruction (Showalter 1996: 7–8; Best 1982: 59). Europe's pre-revolutionary armies were small and inefficient. Rarely exceeding 60,000 men, they lacked the manpower and mobility to destroy. In wartime, European regiments were hastily and unsystematically bundled into 'columns' that limped into enemy territory burdened with supply convoys that Guibert likened to 'leg irons'. Because eighteenth-century communications were sketchy, army columns had to be spread thin to cover every conceivable point of invasion or attack. This was 'cordon strategy', and cordon battles were necessarily limited in scope. Even military geniuses like Prussia's Frederick the Great, who campaigned intermittently from 1740–86, lacked the manpower, guns and logistical support to push tactical successes forward and convert them into strategic victories. When, for example, Frederick shattered the Austrian army at Leuthen in 1757, the Austrians merely gave ground, and regrouped beyond the reach of Frederick's weak pursuit. The physical inability of either side to finish the other off made the Leuthen campaign part of a seemingly interminable Seven Years War. The small size and inflexibility of the old regime army all but precluded war-ending envelopments (Parker 1988: 147–50; Showalter 1996: 203–6).

The French Revolution gave an urgent new impetus to French military reforms. In 1792, revolutionaries in Paris proclaimed a republic; in January 1793 they executed King Louis XVI. An indignant coalition of conservative powers, led by Austria and Prussia and financed by England, invaded France to suppress the 'regicide republic' and restore the Bourbons. This was the War of the First Coalition, which lasted until 1797 (Blanning 1986: 73–80, 85–9). Hard-pressed by the foreign invasion and a royalist counter-revolution inside France, France's revolutionary government – which passed into the hands of the radical Jacobins in 1793–4 – introduced mass conscription. The Jacobin *levée en masse* of 1793 decreed that 'every Frenchman is permanently requisitioned for service with the armies'. This was the first total mobilization of a society for war. Young bachelors were to sent to the front; married males and middle-aged men were put to work in French arsenals; French women made sails, packs and uniforms, or nursed sick and wounded men in the field hospitals. Even French children and the elderly were conscripted, the former to manufacture lint and bandages, the latter to congregate in village squares 'to raise the courage of the warriors and preach the unity of the republic and hatred against kings' (Rothenberg 1978: 100–1). France's total effort was all the more threatening because France in 1800 was the most populous state in Europe after Russia. It had a young, growing population of 33 million; the sprawling Austrian Empire had only 20 million subjects, Britain 15 million, Prussia just 6 million (Horne 1996: 49).

Though quite a spectacle, France's 'mass levy' was fraught with difficulties. Peasants hated it, yammering at their city-bred officers in Norman, Breton, Picard, Auvergnat, Gascon, Provençal and Languedocian, and evincing a general European problem: that of extending the urban ideal of 'nationalism' from educated elites to the provinces. Indeed, fewer than half of the peasants drafted by the French republic to 'save the fatherland' even reported for duty. Of these, thousands deserted to return home or to form anti-republican gangs like the Royal Catholic Army of the Vendée, 100,000 strong in 1793. On average, the French army lost 200,000 men a year to desertion in the early 1790s, a rate of loss that was manageable only because France's was the first mass army. 'Isn't it enough to serve the country by supplying our brothers in arms with something to eat', a typical French peasant remarked in 1793 (Griffith 1998: 29–31, 252–5; Elting 1988: 29–35, 40; Bertaud 1988: 111–12, 117–42). Men like this were forcibly inducted or summarily executed. Those that reported for duty and stayed with the army were saturated with propaganda. Tim Blanning estimates that 'political commissars' sent from Paris delivered no fewer than 7.5 million revolutionary journals and 100,000 'republican songbooks' to French troops at the front in 1794 (Blanning 1996: 118–20).

By dint of brutal coercion – the 'Reign of Terror' claimed 80 per cent of its victims in rural departments far from Paris – the Jacobins succeeded in raising an army of 800,000 men by 1794 (Greer 1935: 164). This 'republican army', which mixed royalist veterans, revolutionary volunteers and streams of draftees, was ten times larger than the armies fielded in the eighteenth century; it posed mind-boggling logistical, operational and tactical problems. Yet France's republican leadership solved them, slowly and deliberately setting modern war on its destructive way forward. To equip and feed the new army, the French revolutionaries commandeered France's infant industry and bent it to the needs of war. Forges and workshops were established to manufacture armaments; in Paris, the Tuileries Gardens and the Place des Vosges were fitted with open-air war factories. By spring 1794, 3,000 French workers were making 700 muskets a day, a sum equal to the total daily production of the rest of Europe. French tailors and dressmakers were also put to work sewing uniforms and kit; French cobblers were commanded to make ten shoes a week for the army. In this way, the mass army clothed and equipped itself; still, many regiments would mobilize in 1793 armed with nothing more than picks and axes (Bertaud 1988: 241–51; Blanning 1996: 121). France was not yet industrialized and lacked the roads and transport to move men, raw materials and finished goods efficiently.

In terms of logistics – a baffling problem with nearly a million men under arms – the Jacobins made more momentous changes. To move France's big armies, republican generals like Napoleon Bonaparte shed their tents and supply trains, and ordered their men to live off the land *à la* Guibert. Here was the source of the French *vitesse* that so amazed France's enemies. A German pastor observing the passage of a French army through Bavaria in 1796 noted its stripped-down efficiency:

> One did not see many wagons or much baggage. ... Everything about these Frenchmen was supple and light – movements, clothing, arms, and baggage. ... The greater part of their infantry was without uniforms, shoes, money, and apparently lacking all organization, if one were to judge by appearances alone. But each man had his musket, his cartridge box, and cockade of national colors, and all were brave and energetic.

Of course France's barebones organization exacted a social price. As Guibert had predicted, war in this manner placed civilians and their chattels squarely in the battlefield. Indeed, requisitioning and quartering at the expense of civilians became standard practice during the French Revolution. Initially, French peasants were forced to contribute pigs, bread and wine to the Revolution. If they refused, they were generally branded 'counter-revolutionaries' and killed (Cobb 1987: 253–88; Griffith 1998: 252–4). This problem solved itself after 1795, when the French army drove out the last foreign invaders and carried the War of the First Coalition into enemy territory. Thereafter, until war returned to France in 1814, the French army lived in large part from plunder, establishing a so-called commerce agency to loot foreign art galleries, treasuries and banks. (The practice – begun by the republic – was expanded by Napoleon, who installed the best plunder in the Louvre, where it remains to this day.) At first, revolutionary France tried to target only rich foreigners with the slogan *guerre aux châteaux, paix aux chaumières* ('war to the castles, peace to the cottages'), but this proved impossible, for the wealthy landowners had long since packed up their most valuable possessions and fled, leaving the poor cottagers to bear the brunt of French rapine (Blanning 1996: 158–9). In 1796, German peasants – the first Europeans to experience French savagery – reported that French soldiers carried hatchets and crowbars into action and took time out from battles to burgle even the meanest peasant dwellings, smashing in walls and prying up floorboards in search of money, food and drink, while bawling their five words of German: 'Landsmann Wein! Landsmann Geld! Dépêches-toi, oder kaput!' ('Give me wine! Give me money! Make it snappy or you're dead!') (Bertaud 1988: 286–300). Even Bonaparte, surely one of the most ruthless

French generals, confessed that his troops routinely committed atrocities 'so horrific as to make him tremble'. In 1793, an officer in France's Army of the Moselle deplored the conduct of his men in Germany:

> From time to time ... we would make expeditions into enemy territory ... We would leave our camp after dark, followed by some 50 vehicles; we would fall suddenly on a village which we would devastate. We loaded the wagons with all we could find ... the peasants were abused, sometimes killed; the women raped; everything was permitted.
>
> (Elting 1988: 46–7; Blanning 1996: 164)

Driven by generals like Bonaparte – who routinely forced even small towns to provide him with wine and rations for 50,000 men – war became total during the French Revolutionary and Napoleonic Wars (Blanning 1996: 161–3). Civilians were drawn inexorably into the fighting and brutally sacrificed. Methods of strategy and tactics also changed. The British, Austrians, Prussians and Spanish had invaded France in 1793 with rigorously trained old-regime armies. These allied infantrymen had averaged ten years with the colours, cavalrymen and gunners even more. Advancing in flawlessly dressed lines drilled to manoeuvre and fire fluidly, the old musketeers – 'walking batteries' in Frederick the Great's phrase – had scorned France's mob of green conscripts, a sentiment they came to regret, for the Jacobin government that introduced conscription also produced a brilliant military reformer: Lazare Carnot. Though it would be left to Napoleon to perfect the military innovations of the French Revolution, it was Carnot – the 'organizer of victory' – who slapped them together in the life-or-death crisis of the early 1790s.

To counter a half-dozen threats at once – a French civil war between republican 'blues' and royalist 'whites', and foreign invasions from all points of the compass – Carnot took up Bourcet's divisional concept and grouped the French revolutionary army in divisions of 12,000 men, which were small enough to move and provision efficiently. Five or six divisions joined on the battlefield comprised an army. Operationally, Carnot's divisions were a great success; they permitted an army general to radiate his divisions out like spokes on a wheel, using every available road and track to rush his troops into battle. Since a division in march columns required six or seven miles of open road and lots of requisitioning at roadside farms, the advantages of this controlled dispersal were obvious.

To overcome the tactical advantage enjoyed by the long-service, professional armies of Britain, Austria and Prussia, Carnot increased France's artillery establishment – providing each of his divisions with thirty-eight guns – and introduced infantry 'shock tactics'. Shock tactics were designed to bring the largely untrained French infantry quickly to grips with deadly, rapid-firing lines of enemy musketeers (Black 1994: 168–76; Chandler 1966: 66–70; Rothenberg 1978: 114–18). Because professional infantrymen deployed in line in three files could fire without interruption – the first file resuming fire after the second and third had discharged their volleys – French recruits, who scarcely knew one end of the musket from the other, had to be rushed across the killing ground to the point of attack. Carnot's solution was to compress the French line into battalion-strength 'attack columns' of eight companies, which would mass themselves one behind the other – or two companies abreast, four deep – and sprint at the enemy with the bayonet. Though this unsophisticated tactic solved the problem of discipline (the men could be driven into action like cattle), it was careless of human life, for well disciplined enemy lines were able to pour salvos into the massed French columns and inflict punishing casualties. Indeed, French casualties were kept within sustainable limits only by the speed of the infantry columns, the covering fire of their divisional artillery, and the harassing fire of their *tirailleurs en grandes bandes*, whole battalions of skirmishers that the French sent forward to snipe at the enemy firing line and conceal the approach of the 'shock columns'. Still, shock tactics were a crude expedient. The French routinely absorbed 20 per cent casualties, 'pitching in one demi-brigade after another until the last ones drowned the worn-down enemy', in what an Austrian critic called 'une mer de sang' – 'a sea of blood' (Elting 1988: 50; Bertaud 1988: 154–6; Blanning 1986: 87). This was generally the outcome only because old-regime armies were small and predisposed to limit their losses. Though French 'storm attacks' at Jemappes in 1792 and Wattignies in 1793 left droves of killed and wounded men in their wake, they won through by sheer weight of numbers. Even when the French were defeated – Neerwinden and Valenciennes in 1793 – Carnot merely shrugged. He could always replenish the French armies with fresh drafts from the mass levy, which provided cheap and abundant reserves (Griffith 1998: 230–4; Black 1994: 171; Blanning 1996: 120, 123). The Prussians and the Austrians, who invested years of training and upkeep in a soldier, were astounded by this contempt for human life. Rather than sacrifice their own men in this way, they gave ground before the French bayonet charges. And who could blame them? John Elting sympathizes with these early victims of French revolutionary tactics, which combined shock, skirmishing and the cannonade in an unprecedentedly destructive package:

> Put yourself in their place. Swarms of skirmishers have enveloped your tight, strictly-dressed formations, firing from behind cover in a most unsoldierlike fashion. If you charge them with the bayonet, they drift away – still shooting – and follow you when you return to your original position. Eventually your lines are in tatters. Then suddenly, out of the smoke, comes a howling, trampling, caterwauling rush of battalion columns, the bayonets and bull-weight of twelve fresh men against every yard of your exhausted line (which was only three deep when the action began) at their chosen point of impact.
>
> (Elting 1988: 51)

Carnot's divisional system and shock tactics pushed forward a new generation of generals. Leadership in the republican style required youth, zeal, technical competence and bravery. Carnot ushered out the old generation of military men – many into exile, others to the guillotine – and entrusted his new divisions to France's best and brightest young officers. It was a magical moment in French military history: the end of the elaborately structured Enlightenment, and the start of a brash romantic age. Carnot gave romanticism a military dimension by overturning the desks in the French war department, expelling time-servers and regrouping the army around a core of young fighting soldiers: Jean-Charles Pichegru, André Masséna, Jean-Victor Moreau, Lazare Hoche, Jean-Baptiste Jourdan, Louis Desaix and Napoleon Bonaparte. All of them shared Bonaparte's no-nonsense formula for command, which distinguished them from their stand-offish old-regime predecessors.

> 'You must be a soldier, and then a soldier, and again a soldier; bivouac with your advance guard, be in the saddle night and day, and march with your advance guard to have the latest information. ... With an army of 200,000 men, I am at the head of my skirmishers'.
>
> (Elting 1988: 41–4, 67)

Trusting in their generals, Carnot and the republican leadership in Paris organized France's million-man army into semi-autonomous groups of several divisions. This process of decentralization, coordinated by Carnot's Topographical Bureau, an early version of Napoleon's general staff, permitted the French army to operate more effectively on a broad fighting front that extended from Holland to Italy. General Bonaparte – just twenty-seven years old in 1796 – was given command of France's 'Army of Italy': 50,000 men grouped in six divisions with 600 guns (Rothenberg 1978: 40–1). The victories Bonaparte wrested from the Austrians and Piedmontese in North Italy in 1796–7 vaulted him into the public eye.

Napoleon's Italian campaign of 1796–7 demonstrated the great superiority of the briskly evolving French method of war. Dispersed in mobile divisions, Bonaparte moved into Piedmont, and took up a central position between the converging Austrian and Piedmontese armies. In a sequence of battles in April and May 1796, Bonaparte prised the allies apart and smashed them separately. He knocked the Piedmontese out of the allied coalition altogether, and pursued the Austrians into Lombardy. After beating them at Lodi, where Bonaparte led from the front and exposed himself to fire, Napoleon trapped 20,000 Austrians in the fortress of Mantua. Emperor Franz of Austria made four attempts to raise the siege of Mantua, and Napoleon, operating at the ends of his supply lines deep in enemy territory, repulsed them all: at Lonato, Castiglione, Arcola and Rivoli. Grouped in mutually supporting divisions, Napoleon's Army of Italy was able time and again to defeat big Austrian armies, which advanced in unruly columns and were easily outnumbered and beaten by the concentrated French army. Mantua fell in 1797, and Austria signed the Treaty of Campo Formio, which ceded Belgium and Lombardy to France and ended the War of the First Coalition. The British taxpayer, who had paid a subsidy of £1.75 million for every 100,000 Austrian troops mobilized against the French, quietly fumed while France applauded a new hero: Napoleon Bonaparte.

Bonaparte, the political soldier *par excellence*, did not delay in exploiting his popularity. After leading a military expedition to Egypt in 1798–9, Napoleon returned to Paris and seized power from France's increasingly corrupt republican leadership (Ross 1979: 115–75). This 'coup of 18 Brumaire' was popular, particularly among French peasants, who resented the revival of conscription and excise taxes by the *gros-ventres* or 'big-bellies' of the Directory. Backed by the army (Jourdan concurring that the Directors were 'vampires, who devour the substance of the people'), General Bonaparte rather easily ousted the French republic's civilian leadership and made himself 'General-in-Chief' and 'First Consul' of France (Elting 1988: 45). In 1800, Bonaparte introduced the army corps: a tactical unit of 30,000 men that comprised three infantry divisions, a cavalry brigade, and forty-six guns. This further refined the process of command and control in the French army. With each French corps entrusted to a demonstrably competent 'Marshal of France', Napoleon could briskly transmit orders to his largest tactical formations and count upon their prompt execution at all levels.

In May 1801, faced with a second, British-led coalition, Napoleon led an army of 60,000 men into Italy to beat the Austrians again and deprive England of its strongest continental ally. At Marengo, Bonaparte was set upon by a large Austrian army and nearly beaten. Significantly, he was rescued by a detached corps under General Louis Desaix, which belatedly swung its two divisions into the Austrian flank and clinched the battle (Connelly 1987: 66–8). Once again, the modern structure of the French army brought victory. The Austrians, loosely joined in old-fashioned columns, broke under the concerted fire of the French attacks and failed to finish off Napoleon's isolated troops before the arrival of Desaix's. Emperor Franz of Austria capitulated again, and even England recognized the futility of prolonging the war. At the Anglo-French Peace of Amiens in 1802, the British conceded Bonaparte mastery of Europe.

Between 1802 and 1805, Bonaparte consolidated his authoritarian regime at home. In 1804, he crowned himself 'Emperor of the French' and made more reforms to the French army. France's reorganized corps and divisions facilitated the classic Napoleonic attack: the *manoeuvre sur les derrières*, in which a single French corps or division would fix the enemy force and permit the bulk of the French army to curl around its flank and rear (Strachan 1983: 44). Under Napoleon, shock tactics were no longer a desperate expedient, they became the cutting edge of the French army. Employing *l'ordre mixte* – a tactical transition from firing line to shock column smoothly executed by battle-hardened veterans – France's infantry became the best in Europe (Bertaud 1988: 278–9). Napoleon himself was an artillery officer by training, and under his leadership the French artillery hit harder than ever. As Consul and Emperor, he added hundreds of guns to the French army; the new pieces were concentrated in 'batteries' of four to eight cannon and fitted with horse-drawn limbers containing 300 rounds of ammunition; these innovations conferred speed and endurance on the French guns (Rothenberg 1978: 74–80; Elting 1988: 258–60). While Napoleon's enemies placed their guns in static lines well behind the fighting front, Napoleon set his cannon – *belles filles* he affectionately called them – in perpetual motion, shunting them about to deliver concentrated, devastating fire at every vulnerable point. 'Skill consists in converging a mass of fire on a single point', he liked to say. In action, Napoleon invariably pushed his guns forward to 'ripen' the battle and force a favourable outcome (Elting 1988: 249, 259).

Under Napoleon – who standardized the calibre of French field guns in 1803 to simplify production and maintenance – the ratio of guns to infantry in the French army steadily increased, from 2 per 1,000 at Austerlitz in 1805, to 3 per 1,000 at Borodino in 1812, to 3.5 per 1,000 at Leipzig in 1813 (Strachan 1983: 51–2). France's corps and divisional organization easily absorbed the influx of artillery. Napoleon allotted each of his divisions twelve cannon and reserved a 'super battery' of 100 guns for himself, ensuring that they were usefully employed in all phases of a battle. Needless to say, combat became more hazardous in the early 1800s. The eighteenth-century cannonade, which had aimed to shatter or dismount an enemy's guns, was replaced by a seamless curtain of anti-personnel fire delivered by mobile field guns firing solid shot, grape and canister. In 1804, a British artillery officer named Henry Shrapnel invented a new anti-personnel round that was effective at long range. Shrapnel was a fused, cast-iron shell crammed with powder and musket balls; the shell burst in flight exploding its contents in the face of advancing troops. The shrapnel shell was the ultimate 'force multiplier' for the time: a single well placed round delivered the punch of an entire company of musketeers. Though most guns still fired softball-sized round shots, they carried plenty of shrapnel, canister and 'common shell' – a fused metal sphere loaded with gunpowder – in their limbers for close-in fighting (Muir 1998: 31). The modern 'artillery battle' – in which masses of infantry would be pulverized by masses of artillery – was already revealing itself. In 1814, artillery fire inflicted 20 per cent of battle casualties; by 1914 it would account for 75 per cent.

In 1805, the British and Austrians formed a third coalition to wrest control of Europe from France. With most of the French army deployed on the Channel coast to invade England, Emperor Franz of Austria thought the moment ripe to breach the Peace of 1801 and invade France via Lombardy and Bavaria, the one a French satellite state, the other a French ally. This was the start of the Austerlitz campaign, the focal point of the War of the Third

Coalition. Although the Russians joined the Anglo-Austrian coalition, they were slow to mobilize, giving Bonaparte time to reroute his 100,000 man *Grande Armée* from the Channel Coast to Germany. Organized in mobile corps and unencumbered by tents and cook wagons – the French would scrounge instead – the Napoleonic army fairly flew from France to Bavaria, while the Austrians and Russians, weighed down by canvas, food and fodder, staggered there.

En route to Austerlitz, Napoleon eliminated 60,000 Austrian troops gathered under General Karl Mack at Ulm. The British took a keen interest in Mack's army, because they had paid for it with receipts from an income tax levied in 1797 to defray the cost of the long struggle with France. London received scant return on its investment. Napoleon swept up to Ulm in six great columns, encircled it, and forced Mack's surrender (Rothenberg 1982: 88–93). Ulm exemplified Napoleon's operational art; it was a classic envelopment, a successful, annihilating *manoeuvre sur les derrières*. The Austrians were frozen in place, likened by Correlli Barnett to 'a tethered goat in an Indian village awaiting the visit of a tiger' (cited in Horne 1996: 116). This successful French strike at Ulm would profoundly influence Napoleon's most successful imitator: Prussia's General Helmuth von Moltke.

Speed was always the secret of Bonaparte's success. On the Napoleonic battlefield there was no place for the lumbering siege parks, magazines and convoys of the eighteenth century. 'Marches are war', Napoleon often said. 'Time is the grand element' (J. Fuller 1992: 50). He appeared at Ulm much earlier than the Austrians had anticipated, and cut across Mack's lines of retreat, taking 60,000 prisoners. Although the French infantry protested at the exhausting pace – earning the nickname *grognards* or 'grumblers' – they came to appreciate that the element of surprise spared lives. After Ulm, Napoleon's men joked that 'the emperor has discovered a new way of waging war; he uses our legs instead of our bayonets' (Chandler 1966: 148–51).

Yet Ulm was only a partial victory. Several thousand Austrians escaped to the east, where they united with an Austro-Russian army of 90,000 men in the Habsburg province of Moravia. The Allies assumed that Napoleon would settle into winter quarters in some snug Bavarian town; instead, Napoleon pursued them through the ice and snow. 'No rest', he wrote Joachim Murat, his best cavalry general. 'Pursue the enemy and keep your sword in his back' (Muir 1998: 13; J. Fuller 1992: 49). Here was another change in warfare; the French fought day and night, in fair weather and foul, anything to seize and exploit a military advantage. While Murat's cavalry rode the Austrians down, Napoleon followed with the infantry and guns and took Vienna in November. (There Napoleon sat in the Habsburg emperor's box for the première of Beethoven's *Fidelio*; the new opera, like the Austrian army, had been overtaken by the stormy French advance.)(Horne 1996: 127.) Reduced by casualties and detachments to just 65,000 men, and threatened by two vast enemy armies – the 90,000 Austrians and Russians assembled in Moravia and 50,000 more

Austrians marching up from Italy (where Emperor Franz had mistakenly believed the main French attack would come) – Napoleon turned to face the nearer of the two, the allied army in Moravia (Rothenberg 1982: 93–102). On 2 December he routed the Austrians and Russians at Austerlitz, killing, wounding or capturing 30 per cent of their effectives. It was another victory for Napoleon's modern, articulated force, which landed crippling blows on the front, flanks and rear of the ponderous Austro-Russian armies. Napoleon's corps and divisions swarmed around the Austrian and Russian flanks in a way that Prussia's Moltke would consciously imitate in the 1860s and 1870s: a *masse primaire* lured the enemy into the open, a *masse de manoeuvre* uncovered his flanks and rear, and a *masse de rupture* – the Imperial Guard – charged home to victory. This was the rather simple secret of Bonaparte's success and it worked like a charm until 1805, when the shock of Austerlitz persuaded Napoleon's adversaries to begin slowly adopting French methods: the corps and division, shock tactics, and a more aggressive operational tempo. The last Napoleonic Wars would unfold quite a bit differently from the first ones (Epstein 1994: 40, 174–83; Muir 1998: 239–40).

The Napoleonic Wars at sea

Having beaten the Russians and the Austrians, Napoleon would have liked to resume the invasion of England he had planned for 1805. Yet Napoleon's expansion of the French army after 1804 had been at the expense of the French navy, which in 1805 could muster just ninety-six battleships to Britain's 136. As would be the case until 1945, Great Britain took pains to maintain a bigger navy than any European adversary. In 1805 the Royal Navy counted 1,000 ships and 142,000 sailors, making the Napoleonic Wars that proverbial contest between the (British) 'whale' and the (French) 'elephant'. The *Grande Armée* indisputably ruled Europe, but the Royal Navy ruled the waves, and was able to impose a crippling embargo on French trade, supplies and movements (Kennedy 1976: 123–47). Furthermore, in terms of naval training, the British were far ahead of the French, who had purged most of their naval officers during the Revolution. Between 1789 and 1792, the French navy had lost twenty-two of twenty-seven admirals and 128 of 170 captains; most had sensibly chosen exile over death when threatened by their *sans-culotte* crews (Blanning 1996: 196–9; Griffith 1998: 131–2; R. Harding 1999: 273–7). With attrition like this in the skilled cadres, it was no wonder that the French failed to win a single major sea battle with the British in all of the French Revolutionary and Napoleonic Wars.

Multi-deck ships of the line were the heart of the eighteenth-century navy. These lofty battleships – built to a great height to accommodate gun decks and facilitate boarding – displaced up to 3,000 tons, carried up to 150 cannon in their broadside batteries, and could throw a greater weight of metal in a single salvo than all of Wellington's artillery had fired at the Battle of Vittoria

(Glover 1980: 55). Yet the battleships were only the most visible part of a global naval campaign in which the British targeted France's trade and supply lines. Overall, it was Britain's cruiser fleet – 160 single-deck, 1,000-ton frigates, each mounting forty guns – that bore the brunt of the Napoleonic Wars at sea, projecting British sea power across the globe and sapping Napoleon's strength no less effectively than the coalition armies of Russia, Austria and Prussia (R. Harding 1999: 253–5, 257–77; Mahan 1890).

In 1805, squeezed by Britain's close blockade of the French ports and its seamless patrols along the rest of the European coast, Napoleon resolved to combine his Brest and Toulon fleets in the English Channel, drive off the Royal Navy, and transport an army to England, where he would take London and dictate terms to his most redoubtable enemy. The plan failed, chiefly because Britain raised the Third Coalition in time to distract Napoleon from the cross-Channel invasion and redirect him into Central Europe, where the Austrians eventually mobilized 180,000 men with dismal results. As Bonaparte closed on Vienna, he impatiently ordered his chief admiral, Pierre de Villeneuve, to break out of Cadiz – where the allied French and Spanish fleets were shut in by the British – and join the intensifying attack on the Austrian Empire. As Villeneuve ran from Cadiz for the open sea, Admiral Horatio Nelson's Mediterranean squadron intercepted him at Cape Trafalgar. Nelson, who would be killed in the fighting by a French sharpshooter, sank, burned or captured twenty-two French and Spanish ships (losing none of his own) and inflicted 10,000 casualties on Villeneuve's fleet. (With the French fleet bottled up in port, it would be almost impossible for France to replace these casualties with trained sailors.) As always, bold tactics accounted for Nelson's victory. Whereas Villeneuve deployed in line ahead, Nelson cut across the French line, broke it in two, and then encircled Villeneuve's confused fragments, pounding them down to the waterline with his broadside guns.

After Trafalgar, Napoleon stopped trying to beat Britain at sea. Complaining that 'wherever there is enough water to sail a ship, there is to be found an English ship of the line', he searched for some other means to defeat the British (Kemp 1969: 152). The search produced a French-imposed reconstruction of Europe: the Great Empire and Continental System of 1806. The Great Empire was a vastly enlarged France that incorporated Dutch, German and Italian territory (Map 1.1). The Continental System was a French-run economic bloc embracing all of Europe, from Antwerp to Moscow. Since more than 60 per cent of Britain's exports went to Europe at the time, Napoleon hoped to force the British to the peace table by stopping their European trade. Predictably, the Continental System failed, for Britain's command of the sea permitted the Royal Navy to blockade France, launch peripheral operations like the defence of Spain in 1808 and the landing near Antwerp in 1809, smuggle goods more or less freely into Europe, and punish French collaborators. In one such punitive expedition, a British squadron rained shell on Copenhagen in 1807, blasting its houses and shops to rubble, killing and wounding 2,600 civilians, and forcing the Danes to reconsider their French alliance. Even neutral states that trafficked with France were not spared. The United States, which had just freed itself from British rule, resented the Royal Navy's embargo on American trade with France, and unsuccessfully declared war on Britain in 1812. The Royal Navy pressed America's Atlantic fleet back into its ports, stopped France's mutually profitable trade with the US, and burned the new American capital at Washington to the ground. Meanwhile, French society was made to feel the pain of Napoleon's wars. Prices rose, and the 'tropical commodities' that made life worth living – tobacco, coffee, tea, chocolate, sugar and rum – all but vanished into the holds of British frigates and privateers. Those French families fortunate enough to procure a lump of sugar after Trafalgar would dangle it from the kitchen ceiling on a string and lugubriously press their watery morning coffee against it (Horne 1996: 233).

From Jena to Waterloo: the emergence of modern war

After Trafalgar and Austerlitz, the British approached the Prussians and persuaded them to join Britain and Russia in a fourth coalition against Napoleon. The Prussians agreed in 1806, only to be invaded and beaten at the twin battles of Jena and Auerstädt. Bonaparte then thrust into Poland, and beat the Russian army at Friedland in June 1807 after a long pursuit through inhospitable country. At the Treaty of Tilsit in July, Napoleon stripped away most of Prussia's territory in Poland and all of it in western Germany – more than half of the Prussian kingdom – and forced Tsar Alexander I to attach Russia to the Continental System. Bonaparte was at the peak of his powers. Like Louis XIV, he appropriated to himself the title *le Grand*, as in 'Napoleon the Great'. He also ordered construction of the elephantine *Arc de Triomphe* to immortalize his victories (Horne 1996: 231).

Of course, Napoleon owed his greatest victories to the incompetence of his enemies, which amplified his own undoubted greatness. Until Tilsit, the Austrians, Prussians and Russians had stolidly fought in the eighteenth-century style. Rather than adopt French-style corps and divisions, they had kept regiments as their highest tactical formations, bundling them into hastily improvised brigades, columns and detachments in wartime (Rothenberg 1982: 85). The allied armies were also late to form French-style general staffs, leaving the planning and execution of campaigns in the hands of overworked field commanders, or fainéant courtiers. Instead of experimenting with French shock tactics, they had retained eighteenth-century fire tactics, which left their rigidly dressed lines of musketeers vulnerable to French gunfire, cavalry charges, skirmishing and assaults with the bayonet. The allies were also slow to introduce Napoleon's 'battery system', which grouped six guns in a mobile battery and inflicted far more damage than single pieces or long-range cannonades. Moreover, fearing that mass conscription would upset economic

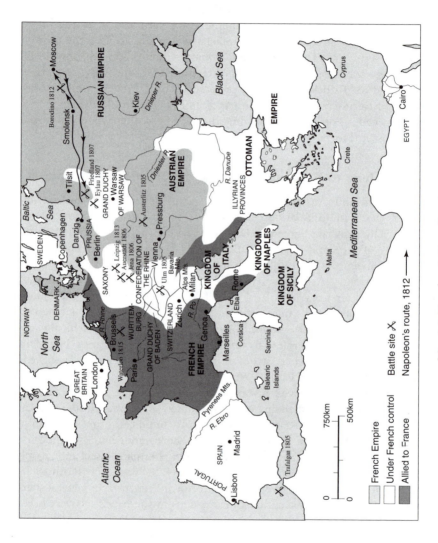

Map 1.1 Napoleon's Great Empire

and social relations in their monarchies (depriving mills of their workmen and landlords of their serfs), the British, Austrians, Russians and Prussians had hesitated to draft mass armies, conferring an inestimable advantage on the French until 1806, when the three eastern monarchies began finally to appreciate the necessity of change. Finally, the allied coalitions had consistently failed to *coordinate* their campaigns against the French in the years between 1792 and 1807. Napoleon and his generals had been able to knife between Austrian, Russian and Prussian armies to beat them separately. After 1807 the balance began to shift. Learning from past mistakes, the allied powers began to adopt French methods and concert their efforts. Noting this development, Robert Epstein has recently broken the Napoleonic Wars into two quite distinct phases: the wars before 1807, when Napoleon battered his unreformed, old-regime adversaries into the dust, and those after 1807, when the allied armies absorbed French methods and delivered war between huge, well armed and well organized armies into the modern age (Epstein 1994: *passim.*).

Though not all historians agree with Epstein's timing, it is a fact that the Austrians, Prussians and Russians introduced significant reforms after the disasters of Austerlitz, Jena and Friedland that would shape all subsequent military development. They aimed to discover the secrets of Napoleon's success and make these their own. In February 1806, Emperor Franz of Austria authorized his brother – Archduke Karl – to rebuild the Austrian army. This was a daring step, for Franz and Karl were fierce political rivals, and the Habsburg army was a flabby bureaucracy that cushioned legions of well connected courtiers and businessmen. Although root-and-branch reform might weaken the dynastic rule of the Habsburgs, France's military pressure was so exhausting that Franz felt that he had little choice but to accept the political risk. Archduke Karl, an energetic reformer, set to work at once (Rothenberg 1982: 103–19). Although he hesitated to introduce conscription, which Austria's litigious Hungarian minority refused to sanction, he did succeed in creating a vast reserve militia, the *Landwehr*. Under the *Landwehr* law of 1808, all Austrian males between eighteen and forty-one years of age were made liable for military service, an important step that would furnish a reserve army of 180,000 trained men in a crisis (Rothenberg 1982: 70–1, 119). To improve morale, and awaken something of the patriotic fervour that drove French troops, Karl tried to Germanize the Austrian army in order to infuse it with a missionary zeal to 'liberate' the German states of Napoleon's Confederation of the Rhine, which were suffering from French taxes, requisitions and conscription. Although this attempt foundered on the fact that 70 per cent of Austrian troops were non-Germans – Slavs, Hungarians, Rumanians and Italians – Archduke Karl did relax the harsh discipline of the Austrian regiment, greatly improving the morale and fighting quality of Austrian troops. Finally, Karl reorganized the Habsburg army into French-style corps and divisions and supplied each with its own artillery. He adopted infantry shock tactics and massed Austria's cavalry in the light and heavy brigades favoured by Murat. By 1809, the Habsburg army had transformed itself into a copy of the French force that had crushed it at Marengo, Hohenlinden, Ulm and Austerlitz (Chandler 1966: 664–7).

Not coincidentally, the Austrians beat the French for the first time in 1809. Emboldened by events in Spain – where 300,000 of Napoleon's best troops were pinned down fighting a Spanish revolt and an English expeditionary force based in Portugal – Emperor Franz joined Britain's Fifth Coalition. To beat the Austrians and clear his supply lines to Spain, Napoleon promptly placed himself at the head of a large army, and marched on Vienna. Archduke Karl, leading the reformed Austrian army, clashed with Napoleon near the capital at Aspern, and defeated him. Bonaparte retreated to Wagram, a village north of Vienna. There he counter-attacked and beat the Austrians. Wagram, however, was a different, far bloodier, far more terrifying battle than any that had preceded it. To neutralize French firepower, Archduke Karl had added batteries of guns to the Austrian army since Austerlitz. Both sides brought 500 cannon to Wagram and, thanks to their efficient corps structure, were actually able to use them, pouring tons of shot into each other, and inflicting stupendous casualties: 33,000 French and 37,000 Austrian dead and wounded. Napoleon, who had become accustomed in the old days to droves of demoralized enemy prisoners and ranks of captured cannon (the ultimate trophy of war), angrily muttered: 'war was never like this: neither prisoners nor guns; this day will have no result' (Muir 1998: 42; Rothenberg 1982: 168). Indeed there were few prisoners and captured guns, but lots of dead and wounded. Casualties on the scale of Wagram (25 per cent of effectives) would have destroyed the old Austrian army, yet the new army was able to take them in its stride (Chandler 1966: 708–32). Modern corps and divisions replenished from the *Landwehr* proved far sturdier than the old-regime mercenary armies. The Austrians withdrew from the fight in good order and might have resumed the battle were it not for Karl's timidity. Though a bold reformer, he was a cautious soldier, and he surrendered to Napoleon after Wagram, taking Austria out of the war and ceding France swaths of territory in Poland, Croatia and Slovenia (Rothenberg 1982: 170–1). Furious, Emperor Franz sacked his brother, ensuring that Karl would live on only as a military theorist. Wagram was his last battle

Meanwhile, France, its empire, and its 'satellite states' had been at war for an entire generation, heaping up casualties and misery as well as conquests. How did Napoleon keep French-occupied Europe and the multinational *Grande Armée* going? The examples of Spain and Calabria, where the French never succeeded in suppressing popular insurrections, hinted at the difficulties of ruling an empire of 500,000 square miles and 45 million subjects, only 30 million of whom were actually French. In brief, Napoleon kept Europe down by a combination of hope and fear. Local elites – Polish aristocrats or Italian *mafiosi* – were often permitted to keep their feudal privileges (in defiance of the Napoleonic Code), while middle-class progressives were strung along with the largely empty promise of a 'Napoleonic Project' for Europe. The 'Project' – never realized – would have levelled social classes and modernized the economies of every European state. And yet anyone familiar with Bonaparte would have understood that he was incapable of *comprehensively* implementing such plans. His taxes, tariffs, conscription and Continental System – all designed to shift the burden of the French Wars from the French people to their satellites – undercut rather than strengthened the economies of most of the European states, which were deprived of British technology and 'pastoralized' to feed the growth of France's infant industry. The once booming seaports of Europe – Genoa, Barcelona, Cadiz, Bordeaux, Antwerp, Amsterdam, Hamburg and Lübeck – were ruined by the Continental System and the retaliatory British blockade, to which Napoleon had no answers after 1805. With these great cities went their industries: textiles, tobacco, sugar, distilling and shipbuilding; all were depressed or wiped out by French domination.

Politically, Napoleon's overcentralized, authoritarian rule – which never hesitated to make cynical compromises with local grandees – nullified any democratic impulse in the Empire. Though the emperor abolished serfdom in Prussia, Poland and Naples, he saw to it that the expropriated estates found their way not into the hands of the peasantry but rather to French political allies, often the original owners. This was how Bonaparte oiled his machine; his peasants were henceforth free but landless (Lyons 1995: 229–40; G. Ellis 1997: 136–41; Esdaile 1995: 104–6, 301–7). As hope dwindled, fear and repression were increasingly the only means with which Napoleon could keep occupied Europe in check. 'Forced loans' and 'subsidies' were extorted everywhere the French went; Napoleon bankrupted Holland and, before the arrival of the British, demanded a monthly gift of 6 million francs from Spain and 16 million francs from Portugal. Cities and towns that hesitated were sacked, hostile villages burned to the ground, women raped or pressed into service as prostitutes, peasants raked into the French army or lynched and left hanging from trees *pour encourager les autres*. War Minister Soult's unvarying refrain summed up the Napoleonic style: 'You must assist us, even if it means providing the army with your last kernel of corn and your last forkful of fodder' (Schom 1992: 35; Finley 1994: 26–7, 66; Esdaile 1995: 17, 106–14).

Though well looked after, the French army was not always a reliable instrument. It had mutinied several times under the republic, rioting against low pay, poor rations and long campaigns. Napoleon solved this problem by forging a close, personal link with the army, a link that future soldier politicians – men like Austria's Franz Joseph and France's Napoleon III – would try with conspicuously less success to emulate. To the end, Napoleon succeeded in the pose of a simple soldier. To the men, he was the 'little corporal', always dressed in a grey duster and slouch hat, disdaining badges, sashes and medals (Horne 1996: 117). He entered enthusiastically into the life of his troops, plunging without ceremony into their camps, sampling rations, and carefully memorizing the name of every private soldier he met, so that he could greet him later – sometimes years later – in familiar tones: 'You were with me in Egypt. How many campaigns since? How many wounds?'. In the Napoleonic army there was no higher distinction than to have one's ear painfully grasped and twisted by the emperor, an exercise Bonaparte made sure to perform at least once on every line of men drawn up before him. A genuine love for Napoleon shot through the ranks: when the emperor lost his way in the dark on the night before Austerlitz and stumbled through a French bivouac, the men spontaneously rose from their sleep and burned their straw pallets – all that separated them from the cold, wet ground – to celebrate the emperor's passage through their camp. When Napoleon was shot in the heel at Regensburg, imperial adjutants and staff officers had to be sent flying in all directions to reassure the army that the emperor was only lightly wounded (Muir 1998: 3, 152). Napoleon's marshals also constituted an important link with the rank-and-file; like the emperor, they routinely exposed themselves to fire and shared the risks of battle. Three of the twenty-six marshals – Lannes, Bessières, and Poniatowski – were killed in action, and the rest received twenty wounds between them. To the men, this was reassuring (Muir 1998: 161).

Like other dictators, Napoleon made sure to satisfy the greed and ambition of his men. 'A man does not have himself killed for a few pennies a day', he liked to say. To raise the stakes, Bonaparte invented a whole inventory of military decorations, which came with cash prizes and pensions for conspicuous bravery. After Ebelsberg in 1809, he inspected a light infantry unit that had taken dreadful casualties in the battle and casually bestowed an imperial barony on Lieutenant Guyot, reportedly the bravest officer in the fight. The bravest enlisted man was made a *chevalier* of the Legion of Honour and, like Guyot, provided with a hefty annuity (Muir 1998: 152). Bonaparte induced his generals to keep a clear head in war and support his regime in peace with even more lucrative awards: duchies, principalities and even kingdoms (Chandler 1966: 155–7). To show his gratitude to Marshal Louis Davout for routing the Prussian army at Jena with a single corps, Napoleon made Davout 'Duke of Auerstädt' in 1806, a title that included substantial estates in Germany as well as a Parisian townhouse, a château in the Loire valley, and a princely salary that Davout more than repaid in 1809, crushing Archduke Karl in Bavaria and earning the title 'Prince of Eckmühl'. In all, Napoleon bestowed 3,400 imperial titles, not bad for a man who had begun his career as a Jacobin revolutionary. Though real aristocrats sneered at Bonaparte's new men – Marmont was 'Duke of Ragusa', Ney 'Prince of Moscow', Bernadotte 'Prince of Pontecorvo', Masséna 'Prince of Essling' – each jump up the ladder netted tremendous wealth and power, which helped cement Napoleon's *régime du sabre* (G. Ellis 1997: 132–6; Schom 1992: 36).

While Napoleon consolidated his rule in France, the Austrians put finishing touches to a modern, fire-intensive, manoeuvrable army. At Wagram, Archduke Karl stymied the French for sixteen hours and forced Napoleon to abandon his usual, artful manoeuvres and try instead bloody frontal attacks, which wasted French manpower and depressed morale. The Prussians and Russians were as buoyed by the results as the Austrians. They too had spent the years after 1806 reforming their armies to counter the French. Change had been most urgent in Prussia, which had retained every aspect of the old Frederician army until 1806: long-service, pressed and mercenary troops, inhuman discipline, unprofessional officers and rigid linear tactics. Prussia's catastrophic defeat at Jena-Auerstädt in 1806 had awakened Berlin from its long slumber. After losing half of his territory and population to the French at Tilsit, Prussia's King Friedrich Wilhelm III dismissed his elderly generals and admitted a younger generation of French-inspired reformers to the corridors of power: Gerhard von Scharnhorst, August Wilhelm Gneisenau, Hermann von Boyen, and Karl von Clausewitz. Together, these men crafted the reforms that would jerk Prussia into the nineteenth century, and pave the way for Prussia's forceful unification of Germany in 1866 and 1870.

Between 1807 and 1813, the Prussians developed a French-style general staff to centralize and expedite the conception and transmission of orders. Like the Austrians, the Prussians adopted the French corps and division, as well as French tactics. Prussian guns were concentrated in mobile, horse-drawn batteries, and the Prussian infantry began to skirmish and charge as effectively as the French. The Prussians also introduced a kind of conscription – the *Krümper* system – and created an Austrian-style *Landwehr* that would nearly quintuple Prussia's 66,000-man royal army to a strength of 300,000 in time for the final campaigns against Napoleon at Leipzig, Paris and Waterloo (Craig 1955: 37–53).

The Russians too hastened to reorganize and reequip, forcing Napoleon to invade Russia with an army of 600,000 men in 1812 to preempt what he regarded as an inevitable Russian attack on France and its satellite states. Pressed by Britain's unrelenting blockade and by the ongoing war in Spain – Napoleon's 'Spanish ulcer' – Bonaparte felt constrained to win breathing room in the east, where the Russians were creeping into Poland and the Balkans, challenging the frontiers and spheres of influence established in 1807 (Chandler 1966: 739–50). Bonaparte's invasion of Russia – planned as a sweeping envelopment of the Russian army by three French armies on a 250-mile front – miscarried. The Russians had improved themselves since Friedland; they had expanded conscription, rearmed with a better musket and field gun, and adopted the Napoleonic army corps (Epstein 1994: 177–8). They were more nimble and dangerous than ever, and successfully eluded Napoleon's attempted envelopment, which would have been the greatest *manoeuvre sur les derrières* of his career. When the Russians did finally offer battle, it was a mutually destructive, indecisive, Wagram-style affair, at Borodino near Moscow. Twelve hundred French and Russian cannon fired an estimated 90,000 artillery rounds in the course of the fight, ripping bloody gashes through the opposing armies (Clausewitz, who took part in the battle, remembered a field curiously devoid of men because of the ceaseless pounding of the artillery)

(Muir 1998: 236). Unable to flank the more manoeuvrable, well protected Russian corps, Napoleon resorted again to a bloody frontal attack. As at Wagram, the casualties were astounding: at least 80,000 dead, wounded and missing. Before closing with the bayonet, the French and Russian infantry fired off an estimated two million cartridges (Chandler 1966: 806–7). Here at last was modern war: mass armies and mass slaughter, with no immediately apparent result. (Of course the fact that fewer than 80,000 men were injured by 2.09 million projectiles indicated just how far 'modern war' had yet to go to become truly modern.) At Borodino, the armies absorbed their losses, recoiled and prepared to resume the bloody fight. The tactical flexibility conferred by the corps system and the vast reserves furnished by conscription allowed generals to recover their balance, replenish their strength and fight on. Unwittingly, Napoleon – the master of the short, decisive stroke – had begun the process by which battles became not brilliant, one-day affairs, but wretched, year-long slogs.

After Borodino, the Russians burned Moscow to the ground, deprived France's Grand Army of its winter quarters, and forced Napoleon to retreat westward. The French troops and their allies were shortly overtaken by winter weather, and destroyed by the attacks of Russian regulars and Cossacks, who marched parallel to the French retreat and kept it under constant attack. Of the 600,000 men Bonaparte took into Russia, no more than 60,000 came out. The rest were either lost along the route – to desertion, exposure, hunger and disease – or killed in action. Napoleon's men were so weakened by the march that the Cossacks could ride into their midst and flog them with knouts, taunting: *Alors, marchez, camarade!* (Walter 1991). With his army effectively immobilized by the loss of horses, who perished even more quickly than the men, Napoleon deserted his floundering army and raced back to Paris, where he began arming deserters, pensioners and adolescents for a last-ditch campaign (Muir 1998: 258; Horne 1996: 217; Chandler 1966: 852–3; Esdaile 1995: 259–61).

In 1813, the reformed armies of Austria, Prussia and Russia – buttressed by British sea power and subsidies – formed a sixth coalition to bury the French Empire. Napoleon returned to Germany with a hastily raised army, intending to knife between the coalition armies to beat them separately before they joined. He failed, for the *Grande Armée* – gutted by desertions and casualties – was by this late date a shadow of its former self. Moreover, the Allies had by 1813 completely digested French methods. The Austrian and Prussian armies were hustled into action by able general staffs: Joseph Radetzky's in Austria, and August Gneisenau's in Prussia. (The latter was so efficient that Field Marshal Blücher famously agreed to accept an honorary doctorate from Oxford University after the wars only if Gneisenau were made his honorary pharmacist!) (White 1996: 270). At the battle of Leipzig in October 1813, 360,000 Russian, Austrian and Prussian troops with 1,500 guns converged on 200,000 French troops with 800 guns. Leipzig was the biggest battle of the nineteenth century. It dragged on for three entire days, portending the bloody slogs of the future. While the allied armies struggled to press Bonaparte into a pocket and destroy him, he manoeuvred between the converging forces, dealing blows left and right before finally succumbing. At Leipzig, the first great allied victory over Napoleon, the Austrians, Russians and Prussians inflicted 73,000 casualties on the French, suffering just 54,000 of their own. The battle was a veritable firestorm; the French artillery fired off 200,000 shots and shells; the allies matched them round for round (Horne 1996: 342; Esdaile 1995: 268–72). Beaten, Napoleon fell back on France. As the allied armies came on in pursuit, they carried the war into France's towns and villages, another sad characteristic of modern war with its masses of hungry, intermittently idle troops. The Prussians were the worst offenders. A British officer who rode behind the Prussians described their depredations:

> After the forest of Pontarme a sudden and disagreeable change took place in the aspect of the towns and villages. We had got on the route of the Prussian army, which was everywhere marked by havoc and desolation. What a contrast! In Senlis, a few miles back, all was peace, plenty, and confidence, – here traces of war in its most horrid form, desolation and desertion. The inhabitants had everywhere fled, and we found naught but empty houses. Troops and their usual followers were the only human beings we saw now. The village of Loures, where we arrived about noon, presented a horrid picture of devastation. A corps of Prussians halted there last night, and, excepting the walls of the houses, have utterly destroyed it. The doors and windows torn out and consumed at the bivouac fire – a similiar fate seems to have befallen furniture of every kind, except a few chairs and sofas, which the soldiers had reserved for their own use. ... Clothes and household linen, beds, curtains, and carpets, torn to rags, or half-burned, lay scattered about in all directions. The very road was covered with rags, feathers, fragments of broken furniture, earthenware, glass, etc. Large chests of drawers, *armoires*, stood about broken or burned. The very floors had been pulled up and the walls disfigured in every possible way. No human being was to be seen amidst this desolation.

> (Mercer 1985: 231–2)

In this way, the brutal French way of war rebounded on itself. Napoleon was encircled in the course of 1814, deposed, and exiled to Elba, a sun-dappled Mediterranean islet next to his native Corsica. Although he escaped from Elba in 1815 and restored the French Empire for one hundred days, he was crushed a final time at Waterloo in June 1815. Waterloo – which pitted 70,000 British and 40,000 Prussian troops against 72,000 French – confirmed that the modernization of warfare begun by Napoleon had ultimately done him in. The British – alone against the French for most of the day – stood their ground, parried Napoleon's every thrust, and, with the Prussians pressing in on the French flank and rear, forced Bonaparte to attack them frontally, wasting his magnificent cavalry and guardsmen in suicidal lunges at the British line. Overall, Napoleon lost 44,000 men at Waterloo, 60 per cent of his strength. Wellington, who had led Britain's hugely successful Peninsular Campaign in Spain and Portugal, shot the French down and expressed his disappointment at Bonaparte's surprising lack of finesse: 'Damn the fellow; he's a mere pounder after all' (Muir 1998: 8; Nofi 1993: 227, 258). True enough, but the change was due to improvements in the strategy, operations and tactics of Napoleon's adversaries, who ultimately beat the French emperor with his own weapons. From the moment the seventh and final coalition was assembled at Vienna in March 1815 until the last shot was fired at Waterloo in June, the allied armies had operated smoothly and efficiently. Even had Bonaparte won at Waterloo, he would have met a second wave of Austrian and Russian troops, which invaded France to reinforce the British and Prussians in June. The Russians were in such a hurry to reach Paris that they entered French taverns, straddled the benches, and shouted *bistro!* – 'quickly' – suggesting a new gastronomic concept to the French: fast food. Observing the rapid progress of the Russians through Bavaria en route to France, Alexandre Berthier, Napoleon's erstwhile chief of staff, despondently downed a bottle of champagne and threw himself from the third storey of his wife's summer palace. He had much to be despondent about. Napoleon had given him not one but *two* principalities – Neuchâtel and Wagram – which made Berthier one of the richest men in Europe in 1815 (G. Ellis 1997: 134). He was about to lose it all. Berthier's battered corpse – clad in the green coat of the Napoleonic staff with a Bourbon rosette in the buttonhole – seemed to symbolize the tension between revolutionary action and conservative restoration that would unsettle Europe in the years after Napoleon (Nofi 1993: 250–1).

CHAPTER TWO

Restoration and revolution, 1815–49

After the orgy, revulsion set in. An estimated four million Europeans had died in the French Wars, and *La Grande France* – Paris' intoxicating name for the Great Empire – had bitten off vast chunks of the continent, annexing or enthralling entire non-French peoples. In repeated wars with Austria, Paris had stripped the Habsburg monarchy of territory in Italy, Germany, Poland and the Balkans. In the years after 1800, the French had annexed Switzerland and Piedmont, lumped Lombardy into a French-run 'Kingdom of Italy', and usurped the Pope and the Bourbons of Naples, transferring control of South Italy to a succession of French governments. After Austerlitz and Jena, Bonaparte had reorganized Germany, abolishing scores of German statelets and feeding their confiscated territory into France and its enlarged German client states, chief among them Saxony, Bavaria, Württemberg and Baden (Schroeder 1994: 291–3; Horne 1996: 388; Esdaile 1995: 298–301). At Tilsit, he seized Prussia's western and Polish provinces, made some of them French departments, and fashioned the rest into French satellite states: the Duchies of Berg, Westphalia and Warsaw (Connelly 1965: 333–46). He did the same to the Russians in 1807, crushing them at Friedland and adding their wedge of Poland to the growing Duchy of Warsaw, which the Russians rightly took to be Napoleon's hammer in the east. In 1808, Napoleon invaded Spain to overthrow the Bourbon monarchy and implant a more modern, enlightened and tractable French regime in its place. Although this invasion failed – miring France in five years of bloody guerrilla warfare – it was a classic Napoleonic action in that it was both strategic and political, intended not only to augment French power, but to spread the Napoleonic ideals of order, science and progress.

This, then, was the essential problem with Napoleon. Though a despot, he was also an enlightened one. In France, he retained key revolutionary reforms like the tricolour flag, the metric system and the *départements*, and, in the conquered territories, he made popular changes. He abolished serfdom, suppressed aristocratic and clerical privileges, employed the middle class in record numbers, built universities and extended secondary education, made all citizens equal before the law, and introduced the jury trial. In the French satellite states, Napoleon's hand-picked princes – reformers like Marshals Davout, Marmont and Murat in Poland, Croatia and Naples – swept away reactionary elements like the Church and the aristocracy to impose a uniform, modern culture on Napoleon's Great Empire and satellites. Although French rule was subsequently condemned for the graft, taxes and conscription required to maintain Napoleon's place-men and *Grande Armée*, many relished it for the jobs and opportunities it created (Johnson 1991: 65–8; Lyons 1995: 229–43; Best 1982: 191–203; Esdaile 1995: 286–7). For Croats and Slovenes accustomed to Austrian neglect, Marshal Auguste Marmont's Illyria represented a great improvement. Besides investing heavily in roads, schools and public works, Marmont broke up the feudal estates of Croatia and Slovenia and distributed the land to the peasantry (Jelavich 1983: I, 162–3). In Naples and Sicily, Marshal Joachim Murat – whom Napoleon made King of Naples in 1808 – declared war on the corrupt priests, landowners and *mafiosi* who had traditionally taxed and worked the Italian *contadino* to an early death. Like Marmont, Murat built schools, roads and ports, drained marshes, established workhouses, and laid down a profitable merchant marine (di Scala 1998: 32–3, 38–40). Elsewhere in Europe, Napoleon was the first monarch to outlaw attacks on Jews and concede them full civil rights. Needless to say, this made him enormously popular in the *shtetls* of Eastern Europe and the ghettos of the West (in 1815, a grateful Jewish battalion would join French and Polish troops in the defence of Warsaw against Russian reoccupation) (R. Palmer 1971: 137).

Napoleon was, in short, a dangerous figure, even in exile and death. Although undoubtedly a warmonger and a criminal (Napoleon personally pilfered an estimated £8 million – $800 million today – in the course of his conquests), millions remembered him fondly for his social action (Kaiser 1990: 246–9; Johnson 1991: 67). He had rattled the old regime, and injected the ideas of liberalism and nationalism into Europe's political culture by employing middle-class officers and functionaries and redrawing the map of Europe to facilitate trade and national unification. His last act before Waterloo had been to give the vote to thirteen million Frenchmen (the entire adult male population), a bitter legacy for Louis XVIII (R. Palmer 1971: 163–94). This radical Napoleonic legacy explained the fury with which Europe's restored dynasties obliterated most vestiges of the Napoleonic system at the Congress of Vienna, convened from March 1814 until June 1815. Led by Prince Klemens von Metternich, Austria's conservative foreign minister, Europe's emperors and kings undid most of the changes wrought by Napoleon in the years since 1804. Bonaparte was banished to St Helena, a rat-infested islet in the South Atlantic. Elderly Louis XVIII was recalled from exile and placed on the French throne, where he commenced a 'white terror' against those who had too ardently served the Revolution and Empire: prefects and officers were murdered, newspapers shut down, 'liberty trees' pulled up from their roots (Esdaile 1995: 288–9). While Louis XVIII restored 'order' in France, the Russians and Prussians moved back into Poland, snuffing out the Grand Duchy of Warsaw. The Austrians destroyed the Napoleonic Kingdoms of Italy and Naples: taking Lombardy and Venetia for themselves, restoring the Bourbons to Naples and Palermo, and returning the Pope to the Papal State, and the House of Savoy to Piedmont. In Turin, Jews were hounded back into the ghetto, and Protestants were carefully watched (Woolf 1979: 229–52).

In Germany, Prussia reaped the fruits of victory at Leipzig and Waterloo by annexing the Rhineland, Westphalia and Posen, which put paid to three more Napoleonic satellite states, and made Prussia 'gendarme' of North Germany. Although Austria and Prussia hesitated to restore the old regime in Germany – they had both profited from Napoleon's abolition of the Holy Roman Empire in 1805, Austria taking Salzburg, Prussia Anspach and Bayreuth – they did restructure Napoleon's 'Confederation of the Rhine', renaming it the 'German Confederation' placing themselves atop it in a senatorial role, and pointedly excluding France and all French influence (Schroeder 1994: 291; Kaiser 1990: 235–7). In 1819, Austria and Prussia moved to eradicate the last traces of French-inspired nationalism in Germany; they jointly issued the Karlsbad Decrees, which censored the press, schools and universities in all of the German states, outlawed student fraternities, and proscribed even casual references to democratic reform or the 'German nation'. In the 1820s, a German schoolmaster only half-jokingly quipped that officials in Berlin and Vienna were 'working on a law that will lay down how high birds may fly and how fast rabbits may run' (Beck 1995: 37–8; Johnson 1991: 115).

Even liberal England joined the reactionary fray for a time (Nicolson 1974: 266). From 1812 to 1822, Lord Castlereagh – a friend and admirer of Metternich – ran the British foreign office. He applauded the Karlsbad Decrees ('we are always pleased to see evil germs destroyed') and gave political support to Austria's annexation of North Italy and Russia's repression of the Poles. These very un-English excesses prompted Percy Shelley to write one of his most blistering sonnets: 'England in 1819'.

> An old, mad, blind, despised, and dying king, –
> Princes, the dregs of their dull race, who flow
> Through public scorn, – mud from a muddy spring, –
> Rulers who neither see, nor feel, nor know,
> But leech-like to their fainting country cling,
> Till they drop, blind in blood, without a blow.

While Shelley's 'despised and dying kings' restored their grip on Europe after 1815, old-regime generals (Shelley and the romantics called them 'liberticides') took back the European armies, taking care to rinse out the reformers who had introduced French methods during and after the Great Revolution. Naturally the process began in France itself, where the restored

Bourbons abolished conscription, purged 15,000 Napoleonic officers, and shrank enrolments at Napoleonic military schools like the Ecole Polytechnique, which came to be regarded as nests of liberalism. Fat, gouty Louis XVIII – 'Louis the pig' to most Frenchmen – reclaimed the French throne after Waterloo and promptly reactivated foreign guards and aristocrats – the so-called *voltigeurs* of Louis XIV – to run the Bourbon army. Roman Catholic chaplains were insinuated into every battalion to spy on officers suspected of 'Bonapartism'. Alfred de Vigny, one such officer of the Bourbon Restoration, called his years of service 'one long mistake. … The days dragged by, and thus we lost precious years dreaming of the battlefield as we drilled in the Champs-de-Mars, frittering away in tattoos and private feuds our potent but useless energies' (de Vigny 1964: 11). For French soldiers, the psychological impact of this inertia was crushing:

> The world of great issues [and] opportunities had disappeared in 1815. … The government, the civil service, and the army aged. A young soldier could no longer hope to imitate the career of Marshal Ney: son of an artisan, volunteer in 1787, and Marshal of France in 1804 at the age of 36. The Restoration only offered the 62 year-old Prince de Hohenlohe, promoted to Marshal in 1827.
> (Porch 1974: 1–7, 30–1, 90–1; Cox 1994: 41–51)

In Prussia, Scharnhorst, Gneisenau, and Clausewitz – the visionaries who had rebuilt the royal army after Jena, introduced conscription and the *Landwehr*, and spread the idea of the 'nation in arms' after Leipzig – found themselves at loose ends after 1815, when reaction descended on Berlin (Paret, in Howard 1966: 34–9; Beck 1995: 51–61; White 1996: 272–7). King Friedrich Wilhelm III now considered the reformers who had saved his throne after Jena 'Jacobins', and rudely kicked them upstairs or into retirement. General Clausewitz was banished to the Prussian Kriegsakademie, where he was lumbered with administrative tasks and an outdated curriculum (Gatzke, in Clausewitz 1960: 4–5). There he found plenty of time to write his enduring classic: *On War* (Craig 1955: 65–81). In Russia after 1815, Tsar Alexander lost all interest in the reforms he had propagated at his coronation in 1801 and became a mystical Christian revivalist instead. In the Russian army, Alexander pushed young, progressive officers – who made political and economic modernization a prerequisite for military greatness – to the sidelines. There they plotted the Decembrist Rising of 1825, a botched liberal *coup* that was viciously put down by Alexander's ultra-conservative heir, Tsar Nicholas I, who was committed only to the spread of Russian 'Orthodoxy and Autocracy', his slogan in fact (Johnson 1991: 112–15, 838–48).

In Austria, Field Marshal Joseph Radetzky – Austria's most talented staff officer in the Napoleonic Wars – rose steadily after 1815. A charismatic, able soldier, he was also a stony-hearted reactionary, who defeated every impulse toward reform and every concession to nationalism in the Habsburg Monarchy in the years between 1815 and his death in 1858. Under Radetzky, the Austrian army acquired the form it would cling to until 1866: an elephantine bureaucracy that duplicated the functions of the Austrian civil service, and – in the field – massed, white-coated columns of illiterate Slavs, Hungarians and Italians under the direction of German officers, who proverbially 'knew only how to curse and criticize in the language of their men' (Schmidt-Brentano 1975: 476–7; Brandt 1978: II, 603–24; Wawro 1996c: III, 42–65). Under Radetzky, the Austrian army became not a 'school of the nation' – for there was no single nation in multinational Austria – but rather an instrument to denationalize Austrian youth. Austrian conscripts were first instructed in the German 'language of command' – eighty words like *Marsch*, *Halt* and *Feuer* – and then forbidden all contact with 'national parties': Czech, Croatian, Polish, Hungarian or Italian patriots committed to the reformation of the Habsburg Monarchy into ethnically delimited, self-governing crownlands or nation-states.

The riddle of Napoleon: Jomini and Clausewitz

Resurgent conservatism also influenced the study of war, for Napoleon's sudden disappearance after 1815 prompted a nervous search for the roots of his genius. There were two schools of thought in this inquiry. One concluded that Bonaparte had simply exploited the national and liberal innovations of the French Revolution and made himself the champion of a new democratic age. He had, after all, named himself Consul and Emperor not by divine right, but by plebiscite, earning himself a popular following. A second school of thought ignored these troubling political questions and confined analysis of Napoleon to the military sphere, arguing that Napoleon's fame and victories stemmed from purely military factors that any regime – imperial or national, reactionary or liberal – could successfully imitate. Naturally, the post-war French, Austrian, Prussian and Russian armies scrambled to adopt the latter perspective, which unhitched the study of war from the troubling social, political and economic changes wrought by the French Republic and Empire in the years between 1792 and 1815.

The tribune of this conservative school was a former Napoleonic staff officer, General Antoine-Henri Jomini. A Swiss citizen born in 1779, Jomini passed most of the French Revolution peacefully, clerking at a bank in Basle. When Revolutionary France forced the Swiss cantons to form a French satellite state in 1798, Jomini, discerning an outlet for his ambitions, joined the army of the newly created Helvetic Republic and rose swiftly to the rank of major. Jomini's ambitions were chiefly pecuniary, and he served in the Swiss war ministry only until 1802, when he was discharged for soliciting bribes from a military contractor. Jomini fled to Paris, joined the French army, and found a place on the staff of Marshal Michel Ney, the commandant of Napoleon's VI Corps (Shy, in Paret 1986: 143–85).

Secure at last in the entourage of one of Napoleon's favourite generals, Jomini began to write. Though he had little military experience, he had read enough of the eighteenth-century military theorists like Henry Lloyd and G. F. von Tempelhof to begin spinning some theories of his own. Like Lloyd and Tempelhof, Jomini believed that all wars could be rationally explained, and reduced to a simple formula, one that Jomini published in 1803 and merely elaborated in subsequent works. The formula was pure Napoleon. It went like this:

> Strategy is the key to warfare [and] all strategy is controlled by invariable scientific principles. ... These principles prescribe *offensive action* to *mass forces* against weaker enemy forces at some *decisive point* if strategy is to lead to victory.
>
> (Shy, in Paret 1986: 146)

This facile maxim contained two pernicious tendencies: the nineteenth-century soldier's unswerving faith in the massive concentration of troops on a single 'line of operations', which could really be accomplished only by small armies, as the Austrians, Americans, French and Russians would discover in the great wars of the 1860s and 1870s, and the tactical 'cult of the offensive', which led the French in 1859, the Austrians in 1866, the Americans throughout their Civil War, and the Russians in 1877–8 to attempt needlessly bloody frontal attacks (Howard 1966: 18–19; Luvaas, in Howard 1966: 78–9). As weapons improved – shrapnel was introduced in 1804, the infantry rifle in the 1840s, the Gatling gun in the 1860s – offensives became chancier propositions. Moreover, massing troops on a single line had already proven problematic in the Napoleonic Wars, when wayward supply trains carrying vital stores of food and ammunition had lost themselves in the crush of infantry, cavalry and guns on the march route (Glover 1980: 35–51). The obvious problem with Jomini – who wrote and published prolifically from 1803 until his death in 1869 – was that he oversimplified combat. He plucked war from its logistical, social and political context, and extruded its 'fog and friction': stupidity, fanaticism, blunders and foul weather. A shrewd businessman who earned handsome royalties from his publications, Jomini marketed war as a more or less exact science that was best left to the professional military. In his studies of the Napoleonic Wars, he hardly mentioned the fanatical Calabrian or Spanish peasants who had joyously ambushed, mutilated and crucified French troops or their *afrancesados* foolish enough to leave the beaten track (Esdaile 1995: 126–31; Gates 1986: 34–6, 73–7; Finley 1994: 26–7; Tone 1994: 132–4). Similiar atrocities in Russia and the German states – some inflamed by religion, others by local politics or nationalism – also escaped Jomini's notice. Though he had been with Ney during the French retreat from Russia and had witnessed first-hand the guerrilla war in Spain, Jomini reduced war to the comforting principle that any army efficiently concentrated in the vicinity of a divided enemy could win by combining its strength sooner than its foe. He impatiently waved away the foulest aspects of war; acknowledging that Napoleon had pushed the limits, he observed that 'one might say that [Napoleon] was sent into this world to teach generals and statesmen what they ought to avoid' (Esdaile 1995: 295). This, of course, was wishful thinking: war can never be put inside a bottle and corked.

Jomini's guiding principle, which he elaborated in his multi-volume analysis of the French Revolutionary Wars and summarized in his most famous work, *Précis de l'Art de la Guerre* (1838), struck a responsive chord with professional soldiers after 1815 (Strachan 1983: 68–9). Jomini seemed to have solved the riddle of Napoleon. According to the Swiss thinker, Napoleon had swept to victory not because he had successfully mobilized all of France for war and integrated key reforms of the French Revolution into his own authoritarian regime (making it expansive and popular); he had won simply because he had chosen his battlefields more carefully and manoeuvred more adroitly than his enemies (Jomini 1965: 68–99, 159). Even at Waterloo, Napoleon's downfall, the French emperor had nearly beaten the British and the Prussians by thrusting between their converging armies and hitting them separately, first the Prussians at Ligny, then the British at Waterloo. Only Blücher's unexpected return to the battlefield with the rump of his army had saved Wellington and doomed Napoleon.

Yet was this not the essence of war? War never kept to a formula, Jomini's 'regulating principles'. It was by nature unpredictable, and in the new age created by the French Revolution always liable to burst its professional boundaries and spill into the populace, where armed, impassioned mobs could join insurrections and rip the social fabric once war was declared (think of France in 1870–1, Russia in 1905, Germany in 1918). Although Jomini would have escaped many of war's horrors amid the relative comfort of the general staff, he had seen enough of the Russian and Spanish campaigns to know that wars were messy affairs (in the *Précis* he rued 'that frightful epoch when priests, women, and children throughout Spain plotted the murder of isolated soldiers') (Jomini 1965: 34–5). Nevertheless, his professional clientele craved a simple answer to the great riddle posed by Napoleon: how had Bonaparte pushed France through fifteen years of war, heaping up victories along the way? There had to be social, political and cultural explanations for this, yet Jomini confined himself to military ones: mass, initiative and the offensive spirit were all. In this way Jomini became 'the high priest of Continental *grande guerre* orthodoxy', very consciously inspiring a pull back to the more orderly eighteenth-century style of war (Strachan 1985: 5).

Jomini's Prussian contemporary and rival, Karl von Clausewitz, was a shrewder, more penetrating critic of war and the modern age. Born at Burg near Berlin in 1780, Clausewitz had already begun to appreciate the unconventional nature of a 'people's war' at the age of twelve, when he had enlisted in the Prussian army and spent four years fighting the French in western

Germany. In 1807, he was among the military reformers summoned by King Friedrich Wilhelm III to reorganize the Prussian army after its collapse at Jena. In Berlin and Königsberg, Clausewitz helped Scharnhorst and Gneisenau overcome conservative opposition to their military reforms, which were enacted between 1807 and 1811. These reforms included the relaxation of Prussia's notoriously harsh discipline (to improve troop morale), the introduction of conscription (to mobilize Prussia's untapped reserves of manpower), the creation of a *Landwehr* or national guard ('to unite warrior and civilian society'), and the adoption of French skirmishing and shock tactics, which Prussian traditionalists decried as an impertinent slap to Frederick the Great's chief legacy: the flawlessly drilled line of musketeers (Craig 1955: 69–70).

In 1811, Prussia's king meekly bowed to French demands that he contribute 20,000 men to Napoleon's Grand Army and make his country a staging area for Bonaparte's invasion of Russia in 1812. For the Prussian reformers, whose hopes of liberation had risen briefly in 1809 only to be dashed at Wagram, this last Prussian surrender proved too much. Scharnhorst, Clausewitz and the rest resigned their Prussian commissions and joined the Russian army. For the remainder of the French Wars, Clausewitz would serve as a Russian colonel. In 1813, he was instrumental in detaching Napoleon's Prussian contingent from the *Grande Armée* and enlisting it in the Sixth Coalition instead. This treasonous act alienated him completely from King Friedrich Wilhelm III of Prussia, who henceforth took for granted that Clausewitz was a mutineer and a revolutionary. Clausewitz shortly proved him right. To harry the French and disorganize their retreat through Prussia, he armed 20,000 Prussian peasants in 1813 with captured weapons; this was the *Landsturm*, a Prussian mass levy akin to Carnot's *levée* of 1793. As usual, Friedrich Wilhelm III opposed the measure, yet Clausewitz went ahead. To him, modern war was 'a trinity' that joined three elements: army, state and society. The Prussian king, a product of the old regime, could only conceive of the first two elements. Clausewitz, a product of the revolutionary age, stressed the third. Purely dynastic wars were finished he argued, for 'the passions that are to be kindled in war must already be inherent in the people' (Clausewitz 1976: 89; Esdaile 1995: 262–8). Wars would increasingly be national struggles.

After the conservative restoration of 1815, Clausewitz vanished into the depths of the Prussian bureaucracy. The king could not sack such a visible hero of the 'Wars of Liberation', so he did the next best thing. He made Clausewitz director of the Prussian war academy – a backwater – and forbade him to make changes to the hoary curriculum. With little to do in the years between 1818 and 1830, Clausewitz sank his energy into his great unfinished work, *On War*, which appeared finally in 1832, a year after Clausewitz contracted cholera and died at the age of fifty-one, 'pushing aside his life like a heavy burden' (Clausewitz 1960: 5).

For many years *On War* attracted none of the attention enjoyed by Jomini's *Précis*. Whereas Jomini wrote plainly, Clausewitz – an admirer of the Prussian philosopher Immanuel Kant – tried to sound philosophical, with disappointing results. Indeed it is hard to dispute J. F. C. Fuller's opinion that *On War* is 'largely a jumble of essays … prolix, repetitive, full of platitudes and truisms, and in places contradictory and highly involved', or Jomini's own waspish critique of Clausewitz: 'This facile pen is at times a little vagrant, and is above all too pretentious for a didactic discussion, in which simplicity and clarity ought to come first' (Jomini 1965: 42; J. Fuller 1992: 60; Howard 1966: 11). And yet for all of its stylistic faults, *On War* contained profound insights that added a valuable, new dimension to the study of strategy. In contrast to Jomini, who divided warfare and society, Clausewitz insisted that 'war belongs to the province of social life'. He argued that if war were limited it was only because generals, statesmen and rabble-rousers agreed to keep it within bounds; one or both parties to a conflict could as easily unleash the 'dogs of war', with catastrophic results (Strachan 1985: 7–8; J. Fuller 1992: 62). In the modern age of mass armies and emergent nationalism, war was riskier than ever. Napoleon had found this out the hard way. Indeed, Clausewitz's insistence that war always be fitted to an achievable political object derived in large part from his study of Napoleon, who had never done this.

While Jomini confidently assured soldiers that war could be a limited enterprise – controlled by masterful military strokes – Clausewitz sowed doubts that would later prove justified. To him, war was anything but controllable; war was a destructive, unchained beast. Once let loose, it invariably ran amok. While Jomini described military 'keypoints' and 'lines of operation', Clausewitz considered the actual experience of battle. Wars and battles were 'chancy', 'unpredictable', and 'dangerous'; they swayed back and forth and were managed not by theories, but by men, who struggled to overcome the 'fog and friction' of war and make order from chaos. Here of course was the intellectual seed of *Auftragstaktik* or 'mission tactics': the legendary Prussian emphasis on individual initiative and problem-solving (Paret, in Howard 1966: 27–8). Whereas Jomini – who rejected *On War* as 'a declamation against all theory of war' – would have embarked upon war lightly so long as 'massive force' had been concentrated at 'decisive points', Clausewitz condemned this narrow technical outlook and insisted that war always be viewed as a 'political instrument' that could deliver great gains or disasters (Jomini 1965: 42; Howard 1966: 11). Clausewitz warned that the professional military, even in possession of Jomini's recipe for victory, ought never to embark on military *adventures*, or drift away from civilian decision-makers because 'war is a continuation of political activity by other means' (Clausewitz 1976: 86–7). Generals would ignore this at their peril; to do so would be to risk the support of their own governments and people, essential struts in a modern war of nations.

Unfortunately, the philosophical cobwebs shrouding so much of Clausewitz's work hung thickest on his strategic and political thoughts. As a result, they were often overlooked. His emphasis on battle ('victory is purchased by blood') was clearer, and this is what endeared him most to future Prusso-German strategists. Field Marshal Alfred von Schlieffen later called *On War* 'in content and form the greatest book on war ever written' (Clausewitz 1960: 5). Having watched Bonaparte twist and wriggle his way through twenty years of fighting with powerful but disjointed coalitions, Clausewitz believed that war – once embarked upon for a statesmanlike, achievable purpose – had to be driven home with merciless violence. 'To introduce into the philosophy of war a principle of moderation would be an absurdity', he wrote. 'War is an act of violence, pushed to its utmost bounds'. The enemy army had to be destroyed, the enemy capital occupied, and the enemy population pacified. The enemy in short had to be trounced. Clausewitz spoke of the 'overruling importance of the destructive principle', which was best applied through brutal, thrusting offensives (Clausewitz 1976: 77, 90–9). On this point, Jomini and Clausewitz agreed, though Clausewitz rejected Jomini's rather innocent view that war and its impact could be contained by surgical military operations (Howard 1966: 16–17). *On War* insisted that the French Revolution had changed the conduct of war forever by arming and inspiring whole nations:

> War ... took on an entirely different nature, or rather approached more nearly to its true nature, its absolute perfection. The potentials that were mobilized had no apparent limits, instead these disappeared in the energy and enthusiasm of governments and their subjects. ... War, freed from every bond of convention, had again broken loose in all its elemental fury.
>
> (Paret, in Howard 1966: 27–8)

Improving the 'means of destruction': key changes in weapons technology, 1815–49

In his *Summary of the Art of War* published in 1838, Jomini noted that rapid advances in weapons technology were making war bloodier and more difficult with each passing year:

> The new inventions of the last 20 years seem to threaten a great revolution in army organization, armament, and tactics. ... The Congreve rockets ... the shrapnel howitzers, which throw a stream of canister as far as the range of a bullet, the Perkins steam-guns, which vomit forth as many balls as a battalion – all will multiply the chances of destruction, as though the hecatombs of Eylau, Borodino, Leipzig, and Waterloo were not sufficient to decimate the European races.
>
> (Jomini 1965: 58)

An invention that Jomini neglected to mention was the modern infantry rifle, which was being introduced even as he published his *Précis*. Throughout the Revolutionary and Napoleonic Wars, French and allied troops had carried flintlock muskets, which misfired 20 per cent of the time and were surprisingly inaccurate even at short ranges. The misfires occurred in rain, fog or damp, which wetted the flint and gunpowder. British engineers began solving this problem in the 1820s by introducing the percussion cap, a metal tube of mercury and potash detonated by a blow from the hammer. This watertight 'percussion system' all but eliminated misfires; and when combined with rifling in the barrel, it transformed the old infantry musket into a truly formidable weapon.

The first 'rifles' were simply muskets with grooved barrels. All armies had employed riflemen since the eighteenth century, but because it was difficult to force a musket ball down a grooved barrel and then aim a shot at a distant, moving target, only small numbers of 'sharpshooters' and 'fusiliers' had ever been issued rifles. In 1848, however, a French officer, Claude-Etienne Minié, invented a grooved, tapered, cylindrical bullet that could be rammed down the muzzle of a rifle as smoothly as a ball down a smoothbore. The new 'Minié rifles', which were cheaper to produce than the early rifles and could be fitted with bayonets, were eagerly procured by every European great power in the course of the 1840s and 1850s. The Minié rifle quadrupled the effective range of line infantry, from 150 to 600 yards. Minié's conical bullet also flew flatter and hit harder than the musket ball that it replaced. At 150 yards, the Minié rifle was twice as accurate as the smoothbore musket; at 400 yards it was eleven times more accurate. At longer ranges – 500–600 yards – British officers observed that 150 riflemen inflicted substantially more damage than 525 musketeers (Strachan 1985: 37–43).

As each power rushed to manufacture its own version of the French rifle – the British Enfield, the Austrian Lorenz, the American Sharps – Nikolaus Dreyse, a Prussian engineer who had apprenticed with the American firm Remington, sought in 1849 to leapfrog the competition by inventing a bolt-action, breech-loading rifle that would fire four or five times quicker than a muzzle-loader. This was the Prussian 'needle rifle', which would devastate the Austrian army in 1866. However, early models of the Dreyse rifle were spurned by Prussia's neighbours. The needle-shaped firing pin was brittle and badly forged; the bolt action tended to jam in place or rip open the paper catridges that encased the Minié bullet; the cork seal around Dreyse's breech functioned badly, dissipating much of the needle rifle's velocity before the bullet even left the barrel. This catalogue of defects, added to the rifle's gluttonous consumption of ammunition (which would overtax any army's horse-drawn supply lines), sufficed to discredit breech-loaders in the eyes of military experts until the Austro-Prussian War of 1866 conclusively demonstrated their great merits.

Countdown to the revolutions of 1848

In the decades between 1815 and 1848, educated Europeans chafed at the reactionary regimes restored to power by the Congress of Vienna. They balked at the tactless revival of hated symbols like the Bourbon lily in France and the Habsburg eagle in Milan and Budapest, and resented the stultifying erosion of civil liberties at the hands of statesmen like Metternich, who called himself a 'moral power' sent to save Europe from itself (Nicolson 1974: 266–7). Even before the Congress of Vienna had adjourned, European liberals had begun to agitate, forming secret societies and radical clubs like Italy's *Carbonari* or France's Society of the Rights of Man, to undermine the restored monarchies. Violent revolutions flared in Italy, Germany, Spain and Poland in 1820 and 1830. Still, the impact of revolutionary organizations and their revolutions was slight. Peasants comprised 80 per cent of the European population in the early 1800s, and they had little national or political consciousness. Indeed, it was quite rare to meet a European outside of the cities who could read. When Louis XVIII returned to France in 1815, 25,000 French communes still had no primary or secondary school at all, and France – with a population of 28 million – sent just 10,000 children a year to high school. By 1842, the number of French high school students had risen to just 19,000. Russia at the time – with a population of 68 million – educated only 20,000 children a year (Hobsbawm 1987: 168–9; Bury 1989: 16). This negligence was not accidental, for Europe's restored monarchs correctly equated education with liberalism. Emperor Ferdinand of Austria (deposed in 1848) seriously believed that universities belonged inside the walls of garrison towns, and King Carlo Felice of Savoy, who ascended the throne of Piedmont in 1821, spoke for his peers when he said: 'the good people are ignoramuses; the bad ones are educated' (Schmidt-Brentano 1975: 300; Barzini 1986: 16). The vast majority of Europeans in the early nineteenth century were illiterate or semi-literate peasants concerned only to scrape a living from the land; this suited their restored masters perfectly.

Urbanization and industrialization after 1815 altered the landscape. The industrial revolution, which commenced in England in the 1780s, had already worked major social changes there. Labour agitation against low wages and cruel working conditions prompted calls for political and economic reform, and sharp, polarizing clashes with the state. The most sensational was the 'Peterloo Massacre' of 1819, when mounted British militiamen rode into a crowd of working-class demonstrators in Manchester, killing ten, wounding several hundred others, and inducing another primal scream from Shelley: 'I met Murder on the way – He had a mask like Castlereagh' ('The Mask of Anarchy'). In the 1820s, the term 'working class', which connoted economically determined class conflict, gained currency in Britain and Europe. Labour organization also increased. In France, trade unionists adopted the military term *avant-garde* to describe their function – an advance guard that would penetrate the *mur d'argent*, the 'wall of capital' – and Auguste Blanqui coined the term 'industrial revolution' to explain the radical changes in French society (R. Palmer 1971: 251–70). In Britain and Europe, workers formed unions, mutual aid societies, schools and reading clubs, and began experimenting with a new weapon to wound industry and the conservative state: the strike. Newspapers began increasingly to publish social and political criticism. In Prussia, a liberal law student named Karl Marx took too keen an interest in the burgeoning labour movement and was forced into exile by royal authorities in 1840. Marx settled in London, and there – at the age of thirty, comfortably maintained by a wealthy textile manufacturer named Friedrich Engels – wrote the *Communist Manifesto* in 1848.

European monarchs were not all daft. Some chose to introduce measured reforms to defuse the smouldering social crisis. In 1830, Duke Louis-Philippe d'Orleans – a cousin of the French king – preempted revolution in Paris by ousting seventy year-old Charles X, who, in the six years since Louis XVIII's death, had governed in an almost inconceivably unpopular way: restoring Versailles at public expense, indemnifying the old aristocracy for the loss of their estates during the Revolution, returning education to the Catholic church, and suppressing France's legislature (de Bertier de Sauvigny 1966: 365–460). Louis-Philippe, who reigned from 1830 to 1848, formed a striking contrast. He strolled about Paris in a simple frock coat (surviving eighteen assassination attempts by unappeased radicals) and sent his children to re-secularized state schools. He called himself a 'bourgeois monarch', and took care to honour and employ France's expanding middle class. Yet such was the march of social change that Louis-Philippe's reforms did little to appease Europe's most dangerous class: not the bourgeois liberals or even Marx's 'factory proletarians', but the craftsmen and artisans – printers, tailors, shoemakers and weavers – who were steadily losing their jobs and way of life to 'bourgeois industrialism' and the assembly line. The 'novelty of the situation after 1815', Eric Hobsbawm has observed, 'was that the [labour movement] was increasingly directed against the liberal middle class as well as the kings and aristocrats' (Hobsbawm 1987: 258–61). On the land, European peasants were no less restive. Cold weather, bad harvests, price inflation, conscription and rising taxes eroded even rural support for the conservative monarchies in the 1830s and 1840s.

'Champions of justice and right': war as a tool of national integration

Just fifteen years after Waterloo, European leaders looked anxiously for ways out of what was fast becoming a social and political crisis (Price 1989: 1–33). Louis-Philippe's popularly-sanctioned *coup* in 1830 had triggered revolutions in Germany, Italy and Poland that had ultimately to be put down by the great powers (Clausewitz, a general in 1830, contracted cholera and died while restoring order in Posen, Prussia's wedge of Poland). In Britain in 1838, millions of workers signed the 'People's Charter', which demanded universal male suffrage and the secret ballot, to no avail. When Welsh miners attempted to enact the Charter in 1839, they were set upon by British troops. From London to Moscow, the central political question of the nineteenth century emerged in sharp relief: how could governments head off protest without fundamentally changing their economic and political systems? Oddly, Europe's armies and navies seemed to offer a way out of the dilemma. By conducting expansionist foreign policies and 'showing the flag' across Europe and the world, they might rally popular support and distract attention from increasingly virulent domestic–political conflicts (Best 1982: 241–2).

Pressure for change was most acute in France and Britain, where expectations of liberal reform and levels of literacy and education were higher than in Austria, Prussia, Russia or Italy. In Britain, the need for reform was already apparent in 1815, when anti-Corn Law riots exploded across the kingdom in response to a tariff on foreign grain that protected wealthy landowners at the expense of the poor. In London, a hungry mob had attacked Parliament and pulled members from their coaches, forcing the household cavalry to charge down Whitehall to the rescue (Johnson 1991: 372–3). Thereafter, British statesmen combined halting political reforms with a grand foreign policy that aimed to rally Britons of all classes behind the 'civilizing mission' of the British armed forces. Britain's campaign against the slave trade in the years after 1815 was a perfect example of this phenomenon. Castlereagh had inserted a clause in the Treaty of Vienna outlawing the slave trade. At the time, other powers thought this little more than British sanctimony, yet the reluctance of French, Spanish, Portuguese, Brazilian and American slavers to observe the clause gave Britain something to do with its 300-ship navy in the years after 1815. Braving repeated diplomatic incidents with France and the United States, the Royal Navy declared war on pirates and slavers, bombarding Algiers in 1816 and creating the West African Squadron to patrol the 3,000 mile-long 'Slave Coast' from Senegal to the Congo. When Parliament questioned the expense of the enterprise – British cruisers impounded 1,500 vessels and freed 160,000 slaves over the years – one British prime minister replied that cost was irrelevant in this 'high and holy work against ... the curse and the crime of slavery' (H. Thomas 1997: 737–8; Kennedy 1976: 164–8).

Castlereagh slit his throat in 1822 in the midst of this humanitarian operation, conferring leadership of the Conservative Party's foreign affairs to his arch-enemy, George Canning. Whereas Castlereagh had aligned Britain with the reactionary powers (the 'repose' of Europe was always his aim), Canning embarked on a more dynamic, liberal foreign policy that did not shrink from revolution, whether in Greece or Argentina. Metternich was duly appalled; he called Canning 'the devil incarnate', the 'evil genius of revolution', and a 'Jacobin democrat'. Yet Canning forged ahead; throughout the 1820s he railed successfully against 'the areopagitical spirit' of Metternich, Tsar Alexander and his own predecessor. In 1822–3 he joined the United States in supporting the new South American republics of Colombia, Chile and Argentina against a Spanish reconquest. After US President James Monroe issued his famous doctrine warning the European powers off of the Americas, Canning boasted that he had 'called the New World into existence, to redress the balance of the Old'. This sort of rhetoric played well in Parliament and in Canning's Liverpool constituency.

Between 1825 and 1827, Canning rode the romantic wave that was sweeping England in the wake of Byron's colourful death at Missolonghi; to public acclaim, he stitched together a European coalition to induce the Ottoman Empire to give the Greeks their independence and stop slaughtering Greek islanders in the Aegean. This early exercise in peacekeeping culminated in the last great naval battle of the age of sail, when an English-led allied fleet anchored up against the Turkish navy at Navarino Bay and blasted it to smithereens. The battle on the Greek coast conclusively proved the superiority of European gunnery. While the European fleets lost just 178 men in the close-quarter action, the Turks lost 10,000, most to European shells and drowning, the rest to fires lighted by their own officers on board the crippled Turkish ships. Though a human tragedy, Navarino paid rich political dividends in England. The British public applauded the victory over 'Turkish tyranny', and King George IV showered the victor – Admiral Edward Codrington, one of Nelson's captains at Trafalgar – with decorations. A London newspaper boasted that 'the Turk never before felt the British eloquence of our guns', which perfectly described popular sentiment (Gildea 1996: 65–7; R. Harding 1999: 278–9; Johnson 1991: 696–8). All of these adventures – which served British no less than humanitarian interests by securing American markets, seizing strategic points and curbing the expansion of France and Russia in the Middle East – flowed through the British political system like an invigorating tonic (Bourne 1970: 12–17).

Canning was succeeded at the Foreign Office by an even greater imperialist: Henry John Temple, Viscount Palmerston. Palmerston, a Tory turned Liberal, was Britain's foreign secretary from 1830–41, 1846–51 and 1855–65. In the 1830s and 1840s he conducted a vigorous foreign policy that was designed, as he put it, to make Britain 'the champion of justice and right'. His real aim was to steal the thunder of Parliament's Radical Liberals, who were demanding democratic reforms at home. Palmerston – 'Pam' to his admirers – masterfully changed the subject by shifting the British public's attention abroad with a sequence of showy wars and incidents. In 1840–1, alarmed by French attempts to detach Egypt from the Ottoman Empire, he threatened war and dispatched the Royal Navy to bombard France's Arab allies in Beirut and Acre. In the Far East, he dispatched gunboats to open Chinese ports to British trade and secure the island colony of Hong Kong. In North America, he backed Mexico in its war with the United States and tried to push the border of British Columbia into America's Oregon Territory. In European affairs, he repeatedly squared off with the conservative powers, most notably in 1849, when he gave political asylum to Hungary's Lajos Kossuth, who had called for the overthrow and murder of the Habsburg emperor in 1848.

Palmerston is perhaps best remembered for the Don Pacifico Affair, a spectacular piece of theatre that combined war (or the threat of it) with politics. In 1850, an Athens-based Portuguese merchant named Don Pacifico, who held a British passport only by the accident of his birth at Gibraltar, demanded British support for the restitution of business losses and got it. Palmerston sent Britain's Mediterranean Squadron into the port of Athens and betook himself to Westminster, where he gave the *Civis Romanus sum* speech, which rather famously boasted that the global reach of British sea power had made England the rightful heir of ancient Rome:

> as the Roman, in days of old, held himself free from indignity, when he could say *Civis Romanus sum*; so also a British subject, in whatever land he may be, shall feel confident that the watchful eye and the strong arm of England, will protect him against injustice and wrong.
> (Jenkins 1994: 78–9; Best 1982: 241–2; Bourne 1970: 301–2)

For Palmerston no less than Canning, bellicosity had powerful electoral appeal, and became an important facet of British politics in the Victorian period. Elections frequently turned on imperial issues, which was hardly surprising in a culture where the voting classes indulged in a mania for military fashions. Victorian women wore green velvet 'rifle dresses' and hussar jackets; boys dressed as sailors or kilted highlanders, and British gentlemen wore suits of 'Waterloo blue' and 'Alma brown' (Myerly 1996: 149–50). As Great Britain ascended to the peak of its world power, the British public joined enthusiastically in the venture.

French statesmen also resorted to foreign adventures to popularize themselves. In 1823, Louis XVIII had launched a military expedition calculated to stir popular passions and distract attention from his sagging regime, which was more or less fairly characterized by one liberal critic as a 'gerontocracy ruled by seven or eight thousand asthmatic, gouty, paralytic [men] with enfeebled faculties' (Sauvigny 1966: 238–9). This was the French invasion of Spain – authorized by Metternich's Congress of Troppau in October – to crush liberal forces and restore the deposed Spanish king. One hundred thousand French troops crossed the Pyrenées and marched to Cadiz, where they defeated the 'constitutionalists' and snatched back the king from his captors. In Paris, Louis XVIII's government used the excursion to dissolve parliament, call new elections and secure a solid majority on the strength of the military success. A clear-sighted French officer summed up the real aim of the campaign: it was a 'Don Quixotiade' contrived to impress public opinion (Hall 1909: 310–48; Sauvigny 1966: 186–97). As if to confirm that impression, Louis XVIII named the imposing height opposite the Champs-de-Mars in Paris after the fortress at Cadiz: Trocadéro.

Charles X's foray into Algeria in 1830 ran in the same vein; it was only partly intended to destroy North Africa's Barbary pirates, who preyed on France's Mediterranean trade. In fact, Charles X snidely referred to Algeria as 'France's opera box', and his successor, Louis-Philippe, who was shortly engulfed by his own political problems, called the growing Algerian colony 'a distraction to keep our turbulent imaginations occupied'. Indeed, the Mahgreb was a colourful place, and France's gradual conquest of it between 1830 and 1857 was undertaken for strategic and economic reasons to be sure, but also to furnish the French press and public with a steady diet of adventures which would win acclaim for the government (Collingham 1988: 248–9; Vandervort 1998: 56–62; Bury 1989: 42–3, 58–9; Glover 1980: 40–6). One reason the Bourbon Monarchy found itself unprepared for the Orleanist revolution of 1830 was that Charles X had assumed that the French conquest of Algiers – completed in the summer of 1830 – would rally France behind him (Porch 1974: 34–5).

For the 'July Monarchy' of Louis-Philippe, who seized the crown from Charles X and ruled France from 1830–48, foreign and military policy bulked even larger. Because Louis-Philippe took power by revolutionary means, ousting the Bourbons and reinstating conscription and the tricolour flag, many at first took him for a new Napoleon (Cox 1994: 94–120). French radicals expected him to retake territory lost in 1815 and carry national revolutions into Poland, Italy and the Middle East, where the French backed the Egyptians for a time against the Turks. The new king, however, was a timid statesman and an unprepossessing figure. People called him 'the crowned pear', and his chief minister, François Guizot, evinced a complete ignorance as to the domestic-political uses of military expansion:

> Let us not talk about our country having to conquer territory, to wage great wars, to undertake bold deeds of vengeance. If France is prosperous, if she remains free, rich, peaceful, and wise, we need not complain.
>
> (Bury 1989: 59)

Halcyon opinions like these ultimately disgraced the July Monarchy, revealing anew the link between war, society and politics. As H. A. C. Collingham, the July Monarchy's most recent historian, has convincingly demonstrated, Louis-Philippe was perpetually trapped 'between the needs of a British alliance and fear of French opinion'. The British wanted France to accept the borders of 1815 and stay out of the Mediterranean; the French public wanted 'revenge for Waterloo' (border adjustments in Belgium and Germany, satellite states in Poland and Italy) and colonial expansion in the Middle East and Africa. In the end, Louis-Philippe abandoned his riskiest ventures – in Poland, Italy and Egypt – and contented himself with the gradual colonization of Algeria (Collingham 1988: 186–98). Although the French king never really approved of the Algerian conquest, Collingham shows that he willingly sponsored it for its domestic-political benefits: to lionize his sons and heirs in colonial combat, to satisfy the French army's appetite for expansion, and to convince the French public that he was taking a hard line with the Anglo-Saxons (Collingham 1988: 248–56). Another historian of the July Monarchy, David Pinkney, stresses the emotional importance of Algeria for Louis-Philippe's and subsequent French governments:

> The old colonies had never engaged popular emotions among the French people. They were commercial ventures, free of any involvement with national honor or prestige. The conquest of Algeria, its skirmishes magnified by the daily press into heroic battles, became associated in the public mind with national military glories (which had been in short supply for the French since the fall of Napoleon). The new possession in North Africa acquired a patriotic and national importance that the old colonies had never had. That emotional, even irrational attachment lasted for more than a century.
>
> (Pinkney 1986: 141–5)

Still, Orleanist imperialism was half-hearted at best, and this faintheartedness would ultimately destroy Louis-Philippe's credit with the French people and leave a stain on the French army. Under the July Monarchy, the French aristocracy and middle class gradually abandoned the unambitious army as a career, leaving the French officer corps to the poorly educated lower-middle class. These were the years when dimwits like Achille Bazaine – who failed the entrance exam to the Ecole Polytechnique and despairingly joined the infantry as a private – infiltrated the French army and began rising to positions of power, where they would resentfully cultivate the anti-bourgeois, anti-intellectual spirit that would lay France low in 1870 (Porch 1974: 66–7). These were also the years when Marshal Thomas Bugeaud ruled France's Algerian annexe with an iron hand, training a whole generation of French officers – who would attain senior commands under the Third Republic – to despise civilians, parliaments and the rule of law (Vandervort 1998: 62–7; Pinkney 1986: 143–6). Of course, none of this was immediately apparent to Louis-Philippe, who in 1840 made a final, rather pathetic attempt to buck up his army and coopt French nationalists by transporting the dusty remains of Napoleon from St Helena to Paris. The ceremony was a flagrant appeal to Napoleonic memories. Louis-Philippe had Bonaparte's remains encased in a red marble tomb and paraded down the Champs-Elysées by elderly veterans of the Grand Army to shouts of *Vive Napoléon! Vive l'Empire!*

1848: The 'springtime of the peoples'?

Stunts like this would not save the July Monarchy. By 1848, Paris was home to one million people, twice the population of 1800; like other European cities, it was feeling the strain. Housing and working conditions were squalid, public health appalling, and republican and communist nostrums increasingly attractive. For the first time, French workers had begun to call themselves *prolétaires*: class enemies of the capitalists (Hobsbawm 1987: 211–15; Bury 1989: 50–3; Collingham 1988: 365–83). Alexis de Tocqueville, a worried liberal, rued Louis-Philippe's inaction on the all-important social question: 'We sleep now that we are on top of a volcano' (Collingham 1988: 385–418). Proudhon, a less sympathetic critic, blasted the king's 'immobilisme'. In February 1848, workers in Paris finally rose against the July Monarchy, and demanded a republic. Deserted even by his middle-class supporters – the 'greengrocer janissaries' who had helped suppress the Lyon Insurrection of 1831 and every other proletarian rising until 1848 – Louis-Philippe handed power to a republican committee and fled into exile. The easy triumph of republicanism in France sparked revolutions across Europe.

In Austria, Emperor Ferdinand, a mentally retarded young man called 'the dumpling' by his subjects, was driven out of Vienna by a revolutionary crowd. Students, artisans, workers and even respectable bourgeois invaded the imperial palace and arsenal demanding reform. Though Metternich got away, a mob trapped the Austrian war minister Count Theodor Baillet de Latour, beat him to death and hung him from a streetlamp. In the Habsburg crownlands, frustrated nationalism sharpened the liberal revolution. 'Young Czechs' stormed the Habsburg palace in Prague and demanded official recognition of their language and culture. In Hungary, nationalists went further; they overthrew the Habsburg emperor and proclaimed a republic. In Milan and Venice, Italian nationalists rose against the Austrian Empire and summoned the Piedmontese army to deliver Italy from foreign domination (Sked 1989: 89–134; Rothenberg 1976: 22–37; Price 1989: 37–9, 71–6). In Germany, liberal and nationalist opponents of the Confederation of 1815 ousted their princes and convened a 'German parliament' at Frankfurt to draft a unitary constitution for all of the German states (Sheehan 1989: 656–729). In Poland, a national committee claimed sovereignty over the Polish provinces of Russia, Austria and Prussia. In Prussia, King Friedrich Wilhelm IV fled his capital before a howling mob. Significantly, the revolutions were urban; workers, artisans, clerks, shopkeepers and professionals spontaneously united to form revolutionary fronts. However, the fronts just as quickly dissolved when the wealthy merchants and professionals who headed them came to fear the socialist, democratic demands of their lower-class colleagues, and when German-speaking liberals deserted the Czech and Polish national movements for fear that they might be 'shut out' of the successor states. As the revolutionary movements splintered, the European peasantry – which would form the conservative core of European armies and politics until 1914 – began finally to stir.

Until the late nineteenth century, the population of Europe was chiefly rural. In the eastern empires of Russia and Austria, only one person in ten lived in a town or city. In more industrialized societies like France and Prussia, the ratio was three in ten, in Britain just five in ten in 1848 (Hobsbawm 1985b: 205). These demographic facts had political ramifications, for nineteenth-century peasants were indifferent to the urban ideals of nationalism and liberalism, and positively hostile to revolution, which they equated with anarchy, inflation and new taxes (Corbin 1992: 19–38). To the end of his days, Marx feared the peasant; he resented the countryman's uncomplicated world-view, invariably expressed in proverbs ('the peasant farts when his belly is full, the bourgeois when his belly is empty'), and prejudged him a counter-revolutionary (Marx 1969). In this he was quite correct, for once. When a Polish nationalist named Ludwik Mieroslawski attempted in 1846 to raise the Polish and Ukrainian peasants of Galicia against the Austrians, the peasants responded not by joining, but by handing Mieroslawski's agents over to the Habsburg police, and then looting and torching the country houses of Mieroslawski's gentry (Best 1982: 293–4). (It was in the midst of this counter-revolutionary jacquerie that a thirty-five year-old Austrian infantry officer named Ludwig Benedek, who would make a hash of Austria's war with Prussia in 1866, made a name for himself by plucking a Polish lord from the clutches of his furious peasants.) Peasant conservatism showed itself most clearly in 1848. After the urban revolutions had run their course and produced liberal constitutions in France, Austria, Prussia and the German and Italian states – the monarchs retook their capitals and crownlands with the aid of large, obedient peasant armies.

In Paris, the radical republic was crushed in June 1848 by General Louis Cavaignac, who stormed the proletarian districts of Paris with reliable peasant troops trucked in from the suburbs and provinces on steam trains. The French army had been preparing for this eventuality since the 1830s, when, in the Austrian style, it had begun rotating its regiments quickly through urban areas to prevent their contamination with republican ideas, which festered in the cafés and brasseries of garrison towns (Porch 1974: 87–90). In Paris, the 'June Days' of 1848 saw vicious fighting with a perceptible class character. As a French officer watched his men slaughter the revolutionaries (whom the peasants considered parasites living on tax money raised in rural areas), he noted that the streets around the barricades literally 'ran with blood'. Quarter was rarely given and at least 3,000 insurgents were killed. Fifteen thousand more were deported to the 'dry guillotines': penal colonies like New Caledonia and French Guiana, where death from tropical diseases was a dead certainty. The 'June Days' would be considered a singularly ugly episode of fratricide in the land of *fraternité* until exactly the same thing recurred in 1871 in the fight for the Paris Commune. Marx called the 'June Days' a 'modern

Vendée' (a reference to the French counter-revolution of 1793–4) and 'a reaction of the countryside against the town' (Price 1989: 61–7; Marx 1969: 20–3, 31, 110). France remained a republic, but a deeply conservative, socially divided one. Thanks largely to rural and middle-class support, Napoleon's ambitious nephew Louis-Napoleon Bonaparte was elected president of France in December 1848. Though he spoke French with a noticeable accent (having lived his entire life in exile), he trounced every radical candidate put forward by the cities and rallied the peasantry, who went to the urns chanting a mixed-up philosophy that made sense only to rural folk who lived steeped in seclusion and rumour: 'No more taxes; down with the rich; down with the republic; long live the emperor!' (Gildea 1996: 88–90; Hobsbawm 1985b: 40). Sceptical of radical ideals (like the 'right to work' proclaimed by France's Second Republic), the peasant cultivated his garden and hewed to the rustic philosophy of Marshal Bugeaud, France's no-nonsense 'soldier-peasant' of the 1840s: 'After God, your wife and your children, it is clover you must adore' (Porch 1991: 71; Vandervort 1998: 65–7).

In Austria, Archduke Franz Joseph inherited the Habsburg throne from half-mad Ferdinand in December 1848 and easily retook Vienna with the help of Croatian *Grenzer*. These Balkan borderers, the Austrian equivalent of Don Cossacks, made short work of the student and *Bürger* legions deployed in defence of the revolution and then contentedly staked out billets in the parks and streets of the capital. When asked why they joined the Habsburg counter-revolution, the Croats simply replied: 'We are poor; we need someone to give us bread' (Sked 1979: 69; Deak 1992: 36–40). As was the case in France, the Austrian army insulated itself against liberal ferment by recruiting provincials, most of whom swore allegiance to the Habsburg government for the simple reason that it had abolished feudalism in the midst of the revolution. Austrian genre prints of 1848 depict leering, mustachioed 'Pandours' and 'Saracens' – Franz Joseph's Croatian irregulars – guarding the Hofburg and turning away even the most respectable visitors with their two words of German: 'nix Deutsch' – 'no German'.

Elsewhere – in Poland, Hungary, Italy and Germany – the well equipped dynastic armies of the Habsburgs, Hohenzollern and Romanovs crushed the national revolutions. Eighteen forty-eight saw the first military use of the railway when Prussia used the German railways to crush a popular rising in neighbouring Saxony, and Austria used its western and southern lines to move troops to Verona and Milan. In 1849 – prodded by a pope in exile and Catholic voters in France – President Louis-Napoleon Bonaparte rushed a corps into Italy by rail to crush Giuseppe Mazzini's short-lived Roman Republic. Steam locomotives pulling fifteen cars conferred unheard-of mobility on infantry battalions, which could now cover a week's march in a matter of hours. After 1848, the Prussians moved fastest to bring public and private railways (and all new construction) under military control, which helped explain their lightning victories over Austria and France in 1866 and 1870 (Showalter 1975).

Aside from technology, the reactionary armies had one inestimable advantage in the counter-revolutions of 1848–9: the political adherence of Europe's peasants. Marx protested that the peasants had behaved 'like potatoes in a sack', dumbly adhering to their officers and smashing down the barricades of the urban revolutionaries (Marx 1969: 108–9). The Russian tsars Alexander and Nicholas had long planned for this day. Worried after 1815 that the germs of nationalism and liberalism would spread to Russia, they had taken care to settle 'military colonies' – peasant villages administered by the army – among Russia's minority nationalities and near the empire's growing towns. In the military colonies, regiments of Cossacks – irregular soldiers paid by the tsar – were groomed for the day when they would be unleashed against external enemies or internal 'subversives'. The military colonies proved their worth in 1848, when Nicholas I was able to drown the Polish and Hungarian revolts under waves of regular and irregular peasant troops (Best 1982: 223–30). In Russia and elsewhere, peasants fought to restore order and to punish city-dwellers, whom they considered slackers, atheists and regicides. Whatever their personal motives, the sheer number of peasants made them formidable (this is why Mao Zedong later called the peasantry 'the sea in which revolutionaries must swim' in any agricultural society). Russian, Prussian and Austrian peasants fought simply because they had orders to fight. Few shared liberal or national ideals of 'progress', a fact that some urban revolutionaries seem to have appreciated. Their appeals to the peasants in 1848 generally centred on the price of bread. A revolutionary Piedmontese 'catechism' circulated among Austrian troops in Lombardy posited better food and wages as the ultimate aim of the Italian revolution:

Q.   Who is your leader?
A.   Our leader is Hunger.
Q.   Do you like your Emperor?
A.   No, because the Emperor does not pay us and makes us die of hunger.
Q.   Where is your homeland?
A.   Where we can eat.

(Sked 1979: 231)

The social conservatism of the European peasant was a key strut of the European army, and one that made it a potent *political* force until the 1890s, when mass conscription and urbanization began finally to dilute every European army's peasant base. In 1848, and for years afterwards, European armies could safely innoculate themselves against the spread of liberal nationalism, socialism and anarchism by recruiting peasants. In this way the European armies became a stout bulwark against social revolution, and a sure weapon for territorial expansion.

CHAPTER THREE

Napoleon III and the militarization of Europe, 1848–66

As Napoleon neared his end on the island of St Helena in 1820, he prophesied that 'in twenty years, Europe will be either republican or Cossack'. He anticipated, in other words, a great collision between Western liberalism and Russian conservatism, between progress and reaction. Oddly, considering that Napoleon was himself a 'Cossack republican', an authoritarian soldier with a cynical appreciation for the uses of limited, controlled democratization, the French emperor never detected a *new* phenomenon: what we might call 'Cossack republics', conservative monarchies just liberal enough to forestall revolution, but not so liberal as to endanger the power and prerogatives of traditional elites. In these 'Cossack republics', war would serve as an integrating tool. Governments could resort to it as much for political and social reasons – to distract or titillate rival parties – as for strategic ones. Indeed it is striking that right down to the Great War, European leaders would tend to view war as an acceptable trump to be played in times of political crisis: to rally political opponents and fabricate parliamentary majorities in 'khaki elections' unfailingly called on the eve of war or in its celebratory aftermath.

Neo-absolutism

The 'Cossack republics' rooted themselves deeply in the soil of 1848. Peasant armies had crushed the republican revolutions of that year, and the monarchs of Europe moved quickly to consolidate their victory. In Habsburg Austria, Emperor Franz Joseph did this by a process called 'neo-absolutism'. What was 'new' about this latest version of Austrian absolutism was the emperor's paradoxical recruitment of the liberal middle class to staff it. Though a self-proclaimed 'monarch of the old school', who despised even the idea of constitutional government, eighteen year-old Franz Joseph saw the need in 1848 to coopt Austria's growing middle class and make it a part of his military state. Thus, in the decade from 1848 until 1859 – when neo-absolutism collapsed in the wake of the disastrous Franco-Austrian War – the Austrian emperor grafted modern men and ideas – what A. J. P. Taylor called 'a government of

Jacobins' – onto an absolute monarchy (Taylor 1988: 85; Brandt 1978: 247; Bled 1992: 72–84).

The way Franz Joseph did this was interesting. Sure of his peasant masses, who had given proofs of their loyalty in the counter-revolutions of 1848–9, Franz Joseph needed only to tame Austria's restive bourgeosie: students, professional men and merchants – many of them Protestant – who resented the aristocratic and clerical elites in Franz Josephan Austria. To capture these dissidents, the emperor appealed to their vanity and economic interest: he offered educated Austrians secure, tenured employment in an ever-expanding bureaucracy and the opportunity to introduce moderate political reforms. Even the most intransigent revolutionaries of '48 could not resist the temptation. First to succumb was Alexander Bach, a fiery reformer and German nationalist, who discarded his radical past and accepted the all-powerful Habsburg Ministry of the Interior in 1849, earning the sobriquet *Barrikaden-minister* from the emperor's jilted conservatives. Bach eagerly set to work, spinning a seamless tapestry of government *bureaux*. To snatch power away from the empire's landed families – the Liechtenstein, the Kinsky, the Trautmannsdorf, the Batthyány – he carved the Austrian Empire into hundreds of *Kreise* and *Bezirke* – the Austrian equivalent of the French Revolutionary *départements* and *communes* – and staffed them with German-speaking liberals like himself. It was Bach and his revolutionaries who sowed the seeds of the festooned Austrian bureaucracy that would be notorious by 1914; they created state ministries, agencies and secretariats with the ubiquitous *k.k.* (*kaiserlich-königlich*) prefix for everything from salt production to the registry of wild boar. (*Kaiserlich-königlich*, which means 'imperial-royal', referred to the fact that the Emperor of Austria was never accepted as such in Hungary, where he was only 'king'.) Eager for work in what was still a largely agricultural economy, Austria's middle class joined the burgeoning 'Bach system' in record numbers. For the Habsburg emperor, bureaucratization paid enormous dividends. Since politics in multinational Austria turned on cultural and linguistic issues rather than economic ones, the big, well funded German-speaking army and bureaucracy unified the educated elites of the empire and appeased liberalism by promoting German language and manners at the expense of Slavic and Hungarian culture. One did not need a German surname to participate; one had only to accept the primacy of German *Kultur*. Thus, to the end of the monarchy in 1918, all of the Austrian nationalities mingled in the Habsburg government machine, as this Hungarian lampoon of Austrian government in the 1850s made clear:

> Schmutz, Kozseluch, Tumerauf, Hornecek,
> Hruby, Melichar, Schleimer, Chrobacek
> Satala, Kreimel, Safranek, Weigel
> Wawra, Sucek, Prihoda, Beigl
> Wiplel, Worel, Wrtl, Brix

Popelka, Czibulka, Wawrecska, Dix!
(Schmidt-Brentano 1975: 369)

What was most interesting about the trend – what made Austria a classic 'Cossack republic' – was the way in which the emperor used the *k.k.* civil service and army as a sort of jobs bank for his middle-class constituency. In the 1850s and 1860s, scarcely half of Austrian military budgets went to active duty personnel and weapons procurement. The balance was spent on a growing corps of civilian functionaries – professors, physicians, lawyers, accountants, veterinarians – and on generous contracts tendered not to supply the army and navy at a reasonable price, but to purchase the loyalty of Austrian businessmen. Indeed, the 1850s in Austria were punctuated by scandals and suicides, usually involving a general or war ministry official accused of embezzlement or racketeering (Apfelknab 1984; Wawro 1996c: 48–9). Deliberate overstaffing was a racket in its own right; there was no better illustration of this tendency than the Austrian General Staff, where civilian employees – *Kriegskommissäre* – greatly outnumbered military ones during neo-absolutism.

Perhaps 'war commissars' really were needed, to sift through the mulch of useless chanceries that covered the general staff, so very different from its lean Prussian counterpart. At the Hofburg, the emperor created an *Organisationskanzlei* to duplicate the work of the general staff, while his war minister staffed an *Operationskanzlei* to perform the same functions a third time (von Arno n.d.: VI, 32–3). The fabled Austrian Military Frontier (*Grenze*) created on Austria's Balkan borderlands by Empress Maria Theresa in the 1750s and settled with irregular troops – the fiercely mustachioed 'Pandours' and 'Saracens' who had helped put down the urban revolutions of 1848 – became in Franz Joseph's hands a 'bureaucratic frontier' of the first order, employing four times as many civil servants as army officers by the 1860s (Wawro 1996c: 49–50; Brandt 1978: 622–3). Overall, the Austrian army came to play a costly social-political function in the mid-nineteenth century. It absorbed masses of university-trained professionals, who might otherwise have gravitated to a liberal opposition and, as Geoffrey Best points out, never failed to find places lower down the ladder for 'ex-soldiers, who might embezzle and scrounge but thoroughly understood the importance of obeying orders and making others do so too' (Best 1982: 248). Though the system was politically useful, it was militarily pernicious. Until his death in 1858, Field Marshal Joseph Radetzky scolded the emperor for his 'mind-boggling multiplication of offices', and predicted that neo-absolutism would erode preparedness, a prediction borne out by Austria's crushing defeats in 1859 and 1866 (Regele 1957: 425).

Like Austria, Prussia emerged from the revolutions of 1848 at a crossroads. The year-long Prussian revolution had signalled widespread dissatisfaction with the royal government, and King Friedrich Wilhelm IV had sought to

Wilhelm IV

appease public opinion in 1849 by tendering a constitution. Although Prussian liberals, who formed a majority in the Prussian *Landtag*, demanded a proper constitution that would affirm the sovereignty of the people and the supremacy of parliament, they received something altogether different. The Prussian constitution of 1849 merely reaffirmed the God-given right of the Hohenzollern family to rule Prussia, and empowered Friedrich Wilhelm IV to veto parliamentary legislation at will. This constitution, which would shape the all-German constitution of 1871 and remain in force in Prussia – Germany's biggest province – until 1918, was drafted in large part by Prussian army officers (Craig 1955: 117–24; Gildea 1996: 90–2). Indeed, the whole rightward drift of Prusso-German politics after 1848 stemmed from the steady militarization of Prussian politics after the failed liberal revolution.

Aware that they were living in a more democratic age that required democratic gestures, the conservative Prussian army officers who dominated at court and in the new war ministry sought to construct their own version of a 'Cossack republic' in the 1850s and 1860s. First, they made sure that the constitution of 1849 was little more than a fig leaf. Votes were apportioned on the basis of income, property and education – ensuring safe, conservative majorities – and the king retained control of foreign and military affairs as well as broad 'emergency powers' (Carsten 1989: 110–11). Although Friedrich Wilhelm IV did make his war minister responsible to parliament, he and his successors insisted that 'their' war minister (not the people's) need only explain administrative matters in parliament, not the meatier strategic, operational and organizational questions that remained the exclusive prerogative of the king and *his* general staff. The Prussian parliament, which aspired to British-style government, angrily disputed this prerogative, and the question would remain open until 1866, providing Minister President Bismarck – as we shall see in the next chapter – with the notorious 'gap' between crown and parliament that he, Moltke, and Roon so brilliantly exploited in the 1860s to take control of the Prussian army and vastly expand its powers at the expense of the Prussian legislature.

The militarization of Prussia was more than just political; it was social and cultural as well. In his anthropological study of German militarism, Emilio Willems posits that the revolutionary tumults of 1848–9 had made 'law and order … an indisputable priority in the value system of Prussian society'. The point is arguable, but Willems is on firmer ground noting that Germans looked on more or less indifferently as the Hohenzollern army increased its powers and the cream of the German liberal movement emigrated to America after 1848 (Willems 1986: 66–8; Taylor 1946: 87–8). Under these circumstances, social advancement in Prussia hinged on military rank or recognition – all good gentlemen needed to be reserve officers – and Prussian society was characterized by a ubiquitous military presence. Amazingly, the ratio of soldiers to civilians was 1:25 in the great cities of Berlin and Breslau, 1:22 in Cologne, 1:14 in Danzig and 1:11 in Posen. And these troops were politically active, routinely intervening against strikes and riots, shouldering aside civilian authorities, and flouting civil law with impunity (Best 1982: 211).

This overlap of civilian and military functions occurred in most of the European great powers at mid-century. John Gooch's book *Army, State and Society in Italy* concludes that there both the Piedmontese army and the all-Italian army created in 1861 'had been patterned to conform with the political and social goals of Piedmont's grandees', fracturing the officer corps into progressive and reactionary factions, alienating the royal army from the Italian public, and loosing it on a reckless career under a whimsical king, Vittorio Emanuele II, who fancied himself a heroic soldier (Gooch 1989: 17). Russia was no better off. From 1825 till 1855, the Romanov empire groaned under the hard rule of Nicholas I – 'Nicholas the stick' – who wielded censorship, surveillance and torture to crush all liberal opposition. Nicholas thoroughly militarized Russian society; alluding to his quotidian acts of repression, he remarked in the 1820s that 'the Tsar of Russia is a military commander and each of his days is a day of battle'. Nicholas founded military committees whose sole task was to comb Russia for dissidents and prosecute them. In 1826 he established the Orwellian-sounding 'Third Section', a military intelligence unit with an Orwellian brief: to 'gather information concerning all events, without exception'. Even peasant society was brought under control; Nicholas colonized Russia's Eurasian hinterland with 'military colonies' so rigorous as to 'make Prussia by comparison look more like Rhode Island' (the most permissive corner of the freedom-loving United States).

> Everything was done in military style, including discipline. Peasants had to turn out for drill, classes and 'fatigues' when they were not in the fields supposedly teaching the soldiers billeted on them how to farm. In such circumstances the only things that had made peasant life worth living, the semi-autonomous village community and what little family life it allowed, completely disappeared.
>
> (Lincoln 1978: 79–85, 88; Best 1982: 227–9).

'Marching at the head of civilization': Napoleon III's Second Empire, 1852–70

What made Europe so combustible in the mid-nineteenth century was the existence side-by-side of so many militarized states: monarchies where military men gained control over more pacific civilians. The most destabilizing of the 'Cossack republics' was Louis-Napoleon Bonaparte's French Second Empire, which lasted from 1852 until 1870. Elected president of France in December 1848 on the heels of the great counter-revolution of June, Louis-Napoleon, a nephew of Napoleon I, based himself on the French peasantry and worked for a revival of the Napoleonic Empire that had been extinguished at Waterloo.

Although such a restoration would have violated the Vienna settlement, which had outlawed the Bonapartes in France, Louis-Napoleon, a rather unprepossessing figure, was able to reassure the victors of 1815 that 'the empire means peace' – 'l'Empire c'est la paix'. This Bonaparte, a more agile statesman than his uncle, successfully persuaded France's rivals that the bourgeois prosperity that would flow from his authoritarian, free market empire would, far from threatening the other European powers, actually enrich them and constitute a helpful dam against the democratic and socialist radicalism that was beginning to seep through Europe with the onset of the industrial revolution.

Though wary of Louis-Napoleon, the other European powers had by the 1850s lost their old 1815 solidarity, and could not oppose him with a united front: the British and Russians were vying for control of Central and South Asia ('The Great Game'), the Austrians and Prussians for Germany, the Austrians and Piedmontese for Italy. Thus engaged, the European great powers predictably did nothing when President Bonaparte overthrew France's Second Republic in December 1851 (on the anniversary of Austerlitz) and restored the Napoleonic empire a year later. French students, workers and some peasants offered real resistance by mounting barricades and occupying town halls across France, but Bonaparte – now Napoleon III – used the French army to smash this republican opposition (Price 1997: 18–21). Promised big budgets and action under a Second Empire, the army eagerly backed Louis-Napoleon. In a memorable passage of his *Eighteenth Brumaire of Louis Bonaparte* (1852), Karl Marx accused Louis-Napoleon of plotting the *coup d'état* with military leaders 'over cigars and champagne, cold poultry and garlic sausage' (Marx 1969: 77). Bored by the *immobilisme* of the July Monarchy and affronted by the riots of 1848, the French army saw in this new Bonaparte not only the prospect of glorious wars of expansion, but also the certainty of a swingeing internal campaign against France's growing body of *démoc-socs*: radical advocates of a 'democratic and social republic'.

Indeed, two French historians, Jean-Jacques Becker and Stéphane Audoin-Rouzeau, argue that it was precisely Napoleon III's plans for a domestic campaign to crush the 'red republicans' and stimulate the French economy that permitted him to assure the other European powers that his empire, in contrast to his uncle's, 'meant peace'. According to Becker and Audoin-Rouzeau, the empire meant peace only because this time around Napoleonic wars would be waged internally, rather than externally:

> Napoleon III would revive the old warrior heritage of the nation in an immense internal effort, a French-on-French struggle of political pacification: to ameliorate the living conditions of the poorest, to modernize the country. Louis-Napoleon [spoke] in the following terms: 'All of you who seek the best for this country: you are my soldiers!'.
>
> (Becker and Audoin-Rouzeau 1995: 22–3)

The spectacular city building and public works of the Second Empire must be seen in this light: the reconstruction of Paris and the provincial towns, the quintupling of French railway mileage, and the surge of state-sponsored industrial, commercial and financial expansion in the 1850s and 1860s. These were potent weapons in Napoleon III's struggle to legitimize himself in modern France. He flushed money and jobs through the French economy and blended popular and dictatorial methods in a sophisticated way. In the coup of 1851, Louis-Napoleon crushed the republic with one hand but conceded universal male suffrage with the other by instituting plebiscites on vital national questions. (The first plebiscite, requesting an extension of presidential powers after the coup of 1851, received 7.5 million votes in the affirmative as against just 640,000 'no' votes.) By carefully controlling the press and the vote, via mayors and prefects appointed in Paris, Napoleon III stifled the parties of the left and revived the Roman Catholic church 'to combat evil and ... extend the reign of the good', a pious message that resonated with millions of French citizens (Gough, in Zeldin 1970: 139–40). In 1851, Louis-Napoleon sounded an early fascist note: 'Who exactly are "the people"? The "people" are nothing other than the great mass of the nation that exercises its universal suffrage. *This* is our master in all matters, not those [parliamentary] coteries that blaspheme by calling themselves "the people".' Indeed, the whole ethic of the Second Empire was eerily fascist; it was a regime called into existence to 'depoliticize' government by substituting a charismatic executive for an allegedly corrupt and aimless parliament (Case 1972: frontispiece; Price 1997: 25–6). French peasants, angered by the high taxes and radical slogans of the Republic, voted 32:1 in favour of Bonaparte's plebiscitary empire. The Empire seemed to empower them, not the big-city ideologues who had flourished under the Second Republic. For the first time in the history of modern France, the provinces had imposed a ruler on Paris rather than the other way round (Corbin 1992: 23–38; Price 1997: 12–14, 22–4; Truesdell 1997: 171).

And yet, as James McMillan argues in a recent biography of Napoleon III, orchestrated plebiscites and tractable mayors could not entirely destroy the imperial opposition: wealthy, English-style liberals who resented the authoritarian empire, and red republicans, who seethed and organized underground (McMillan 1991: 60–5). To marginalize this ineradicable opposition, Napoleon III embarked on a series of foreign adventures. He intended these wars to increase the power of France, but also to convert his enemies. Indeed, one of his advisors prescribed 'military glory and marching at the head of civilization' as cure-alls for domestic-political difficulties (Vandam 1897: 297–9). All in all, Marx's prophesy in the early days of the Second Empire that Louis-Napoleon would be 'driven by the contradictory demands of his political situation [to] execute a *coup d'état en miniature* every day' seemed to materialize in the course of the 1850s and 1860s, when the French emperor relied increasingly on diplomatic brinksmanship and war to exalt and legitimize his government (Marx 1969: 135).

To underscore the link between himself and his more famous uncle, Napoleon III made revision of the treaties of 1815 in favour of France his priority. Treaty revision short of war was a popular issue in France, for the nation had lost important strips of its frontier to the Dutch, the Prussians, the German states and the Piedmontese in 1815. To recover them, Napoleon III had to weaken or coopt the Austrians, Prussians and Russians: the three principal guarantors of the state system established by the Congress of Vienna in 1815. Since the task seemed impossible under existing conditions, Napoleon III hatched a revolutionary plan that savoured of his uncle's Great Empire: he would reconstruct Europe. Multinational Austria and Russia could be dismantled or blown apart, their minority peoples reformed into French-sponsored nation-states. Prussia might be permitted to expand into north Germany (Saxony and Hanover were Berlin's chief desires), but would pay for this growth by yielding up its Polish provinces and allying with France. The impertinence of this French plan accounted for Napoleon III's disagreeable reputation among European heads of state. Since France's Second Empire did not enjoy the demographic, economic and military preponderance in Europe that the First Empire had, Louis-Napoleon had no choice but to attempt his plans by devious means. Unable simply to invade and smash every obstacle in the grand style of his uncle, Napoleon III connived ('his mind is as full of schemes as a warren is full of rabbits', Palmerston complained in 1863), hoping to accomplish his plans incrementally through secret diplomacy and occasional, limited wars (Radewahn, in Kolb 1987: 33ff).

War with Russia was central to Napoleon III's foreign policy. Since the Second Empire was always vulnerable to pressure from the republican left – 20 per cent of Frenchmen routinely abstaining from imperial plebiscites to protest Bonaparte's *coup d'état* – Louis-Napoleon took pains to cast himself as a 'progressive' monarch spiritually at war with 'backward' dynasties like the Romanovs and the Habsburgs. Of course, *real* war with Russia suggested itself as an obvious way to rally all Frenchmen to the Bonapartist cause. To conservatives, a Russian war would constitute 'revenge for Moscow': the humiliating rout of the Grand Army in 1812. Republicans would support a war with Russia to punish the tsar's notorious persecution of Poles and Jews, to say nothing of his fellow Russians. This idealistic foreign policy was called 'marching at the head of civilization'; the French army would carry freedom and enlightenment to the captive peoples of Europe. France also had a profound strategic interest in fighting Russia. Until 1854, the Russian tsar was the 'gendarme of Europe'; his million-man army policed the borders of 1815 and, in league with Austria and Prussia, subjected the small nations of East Central Europe to despotic rule. Overall, Russia was the single greatest obstacle to the achievement of Napoleon III's plans for what he grandly called a 'United States of Europe': a chain of French-sponsored nation-states stretching from the Scheldt to the Vistula (Goldfrank 1994: 76–7). Louis-Napoleon needed only a pretext to fight Russia, and Tsar Nicholas I provided it in 1853, when he pushed his army into the Balkans and commenced an invasion of the Ottoman Empire. Since every power in Europe except Russia was committed to maintaining the Turkish Empire to uphold the balance of power, Napoleon III had his pretext. He promptly invited the military leaders of Britain and Austria to Paris and formed an Anglo-French-Austrian coalition that declared war on Russia, the 'pillar of reaction' in Europe (Becker and Audoin-Rouzeau 1995: 25–6).

On the surface, the Crimean War appeared a typical Anglo-Russian struggle for control of the eastern Mediterranean. A closer look, however, reveals that the war was engineered by Napoleon III, largely for domestic-political reasons. Never heartily accepted by French Catholics (who had never forgiven Napoleon I's decision to annex Rome and imprison the Pope in 1807), Louis-Napoleon always sought ways to bind Catholics to the Bonapartist cause, for the church wielded considerable influence in rural France and stood guard against the libertarian middle class – the *bourgeoisie Voltairienne* – in the cities (McMillan 1991: 58–9, 63). For this reason, Bonaparte had dispatched French troops to crush Mazzini's Roman Republic and restore the Papal State in 1849, and had challenged the Russian tsar for control of the Holy Places in Jerusalem in 1850. Louis-Napoleon had learned the lesson of Louis-Philippe's failed July Monarchy: foreign policy had domestic-political consequences; it had to be energetic or it would be despised by public opinion (B. Gooch 1959: 37–8). In the early 1850s, Louis-Napoleon's abundant energy helped trigger the Crimean War.

The Crimean War

At first, Tsar Nicholas I yielded to French pressure on the Holy Places, which amounted to ordering Russian Orthodox priests in Jerusalem and Bethlehem to hand the keys of the Church of the Holy Sepulchre and the Church of the Nativity over to their Roman Catholic colleagues; he later changed his mind. In 1853, Nicholas sent a military mission to Constantinople to demand that Turkey's Muslim government return protection of Judaea – and the thirteen million Christians of the Ottoman Empire – to the Russian tsar and church. When the Turks, assured of British and French support in the meantime, dug in their heels, the Russians mobilized and moved their Black Sea fleet across to Sinope on the Turkish coast. There the Russians demonstrated a powerful new weapon: the shell gun, a rifled cannon that fired fused, explosive rounds rather than solid shot. Invented by the Frenchman Henri Paixhans in 1821, the naval rifle had been procured by every European navy in the meantime and rapidly improved by the Prussians (Krupp), the British (Rodman, Strong and Whitworth) and the Americans (Parrott and Dahlgren). Indeed, Turkey's failure to acquire the new technology was a sure sign of its backwardness;

even the Russians had it. In a desultory six-hour battle that inaugurated the Crimean War, the Russians obliterated Turkey's Black Sea fleet, sinking seven frigates and three corvettes with all hands. Exchanging broadsides of explosive shell for salvos of Turkish solid shot, the Russians lost just thirty-seven crewmen, the Turks 3,000. Sinope marked a revolution in naval warfare; thereafter fleets scrambled not only to rearm with shell guns, but to armour their warships with iron plates as well (Glover 1980: 58). An Anglo-French naval attempt to seize a beach near Odessa in October 1855 succeeded thanks to three French ironclad barges, which drove under the guns of Fort Kinburn, shells pranging harmlessly off of their armor, and silenced them (Greene and Massignani 1998: 22–31, 109–11; Dupuy and Dupuy 1997: 799).

The 'Massacre of Sinope' and Tsar Nicholas's aggressive aims in the Balkans and the Middle East drove the British and the French toward war in 1853. They feared, as the Duke of Argyll put it, that St Petersburg's claim to represent the interests of the Ottoman Christians was really a stalking horse for a larger strategic design: the conquest of the Balkan Peninsula, the Straits, and Constantinople, which the Russians persisted in calling 'Tsargrad':

> It was Russia alone that was always overhanging the flanks of Turkey with her enormous mass and weight. … There was in the mind of all of us one unspoken but indelible opinion: that the absorption by Russia of Turkey in Europe, and the seating of the Russian Emperor on the throne of Constantinople, would give to Russia an overbearing weight in Europe, dangerous to all the other powers and to the liberties of the world. … If the [Balkans] were to be added to what Russia already has, the Black Sea would be a Russian lake, the Danube would be a Russian river, and some of the richest provinces of Eastern Europe and of Western Asia would give to Russia inexhaustible resources in men, money, and in ships.
>
> (N. Rich 1985: 40–1)

Argyll's statement neatly described the fears of the British public, who, prodded by cheap newspapers (an offshoot of the industrial age) began to take a bloodthirsty interest in the shaping conflict. When British regiments mustered in February 1854, excited crowds thronged London's streets, squares and bridges to cheer them on. When the Russians, faced with Austria's tardy intervention on the side of Britain and France, withdrew from the Balkans in August 1854 and tried to end the war, the British public clamoured for escalation (A. Palmer 1994: 42–5; N. Rich 1985: 97, 226; Glover 1980: 78). Though more cautious – French peasants worried that they would bear the brunt of the war – France generally supported the fight with Russia for what a Napoleonic official characterized as the nation's 'gravest and most legitimate interests' (Case 1972: 21, 29). Thus encouraged, Britain's Lord Palmerston ratcheted up allied war aims. Merely to drive the Russians back to the

Dniester, he wrote, 'would be like turning a burglar out of your house only to break in again at a more fitting opportunity'. Palmerston and the British press demanded quite a bit more:

> The best and most effectual security for the future peace of Europe would be the severance from Russia of some of the frontier territories acquired by her in later times, Georgia, Circassia, the Crimea, Bessarabia, Poland and Finland ... she would still remain an enormous power, but far less advantageously posted for aggression on her neighbours.
>
> (N. Rich 1977: 84; Lambert 1990: xx–xxi)

For the British, it was a dangerous escalation of what had begun as a mere 'police action' to contain Russia, not roll it back. Were British strategists driving public opinion with their decisions, or was it the other way round? Thomas Carlyle, a worried onlooker, was in no doubt on this question: 'It is the idle population of editors that have done this to England. One perceives clearly the ministers go forward into it *against their will*' (Glover 1980: 76). This interaction between domestic politics and external policy in an increasingly democratic and literate age, established what was essentially a *social dimension of strategy* (Snyder 1991: 158–63). In France, Louis-Napoleon also felt its prod. The red republicans (who had only their loathing of autocratic Russia in common with the Napoleonic regime), the popular press and the French industrialists all called for war once Russia invaded the Balkans – 'Turkey in Europe'. The parties of the right were no less insistent: they wanted the Russian Church out of the Holy Land (Becker and Audoin-Rouzeau 1995: 31–3). Driven by excitable publics and interested pressure groups (like the ironworkers of Lorraine), statesmen felt constrained to appease them with war, a dangerous tendency that would culminate in the *Hurra-Patriotismus* of 1914, which would carry the European great powers into the bloodiest war yet.

For the British, this pandering on the home front came at a most inopportune time. War had evolved in the decades since Waterloo, yet Britain had been slow to grasp new technologies like the rifle. At Waterloo, only sharpshooters had carried it; now whole armies, including Britain's, were procuring rifles, thus greatly extending the range and effectiveness of line infantry (Showalter 1975: 93–5). Artillerymen – taken under fire by the new rifles, which could decimate gun crews from afar – began themselves to adopt rifling, which permitted the artillery to deploy their guns well beyond the range of the Minié rifle without diminishing their accuracy. In battle, these rifled cannon exceeded all expectations: firing grooved or studded explosive shells down rifled barrels, they hit harder and more accurately than smoothbores, and were utilized by every European army by the 1860s.

No less significant than these improvements in armaments were concurrent improvements in logistics and communications. European armies, led by the French, British and Prussians, began to use railways and steamships to transport troops, ordnance and supplies in the 1850s. The electric telegraph, another recent invention, provided an effective means to direct these swift movements of men and material. Now generals did not have to be with their troops to enjoy what Napoleon had called *coup d'oeil*: an all-encompassing glimpse of the battlefield. In theory, a modern-day general could remain far behind the lines at 'great headquarters' and launch vast operations with little else but a march table, a railway schedule and a secure telegraph.

Most of these thrilling possibilities were simply ignored by the British in the years before 1854. Indeed, as Hew Strachan has revealed, Britain's pre-Crimean army was astonishingly backward (Strachan 1985). Unlike the armies of Prussia, Austria and France, there was not even a veneer of change on the British army. The redcoats still permitted incompetent officers to purchase their commissions and still filled out their 'other ranks' with Swiss and German mercenaries. The quality of recruits for the Royal Navy was even worse: conscriptions of 'cabmen, navvies, butcher boys and riff-raff' were augmented by sociopaths and criminals (Strachan 1983: 70; Best 1982: 233–41). Resting on their Waterloo laurels, the British found themselves utterly unprepared for war with another great power. This unpreparedness influenced strategy in 1853–4. Although French and Austrian generals met in Paris and considered a vast, 1812-style march to Moscow, they were dissuaded by the British, who insisted on a more limited object that could be taken from the sea: Russia's Crimean Peninsula, with its hulking Black Sea fortress and naval base at Sebastopol (K. Koch 1984: 34–9).

Ultimately, the British were fortunate to be up against Russia in the Crimean War (Map 3.1), for the Russians were even more backward than the British in their military arrangements. The million-man Russian army was filled out with rail-thin, vodka-sotted conscripts, who – conscripted for an astonishing twenty-five years of service – died of exhaustion and disease at twice the rate of the French or British armies. Like the Royal Navy, the Russian fleet used pressgangs to man its ships, relying for the most part on Jewish boys seized from the wretched *shtetls* of Belarus, Poland and Ukraine. In the 1850s, fully one third of Russian sailors were Jewish, a curious statistic. The mortality rate in the navy was even higher than in the army, which explained the institution of the 'crippler' in the Russian village: a hired thug who would cut off the toes or fingers of peasant boys or smash out their teeth to render them unfit for military service (Best 1982: 225–6). Indifferently manned, Russia's army and navy were also shoddily equipped and badly led. Russian generals – friends of the tsar – made their British counterparts look accomplished by comparison, and generally came through battles thanks only to the exertions of their staff officers, most of whom were Germans lured to Russian service by good salaries and the promise of a title (Glover 1980: 80). The Russian arms industry – three factories for the entire empire – produced just 61,000 smoothbore muskets per year, an obsolete firearm to begin with and a sliver of the army's needs. Corrupt contractors were also a problem; they were as likely to fill Russian shells and cartridges with cornmeal as with black powder – not that it always mattered, for Russian shells, solid shot and musket balls were frequently cast in the wrong calibre, making it impossible to fit them down the barrel of the gun. Quality control was unheard of in Russian factories; 1,490 of 1,500 muskets shipped from the army's Warsaw arsenal to Sebastopol in 1854 were found to be defective. Finally, whereas the British and French had rearmed their infantry with rifles by 1854, the Russians did not even possess rifle technology. Nicholas I would order his troops in the Crimea to collect French and British rifles on the battlefield and send them to St Petersburg for scrutiny (W. Fuller 1992: 260; Lincoln 1978: 344–5).

The British and French attack on the Crimea was intended to discourage the Russians from future aggression. After isolating the Crimean Peninsula from the sea, the two maritime powers planned to destroy the 35,000 Russian troops garrisoned there through a combination of close blockade, naval bombardment and ground attacks. This rather modest effort almost immediately miscarried. Though a seaborne allied army of 60,000 men landed safely on beaches north of Sebastopol in September 1854, the troops had trouble coming to grips with the Russians, who stood their ground in formidable positions and took full advantage of their limited firepower. In the first clash of the war, the battle of the Alma, a French and British attempt to cross the Alma River and descend on the fortress of Sebastopol nearly broke against Russia's defensive fire. The ground behind the attacking troops was strewn with dead and wounded men, and some British units lost one third of their effectives.

Superior British firepower eventually drove the Russians back. As the British crossed the Alma, their rifled artillery brought the Russian rear echelons under fire, blasting shrapnel in all directions and sowing panic in the enemy ranks. Even more decisive was the deadly accuracy of a British Guards brigade, armed with the latest Enfield rifles, which, as William Howard Russell of *The Times* put it, 'poured in on [the Russian] masses a fire so destructive that it annihilated the whole of their front ranks in an instant, and left a ridge of killed and wounded men on the ground' (Bentley 1966: 87–8; Edgerton 1999: 50–1). Confronted for the first time with percussion rifles and explosive shells, the Russians panicked and ran from the Alma, leaving 6,000 dead, wounded and missing in their wake.

After Alma, the French and British quarrelled. Though the British began the war with expansive aims – to drive the Russians from the Baltic and Black Sea coasts – they had sobered up by the fall of 1854, and were content to deal the Russians a symbolic blow. In possession of good firing positions after the battle of the Alma, the British planned to mount guns on the high ground and begin a leisurely destruction of the Russian fleet clustered in the roads north of Sebastopol. The town and forts of Sebastopol mattered much

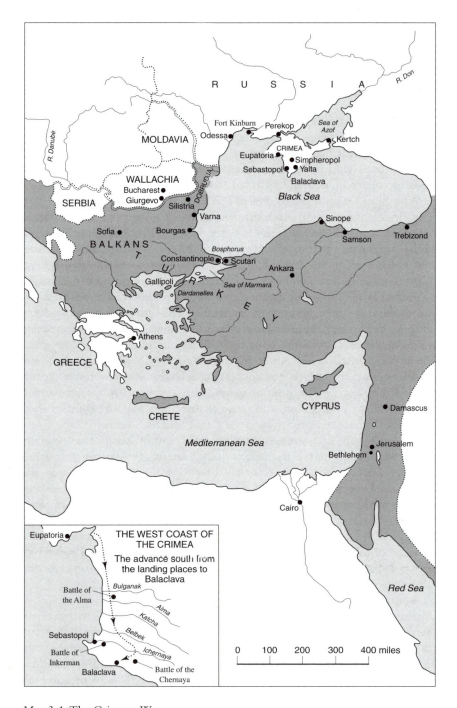

Map 3.1 The Crimean War

less to British strategists. Although perfectly willing to flatten Sebastopol with their guns, the British had no desire to take it by storm. Napoleon III in contrast desperately wanted to do just that, for the capture of Sebastopol would furnish his new empire with a sensational triumph worthy of his uncle (Lambert 1990: 125–6; Gibbs 1963: 197). It was no coincidence that he and Baron Haussmann later named one of the broad new boulevards that they cut through the centre of Paris 'Sebastopol'.

French strategists won the argument, and an exhausting flank march ensued in the name of coalition unity. From the Alma front, the allied armies crept around the fortress works to establish new bases south of the city at Balaclava and Kamiesch. There the British and French fleets could supply the allied land armies, which began entrenching themselves for the great siege of Sebastopol desired by Napoleon III. (Believing victory imminent, Louis-Napoleon tried to rush out to the Crimea to take credit for it, but was put off by the British.) While the British and French completed their change of base to Balaclava, General Alexander Menshikov slipped away with most of the Russian field army, leaving his chief of engineers, Colonel Frants Todleben, with 20,000 sailors and marines to convert Sebastopol into a sandbagged, entrenched fortress. The failure of the allied commanders Lord Raglan and Marshal Armand Saint-Arnaud (given command as partial repayment for his assistance in the Napoleonic coup of 1851) to block Menshikov's escape radically changed the nature of the war. Instead of simply surrounding Menshikov, battering him with artillery and starving Sebastopol and the Russian forces trapped there, the allies had now to fight two campaigns for which they were unprepared: one a conventional siege against Todleben's forts (interestingly described by Tolstoy, who was there), and another against Menshikov's reinforced army of 90,000 men, which spent the next several months trying to drive the Anglo-French army besieging Sebastopol into the sea (Curtiss 1979: 313–16).

In the hard-fought battles of Balaclava and Inkerman in October and November 1854, the allies barely repulsed Russian attempts to seize their coastal bases. At Balaclava, Britain's Light Brigade of cavalry was needlessly thrown away by its oafish brigadier Lord Cardigan, who charged down a valley lined with Russian guns with tragic results. In an age of rifles and explosive shell, massed cavalry formations had lost their utility, a fact that European armies would need years to absorb. Inkerman was no less instructive. There, the Russians drove in old-style shock columns at 'thin red lines' of British infantry armed with Enfield rifles. The British commenced fire from beyond the range of the Russian columns and hammered them with well aimed volleys. After the battle, a stunned Russian officer recorded that 'whole [Russian] regiments melted' under the British rifle fire, 'losing one-fourth of their men while they were coming into musket range', most to panic-stricken flight, the rest to the fusilade (Lincoln 1978: 344–5). Whereas Russian muskets had trouble finding their targets at 60 paces, British rifles were deadly accurate at 200 (Curtiss 1979: 324). This insurmountable difference decided the battle. W. H. Russell, who watched the Russian battalions collapse under the British fire, applauded Raglan's redcoats: 'a thin red streak topped with a line of steel' (McElwee 1974: 31).

The obsolescence of the musket in the age of the rifle was plain; the Russians lost 12,000 men at Inkerman, four times the sum of British dead and wounded. The uselessness of Russia's artillery and war industry was also obvious. At the siege of Sebastopol, allied guns fired 400,000 more shells into the town and fortress than the Russians sent back, revealing again the correlation between national wealth and military might (W. Fuller 1992: 260). Overall, the Crimean War, a proving ground for new technologies, confirmed the preponderance of *defensive* fire on the modern battlefield. Nearly every allied attack on Sebastopol and every Russian counter-attack ended with the same awful result, dolefully described by Tolstoy in his Sebastopol notebook:

> Hundreds of bodies, drenched with fresh blood, of men who two hours before had been filled with various lofty or petty hopes and desires, now lay with stiffened limbs in the damp, flowering valley separating the bastion from the trench, and on the even floor of the mortuary chapel in Sebastopol. Hundreds of men crawled, twisted, and groaned, with curses and entreaties on their dry lips, some among the corpses in the flowery valley, others on stretchers, cots, and on the bloody floor of the hospital.
>
> (Tolstoy n.d.: 115, 121)

The lucky ones died quickly, for medical preparations were appalling. Menshikov's army of 65,000 offered battle with hospital beds for just 1,200 in its rear. After Inkerman, thousands of Russian wounded sat for days in the open in their louse-ridden, blood-stiffened uniforms, while the few Russian surgeons who attended the army worked through the night to clear beds in the overworked lazaret. An eminent Russian physician later wrote of his experiences in the Crimea: 'No one who has not seen with his own eyes can form any conception of the filth, the miserable condition in which our wounded and sick lay from October to December' (Curtiss 1979: 328). British arrangements were no better; indeed, when it was discovered that thousands of ill and wounded British servicemen had died without medical treatment in the hard winter of 1854–5, Lord Aberdeen's government resigned in disgrace and Florence Nightingale was dispatched to the Black Sea front to establish proper hospitals. Until the arrival of Miss Nightingale in 1855, the sole bright spot of the entire war from the medical standpoint was the introduction in 1854 of chloroform as a pain-dulling anaesthetic. Otherwise, there was nothing to applaud; the war became bogged down in squalid trenches, with no end in sight. Britain had always assumed that Nicholas I, spread thinly on four fronts – the Crimea, the Baltic (where the Royal Navy concentrated the bulk of its strength), the Danube (where the Austrians assembled two corps) and the Caucasus (where the Turks pinned down a large Russian army throughout the war) – would recognize the futility of his position and capitulate. Yet the notoriously stubborn tsar would not submit, and Britain and France, who had entered the war seeking an easy victory that would pay domestic-political dividends, found themselves mired instead in a costly, unpopular slog (Ropp 1959: 147–50). The winter of 1854–5 destroyed what little remained of British enthusiasm for the war; all of the steamship capacity in the world could not save British troops from the inefficiency of their military adminis- tration, which dumped mountains of firewood, meat, rice, flour, vegetables, and tea on the wharves of Balaclava, but neglected to build roads or tactical railways to move these supplies to the British troops in the Sebastopol trench lines. Cold and hungry, thousands of British troops in the Crimea fell ill. By January 1855, two thirds of Raglan's effectives were in hospital. The French did no better; they lost 12,000 men to pneumonia, typhus, cholera, dysentery, scurvy, frostbite and gangrene, wholly avoidable losses that scandalized Paris. Indeed, the whole campaign stirred memories of an event that the French press and public had entered the war to forget: Napoleon I's winter retreat from Moscow in 1812 (Case 1972: 30–1).

To break the deadlock, in 1855 France and Britain planned a single, mighty push up and out of the Crimean quagmire: an assault on Sebastopol's key forts, Malakov and Redan. To supply the offensive, the British built the first tactical railway in the history of warfare: a twenty-five-mile track connecting Balaclava harbour and the British trenches; 240 tons of food and war material rolled up and down the track daily (Glover 1980: 93–4). Though tolerably well prepared for a change, this latest allied push – tactlessly launched by the British on 18 June, the fortieth anniversary of Waterloo – came to grief. Enfiladed by Russian muskets and artillery, the French and British lost 4,000 men and retired to their filthy trenches. These latest setbacks revealed the hazards of 'open warfare' against defensive field fortifications and fire. Even large infantry formations well supported by artillery failed to penetrate the granite forts and sandbagged trenches of the Russians. The repulse at Malakov plunged France into mourning; Napoleon III's popularity sank, even in rural areas. Luckily, Russia's Sebastopol garrison was even worse off. Short of every- thing, the Russians attempted to break out in August 1855, only to be blocked and driven back by the French and a newly arrived division of Piedmontese troops at the Chernaya River. Whereas Inkerman had demon- strated the awesome power of the French and British rifles, the battle of the Chernaya exhibited the rifled cannon, which the French would use to even greater effect in the Franco-Austrian War of 1859. The Russians lost 8,000 men on the Chernaya, most of them to explosive shells that gutted their densely packed 'steamroller columns' (Bentley 1966: 239).

Desperate to end the endless war, the French orchestrated a truly brilliant surprise attack on the Malakov in September 1855; it succeeded, breaching the defences of Sebastopol and evicting the Russians at last. The French capture of the detached fort at Malakov anticipated the tactics of World War I; French officers first pushed their trenches to within thirty yards of the objective, then synchronized their watches (the first time that this was done in a military operation) and attacked *en masse* without warning at a prescribed hour, breaking through the Russian trenches and revetments before the startled enemy could react. The British, who supported the French attack with one of their own on the Redan, went 'over the top' in the old helter-skelter style and got nowhere (Dupuy and Dupuy 1977: 907). It was this sort of contrast that accounted for France's reputation as the first army of Europe until 1870.

Inside France, the domestic-political impact of the victory was electrifying. Before the storm, French ministers and prefects had urged the emperor to make peace and remove the cause of so much anti-war feeling in Paris and the provinces. The *coup de main* at Malakov changed all that, loosing a flood of patriotic feeling that Napoleon III and his propagandists sedulously milked. On 10 September, the emperor announced the capture of Sebastopol by firing off a great battery of guns at the Invalides and lighting up every quarter of Paris, from the splendid west side to the gritty east end. In the provinces, Napoleon III wallowed in victory, a fact noted by a prefect in western France, who stressed the connection between war and society:

> The news of the capture of Sebastopol spread through the department with incredible speed. The towns and little hamlets illuminated spontaneously. The following Sunday the occasion was celebrated with the greatest rejoicing, the illuminations were still more brilliant because they had had time to prepare them. Even the isolated houses and farms were lighted up; in almost every commune great bonfires were lighted to cries of 'Long Live the Emperor!' From the heights of the Pouzauges Mountains, the Vendée looked all afire.
>
> (Case 1972: 39)

Napoleon III made sure to hold the peace talks in his capital, and the Crimean War officially ended in March 1856 with the signing of the Treaty of Paris, which drove Russia from the Balkans, neutralized the Black Sea, and denied the Russian claim to protect Turkey's Christians, the original *casus belli*. The war was significant on a number of counts. For the first time, steamships were widely deployed: in the Black Sea to bombard Sebastopol and supply the allied army, and in the Baltic to contain the bulk of the Russian fleet and hammer the tsar's coastal forts (Greene and Massignani 1998: 20–40). Railways figured in a negative way; since there was no railway connecting Moscow to the Crimea, the tsar's inland garrisons had needed three months or more to march to the relief of Sebastopol. Carried on steamships, French and British troops had reached Balaclava in three weeks or less (Glover 1980: 78–80; Gildea 1996: 175). (In 1867, Russia would sell Alaska to the United

States for $7.2 million to cover the costs of new railway construction that the Crimean War had proven necessary (Goldfrank 1994: 295).) Telegraphs also made their military debut in 1854. A British field telegraph from the Sebastopol siege works to Balaclava was carried across the Black Sea to Varna, where it was picked up by French engineers, extended to Bucharest, and there attached to the main European network (Glover 1980: 94). It was of course ironic that the new telegraph facilities were most effectively used by war correspondents like W. H. Russell, who emitted a blizzard of news from the Crimean front (much of it useful to the Russians) that was a constant source of embarrassment to the British and French high command. Here was another first: newsmen – the so-called fourth estate – not only began to shape military affairs, they awakened public interest in the plans of war and the plight of the common soldier, who would no longer suffer bad generalship and neglect in silence (Howard 1976: 98–9).

Although a 'limited war', the Crimean War inflicted terrific casualties. Half a million Russians were struck down by allied firepower and disease, while 300,000 French and British were killed or wounded, two thirds of them succumbing to cold, hunger and illness. Turkish casualties fell somewhere between 200,000 and 400,000 (Goldfrank 1994: 289; Gibbs 1963: 189–90, 197–8). Public opinion everywhere castigated the armies, and forced them to think seriously about *all* of the elements of strategy: war aims and plans, logistics, operations and tactics. As a result of the Crimean War, the Russians finally recognized the extent of their backwardness and began to reform and modernize (Menning 1992: 6–50; D. Rich 1998: 65–73). The British centralized their unruly War Office, moved it to new premises on Pall Mall, and convened no less than eighty-nine military reform committees in the ten years after 1854 (J. Gooch 1974: 3). The French, proud of their easygoing *système D* (*on se débrouillera toujours* – 'one muddles through somehow'), viewed the Crimean War's successful outcome as ample excuse to reform nothing at all. Indeed, the British critic who later proposed that 'the disaster of Sedan was foreshadowed in the victory of Magenta' might well have made the same proposition for Sebastopol (Vandam 1897: 206). Napoleon III's victories in the Crimea in 1855 and Italy in 1859 blinded him to the need for essential reforms, which were not made in time for France's all-important war with Prussia in 1870 (McElwee 1974: 39–40; Cox 1994: 163).

Tactically, the Crimean War spelled (or ought to have spelled) the end of close-order, Napoleonic shock columns, which were easily marked and shattered by the accurate, long-range fire of infantry rifles and artillery. At bottom, the war suggested that the advantage in modern battles had shifted from the attacker (as had been the case in the Napoleonic Wars) to the defender, who could now use precision firearms and field fortifications to repel enemy attacks by inflicting unsustainable losses. In fact, military observers in the Crimea were struck by the sheer quantity of firepower needed to blast the Russians out of their modern fortifications. Ordered to soften up the Russian forts in September 1854, the allied fleet had hit them with 40,000 shells, to no apparent effect (Ropp 1959: 148). Between March and August 1855, the allies subjected Sebastopol to continual land and naval bombardment, killing an estimated 100,000 Russians in a futile attempt to break the town's resistance. To increase the pressure, the French lugged a battery of 13-inch mortars from Paris to the Black Sea front; they aimed a steady fire of heavy projectiles at the Sebastopol fortifications, flattening most of them in time for the final offensive (Browning 1903: 291–2; W. Fuller 1992: 260; Curtiss 1979: 445). Here were portents of the grinding trench warfare of 1914–18.

One of the more interesting aspects of the Crimean War and the conflict that followed it, the Franco-Austrian War of 1859, was the way Emperor Napoleon III very consciously manipulated the crises to create a 'heroic ethic' in imperial France. Denied by the British the chance to lead the allied armies in the Crimea, Louis-Napoleon did what he could to take credit for the victory at home. Months after the war, when the memory of Sebastopol had begun to fade, he gave the victory a final, self-congratulatory shake, parading his veterans through the centre of Paris in the most extraordinary way. French troops assembled for the review not in clean, brushed uniforms, but in the very rags they had worn home from the Crimea. Wounded comrades were not tucked away in convalescent homes, but prominently placed at the front of the procession to stagger along on crutches and wooden legs beneath singed and ripped battle flags (Becker and Audoin-Rouzeau 1995: 29–30; Bierman 1988: 164). Although it was normal for charismatic regimes to glorify war, there was something preternatural about Napoleon III's exaltation of the common soldier, the 'front fighter'. Indeed, the parade was tinged with fascism, one of Louis-Napoleon's own newspapers characterizing the heroic troops as 'characters of iron and fire, of mourning and of glory, the solemn reality of war'. The route taken by the parade was also carefully thought out. Instead of trudging the well worn path through the Arc de Triomphe and along the Champs-Elysées (the province of the *haute bourgeoisie*), Napoleon III's veterans marched clean across Paris, from the dingy eastern *arrondisements* to the posh western ones, from the Place de la Bastille (symbol of the revolution) to the Place de Vendôme (symbol of wealth and property). The parade in short was an act of political reconciliation; as was customary at festive events during the Second Empire, it moved to the rousing strains of the *Marseillaise*, the normally proscribed anthem of the republic (Truesdell 1997: 145–7).

Though a Russian defeat, the Crimean War merely set back the Romanov empire. It did not destroy Russia or even remove it as a significant factor in European affairs. Thus Louis-Napoleon was no closer after the war to freeing Poland or any other 'captive nation' than he had been before it. Blocked in Russia, he turned his gaze on Austria, and began plotting a war against the Habsburgs that would end with the same partial result as the one against the Romanovs, increasing the political isolation that would help topple Napoleon III in 1870.

The Franco–Austrian War of 1859

The Habsburgs, like the Romanovs, obstructed Louis-Napoleon's bold plan to redraw the borders of Europe along national lines. Their Austrian Empire, patched together over the course of 300 years, sprawled across a dozen Central European nations, joining Italians, Germans, Hungarians, Rumanians, Slovaks, Czechs, Poles, Ukrainians, Croats, Serbs and Slovenes in an anachronistic, multinational state whose capital was Vienna. Ever since his youth as a *Carbonaro*, when Louis-Napoleon – forced by the treaties of 1815 to live outside of France – had conspired against Austrian rule in Italy, the French emperor had dreamed of destroying the Habsburg Monarchy. The Franco-Austrian War of 1859 was his first blow.

The cause of the war was fairly straightforward. Until 1859, Italy was riven into eight states; the strongest of them, Piedmont, sought after 1848 to bring most or all of the peninsula under Piedmontese rule. Piedmont's prime minister from 1852 until his death in 1861 was Count Camillo Cavour, who worked steadily to expand Piedmont and extend the laws and authority of Turin to the rest of Italy. Though wary of France, which bounded and overshadowed Piedmont, Cavour sensed opportunity in Napoleon III, whose frustration with the old European empires matched Cavour's own. In brief, Cavour hoped to turn France against Austria, which would distract Vienna sufficiently to enable little Piedmont to lead a 'war of union' in Italy and make off with Austria's prized Italian crownlands – Lombardy and Venetia – along with the sovereign duchies of Tuscany, Parma and Modena.

Cavour's first step down this road was his decision to lend France 10,000 Piedmontese troops in the Crimean War. The hundreds of Piedmontese troops struck down by Russian fire and by the seething diseases of the Black Sea front may have wondered why they were there, but Cavour was never in any doubt. He saw the Crimean intervention as crucial to his courtship of Napoleon III, and it worked. After the war, the two statesmen drew closer, meeting secretly at the French resort of Plombières in 1858 to plan a war against Austria. By then, Louis-Napoleon's aim had shifted somewhat. No longer the wide-eyed *Carbonaro*, he perceived the danger of a united Italy on France's southern flank, and planned to use the war more to weaken Austria than to strengthen Italy. At Plombières, Napoleon III warned Cavour that Piedmont must confine its annexations to the 'valley of the Po' (i.e. the Austrian provinces of Lombardy and Venetia) and the formerly papal territory of Emilia-Romagna, which might be combined into a Piedmontese-run 'Kingdom of Upper Italy'. Elsewhere, Napoleon III had plans of his own, which plainly compromised Italian national interests. Naples and Sicily would either be returned to the Murats or left in the weak grip of the Bourbons to appease the Romanovs, who had a family interest in the Kingdom of the Two Sicilies. Rome, Lazio, Umbria and the coastal strip around Ancona would be left to Pope Pius IX to placate Catholic opinion in France. Tuscany, Modena

Map 3.2 The Unification of Italy

and Parma would be grouped in a new 'Kingdom of Central Italy' that would be given to Bonaparte's louche cousin Jerôme-Napoleon as partial recompense for the French-led reconstruction of Italy. Savoy and Nice, Piedmontese provinces until 1860, would be detached from Piedmont and ceded to France (Coppa 1992: 80–1) (Map 3.2).

Cavour discerned Napoleon III's real agenda, but gambled that French armed assistance would trigger a nationalist landslide in Italy that would overwhelm all French or Austrian efforts to limit Piedmont's gains. Cavour therefore pressed Napoleon III for a guarantee of armed support in the event of a war with Austria, and received a pledge of 300,000 French troops. This was a substantial force, equal to the Austrian army; if Piedmont's 100,000 troops were thrown in, the Franco-Piedmontese coalition would outnumber the Austrians and have a fair chance of beating them in the field and rooting them out of the Quadrilateral forts at Peschiera, Mantua, Legnago and Verona. Confident of his chances, Cavour moved to provoke a breach with the Austrians in the spring of 1859. He incited Italian nationalists in the Austrian provinces of Lombardy and Venetia and put the Piedmontese army on a war footing. In April 1859, the Austrians ordered the Piedmontese to withdraw their agents from Lombardy and disarm. Receiving no reply, they sent a punitive expedition over the Ticino into Piedmont.

In Paris, Napoleon III had decided that war in Italy served political and strategic purposes. As in the Crimea, war would rally all classes and parties on a patriotic platform: businessmen, workers and peasants would appreciate the lucrative contracts for war stocks, and even republican diehards would join the emperor in 'liberating oppressed peoples', in this case the Italians of Lombardy-Venetia (Truesdell 1997: 150; Case 1972: 72–3). Overarching these economic and ideological inducements was the mere fact of war, which integrated the 'Cossack republic'. In this respect, the French mobilization of 1859 in no way disappointed; it detonated an explosion of patriotic feeling that flabbergasted critics of the regime. 'We're a funny nation', Prosper Mérimée wrote in April 1859, 'Two weeks ago there was only one man who wanted war. ... Today you can take the opposite to be true. ... The people accept the war with joy' (Case 1972: 71). Townsmen and villagers who had ignored the brewing crisis in the winter went berserk in the spring, rushing to join crowds and bellowing slogans like 'long live war' and 'death to the Austrians' when mobilization was announced. As always, Napoleon III latched onto the war fever. When he left Paris for the front in May 1859, he was thronged by masses of Parisians. An eyewitness submitted the following account:

> Departure of the emperor for Italy; it is impossible to give any idea of the enthusiasm with which he was greeted when in field uniform, with tunic and kepi, he emerged from the great portal of the Louvre opposite the Palais Royal. I was right next to the gate, on the front row as usual, at the risk of being crushed. An overwhelming acclamation of 'Long

Live the Emperor!' – 'Long Live Italy!' arose. The sovereign's face was radiant with joy. The immense crowd began to sing the *Marseillaise*; I was thrilled to the very depths of my being, and I ended up by sharing in the common joys and hopes.

(Case 1972: 75)

In terms of military art, the war that followed represented another important lurch forward. For the first time in the history of war, the French used railways to accelerate their mobilization and deployment. While an Austrian army of 120,000 men shambled slowly into Piedmont in April 1859, some units covering less than three miles a day, the French rushed 50,000 men by rail to reinforce Piedmont's force of 74,000. Seventy thousand more French troops deployed to Italy by sea, steaming from Algiers and Marseilles to Genoa. Europe's first large-scale rail deployment was attended by predictable confusion. In their haste to move men, French stationmasters often left guns and ammunition behind, evoking this quip from General Louis Trochu: 'French armies of the past have made their way into Italy without shoes to their feet and without shirts to their backs, but the sight of a French army going to confront the enemy without cannon and without cartridges is an unprecedented one' (Vandam 1897: 210–11). Still, France's rail deployment was a tremendous achievement; it accomplished in two weeks a task that would have required sixty days on foot. The Austrians, who had planned a rather leisurely envelopment of the Piedmontese, were amazed to discover French troops in place at Montebello and Palestro, where the war's first battles were fought in May 1859.

At Montebello, the Austrians tasted a punishing new weapon that would transform war in the 1860s and 1870s: France's rifled field gun, the bronze Napoléon. This devastatingly accurate cannon, which owed its rapid introduction after 1856 to Napoleon III's personal interest in the project, turned every battle in France's favour. Austria's guns in 1859 dated from the Napoleonic Wars; they were smoothbores that fired out to a maximum distance of 2,000 yards. The new French guns could put an explosive shell on target at 3,400 yards. The implications of this were obvious; in 1859, the French artillery could set up beyond the reach of the Austrian guns and smash them with counter-battery fire before crabbing forward to mow down the unprotected Austrian infantry and cavalry with shrapnel and canister.

At Montebello and Palestro, the French and Piedmontese drove the Austrians back across the Ticino and pursued them into Habsburg Lombardy. For Count Ferenc Gyulai, the feckless Austrian commandant, a campaign that had begun in April as a 'military promenade' had rather embarrassingly become a desperate defence of Austria. Napoleon III now joined the French army and publicly vowed to 'free Italy from the Alps to the Adriatic'. The emperor, who had no aptitude for maps, somehow conducted the French army into its first great test at Magenta, where Gyulai paused to defend the road to Milan. The battle justified scepticism about the ongoing revolution in military affairs. The commander of Gyulai's reserve, General Eduard Clam-Gallas, literally lost himself on the rails between Tyrol and Lombardy and never arrived with his corps to join the battle. Telegraphs merely confused both sides, which sent contradictory orders by wire and horseback, causing whole divisions to swerve off course and trickle slowly or not at all into battle (McElwee 1974: 123–4; Glover 1980: 101). In the end, plucky charges by the French infantry and Napoleon III's rifled guns decided the battle, blasting bloody holes through the hinge of the Austrian position at Magenta and forcing Gyulai back on Milan.

After Magenta, Emperor Franz Joseph sacked Gyulai and personally took command of the Austrian army in Italy. He did this partly to settle a feud between his chief advisors Generals Hess and Grünne, and partly to cover himself in glory so that he could return victorious to his capital. Because the Habsburg programme of neo-absolutism, now in its tenth year, leaned heavily on the army for support and legitimacy, Franz Joseph *needed* a military success. It was not to be. At Solferino, a picturesque village nestled in the pre-Alps east of Milan, Napoleon III's army stumbled into Franz Joseph's. A seesaw fight ensued; 40,000 men were killed or wounded before the French finally broke the Austrian line and drove Franz Joseph across the Mincio and into Venetia, Austria's last bastion in Italy.

On the ground at Solferino, most of the wounded died of shock, thirst and infection, for, as in the Crimea, neither side had made adequate provision for casualties. French medical supplies were still piled up in Piedmontese rail terminals, for the army had accorded them low priority in the movement of men and material to the front (McElwee 1974: 41). This disregard for the welfare of the men prompted a Swiss tourist named Henri Dunant, who happened past the battlefield at the height of the fighting, to found the International Red Cross in 1864. The cries of anguish that drew Dunant to Solferino also dulled Napoleon III's appetite for war; he lost his innocence at Solferino and no longer aped the mannerisms of his uncle. The outcry from Vienna – political this time – was no less insistent. Liberals damned the emperor and the *k.k.* army (Gyulai, Clam-Gallas and Grünne were held up as exemplars of the latter, enfeebled institution) and demanded radical reform. Franz Joseph, who had gone to the front to cover himself in glory, was cursed and booed on his return to Vienna. Forced to accept responsibility for the defeat (the emperor had commanded at Solferino), Franz Joseph conceded a liberal constitution in 1860 to dampen public anger.

On the French side, Louis-Napoleon viewed the shocking casualty list at Solferino and his no less shocking lack of reserves, and resolved to free Italy only as far as the Mincio (Cox 1994: 164–5). Rather than strike into Austrian Venetia and besiege the Quadrilateral forts to gain Venice and the Adriatic coast, Napoleon III hastily signed the Armistice of Villafranca in July; it ceded Lombardy to Piedmont but left the Austrians in control of Venetia. Although

Louis-Napoleon had once promised to 'free Italy from the Alps to the Adriatic', he reneged on the promise the moment he realized that the French public was more concerned to exit the bloody war than to finish it. In short, the thankless realities of a long war with Austria (casualties, budget deficits, inflation) outweighed the rather abstract reward (Italian unification). Thus did war, society and politics mix in a potent brew. Austrian liberals actually cheered news of Emperor Franz Joseph's defeat at Solferino and his surrender of Lombardy at Villafranca, knowing full well that these events portended the end of neo-absolutism.

In Paris, Napoleon III tried to reap the rewards of his partial victory. Recognizing that the war had divided, not integrated France – the left resented his abandonment of Piedmont, the right his attack on Austria, which carried Piedmont one step closer to Papal Rome – Napoleon III saw to it that the celebrations and illuminations after Solferino were even more extensive than those in 1855. One journalist noted that 'one really needed to see the poorer quarters' to grasp the social significance of Solferino. 'The smallest street, the most obscure blind alley was transformed, lighted, glittering. ... This was, in the widest sense of the word, a real national celebration' (Case 1972: 78). Doubts were quieted and crowds of Parisians turned out to witness the victory parade in August, which featured the now commonplace fascist symbols: shredded battle flags and maimed veterans. The three year-old crown prince was so frightened by the sight of these *mutilés de guerre* that he had to be bundled inside the Tuileries and sedated (Truesdell 1997: 153–5).

Several months later, Napoleon III extorted Nice and Savoy from Piedmont as the price of French military assistance. Though the annexations were popular in France, they earned the enmity of Italy for years to come. Nice (Nizza) was the birthplace of Garibaldi; Savoy the dynastic home of the Piedmontese kings (Bosworth 1996: 24–5). For better or worse, Napoleon III had used war and its trophies to integrate a socially fractured nation. In a calculated act of magnanimity, he announced a great amnesty after Solferino: political prisoners were released from jail, and exiles were permitted to return to French soil (Brogan 1989: 118). Peasants and workers spontaneously celebrated the French victory; some even used it to isolate imperial opponents in their communities. A Napoleonic official in Besançon described the Solferino festivities there in the following terms:

> I myself visited different sections of the city. The illuminations were general and brilliant, especially in the suburbs and the workers quarters. ... We heard some groups of men say: 'we illuminated yesterday for the emperor; today we want to give a lesson to the "Austrians"', meaning the upper classes and the clergy, who were not very sympathetic toward the war.
>
> (Case 1972: 78–9)

When the last of the French troops returned from the front in late summer, Napoleon III sponsored another victory parade from the Bastille to the Place Vendôme, this time adding a further fascist refinement: the 'cult of the dead'. The infantry companies that tramped through Paris in their soiled battledress left conspicuous gaps in their ranks where fallen comrades had once stood (Becker and Audoin-Rouzeau 1995: 30; Bierman 1988: 200). The gaps were intended to suggest the ghostly presence of dead brothers-in-arms, who theoretically still marched to the drum of the Second Empire. Like the real fascists who followed him many years later, Napoleon III was trying to flog military values into a contented public. The Franco-Prussian War of 1870–1 would reveal the limits of this political tactic.

Did the Franco-Austrian War teach important military lessons? Yes and no. The French had barely won and might have lost had the Austrians only held out, for France had no strategic reserve. Unlike the Prussians, who employed universal conscription and buttressed their regular army with *Landwehr* reserve regiments that would reinforce front-line units, garrison forts and administer supply lines in wartime, the French relied on a relatively small, long-service force, whose reserves existed only on paper. In fact, there were no reserves, as dismayed French generals discovered in May 1859 when the campaign in Italy – which was supposed to draw off a just fraction of the French army, leaving large contingents for service on the Rhine and in Africa – consumed the entire French army. William McElwee once argued that if Prussia had only intervened on the side of its Austrian ally in 1859, or if Austria 'had decided to fight the campaign to a finish, the Second Empire would have come to a much earlier inglorious end' (McElwee 1974: 36). In the event, Napoleon III's gamble succeeded, yet the Prussians noted France's thinness in the Italian War and very deliberately capitalized upon it ten years later, when they drowned the 300,000-man French army under a million Prusso-German invaders (Cox 1994: 164–6).

France's railway deployment in 1859 also impressed the Prussians, who, with their extensive, vulnerable land frontiers, seized upon the railway as a means to concentrate Prussia's army quickly and fling it against an advancing enemy. France's rifled field guns deeply impressed all of the powers, especially the Austrians, who upgraded their artillery in time for Austria's next war with Prussia in 1866. These were important findings, yet observers of the Franco-Austrian War were most interested in infantry tactics: how the three armies held up under the accurate, devastating fire of the rifle. In this regard, the war passed a curious, utterly misleading verdict, which would go a long way toward explaining Austria's defeat at the hands of the Prussians in 1866.

In 1859, the Austrians were armed with better rifles than the French, and employed tactics designed by old Field Marshal Radetzky in the early 1850s to make optimal use of this excellent rifle. In brief, the Radetzky tactics split Austrian infantry battalions into three 'rifle divisions', which were supposed to manoeuvre jointly in battle to bring all rifles to bear and facilitate flanking attacks. Radetzky's fire tactics were designed not only to bring more rifles into action – by opening up the clotted battalion – but also to disperse troops and present a smaller target to enemy infantry and guns. The French in contrast reverted in 1859 to the shock tactics of 1792; they rather rashly concluded that the best way to overcome Austrian firepower was to crush it beneath bayonet charges by massed 600-man battalions. With outmoded tactics like these, curious after the Crimean experience, the French ought to have been slaughtered, but were saved by the haplessness of the Austrian line infantry. Most Austrian conscripts were Slavs and Hungarians, and they simply made no sense of orders bawled at them in German, the Habsburg army's 'language of command'. Vexing at the best of times, this language barrier was all but impenetrable in the excitement of battle. Moreover, most Austrian troops lacked even a primary education; there were few schools in Austria to begin with, and what self-respecting peasant would send a son to school where he would be no use as a field hand? Poorly educated, Austrian conscripts had no success taking ranges or using the backsights on their technically superb new rifles. They simply blazed away and missed their targets nine times out of ten (Wawro 1995a: LIX, 407–34). In this improbable way, the French triumphed at Magenta and Solferino, sprinting in amongst the bewildered Austrian troops with the bayonet and routing them. To the casual observer, moral force – *élan vital* – had beaten technology; men had beaten fire. From this experience the Austrians took the fateful decision to abandon fire tactics and revert to the French shock column. In 1866, they would pay dearly for this underestimation of the rifle.

CHAPTER FOUR

The rise of Prussia and Italy, 1861–6

Prussia until 1866 was the stuff that jokes were made of. *Pauvre comme le roi de Prusse* was a classic French put-down that described the destitution of Prussia's northern plains and the frugality of Prussia's kings, some of whom wore linen coat sleeves to extend the life of their threadbare uniforms. Voltaire, who spent ten years in Berlin as Frederick the Great's court philosopher, called Prussia 'a little kingdom of border strips'. Unlike France, which bound its citizens into a fertile hexagon solidly buttressed by natural frontiers, Prussia had no natural frontiers – no equivalents of the Rhine, Vosges, Alps, and Pyrénées – and its provinces were not even contiguous, hence Voltaire's sneering reference to 'border strips'. Berlin's enclaves in the west were riven from Prussia's eastern heartland by foreign states: Poland and Sweden for a time, then Denmark, Hanover and Saxony. The awful Seven Years War (1756–63) had exposed all of Prussia's vulnerabilities. Attempting to link up his scattered provinces by the conquest of Saxony, Frederick the Great had seen his kingdom invaded and nearly wiped from the map by mightier neighbours: Russia, Austria, Sweden and France. Only English aid, the miraculous death of the Russian empress, and draconian economies inside Prussia had saved the little kingdom from extinction, but not before 180,000 Prussians had fallen in battle, a veritable holocaust for the times (Duffy 1986: 228).

When not disparaging Prussia's size, Europeans ridiculed its manners. To the end in 1918, the kingdom was run by the Hohenzollern kings and their *Junkers*, landed nobles who officered the Prussian army and administered Prussia's rural areas like feudal barons. Although there were brilliant and cultivated Junkers like Count Otto von Bismarck, many were accurately stereotyped as humourless, Bible-thumping brutes: 'with two legs rooted in the Bible, and two in the soil' (Musil, in Pike 1990: 19). In striking contrast to their pious noblemen, Prussia's kings were often notorious for their perversions: *Potsdamie* was a French euphemism for homosexuality that lingered into the twentieth century, deriving from Frederick the Great's alleged fondness for young men.

In sum, no one took little Prussia very seriously until the 1860s. Its conduct in the Napoleonic Wars had been timid and equivocating. The Hohenzollerns had refused to join coalitions against Napoleon until 1813, seeking instead chances to collaborate with the French and undercut Russia, Austria and the German states. None of Blücher's fulminations in 1814–15 could alter this rather embarrassing fact; hence the Austrians had waved off Prussian objections and assumed the presidency of the German Confederation in 1815 with vindictive relish. In 1850, Austria derived no less pleasure disrupting Prussian attempts to split the German Confederation into a Protestant, Prussian-led north and a Catholic, Austrian-led south. When Prussian King Friedrich Wilhelm IV summoned the German princes to Erfurt to approve Prussia's absorption of the north German states, Austrian Emperor Franz Joseph marched an army to the Prussian border and forced Friedrich Wilhelm to resume his subordinate position in a revived, Austrian-led German Confederation. Though the Prussians felt humiliated, most Europeans did not see the events of 1850 as a humiliation at all; they were merely the expression of political reality. Prussia, 'the sandbox of Europe', had descended to its natural position on the ladder of great powers: the bottom rung, a point scathingly confirmed by the editors of *The Times* in 1860:

> Prussia is always leaning on someone, always getting somebody to help her, never willing to help herself; always ready to deliberate, never to decide; present in congresses, but absent in battles. ... She has a large army, but notoriously one in no condition for fighting. ... No one counts her as a friend, no one dreads her as an enemy. How she became a Great Power history tells us, why she remains so, nobody can tell ... Prussia unaided would not keep the Rhine or the Vistula for a month from her ambitious neighbours.
>
> (H. Koch 1978: 250)

And there – on the bottom rung of Europe – might Prussia have remained were it not for three developments: the industrial revolution, the rise of Bismarck, and the military reforms of Generals Moltke and Roon. These three developments were linked. Sitting astride vast coal reserves, Prussia emerged as an industrial powerhouse in the 1850s and 1860s. Industrialization wrought great social and political changes inside Prussia. A radical working class began to take shape, and liberal merchants and manufacturers in Prussia's growing cities – industrial conurbations like Breslau, Essen and Düsseldorf – began to challenge the ancient prerogatives of the Junker agrarians. The Junkers, recognizing that the urban liberals meant to transform their aristocratic 'barracks state' into a British-style constitutional monarchy – in which the king and the counties would lose their historical prerogatives – appealed to King Wilhelm I for support. Wilhelm, who ascended the Prussian throne in 1858, naturally saw things their way and ordered his brightest, most illiberal Junker, forty-six year-old Count Otto von Bismarck, to form a new government that would silence or coopt the progressives. At the same time, to strengthen the Prussian army as a conservative instrument, Wilhelm made General Helmuth von Moltke his chief of general staff and General Albrecht von Roon his war minister. These three men, well funded by Prussia's industrial revolution, would make the 'German Revolution' in the years between 1864 and 1871.

Industrial revolution

Having failed to make a political revolution in 1848, the Prussian middle class settled for an economic one instead. In the years between 1848 and 1870, the Prussian economy took off. Prussian mills in the *Ruhrgebiet* and Silesia added 5,000 steam engines and increased their combined horsepower from 22,000 in 1846 to 137,000 in 1866. Between 1850 and 1870, Prussia's railways tripled in length, from 2,404 miles of track in 1850 to 4,455 in 1860, and to 7,160 by 1870. Growth in Prussian coal production was even more impressive. Prussia's Saar mines, which had yielded 675,000 tons of coal in 1850, produced 2.1 million tons by 1860. Output in Prussia's Ruhr fields more than doubled, from 1.9 million tons in 1850 to 4.3 million tons in 1860. As Prussian industry expanded, publicly owned conglomerates replaced small businesses; this boom in railways, coal, iron and steel spawned big banks and insurance companies, which gathered capital and pumped it into the growing industrial machine. The results were palpable; on a visit to Prussia in 1859, Karl Marx wrote:

> Whoever last saw Berlin ten years ago would not recognize it again. A stiff parade ground has been transformed into the powerful centre of German engineering. When one travels through the Prussian Rhineland and Westphalia, one is reminded of Lancashire and Yorkshire.
>
> (H. Koch 1978: 241-2)

To Marx's delight, industrial capitalism only aggravated social and political tensions inside Prussia. A third belligerent joined the conflict between bourgeois liberals and landed gentlemen: the industrial working class. Prussia's proletarians were revolutionary and republican in their politics, and never reconciled themselves to the rule of the Hohenzollern kings (Hamerow 1972: 207-11).

Bismarck

The industrialization of Prussia brought with it demands for political liberalization (to enfranchise Prussia's middle- and working classes) and national unification (to create a single German state and market). Yet Prussia's rising classes met an immovable obstacle in the Junkers. A military monarchy with an aristocratic ethos since the seventeenth century, the Hohenzollern state found it difficult to integrate new ideas, faces and interests. The Prussian army, which had counted just 695 middle-class officers among a corps of 7,000 in 1806, had made little progress introducing new men since then. In 1861, 65 per cent of officers (and 86 per cent of colonels and generals) were Junkers (Moncure 1993: 50). King Wilhelm I's camarilla was dominated by elderly, aristocratic soldiers, who defended Prussia's traditions (the black-white flag, the 'barracks state', the semi-feudalism) and scorned the ideas of 'nationalism' and 'progress'. Junkers equated the first idea with the revolutionary turbulence of the Napoleonic period, the second with 'bourgeois materialism'. Naturally the landslide victory of Prussia's Progressive Party in the legislative elections of 1861 precipitated a political crisis. For the first time, a liberal Prussian *Landtag* faced a conservative king and clique. To win the face-off, King Wilhelm turned to Bismarck, who boasted that he was a 'white revolutionary', a dedicated monarchist who would derail liberal reform efforts and unify Germany not by offering the German people a liberal constitution (the progressive formula), but by *conquering* them and offering them a nation-state. The catch was that it would be a Prussian-run nation-state: militarized, oligarchic and centred on Berlin.

Bismarck's efforts to break the liberal bloc in parliament were focused on the so-called Prussian army crisis, which convulsed Berlin from 1861 until 1866. Prussian progressives sought an issue to break the back of royal authority, and found it in the army, which, under Wilhelm's pugnacious war minister 'Ruffian Roon' was attempting to triple its active-duty strength and purge its liberal-minded national guard (the *Landwehr*) in an effort to strengthen Prussia's international position and secure the Hohenzollern dynasty against revolution (McElwee 1974: 61–2). Liberals seized upon the army issue as yet another instance of royal despotism. When Roon argued that more soldiers were needed to defend Prussia's interests against France and Austria, liberals replied that what Roon was really aiming at was the 'militarization' of Prussian society. If more men were needed, they asserted, surely the middle-class *Landwehr* would provide them in ample numbers. No, Roon retorted: warfare was becoming more complex; professionals, not militiamen, were needed. War was also becoming more strenuous. Prussia's adoption of fire tactics and small-unit manoeuvre in the 1860s meant that soldiers had to be able to scramble in and out of cover and take rifle ranges with the naked eye, activities that were beyond the capacity of paunchy, bespectacled *Landwehr* men abruptly called up from their civilian trades and professions.

Prussian liberals reacted angrily to the insinuation that they were unfit to defend the kingdom. In rousing speeches, they recalled the glories of 1813–14 – the 'Wars of Liberation' – when the Prussian *Landwehr* had fought shoulder-to-shoulder with the king's blue-coated regulars in the climactic battles against Napoleon. Citing Clausewitz (a liberal in uniform), who had insisted that every successful war effort incorporate the 'passions of the people',

Prussian liberals argued that the *Landwehr*, though relatively old and lax (embodying men up to the age of forty), was the very best way to unleash Prussia's war potential, for it would unleash the 'will of the people' in a burst of popular enthusiasm. Predictably, the debate foundered. Prussian liberals rightly suspected that Bismarck and Roon were manipulating the issue of military reform to kill two birds with one stone. On the military level, they wanted to give Prussia the capability to assert itself as a great power (Craig 1955: 159–74; Howard 1981: 19). On the domestic-political level, they were using the army and its glorious reputation as a wedge to divide and destroy their liberal adversaries. Roon, a blue-eyed, broad-shouldered giant who deliberately cultivated the upturned moustache of a drill sergeant to inflame parliamentary liberals, advised the king in 1859 to defend every royal prerogative against 'confusions of constitutional thought' and the 'seductions of the Mock Monarchy of England' (Goerlitz 1995 [1952]: 79; Hamerow 1972: 153–4). Although he was an efficient administrator, Roon was perhaps best at polarizing Prussian society. Painting liberals as defeatists and cowards, he all but dared them to attempt a revolution ('a cleansing mud bath', he called it), which would justify a military crackdown and martial law (Goerlitz 1995 [1952]: 80).

What made the Prussian army crisis more than a footnote to history was its conduct, its ultimate resolution, and what it told about the future of civil–military relations in Germany. Rather than compromise with the Prussian parliament on the army dispute, Bismarck – himself a civilian and a *Landwehr* major – chose simply to ignore the legislature. Together with Roon, he began to appropriate money for the army illegally, taking tax revenues directly from the treasury and privatizing state assets (mines, forests and railways) to procure still more funds for the war ministry (Stern 1979: 64–75). These financial dodges enabled Prussian army reform to move ahead over liberal protests, lending credence to Mirabeau's jest that 'Prussia is not a country that has an army but an army that has a country in which it is just billeted' (Blanning 1996: 8). By 1862 Bismarck and Roon had largely replaced the *Landwehr* officer corps with retired veterans, and had doubled the regular strength of the Prussian army. With 212,000 peasant conscripts at his disposal and a docile *Landwehr*, Bismarck bid finally for the friendship of his liberal opponents (Deist, in Förster and Nagler 1997: 313–14). In the notorious 'iron and blood' speech of 1862, he argued that a German nation-state, the liberals' chief desire, would never be attained by parliamentary votes or referenda, but by conquest, and for that, the Prussian army – in its most lethal, illiberal form – would be an indispensable tool.

> It is not to Prussia's *liberalism* that Germany looks, but to its *power*. Let Bavaria, Württemberg, and Baden indulge in liberalism; no one will give them Prussia's part for that. Prussia must collect and keep its strength for the right moment, which has been missed several times already. Prussia's frontiers as laid down by the Vienna treaties [of

1815] are not conducive to a healthy national life. It is not by means of speeches and majority resolutions that the great issues of the day will be decided – that was the great mistake of 1848 and 1849 – but by iron and blood.

(Gall 1986: I, 204)

This was Bismarck's first attempt to seduce German liberals with the promise of glory, territorial expansion and national unification, a seduction that Bismarck would consummate in 1871, when, to liberal acclaim, he founded the German Empire, a deeply conservative facsimile of the Kingdom of Prussia. Part of Bismarck's genius was his perception that Prussian liberals, though sticklers for legality at home, craved a minister who would break international law, who would tear up the treaties of 1815, destroy the Austrian-led German Confederation, and unify the thirty-nine German states. Karl Twesten, a Prussian progressive, frankly admitted this in 1861:

If some day a Prussian minister would step forward and say ... 'I have moved boundary markers, violated international law, and torn up treaties, as Count Cavour has done', gentlemen, I believe that we will not condemn him. And if an inexorable fate should carry him off in the midst of his brilliant career, as happened to [Cavour], then we shall erect a monument to him, as the history of Italy will erect one to Count Cavour.

(Hamerow 1972: 171)

Bismarck would one day have his monument – a towering slab in Hamburg – but, like the great Cavour, he was still greatly disliked in the early 1860s. He was distrusted by the right, despised by the left and regarded sceptically by the working classes, who were informed of the chronic abuse of labour on Bismarck's own estates. If, as Bismarck later boasted, he invigorated the stalemated Prussian political system 'like a fresh battalion produced in the heat of battle', it had to be admitted that the outcome of the battle in the 1860s was still in doubt, and would probably hinge on the wars of expansion being planned by King Wilhelm's chief of general staff, General Helmuth von Moltke.

Prussia's military revolution

Born in 1800, Moltke did not become Chief of the Prussian General Staff by chance; he was the philosophical heir of Boyen, Gneisenau, Scharnhorst and Clausewitz, the brainy reformers who had rebuilt Friedrich Wilhelm's shattered army after Jena and decreed in 1808 that 'from this date forward a claim to officer rank shall in peacetime be warranted only by knowledge and education' (Bucholz 1991: 22). It was this new Prussian emphasis on aptitude over birth or connections that accounted for the rapid ascent of the rather grey and bookish Moltke. He was commissioned in 1819 only after passing competitive exams in German, French, geography and history. From 1823–6 he excelled at the Prussian Kriegsschule (renamed the Kriegsakademie in 1859), and rose to the head of his class.

The curriculum at the Kriegsschule ('War School') reflected the Prussian army's emphasis on education over training, and gives some insight into the reasons for Prussia's military dominance after 1860. Sixty per cent of the war college's course offerings were standard arts and sciences: mathematics, physics, chemistry, literature and history. Just 40 per cent were military courses: tactics, gunnery, mapping and war studies. Students were encouraged to think critically, exercise their imaginations, and apply their liberal education to the military art. The course culminated with a three-week final exam that pushed general staff aspirants to their limits. Students were paired off in war games; each was assigned an army and given total authority for its supply and manoeuvre. Though few failed the war college, only a third of graduates were admitted to the hallowed 'red den': the Great General Staff in Berlin. Like everyone else, these graduates pulled on their trousers one leg at a time, but theirs had red stripes, the mark of excellence in the Prussian army. Final evaluations at the Kriegsschule were always laconic; Erich Ludendorff's was a classic: 'A clear head, combined with knowledge, ability, and form' (Clemente 1992: 192–3). Here was the taproot of *Auftragstaktik* (mission tactics), the German army's easy devolution of command to junior officers on the spot. Once provided with the rigorous education described above, most Prussian officers could simply be told to 'take and hold Glogau', rather than 'take and hold Glogau thus … '. Taught to think flexibly and intuitively, Prussian officers were comfortable planning and improvising. This kept offensive operations on the boil and reduced clutter and bureaucracy at headquarters, where basic tasks, not entire procedures, were formulated.

The Prussian army's respect for education was the source of its midcentury revolution in military affairs. Officers like Moltke regularly published on military questions, a pastime that would have earned them nothing but ridicule in other armies, where 'military science' and 'journalism' were considered trivial pursuits. Prussian officers also joined enthusiastically in the mapping, war games and staff rides that differentiated the Prussian army from its rivals. In the Prussian army, academic study was increasingly acceptable, even desirable. The situation in Austria, Britain and France was altogether different. There, staff rides, which involved studying past campaigns in minute detail and then riding over the ground to evaluate the conduct of the opposing armies, were regarded as futile academic exercises (Clemente 1992: 194–5). War games (*Kriegsspiele*), which forced Prussian officers to predict the most likely military conflicts and fight them to a conclusion using current troop strengths (playing both sides of the war to enter into the mind of the enemy), did not feature in any other European army's war preparation. Indeed, when Field Marshal Archduke Albrecht played a *Kriegsspiel* with the Austrian chief of general staff in 1860, he earned the sobriquet *Friedensmarschall* – 'peacetime field marshal' – from sneering colleagues, who refused on principle to make the connection between real and 'gamed' war. The situation in France was no better. As late as 1908 a critic burst out: 'Find me in France a staff that sets aside a little time each week for a staff ride, any outside work, a historical study, a *Kriegsspiel* with a map or a garrison manoeuvre; I defy anybody to name even one' (Porch 1981: 221). In the more serious Prussian army, this kind of philistinism was definitely not in fashion.

Moltke graduated from the Kriegsschule in 1826 and entered the 'red den': the elite sixty-man Great General Staff. He spent the next nine years mapping Prussia, organizing staff rides, and studying the eighteenth-century campaigns of Frederick the Great. In any other army, activities like these would have earned Moltke early retirement; in Prussia, he was regularly promoted, moving in 1841 to the general staff's railroad bureau, where he began integrating railways and telegraphs into Prussian war planning. Throughout the 1840s, Moltke recommended that the Prussian army abandon its crumbling fortresses and plough the savings into rolling stock and railway lines instead. 'Every new development of railways', he wrote in 1843, 'is a military advantage. For the national defence, a few million on the completion of our railways is far more profitably employed than on our fortresses' (Howard 1981: 2). Still, Moltke's was a lonely voice. When Austria threatened war in 1850 to stop Prussia unifying north Germany, the Prussian army tried and failed to counter with a railway mobilization. While the Austrians briskly marched an army to the Prussian border, half a million Prussian troops loitered in railway stations while their officers haggled unsuccessfully with Prussia's private railways for space on their trains. Without direct access to Prussian telegraphs, the army relied on the Ministry of the Interior, which often neglected to transmit vital communications. Prussian war plans were 'timid and confused' (the conclusion of the Prussian chief of general staff himself), wholly defensive, and based on nothing more original than the possession of fortresses and keypoints (Bucholz 1991: 36–8). While the Prussians floundered, the Austrians, led for the last time by the aged but efficient Radetzky, hastened to the Prussian border and called Prussia's bluff. At the Austrian town of Olmütz, hard by the Prussian frontier, Prussian negotiators wisely renounced their bid to unify north Germany. Bismarck, the coming man in Prussia, called this the 'humiliation of Olmütz'. It was caused in large part by military ineffectiveness, and General Moltke's efforts to correct the many problems revealed in 1850 helped propel him to the top of the Prussian general staff in 1857.

When Moltke was named Chief of Prussia's Great General Staff (*Grosser Generalstab*) in 1857, it was far from great. Still something of a neglected backwater, the general staff was resented by the regimental officers and feudal grandees, who wielded considerable power in the Prussian army despite its theoretical commitment to education and intellect. It took the bitter pill of

1850 – which galled reactionaries and reformers alike – and the unwavering support of Prussia's bright new king, Wilhelm I, to create the right conditions for change, which Moltke immediately grasped. Moltke's study of Prussia's mobilization fiasco in 1850 and the Franco-Austrian War of 1859 convinced him that rapid communications were the essential basis of modern war. In 1858, he launched the world's first extensive railway exercise, moving 16,000 men, 650 horses and their supplies by rail in a fraction of the time that would have been required on foot and horseback. The success of this experiment convinced Moltke to 'mechanize' still more elements of the Prussian army. In 1859, when Prussia mobilized to dissuade France from pressing its advantage after Solferino, 80 per cent of the Prussian army – six entire corps – moved to the French border by rail. The performance was good, but not good enough for the exacting Moltke. When the crisis had passed, he added a 'mobilization section' to the general staff, and noting that Prussian units in the field had typically waited 120 hours for their orders from Berlin, shifted the army's correspondence from horseback couriers to the electric telegraph. In Prussia's next war, notification time would be reduced to just twenty-four hours, a 500 per cent improvement (Bucholz 1991: 40).

After 1859, Moltke took pains to integrate state and private railways into Prussian war plans. While other armies still hunted for rail space on the very eve of war, bidding against merchants and travellers at city ticket offices, Moltke appropriated the entire Prussian rail network in advance, advising railway companies that their rolling stock would be made available to the army in case of war, and fitting freight cars with breakaway stalls, benches and hitching posts to accommodate men, horses and guns. He also instituted the 'unit train rule', providing every battalion, squadron and battery with a fifteen-car train that would rush it to its staging area without any time-consuming changes or halts (Showalter 1975: 46–50; Bucholz 1991: 41). After 1860, Prussian war games and manoeuvres routinely involved the railways. When Denmark laid claim to the largely German Elbe Duchies of Schleswig and Holstein in 1862, Moltke, who wanted the duchies to secure Prussia's northern rim, made some rapid calculations and then assured Wilhelm I that Prussia's railways could move a German army into the disputed duchies faster than Denmark's. Events would shortly prove him right. In 1864, the Danes invaded Schleswig by land and sea and Moltke reacted instantly, confronting 43,000 Danes with an Austro-Prussian force of 65,000. The outcome of this Danish War was never really in doubt. Denmark's early victories against the small Saxon and Hanoverian contingents that arrived first on the scene to defend Holstein – a member of the German Confederation – were swiftly reversed when Prussian troop trains thundered up the isthmus to Rendsburg and Kiel and disgorged their battalions. In battles at Oversee, Selk and Düppel, an allied Austro-Prussian army hammered the Danes out of Schleswig-Holstein and forced Denmark's surrender. The Danish War was a tribute to Moltke's careful war planning. Denmark's winter campaign through fortified belts and boggy terrain would have thwarted most armies. Moltke's prewar planning and his use of the German railways for troop movements and logistics facilitated a quick, decisive victory.

Though fast, Prussia's deployment in 1864 was still not fast enough for Moltke. Like other European armies, Prussia's still practised extraterritoriality, breaking its regiments into four battalions and scattering them haphazardly around the country. Although this dispersal provided a rough-and-ready police force in case of strikes or revolution, it slowed wartime mobilization to a crawl, for Prussia's eighty infantry regiments had first to gather in their battalions from 330 garrison towns, and only then begin slotting them into brigades, divisions and corps (Bucholz 1991: 44–5). Between 1864 and 1866, Moltke solved this problem too. He carved Prussia into ten corps districts *permanently* garrisoned with the battalions that would form their regiments, brigades and divisions in wartime. The system left nothing to chance: Prussian boys were born into a local battalion to which they belonged until their forty-second birthday.

Though eminently sensible, the Prussian reform was rejected by Europe's other powers, who feared that territorial organization would encourage provincial separatism or fraternization between government troops and locals. Other states also used their armies as 'schools of the nation', a practice that paid social and political dividends to be sure, but not military ones. The new state of Italy, for example, consciously wielded its army as a social instrument. Southerners were posted in the north to 'civilize' them; northerners were garrisoned in the south to sniff out secessionist intrigues and organized crime. The French employed a similiar 'extraterritorial' system, always taking care to post Parisians in faraway garrisons and rotating other potentially mutinous groups like the Basques, Catalans, Bretons and Corsicans in and out of every French province but their own (Porch 1981: 119–20). The long-term aim, as Eugen Weber has famously argued, was to 'turn peasants into Frenchmen'; the short-term aim to avoid armed revolts and, by rotating every two years, to withhold the vote from French soldiers (Weber 1976: 292–302). The acme of extraterritoriality was of course the Austrian Empire (Wawro 1996c: 52–4). With its twelve jostling nationalities, Habsburg Austria was in a permanent state of ferment. To dampen the national aspirations of his subject peoples, Emperor Franz Joseph scattered them across East Central Europe. Vienna was garrisoned with Ukrainians, Venice with Croats, Budapest with Rumanians, Cracow with Germans, Prague with Hungarians, and so on. Naturally, this political decision to use armies as police squads and melting pots (Austria's Field Marshal Heinrich Hess actually referred to the Austrian army in 1860 as a 'saucepan of the nations') made mobilization a protracted and difficult process for all but the Prussians. Thus Moltke's efforts to reorganize the Prussian army along territorial lines – greatly facilitated by the fact that Prussia contained only one fractious minority, the Poles, annexed in the 1770s and 1790s – permitted him literally to 'steal a march' on his adversaries.

In terms of warfare, the Danish War of 1864 was most remarkable for what it taught about infantry tactics. In this area, no less than communications, organization and logistics, Moltke revolutionized warfare. Whereas the Danes and Austrians still hewed to the shock tactics of Napoleon – massing their infantry in battalion columns and sending them at the enemy behind flapping flags and skirling bands, betting that the enemy would succumb to the *moral* force of the approaching juggernauts – Moltke hazarded something new. While every other European army rejected breech-loading rifles, which could fire four or five rounds per minute compared with the one round afforded by the Minié rifles employed in the Crimean and Italian Wars of the 1850s, Moltke confidently procured one for the Prussian army.

Moltke chose the *Zündnadelgewehr* or 'needle rifle'. It was a controversial choice, for the early breech-loaders (Prussia used an 1849 model in the wars of 1866 and 1870) were, by comparison with the late model Minié rifles, crudely engineered and notoriously defective. When fired, gas leaked from the gasket sealing the needle rifle's breech, blasting sparks and grease into the face of its handler. In the Danish War, Austrian observers noted that nervous Prussian infantrymen often fired from the hip, spoiling their aim, but saving their faces and whiskers from the greasy inferno in their hands. Though discomfiting, these technical problems were nothing beside the larger tactical question posed by the breech-loaders. Until the invention of small-calibre, metal cartridges in the 1880s, rifle rounds were bulky, cigar-sized cylinders. Infantrymen could only cram sixty of them into haversacks already crowded with food and personal effects. This meant that a Prussian infantryman armed with a breech-loader would be able to run through his entire stock of ammunition in just fifteen minutes. A Frenchman or an Austrian, more prudently equipped with the slow-loading muzzle-loader, would need a full hour to exhaust his ammunition.

The muzzle-loader's slower rate of fire gave officers and NCOs time to pace the firing line and correct ranges. It also gave the infantrymen pause to calm their nerves and accustom themselves to the excitement of battle. For this reason General Robert E. Lee made the rather surprising declaration during the American Civil War that 'what we want is a firearm that cannot be loaded without a certain loss of time, so that a man learns to appreciate the importance of his fire' (Luvaas 1959: 42, 173). Indeed, many Prussian officers regretted Moltke's choice of the needle rifle. In 1864, an Austrian officer attached to Prussian headquarters in Denmark noted that even Prussia's best units became overexcited in combat and tended to fire too quickly, wasting precious rounds: 'I repeatedly overheard Prussian officers worrying about the inability of their men to conserve ammunition for the *second, decisive* phase of a battle' (Wawro 1996a: 23). The Austrians also saw weakness in the Bismarck-Roon army expansion, which was well along by 1864. It expanded the Prussian army not by lengthening the service obligation of enlisted men – the practice in Austria and France – but by adding thousands of short-service conscripts, who would serve three years (as opposed to eight in Austria and France, ten in Russia), and then pass into the reserves. From this, Prussia's rivals deduced that Moltke's new model army, when faced with a sterner foe than the Danes, would shoot poorly and be easily put to rout.

To his credit, Moltke anticipated all of this. He saw that fire control would be a Prussian vulnerability, but vowed to offset it with fire discipline and tactical flexibility. While other armies massed their infantry in dense columns (the Austrian and Russian practice) or compact linear formations with narrow fronts and deep reserves (the French and British practice after 1866), Moltke unleashed his army, making companies sometimes even platoons, his standard manoeuvre formations, and authorizing them to rove freely around the battle-field so long as their movements and combats conformed to the overarching battle plan. This development – a further refinement of *Auftragstaktik* – unlocked the full potential of the needle rifle. Small units were able to strike swiftly, probe the flanks of the enemy, and pour fire into them. They could be rapidly reinforced by fast-moving reserve companies, which would 'swarm' into the enemy rear areas, spread panic and envelop the enemy main force in what Moltke called the *Kesselschlacht* or 'pocket battle'.

To ensure that Prussian riflemen held their fire until the decisive moment and then fired effectively, Moltke emphasized (and found money for) marks-manship in peacetime. Whereas the Austrians furnished just eighteen practice rounds per infantryman per year in the 1860s, Moltke provided his men with 100 rounds. And whereas Austrian troops invariably fired their rounds from the same spot at a fixed target (often surrendering their rifles in advance to an NCO, who would align their front and backsights for them), Prussian troops were expected to take their own ranges, set their own gunsights, observe their own shooting, and record the result of each shot in a *Schiessbuch* or 'shooting log' (Wawro 1996a: 22–4; 1995a: 413–15). In this way, Moltke achieved both fire control and tactical flexibility, an invincible combination. To the last, foreign observers were sceptical. French experts thought Moltke's system 'anarchical', and scorned the Prussian *chef* for 'carving his army into tiny, dispersed packets' (Ferri-Pisani 1868: 188–9). The criticism seemed justified, yet would prove the very secret of Prussia's success in the Austro-Prussian War of 1866.

The Austro-Prussian War

Bismarck and Roon had not reformed the Prussian army for purely military reasons. They had always planned to unify Germany under Prussian rule, an aim that would assuredly place them on a collision course with the two guar-antors of a divided, non-national Germany: Austria and France.

Austria's interest in a divided Germany was twofold. On the one hand, the Habsburgs derived considerable prestige from their presidial role in Germany, as Holy Roman Emperors until the Napoleonic era, and as presidents of the

German Confederation after 1815. On the other hand Austria, a wobbly, multinational empire, had an obvious interest in containing the spread of nationalism, whether German, Italian or Hungarian. Were the thirty-nine German states ever to avow the 'national principle' and unite under a single government, what would prevent the Germans of Habsburg Austria (25 per cent of the imperial population) from leaving to join them? For these reasons, Austria declared war on Prussia in 1866 when Bismarck moved to dissolve the German Confederation of 1815 and annex its northern states.

European military experts predicted an Austrian victory. Though the Austrians had performed badly in the war of 1859, they had learned much from the campaign, and had introduced key reforms in the intervening years. Noting the effectiveness of the French artillery in 1859, the Austrians had procured a rifled field gun of their own in the early 1860s, one that was far superior to Prussia's mixed bag of rifles and smoothbores. Impressed by France's athletic shock tactics in 1859, the Austrians introduced their own version in 1864, which were used to good, though misleading, effect in the Danish War. Most importantly, Franz Joseph flushed new blood into his elderly officer corps, abruptly retiring 120 senior officers in 1859 and promoting dozens of younger men to fill the vacant places. The Austrian emperor seemed even to have found a 'second Radetzky' in 1859, General Ludwig von Benedek, who had taken a Piedmontese town by storm and fought a heroic rearguard action at Solferino. In 1861, Benedek was given command of the Austrian army, a position he used to deliver a series of blunt, no-nonsense pronouncements on internal and external affairs very much in the style of Radetzky. In a war with Prussia, Benedek – the 'Lion of Solferino' – would have the resources of a vast empire behind him. Second only to Russia in land mass, Austria dwarfed little Prussia, and had nearly twice Prussia's population: 35 million inhabitants compared with Prussia's 19 million. Naturally Austria's larger population yielded a bigger army, some 400,000 regulars to Prussia's 300,000. The Austrians were not only more numerous, they were more experienced; Prussia had not fought a major war since 1815; Austria had just been through one. For these reasons, European analysts confidently predicted that Austria would win the war which exploded in June 1866.

At a stroke, the wily Bismarck negated Austria's advantage in troop numbers by concluding a secret treaty with King Vittorio Emanuele II of Italy, who had managed to attach all of the Italian peninsula save Rome and the Austrian province of Venetia to his Piedmontese heartland after Solferino. In 1866, Vittorio Emanuele desperately wanted Venetia with its redoubtable forts and splendid port at Venice, and he actually sparked the Austro-Prussian War by deploying 200,000 troops on Austria's southern frontier in April, forcing the Austrians to counter in May, which triggered the Prusso-Italian treaty and provided Bismarck with all the pretext he needed to attack the Austrians in June.

The Italian threat to Austria drew off 100,000 Habsburg troops, evening the odds in Bohemia, where the Austro-Prussian War was fought to a conclusion. Even odds were all that Moltke needed. Although Prussia had not fought a major battle since Waterloo, the professionalism inculcated by Moltke's general staff more than compensated for the lack of experience. As Moltke had predicted, serious training grounded in physical reality – the Prussians emphasized firepower, the Austrians, with their fresh memories of French bayonet charges in 1859, 'moral force' – was the best preparation for war. While Austrian battalions straggled into Bohemia from the Ruritanian corners of the empire, haphazardly forming brigades and scrounging for supplies as they went, Prussia's permanent corps, already organized for war in peacetime, streamed through Saxony, Austria's chief ally. Using every available railway in Prussia and Saxony, Moltke pushed three armies into Bohemia, the richest, most industrialized province of the Austrian Empire. The Prussian advance was breathtaking; within days the Prussians were within striking distance of Prague. This was an early *Blitzkrieg*; there was no other word for it. Benedek, still dawdling at his headquarters in Moravia, a fourteen-day march from Bohemia, had assumed that Moltke would require weeks to invade Austria. It was not the last time that a German army would amaze an adversary by the speed of its movements.

The first noteworthy clash between the Austrians and Prussians occurred at the little frontier town of Trautenau, a picturesque place at the foot of the Sudeten Mountains. There a single Prussian brigade, surprised and cornered on its way into Bohemia, successfully repulsed 'storm attacks' by an entire Austrian corps. The superiority of Moltke's fire tactics, already proven in Denmark, where the Austrians had suffered much higher casualties than the Prussians, was confirmed by the casualty lists at Trautenau, where four Austrians fell for every Prussian. In the days that followed, the Austrian army was decimated by the Prussian needle rifle. At the battle of Skalice on 28 June, the Prussians attacked a fortified Austrian position across open ground and still managed to uphold the 4:1 casualty ratio established at Trautenau. Skilfully handling their rifles, the Prussians killed, wounded or captured 6,000 Austrians, losing just 1,500 of their own. The Prussians repeated the feat the next day at the battle of Jicin, which heaped up more Austrian dead and placed all three Prussian armies within a single march of one another. These were extraordinary results, which Moltke rightly attributed to the tactical system he had built since 1859. Agile Prussian infantry companies slipped into the gaps between Austria's massed battalion columns and poured well aimed fire into their flanks, panicking them into precipitate retreats, which yielded droves of wild-eyed, unwounded prisoners. Both Skalice and Jicin were successful 'pocket battles': the Prussians had found the Austrian flanks and turned them with calamitous results for Benedek (Wawro 1996a: 150, 173–4). Moltke, who had left Berlin on 30 June and moved Great Headquarters to Bohemia, pushed his pincers to the Elbe, and found Benedek's North Army at the fortress of Königgrätz, where it paused to regroup in the first week of July.

Benedek, in the meantime, had fallen from grace. Though a prewar celebrity ('the Lion of Solferino', 'Austria's Blücher'), he failed to parry Moltke's lightning strokes. Whereas the Prussian chief had deployed on a 300-mile arc – from Bavaria to Silesia – using six railway lines and heeding Napoleon's aphorism to 'march separately and combine in battle', Benedek had proven far less imaginative. Seeking safety in numbers, he had massed his army at the entrenched camp of Olmütz and then lumbered slowly into Bohemia, always one step behind the Prussian army. Since Moltke divided his force into three armies, it was able to supply itself and march far more quickly than Benedek's North Army. Benedek had also neglected to make full use of Austria's railways. Though Austria was crisscrossed by public and private railways, few of them were converted to military use in June 1866; indeed, most of the North Army's regiments had marched on foot to Moravia and Bohemia from their farflung garrisons. Many Austrian units walked for forty days in the summer heat, arriving at Benedek's camp exhausted, their spirits broken, their uniforms in tatters, the soles peeling off their dusty boots.

The contrast with Moltke's smooth, mechanical deployment was striking. The Prussian move to the Austrian frontier had gone almost without a hitch, lifting 'the developing relationship between steam and strategy to a kind of symbiosis' (Showalter 1975: 56). Prussian troops had arrived fresh and well supplied at their jumping-off stations round Torgau, Görlitz and Neisse, and had lost no time invading Austria. For his part, Benedek wasted nearly the entire month of June waiting for slow-moving troop columns and filling up his magazines. Though he led badly in the first battles of the war, the North Army had already been substantially weakened by its own chaotic arrangements. Here was living proof of Moltke's aphorism that 'an error in the original concentration of armies can hardly be corrected in the entire course of a campaign' (Holborn, in Paret 1986: 289).

There were other problems with the Austrian army. One historian has suggested that Emperor Franz Joseph deliberately sought war in 1866 to solve otherwise insoluble domestic-political problems. According to this interpretation, the war was a desperate gamble, a throw of the dice, undertaken in the hope that a 'great patriotic war' might rally disaffected Austrian nationalities to the Habsburg cause. There is evidence that the Austrian Empire was experiencing a social and political crisis in the 1860s and sought war as a possible purgative. Its two most intractable nationalities, the Magyars and the Italians of Venetia, were rudely defying the central government in Vienna, denying the authority of the Habsburg monarch and threatening even to secede. In Venice, Italian students scrawled 'death to the emperor' on the walls of their classrooms, and hurled home-made bombs at their German-speaking professors. Venetians refused even to share the pavement with Austrian troops or officials; whenever an *austriaco* appeared, Italians would cross the street. In Budapest the situation was no better; nationalist mobs hunted Austrian officials through the streets, and Hungary's parliamentary delegation actually threatened to withhold support from the emperor in the event of war with Prussia and Italy. Other Austrian peoples – the Czechs, Poles and Croats to name but three – were scarcely more reliable. The Czechs and Croats demanded radical reforms in 1866: federal capitals and home rule in Prague and Zagreb. Austria's Poles tried to suppress German-speaking officials, journalists and even opera singers in Galicia (Austria's wedge of Poland), and called for the reestablishment of an independent Polish state, with or without the Habsburgs. All of these tendencies converged in 1866, prompting at least one Austrian general to demand a 'war against the reigning confusion' (Wawro 1995b: 226–40, 246–8).

The Austrian army that fought the war of 1866 reflected the empire's national divisions. Roughly 60 per cent Slavic, 15 per cent German and 15 per cent Hungarian (the rest Italians and Rumanians), it mobilized reluctantly and fought halfheartedly. In every clash with the Prussians, the Austrians lost far more unwounded prisoners than killed or wounded. (Generally speaking, men who gave themselves up unscathed were a sure sign of demoralization; the same trend resurfaced in the First World War, when the Austrians lost more unwounded prisoners as a proportion of armed strength than any other European army including the Russians) (Wawro, in Cecil and Liddle 1996: 399–412). At the battle of Skalice in 1866, whole companies of Austrian troops surrendered to the Prussians. At Trautenau, an entire Austrian regiment panicked and ran into a nearby forest. The trend would culminate at Königgrätz, where 20,000 Austrians surrendered, more than twice the sum of Prussian dead, wounded and missing in battle. There was nothing to compare with this on the Prussian side, where one rarely encountered unwounded prisoners. Indeed, the evidence of the war led the Prussians to conclude that the Austrian army was demoralized, perhaps even rotten to the core. This was doubtless overstatement – tens of thousands of Austrians of all nationalities fought bravely – but it did hint at a hidden, social dimension to the Austrian war effort, which enormously complicated operations.

The clash with Prussia also posed a question that Austrian patriots would still be pondering in 1914: how to inspire the men of a multinational empire in a modern 'war of nations'. In 1866, Prussian troops fought to seize control of Germany. Their Austrian foes, who ought to have disputed this aim, were in many cases indifferent to it. In 1866, Czech members of the imperial parliament or *Reichsrat* at Vienna objected that the cause of the Austro-Prussian War – the still open question of how to dispose of the conquered duchies of Schleswig-Holstein – was a German, not an Austrian interest. Austria, the Czechs insisted, was really a Slavic power, and ought therefore detach itself from the affairs of Germany (needless to say, this view was angrily disputed by the Germans of Western Austria). In Bohemia, the seat of war, Czech nationalists stirred up peasant conscripts, urging them 'not to follow the German Rider blindly'. In Venetia, the other theatre of war, the Austrian emperor was abashed to learn that Italian nationalists greatly outnumbered Habsburg loyalists, which vastly complicated his efforts to make war on the southern front (Wawro 1995b: 240).

All of this social and political decay contributed to the crushing Austrian defeat at Königgrätz on 3 July 1866. There, Moltke and Benedek each brought 250,000 men to a battle as big as Leipzig, one that would demonstrate the superiority of Prussian strategy, operations and tactics, and cast considerable doubt upon the ability of the polyglot Austrian Empire to absorb the shocks of modern war. Königgrätz was very nearly a *Kesselschlacht*. Once informed that Benedek was at rest on the right bank of the Elbe, his back to the river, Moltke pushed his three armies forward. One engaged Benedek's front, the other two drove at his flanks. Only wet weather (which slowed the advance of Moltke's flanking columns) and the heroic exertions of the Austrian artillery, who held their positions to the last, prevented Moltke from closing a ring around the Austrian North Army and capturing it whole. As it chanced, Benedek was able to wriggle backward out of the trap, but at the cost of his artillery, his supply train, and 44,000 dead, wounded and missing men.

Tactically, Königgrätz demonstrated the superiority of Moltke's new methods. Though the Austrians were deployed in elevated, entrenched positions bristling with 200 guns, the Prussian infantry turned them out and very nearly encircled them. How? By two methods that came to form the basis of Prusso-German tactics. First, the Prussians generally advanced not in lines or columns, but in swarms: small platoon-sized parties that moved rapidly and presented a small target to the enemy guns. Second, the Prussians rarely assaulted the front of an Austrian position. Instead, they skirmished along the front – to fix the Austrians in place – and made their main push against the Austrian flanks. This was both an operational and a tactical procedure. Königgrätz was decided by a Prussian flanking army that swept around Benedek's exhausted right wing late in the day. But the flanking army penetrated Benedek's trenches and battery positions only by carefully applying Moltke's fire tactics. Small parties of Prussian infantry found the edges of the Austrian position and took them in a cross-fire. Startled by thick fire from all sides, the Austrians yielded their trenches and fled back toward the Königgrätz fortress works, creating a massive rout and traffic jam that sparked panic all along the crumbling line. On the skirts of the fortress town, Moltke nearly slammed shut the *Kessel*. For most of the night, Benedek's North Army struggled to cross the Elbe while Moltke struggled to bring up lagging, footsore units to trap them. When 4 July dawned, Moltke learned that he had failed to seal the pocket. Most of the Austrian army had escaped to fight another day. The news disappointed Moltke, but he would learn from the experience. In his next test, at Sedan in 1870, he would apply the lessons of Königgrätz, bringing his own artillery forward and delaying his attack on the French until his flanking armies were all within striking distance of the enemy.

Though safely away from Königgrätz, Benedek could not hold the demoralized fragments of his North Army. Like the battles before it, Königgrätz accented the social decay of the Austrian army. The battle was hotly contested only because the Austrian artillery, which possessed better guns than the Prussians, was able to keep the Prussian infantry at arm's length for most of the day. Once the Prussians broke through to the Austrian lines, the character of the battle changed. It swung from a seesaw struggle to a rout. Many Austrian units fought badly, or not at all. On the left wing, where the first Prussian flanking attack landed, a Czech regiment dissolved on contact with the enemy. On the right wing, where the last Prussian attack landed, Austrian soldiers of all nations – Hungarians, Croats, Rumanians, Italians – simply ran away from the Prussians. A single Prussian division wrested Chlum, the keypoint of the Austrian position, from three entire corps. Late in the day, Benedek gave up his efforts to direct the battle and tried instead to stem the growing panic. He rode up and down the Königgrätz post road crying: 'In the name of the army commandant, everyone must *stop!*' (Craig 1964; Wawro 1996a: 257–60).

Although badly beaten, the Austrians extricated 200,000 men from the leaky pocket at Königgrätz. Since the battle coincided with an Austrian victory against the Italians in the south, which freed an additional 50,000 troops for service against the Prussians, the question arose: why did the Austrians capitulate after Königgrätz, and not continue the war? Here again, Austrian troop morale, society and politics provided the answer. On the fighting front, the North Army disintegrated. A staff officer sent from Vienna to inspect the remnants of Benedek's army noted that it 'was no longer an army, rather a ragtag mob of stupid, lazy, indifferent men' (Wawro 1992: 716). On the home front, most Austrian civilians rejected all thought of partisan warfare – a patriotic *guerre à outrance* – and pressed the emperor to make peace instead.

Whereas Roon and Moltke had taken care to provide the Prussian army with 180,000 *Landwehr* reservists, Austria's service chiefs had taken no such precautions. Appeals from Vienna for new recruits after the debacle at Königgrätz fell on deaf ears. Franz Joseph's governor in Budapest explained the reluctance of the Hungarian peasant: 'Country folk are scared [of the Prussians], and flatly refuse to join a territorial defence'. The emperor's minister of state described the problem in Austria's cities. Middle-class townsmen were 'infected by dubious [liberal] ideas', and industrial workers could not be armed for the simple reason that they would probably turn their guns against the monarchy (Wawro 1992: 753–4). Throughout July 1866, Franz Joseph was buffeted by political attacks. Vandals smeared his palace with defamatory graffiti, crowds hissed the approach of his coach, and Vienna's liberal *Presse* – the most respected paper in Austria – actually inclined toward Prussia in its coverage of the war. A breathless letter anonymously delivered to the Hofburg in July denounced the officers of the North Army and the emperor too: 'blackguards, traitors, dog's bodies, rats, gallows-birds, who'll be stoned if they ever show themselves in public' (Wawro 1992: 758).

On 22 July, Franz Joseph wearily sued for peace. The risk of revolution outweighed the benefits of a protracted war. Austria agreed to pay an indemnity of thirty million florins ($405 million today), withdraw from the German Confederation, and recognize massive Prussian annexations in North Germany. The system of Bismarck and Moltke had triumphed, due in part to their own formidable exertions, and in part to the weakness of Habsburg Austria.

The consequences of 1866

The war of 1866 transformed Europe, and shook the balance of power. Prussia climbed from the bottom rung of the power ladder to the top. Bismarck formalized his July Armistice with Austria in October at Prague, where Austria and the other powers recognized Prussia's dissolution of the German Confederation of 1815 and its outright annexation of 1,300 square miles of German territory (Schleswig-Holstein, Hanover, Kassel, Nassau and Franfurt-am-Main) and seven million industrious German souls. On hearing the terms of the peace, French statesmen were thunderstruck; one protested too late that Bismarck had succeeded in creating 'une Prusse colossale' that would challenge French primacy in Europe. In addition to the direct annexations, Prussia took indirect control of the remaining states of northern Germany – Saxony, Hessia, the scattered principalities of Mecklenburg and Thuringia, and the free cities of Hamburg, Lübeck and Bremen – via a new, Prussian-run *Bund* called the 'North German Confederation' (Wawro 1996a: 276–7) (Map 4.1). Henceforth, Prussia would control not only the foreign affairs of the northern states, but their military affairs as well. As early as 1866, Berlin ordered all of the annexed areas and most of the confederated ones to adopt Prussian military organization, uniforms, insignia, rifles and tactics. In the event of war, the confederate armies would mesh seamlessly in the Prussian order-of-battle. Bavaria would supply two corps, Saxony one, Hessia, Baden and Württemberg a division each. Between 1866 and 1870, the enlarged Prussian army (really a German army in all but name) added seven corps and 400,000 *Landwehr* reservists to its total strength; it became a million-man army (*Österreichische Militärische Zeitschrift* 1869). None of this escaped the notice of Napoleon III's government in France. Indeed, the day that Bismarck had begun to confer with the Austrians at Nikolsburg, Napoleon III's minister of state warned: 'La grandeur est une chose relative; un pays peut être diminué lorsque de nouvelles forces s'accumulent autour de lui' ('Grandeur is relative; a great power can be diminished when new forces accumulate around it' (Imprimerie Nationale 1870).

While Prussia soared, Austria sank. Crippled by the expenses, casualties and disasters of the war, the Habsburg Monarchy wobbled. Ethnic Germans, once

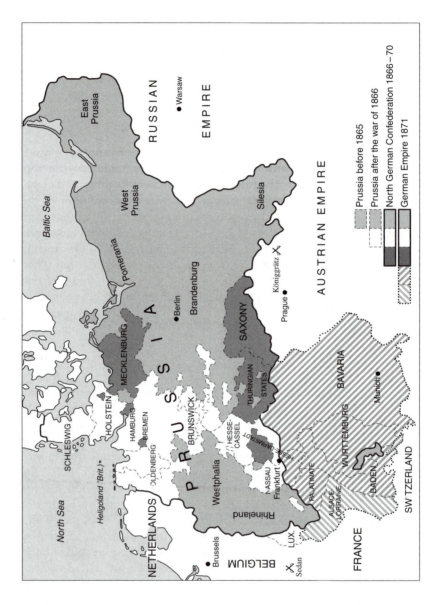

Map 4.1 The making of Germany

the mainstay of the multinational empire, looked to Prussia now that Austria was evicted from the German state system. Franz Grillparzer, the Viennese poet, wondered aloud in 1867: 'Als Deutscher bin ich geboren. Bin ich noch einer?' ('I was born a German, but am I still one?'). Grillparzer saw no future for the Habsburg Monarchy if Bismarck managed to unite all of the German states. In that case, he fretted, Austria would become a Czech or a Hungarian state, for Austro-Germans (a minority in 1866) would abandon the Habsburg cause and gravitate toward the new German Reich in Berlin. He was not far wrong, for Austria came to be dominated by the Hungarians after the Great Constitutional Compromise or *Ausgleich* of 1867.

The *Ausgleich* was born of the Austro-Prussian War; over the ensuing decades, it would corrode Austria (renamed Austria-Hungary in 1867) and all but ensure its collapse in the First World War. Sensing Franz Joseph's vulnerability after Königgrätz, Hungarian politicians, led by Ferenc Deák, demanded a monopoly of power in eastern Austria. Hard-pressed by the Prussian and Italian armies and by his wife Elisabeth, who was Hungary's fiercest advocate in the Hofburg, Franz Joseph granted Deák's demands (Bled 1992: 146–9). He renamed his Austrian Empire the 'Austro-Hungarian Monarchy' and gave Budapest home rule in most of the vast region east of the Leitha river (a muddy stream that curled between Vienna and Sopron.) After 1867, Hungarian Austria would be known as 'Transleithania'; German Austria (the territory west of the Leitha ruled from Vienna) would be called 'Cisleithania'. Although Franz Joseph may actually have believed that Hungarian demands were limited to the right to legislate for themselves, he was rapidly disillusioned. What the Magyar minority of eastern Austria in fact sought was nothing less than the racial domination of East Central Europe.

Together, the Magyars of eastern Austria comprised just 40 per cent of the population; they were outnumbered by the Slavs and Rumanians who shared the region. Thus, for Deák and his more radical colleagues, Hungarian 'liberalism' was a screen for the real business of 'Magyarization', making Hungarians of the non-Hungarian majority in Transleithania. Over the next fifty years, Vienna would frequently repent the great sell-out of 1867. For Slavic and Rumanian national consciousness (and resistance) surged in direct proportion to Hungarian persecution. Hungarian attempts to suppress and 'Magyarize' eastern Austria's Croats, Slovaks, Ukrainians and Rumanians, by outlawing their schools and churches and jailing their priests, teachers, writers and political leaders, sharpened as never before the national rivalries in the Habsburg Monarchy. Abandoned by their 'supranational' emperor after 1867, the eastern nationalities despaired (Bled 1992: 149–52). Millions emigrated to America; those who stayed looked beyond Austria-Hungary for salvation: the Slovaks to Russia, the Croats to Serbia, and the Rumanians, naturally, to Rumania. Needless to say, this made a bad strategic situation worse. By 1900, Habsburg officials would routinely refer to the monarchy's Hungarians as 'der innere Feind' – 'the internal enemy'. By 1905, Franz Joseph was secretly planning to *invade* Hungary, to rescue the non-Magyar peoples. According to this 'Plan U', which was never implemented, an Austrian army composed entirely of non-Hungarian regiments would replay the counter-revolution of 1848–9, marching on Budapest, seizing the parliament, disarming Magyar units and placing all Hungary under martial law.

This extreme level of infighting, which sapped the energies of Vienna and ruined the lives of millions of Austro-Hungarian citizens, was one of the more important and far-reaching consequences of the war of 1866. Largely as a result of the 'dualist' Austro-Hungarian system that sprang from the defeat at Königgrätz, Austria-Hungary would be a social and political invalid by 1914, as will be discussed later. After 1866, Franz Joseph's ramshackle state was more vulnerable than ever to Pan-Slav propaganda (from Russia and Serbia), and a slave to the German alliance concluded in 1879, which, owing to the internal weakness of Austria-Hungary, came to be viewed as Vienna's last resort.

A revolution in naval warfare? The sea battle of Lissa in 1866

The war of 1866 wrought changes in Italy as well. Although a small Austrian force of just three infantry corps and a single cavalry division managed to defeat the entire Italian army – sixteen infantry divisions and four divisions of cavalry – at the battle of Custoza in June, the Italians were saved by Prussia's victories in the north. Forced to move troops from Venetia to defend Vienna after Königgrätz, Franz Joseph could not exploit his victory at Custoza. (Once again, he rued his failure to create a reserve army like the Prussian *Landwehr*, which would have expanded his options after Custoza and Königgrätz.) Austria's evacuation of Venetia in July gave the Italians time to regroup and resume their invasion of Habsburg Italy. By the time the Austrians sat down with the Prussians to negotiate an armistice in late July, the Italian army had pushed most of the way to Venice. Aware that Bismarck was at Nikolsburg trying to end the war to forestall a French or Russian intervention on Austria's behalf, the Italians raced to score a last-minute victory that might earn them territory in addition to Venetia at the peace talks: South Tyrol perhaps, or Austria's rocky Dalmatian coast, which ran from Dubrovnik north to Trieste. This was the rationale for the naval battle in the Adriatic Sea near the island of Lissa (Vis) in late July 1866. Already beaten on land, the Italian government hoped to redeem the galling defeat (and mollify public opinion) with a great victory at sea.

Since the launch of the world's first ironclad warship in 1858, the world's navies had been embracing the 'ironclad revolution' with varying degrees of enthusiasm. The Italians, who had easy access to French loans after 1859, embraced the revolution with gusto. In a flurry of shipbuilding between 1861 and 1866, the Italians had constructed the world's third biggest navy after England and France. Like their counterparts in London and Paris, Italian naval planners believed that maritime operations in the Crimean War and the American Civil War had proven the superiority of the steam-driven armoured ship.

There was considerable evidence to support the Italian view, starting with the Anglo-French naval assaults on Sebastopol, Sveaborg and Fort Kinburn in 1854–5. The American Civil War provided yet more evidence of the power of ironclads. In March 1862 the Confederate Navy had sent their first ironclad frigate, the CSS *Virginia* (formerly the USS *Merrimack*) into Chesapeake Bay, where it had shot two wooden-walled Union frigates to pieces and loosened Lincoln's naval blockade of the southern states. The next day, the Union Navy sent its own ironclad, an armoured 'tower ship' called the USS *Monitor*, into Hampton Roads to engage *Virginia*. The ships wrestled for two exhausting hours, without result. Naval critics were fascinated by the indecisive contest; they had expected *Virginia*, a ten-gun frigate plated with 732 tons of iron, to crush the pesky little *Monitor*. But *Monitor* had scraped through the action intact, circling *Virginia* and pounding the Confederate ship with fire from her twin turret guns (Greene and Massignani 1998: 50–61, 72–81). Subsequent naval actions in the Civil War confirmed the usefulness of tower ships (now called 'monitors'), which, though a liability in high seas, where they tended to ship water and sink because of their shallow draughts, were ideal for coastal fighting, where they did double duty as warships and floating batteries. In the latter capacity, the monitor's low profile concealed it from fortress artillery, which searched the horizon in vain for hostile silhouettes. At the battle of Mobile Bay in August 1864, Union Admiral David Farragut used four monitors to seize the Confederacy's last major port. By 1866, navies all over the world were building hybrid fleets combining armoured frigates like *Virginia* and monitors.

The Italian navy was just such a hybrid. At the outbreak of the Austro-Prussian War it counted eleven ironclads: ten armoured frigates and the *Affondatore*, a twin-turreted British-built monitor finished on the eve of war. Against this potent fleet (constructed in British and American yards), the Austrians fielded just seven lightly gunned and armoured frigates. To exploit Italy's advantage, Admiral Carlo Persano concentrated the fleet at Ancona in July 1866. Persano planned to bombard Austrian forts on the island of Lissa – the so-called Gibraltar of the Adriatic – lure Admiral Wilhelm Tegetthoff and the Austrian navy to its defence and, in a Trafalgar-like action, annihilate the Austrians. Following a successful fleet action, Persano planned to steam as far north as Trieste to assert Italy's claim to Istria and the Dalmatian coast.

It was not to be. Though the Austrians played into Persano's hands, rushing down to Lissa and into the massed broadsides of the Italian fleet, Tegetthoff, whose ships were fitted with iron prows, resorted to a novel tactic. Rather than form a conventional line of battle as the Italians did, he drew his fleet into three closely packed wedges, which ran under the errant fire of the Italian warships and rammed them. Persano and his flag officers were astounded by the crudity of the Austrian tactics. The battle – the first 'blue water' engagement since Trafalgar in 1805 – degenerated into a crude melée. With their view of the enemy obscured by the black, sticky smoke of 1,300 guns, crewmen on both sides fired blindly and made an exasperating discovery: the guns of the day could not bore through the 5-inch iron plates used by both navies. Even the Italians, who mounted the latest 6-inch rifles from Britain's Woolwich works, had no luck against the Austrian ironclads. The Austrians, whose guns were mainly smoothbores, were totally outclassed; four of the eleven Italian ironclads had hulls made entirely of iron and were able to steam carelessly past the Austrian broadsides without incident. Blinded by the pall of gunsmoke, and lightly armed, Tegetthoff exasperatedly ordered his black-painted ships to 'ram everything grey'. The tactic – the same expedient pursued by *Virginia* at Hampton Roads – worked in this case; the Austrian frigates drove at the sides of the bigger, better-armed Italian ships and landed two crippling blows. Tegetthoff himself managed to ram the 6,000-ton pride of the Italian navy at the climax of the battle, the 26-gun *Re d'Italia*. She sank in minutes. Disgraced, Persano and his shipmates straggled back to Ancona. Many proclaimed that the world had witnessed a revolution in fleet tactics: the bow ram had replaced the gun as a ship's principal armament (Sondhaus 1989; Greene and Massignani 1998: 211–46).

Had it really? Naval experts were sceptical, and justifiably so. Indeed Lissa witnessed little that was new. Faced with a poorly handled Italian fleet, Tegetthoff simply resorted to the old Nelsonian tactic of breaking the enemy line and sowing confusion. His decision to ram the Italians was taken only because the Austrian fleet entered the war without the Krupp cannon that the Prussian manufacturer had promised for 1866 but then withheld once Austria declared war. Had Tegetthoff's ships been properly armed, they would naturally have used their guns in preference to their brittle iron rams. (Persano, aboard *Affondatore*, which mounted a lethal-looking 26-foot ram, dared not use it for fear it would stick in an Austrian ship and drag him down with it.) Once engaged, the Austrians found it almost impossible to ram the Italians, for steam propulsion permitted rapid changes of course. Most of the Austrian ram attempts failed; their intended victims merely drove forward or backward, or turned away from the blow. Indeed *Re d'Italia* fell into Tegetthoff's clutches only because a lucky Austrian broadside had smashed her rudder, leaving the Italian frigate vulnerable to the ram stroke that tore a 20-foot gash in her side. The only other victim of the day was the lovely frigate *Palestro*, which, with its all-iron hull, successfully resisted everything the Austrians threw at her until a chance shot carried into the ship's unprotected wardroom and burned its way into the powder magazine, exploding the ship from within.

In short, Lissa was not a revolutionary event. It merely reinforced what sailors already knew: that fluid manoeuvre and accurate gunnery were the keys to naval warfare. Yet many drew the opposite conclusion. When the Royal Navy's chief constructor retired in 1870, he predicted that British battleships of the future would rely chiefly on their rams. Rifled cannon would serve as a defensive armament of last resort, if the ram stroke missed or failed to cripple the enemy ship. The view defied common sense, but was widely shared and reinforced in the years after Lissa by the accidental sinking of seven British warships by the rams of their sister ships (McElwee 1974: 257–64). Because of these mishaps, the world's navies wavered between the ram and the gun for forty years. Only after the great clash in Tsushima Strait in 1905, when Japanese battleships obliterated the Russian Baltic Fleet with their guns to end the Russo-Japanese War, did the last advocates of the ram sink quietly from sight.

The unification of Italy, 1866–70

As Italian troops tramped into Habsburg Venetia in June 1866, King Vittorio Emanuele II (King of Piedmont until 1861, 'King of Italy' thereafter) proclaimed: 'This war cry of joy *completes* our national unification'. The proclamation was premature, for Vittorio Emanuele's army stumbled badly in 1866. Though the Italians brought 220,000 men to the war against Austria's little South Army (80,000 men in all), they failed repeatedly to liberate Venetia. What was perhaps most interesting about the Italian war effort in 1866, was what it reflected about Italian society. Far from being a united, fervently nationalistic country artificially divided by foreign 'occupiers', Italy proved to be a rather apathetic patchwork riven by class, region and culture. Exposed to the shock of war in 1866, the new nation-state nearly collapsed.

There were political reasons for this. Camillo Cavour had died at the worst time imaginable – in 1861, at the onset of unification – and had left no obvious successor. Indeed Italy ran through five different prime ministers between 1861 and 1866, none serving long enough to set the young nation on course to redeem its lost provinces, balance its budget and solve its deep-rooted social problems. A principal cause of this drift was the personality of the king himself. Vittorio Emanuele II was a coarse, despotic man, altogether lacking in tact and common sense. Intimidated by Cavour, he resolved afterward to appoint only weak or tractable prime ministers like Luigi Farini in 1863, a senile old man. Men like Farini did nothing to solve the severe social problems created by national unification. These included endemic brigandage in the south (caused in part by the abrupt dismissal of the old Neapolitan army in 1861) and constantly rising, regressive taxes on salt, oil, wine and flour that bore most heavily on the poorest members of Italian society. By 1866 even the Italian government in the new national capital of Florence had to admit that there was considerable nostalgia in the newly 'liberated' zones of Italy for the 'foreign occupiers' (*stranieri*) of the past. Tuscans spoke fondly of the 'good old days' under Duke Leopold Habsburg, who had been usurped by Vittorio Emanuele's army in 1859. In April 1866, Italian police in Modena were startled by the appearance of a mob demanding the return of *their* Habsburg duke, Francesco V, also ousted by the Piedmontese after Solferino.

Italy's internal political situation was so grim by the mid-1860s that Vittorio Emanuele actually feared a military coup or a civil war. In 1865, General Alfonso La Marmora (the king's latest prime minister) warned parliament that 'the country is full of reactionaries. ... Behind us is the abyss, and a single step backward will invite the horrible ruin of us all. *We must keep advancing to complete the national programme*'. This was a dangerous line for Italy's prime minister to take, for it made the survival of Italy dependent on foreign adventures at a time when the nation was poor, divided, backward, and in desperate need of internal development (Bosworth 1996: 21; Wawro 1996b: 13–16). Although Italian propagandists would call the 1866 campaign the 'Fourth War of Union' (1848 had been the first, 1849 the second, 1859 the third), few Italians seemed to care. Royal appeals for volunteers were largely ignored, and the king had to exclude Italy's new southern regiments from his invasion plan for fear that they would desert to the Austrians. When the Italian war ministry conscripted 105,000 eighteen year-olds in 1866, it pointedly excepted 'all Neapolitans, Sicilians and Sardinians' from the call-up (Wawro 1996a: 83–7).

Clearly, Italy did not embark on the war of 1866 under the most favourable circumstances, and its rout at Custoza can be explained in largely social and political terms. The Italian army itself was split on the eve of Custoza into two, unconnected halves, the one (the Po Army) under General Enrico Cialdini (the dashing tribune of Italy's republican left), the other (the Mincio Army) under General Alfonso La Marmora (the greying head of the 'Piedmontese camorra', the king's reactionary clique). When La Marmora invaded Venetia on 24 June, Cialdini declined to support the invasion, largely for personal reasons. While La Marmora clashed with the entire Austrian South Army on the hilly ground between Verona and Villafranca, Cialdini remained at rest on the lower Po with 80,000 men. Though La Marmora still outnumbered the Austrians on the Mincio, he led badly (conveying scarcely half of his available troops across the river in the course of the day), and his troops displayed a remarkable lack of zeal in battle. Italian infantry units yielded hilltop positions and melted away under Austrian attacks. The Italian cavalry milled about uselessly on the wrong side of the Mincio, and the Italian artillery, firing singly, not in batteries, did little damage to the Austrians. After the battle, the Austrians discovered that 3,500 of their 4,500 Italian prisoners were unwounded. Many of them ran over to Austrian lines crying: *Eviva la Austria!* – 'Long live Austria!'. The South Army's commander, Field Marshal Archduke Albrecht, the emperor's uncle, considered the result at Custoza 'a sympton of [Italy's] utter demoralization' (Wawro 1996a: 118).

After the battle, some of Albrecht's generals urged him to pursue La Marmora into Lombardy to put more pressure on the tottering, scandalized Kingdom of Italy. If the South Army had succeeded in destroying the Mincio and Po Armies, who can say what might have followed? Austrian agents were already busy in southern Italy funding and organizing an insurrection to be led by ex-Neapolitan officers and Albanian mercenaries. Sicilians, who resented the Piedmontese officials sent south after 1861 to introduce northern practices, exploded into open revolt in November 1866. But Albrecht chose not to exploit his victory. He had suffered heavy casualties at Custoza, where the Austrians had employed the same lumbering shock columns they had used with such disastrous results in Bohemia. These densely packed, slow moving battalion masses had proven irresistible targets even for jittery Italian troops, who had poured fire down from their hilltops, killing or wounding 5,000 Austrians (including 300 officers), 7 per cent of total Austrian effectives. With a bigger war raging in the north, the Austrians could not replace losses on this scale. Custoza even more than Königgrätz discredited shock tactics in the age of the rifle. Had the Italians only been armed with a breech-loader like the Prussian *Zündnadelgewehr*, they would almost certainly have won the battle.

Much reduced in numbers and mindful of Benedek's troubles on the Prussian front, Albrecht elected to remain on the defensive after Custoza. After Königgrätz, he marched his army to Vienna, reluctantly ceding all of Venetia to Cialdini's Po Army, which trailed Albrecht's South Army up to Udine, taking possession of Venetia as they went. In this rather inglorious way, the Italian army 'redeemed' Venice in July 1866. In 1870, they completed their national unification by taking Papal Rome. As in 1866, they waited for the 'foreign occupier' (in this case the French) to withdraw, and then struck, fighting a brief, theatrical battle at the city gates against the outnumbered papal guards before annexing Rome and Lazio, and completing the territorial unification of Italy.

Because France was engaged in a war with the Prussians in 1870 and could spare nothing to defend the Pope's 'temporal power', Italy ran no risk by taking Rome. But by threatening Venice – the jewel of the Austrian Empire – in 1866 King Vittorio Emanuele had put his new kingdom at risk. Though his gamble succeeded (thanks largely to the efforts of Bismarck and Moltke on the northern front), it left the Italian military with a dangerous 'Custoza complex'. In the decades after 1866, edgy Italian statesmen and soldiers sought to erase the stain by resorting to dubious adventures, like the failed invasions of Abyssinia in 1881 and 1897, and the costly Libyan War of 1911–12. Haunted by its past, Italy became the classic 'jackal state', hunting around the fringes of Europe and Africa for easy 'kills', periodically upsetting the peace of Europe.

CHAPTER FIVE

The Franco-Prussian War of 1870–1

> This war represents the German Revolution, a greater political
> event than the French Revolution of the last century. ... It has
> created a new world ... new and unknown dangers with which
> to cope.
>
> (Benjamin Disraeli commenting upon Prussia's defeat
> of France in February 1871 [Lowe 1994: 41])

Until 1866, Paris was considered the 'capital of Europe'. While British sea power 'ruled the waves,' the French army ruled the European Continent. France had hammered the Russians out of the Balkans in the Crimean War, and the Austrians out of Milan in the Italian War. Elsewhere, the French army and navy were continually in action during the 1860s, invading Mexico, expanding their African colonies, beginning the conquest of Indochina, all the while building a corps of hardened troop commanders such as existed nowhere else in Europe. Of course, the foundation stone of French power was German disunity; successive French regimes had stood against German unification since at least the 1600s to ensure French primacy. But what would happen to France's leading role if the German states united? The effect would be nothing short of revolutionary, for a unified Germany would be richer, more populous and more industrialized than France. It would transform the European balance of power at a stroke.

When the Austro-Prussian War broke out in June 1866, Napoleon III took the measure of the two sides and confidently predicted that the war would last through the winter and into the following year. The French emperor felt certain that he would have plenty of time to extort concessions from both of the German powers in return for French neutrality in the war. As a down payment on the expected concessions, Napoleon III received Bismarck's vague assurance that Prussia would permit a benevolent France to annex unspecified parts of western Germany as well as Belgium and Luxembourg after the war. From Austria, Louis-Napoleon received something concrete for his neutrality: the long-sought province of Venetia, which Franz Joseph reluctantly ceded to France in June 1866. For France, the Austro-Prussian War therefore began well. Like most Europeans, Napoleon III assumed that the Austrians would win, and was thrilled to have Venetia in advance. The province paid a double dividend. It fulfilled at last the French emperor's boast that he had 'unified Italy from the Alps to the Adriatic' (a project that was dear to France's republican left), but also gave him leverage over the upstart Kingdom of Italy, which, with its constant threats to take Papal Rome, was upsetting Napoleon III's Catholic supporters. After the war, Napoleon III planned to offer Venetia to the Italians in return for their pledge not to annex Rome. He might thus satisfy all constituencies in France, maintain Italy as a French satellite state, and further weaken the Austrian Empire, which would bring him closer to his goal of reorganizing Europe on national lines.

As for Prussia, Napoleon III planned to intervene in the war to rescue Bismarck sometime in 1867. Naturally the price of a French rescue would be high: German territory on the left bank of the Rhine as well as Belgium and Luxembourg. If the British threatened war to defend neutral Belgium, Napoleon III assumed that the Prussian army and navy would weigh in on his side (Mosse 1958: 260–70). In short, Napoleon III decided early on to use the Austro-Prussian War to fortify his commanding position in Europe. Domestically, French expansion into Belgium, Luxembourg and the Rhineland would be viewed as a Bonapartist achievement, and would strengthen the dynasty's weakening grip. Abroad, it would create useful buffers, strengthen France militarily and economically, and discredit Berlin, which, as in the French Revolutionary Wars of the previous century, would appear to be dealing German territory to the French to ensure the survival of Prussia. It seemed an excellent plan, and the wrath that drove Napoleon III to declare war on the Prussians in 1870 over a diplomatic trifle derived from the crushing disappointment he felt in 1866, when the Prussians thrashed the Austrians and forced them to the peace table in just four weeks. The French called this the *surprise de Sadova*. It left no time for a preventive mobilization, and it permitted Bismarck to annex the North German states and renege on the vague promises he had made the French in 1865. Virtually overnight, France was confronted with a new and unexpected threat: a German state that was France's equal in population, resources and industry. Well before the last shot was fired in the Austro-Prussian War, a Franco-Prussian war was in sight.

The French army, 1866–70

Officially, the French army declared itself unimpressed by the Prussian victory at Königgrätz. Napoleon III's military organ, the *Moniteur de l'Armée*, judged Moltke's brilliant campaign little more than a copycat variation on Bonaparte's three-pronged descent on Mantua in 1796. Moreover, the *Moniteur* harrumphed, 'the slightest scrap of Napoleonic spirit in Benedek's headquarters on 3 July would have won the Battle of Königgrätz for Austria ten times over' (*Österreichische Militärische Zeitschrift* 1868). The French, in short, saw nothing magical in the Prussian method of war. Moltke had merely used Napoleonic methods to thrash an incompetent opponent; it went without saying that the French would play this game better.

After absorbing the *surprise de Sadova*, the French army set to work applying its lessons. Like Carnot and Napoleon in the 1790s, Moltke had revolutionized tactics in the 1860s, and the French were determined to keep pace. They promptly discarded the last of the muzzle-loading rifles they had campaigned with in 1859, and procured the world's finest, most advanced breech-loading rifle: the Chassepot, named after its inventor. The new French rifle was far superior to the Prussian *Zündnadelgewehr*, which by 1867 was long in the tooth, having been introduced twenty years earlier. Whereas the needle rifle fired to a maximum range of 600 yards, the Chassepot, when properly aimed and elevated, could hit targets at 1,500 yards. Chassepot cartridges also had a smaller calibre than the Prussian ones, which meant that French infantrymen could carry more of them, and blanket the field with fire. Moreover, French marksmanship would be unaffected by the eruptions of sparks and grease that afflicted the Prussian rifleman. The breech of the Chassepot was sealed by a rubber ring (imported from plantations in the new French colony of Vietnam), a novel safety feature (Howard 1981: 35–6).

The Chassepot was quite frightening enough, yet Napoleon III, who took a personal interest in weapons procurement, augmented its fire with an even more intimidating firearm: the *mitrailleuse*. Like the American Gatling gun, the French *mitrailleuse* was a 'revolver cannon,' a ring of twenty-five gun tubes, each successively detonated by a hand crank. Once the last tube had fired, the gun crew ejected the spent cartridges, slid reloads into the breech, and resumed cranking. In trained hands, the 'coffee grinder' (the gun's sobriquet) could rattle off four or five wheels of ammunition every sixty seconds, which amounted to 100–200 rounds per minute, a blistering rate of fire for the 1860s. Not surprisingly, the Germans had a different name for the gun; they called it the *Höllenmaschine* – the 'hell machine' – but shrewdly noted its vulnerabilities. Unlike the Gatling gun, the *mitrailleuse* was not accurate at long range, and had therefore to be deployed well forward, where its gun crews would be exposed to enemy shrapnel and rifle fire and easily overrun (Musil 1868).

What the French needed to do after 1866 was wed the Chassepot and the *mitrailleuse* to new tactics that would fully exploit their features, and this they attempted to do. Between 1866 and 1870, the French discarded the shock tactics they had used in 1859 and moved in a new direction. To grasp the reasons for France's defeat in the Franco-Prussian War, it is important to recognize the key differences between French and Prussian tactics as they evolved after 1866. Though impressed by the agility of the Prussians in 1866, the French perceived weaknesses in the Prussian system. In particular, they criticized the 'tendency toward fragmentation' in Prussian tactics, the heretical willingness 'to break connections between lines and columns on the battle-field to deliver *partial* attacks'. In other words, the French criticized the very quality that had done so much to bewilder, panic and entrap the Austrians: the sliding, successive onslaught of Prussian rifle companies, arriving at the run, seemingly haphazardly, from all directions. In a study of Prussian tactics published in 1868, a French staff officer concluded that Prussia's small-unit tactics enhanced firepower for a moment, but left the Prussian army sprawled awkwardly across the battlefield. A better adversary than the Austrians would have counter-attacked the small Prussian units and crushed them in detail. The French tactician compared Prussian tactics in 1866 to the tactics adopted by the French Republic in 1792 – 'uncontrolled, small columns, converging from all points of the compass' – and insisted that Moltke would have to take his army in hand after 1866, just as Napoleon I had been forced to modify French tactics after 1800 (Ferri-Pisani 1868).

In fact, the Prussians would change little. What the French failed to notice was that *Auftragstaktik* – 'mission tactics' – permitted orderly decentralization, for Prussian troop commanders, fully briefed on the aims of the battle before them, were only *apparently* isolated from one another. In fact, they were oper-ating together, struggling toward a common objective, and were widely spaced only to maximize the fire from their field guns and rifles. The French did not grasp this fact; they saw only chaos in the Prussian tactics and devised an opposite system, one that would permit the stately, controlled development of a battle.

French tactics after 1866 emphasized the defensive. To offset the Prussian firepower displayed in the Austro-Prussian War, the French army provided each of its brigades with 1,000 shovels and axes, and trained each battalion to scrape out a three-foot trench in twenty-five minutes or less. Whereas the Prussians spread their battalions across the battlefield, the French packed theirs into narrow, prepared positions bristling with rifles, *mitrailleuses* and cannon. According to French doctrine (revised in the wake of the Austro-Prussian War), the Prussians would be made to attack the French trenches, and when they did, would be mowed down by the accurate, rolling fire of entire battalions with their artillery. Whereas the Prussians were permitted to fire at will once they got within range of the enemy, French infantrymen were forbidden to fire more than five cartridges at a clip. Accuracy was then checked by an officer who would also give the order to resume fire. It was a disappointingly bureaucratic system, but one intended to conserve ammuni-tion for the French speciality: the *feu de bataillon*. Entrenched or lying across their knapsacks, French infantry placidly awaited the approach of an enemy column and then, on a signal from their officers, opened fire, not at once, but gradually. Fire flared on the left wing and rolled like thunder to the right, devastating the ground in front. To all appearances, it was a perfectly rational response to the military events of 1866, yet it overlooked the basic features of Moltke's fire tactics: the widening of the fighting front by scrambling small units, and the flanking attack, which would only be facilitated by the narrow, fixed positions selected by the French. The French would have done well to study Moltke's published analysis of Prussian autumn manoeuvres in 1869; in it, Moltke concluded that the essence of Prussian tactics remained unchanged after Königgrätz: 'the secret of our success is in our legs; victory derives from marching and manoeuvring' (Schmedes 1871). It was not for nothing that Prussian infantry ruefully called themselves *Kilometerschweine* – 'kilometre pigs'.

Besides tactics, the French took other, no less important lessons from the Austro-Prussian War. They freely admitted the brilliance of the Prussian general staff, but found themselves helpless to imitate it. This was a peculiarly French problem. Selection for the French staff college was like that for any of the *grandes écoles*: brutally competitive. But once in, French staff officers were set for life, rather like their peers at the School of Administration or the Ecole Polytechnique. Unlike the Prussian army, where the general staff was continually refreshed, the French staff developed a rigid seniority system. The eldest graduates took the best jobs and remained in them forever. A Breton officer fond of Nantes might attach himself to army headquarters there and never move. Regimental colleagues would come and go, but the general staff cadre would remain in place, a little bit fatter and older with each passing year. Despised as 'bureaucrats' by the line officers, who rotated past them every three years, French staff officers inevitably lost touch with the realities of modern war and faded into the woodwork. In 1870, Napoleon III was astonished to discover that his general staff had no plans for a war with Prussia, and little specialized knowledge of the German theatre of operations (Andlau 1869).

Awed by the efficiency of the Prussian general staff, the French were no less impressed by the large and ready reserve that the Prussian *Landwehr* had furnished in 1866; two years later, the French army established the *Garde Nationale Mobile* to perform the same function. France's mobile guard was the brainchild of Marshal Adolphe Niel, Napoleon III's war minister from 1867–9, an admirer of Moltke's institutional reforms who strove to match them. Niel watched two developments with particular misgiving: the alarming decline of France's population, and the no less alarming expansion of the Prusso-German armies after 1866. Caution and contraception were so ingrained in French peasant culture that the nation had not seen growth in its pool of twenty-one year-old males since 1835. (And growth had occurred in that year only because so many French women had been accosted in the course of the Russo-Prussian march across France twenty-one years earlier, yielding, incidentally, the nineteenth century's tallest class of French conscripts [*Journal Officiel de l'Empire Français*, 24 March 1870]. Infused with Slavic and German seed, the lanky French conscripts of 1835, with their average height of 1.67 metres, were not surpassed in height until the twentieth century.) By 1867, a disastrous situation was at hand: the Prussians were able to deploy a million German troops against the French, who would be hard pressed to find half that total for the defence of France. Needless to say, the French urgently needed their own version of the *Landwehr*, which would assume garrison duties in France and Algeria, and reinforce the field army in a crisis. With the Military Law of 1868, Niel reckoned that he had closed the gap with the Prussians. France's army would double in size: 400,000 regulars would be joined by 400,000 *Mobiles*. But Niel never reckoned with France's *Corps Législatif* or parliament; confronted with Niel's Military Law, the *Corps Législatif* refused to pass it.

The growing republican wing in the *Corps Législatif* rejected the very notion of a mobile guard, which, one deputy objected, 'would compel young Frenchmen to abandon their jobs and their families for a corrupting life in the barracks' (Montaudon 1898: II, 52–4). This was a common complaint. All of the republican orators, including Jules Favre and Leon Gambetta (future heads of the Third Republic), protested that Napoleon III's army was 'corrupt' and 'caesaristic', no place to consign France's unblemished youth. The imperial army fought back, calling the republicans *phraseurs*, *utopistes* and much worse. Yet the army itself was deeply divided on the question of the *Mobiles*. Most French officers actually opposed Niel's national guard, fearing that once armed the *Mobiles* would become 'a revolutionary enemy of government and society' (Jarras 1892: 35–6). Under fire from left and right, Niel's national guard legislation passed through parliament with crippling amendments. It was deliberately underfunded and rendered all but useless by Gambetta's insistence that *Gardes Mobiles* never be deployed outside their native regions. This was a mischievous stipulation; the utility of the Prussian *Landwehr* was the ease with which it could be moved between forts, depots, supply lines and even front-line units as an all-purpose reserve. France's *Mobiles*, by contrast, would not be mobile at all; they would be effective only as a local defence force, and would do nothing to arrest the army's demographic slide. Niel died in 1869 an unhappy man. His successor was instructed by the emperor to appease the *Corps Législatif*; accordingly, he suspended formation of the *Garde Mobile* and agreed to broad cuts in the regular army as well. Despite Niel's best efforts, the French army would go to war with Prussia at a steep disadvantage, with just 400,000 men against Prussia's million.

The July crisis of 1870: a French 'escape forward?'

By the late 1860s, Napoleon III had been Emperor of the French for an entire generation. He had grown old, and France's youth, none of whom could remember the anarchy and excesses of 1848, began to question his mildly repressive regime. To make matters worse, the weary emperor displayed none of the creativity on social and economic questions that had formed the Second Empire. He retired from public life, spent more and more time away from Paris, and surrounded himself with a court that even by Gilded Age standards was spectacularly corrupt. Indeed, the last years of the Second

Empire (it was to fall in 1870, in the midst of the Franco-Prussian War) were punctuated by scandals, most of them involving Bonaparte princes or cronies. The relevance of all this to war and foreign affairs was plain. With his domestic support ebbing away, Napoleon III relied increasingly on foreign adventures to popularize his regime. As a contemporary observer put it, Louis-Napoleon 'made foreign politics the handmaiden of home politics ... the overflow tank for the uneasy spirit of the French nation' (Vandam 1897: 296). Though chronic illness made him indifferent to his own future, the emperor wanted desperately to 'refound the empire' for the benefit of his son and heir, Louis, born in 1856. Someone else had high hopes for *Lou-Lou*: his mother, the beautiful, intensely ambitious Empress Eugénie.

Eugénie loathed her rather dissipated husband, but adored her son, and as her loveless marriage to Napoleon III petered out, she too pressed for war with Prussia as the best way to prolong the life of the fading dynasty. From 1867–70, Napoleon III and Eugénie were behind an annual series of Franco-Prussian crises, each ignited by the French (and discreetly fanned by Bismarck) in the hopes of war. For Bismarck, this Napoleonic thirst for action was convenient. It permitted the Prussian minister president to choose the optimal moment for war, rally the German states to the national cause, and portray Prussia as the innocent victim of French bullying. In 1867, Bismarck skewered Napoleon III on the issue of Belgian neutrality, first seeming to promise France Belgium, then withdrawing support, leaving France – its fist raised against 'brave little Belgium' – isolated before the world (Mosse 1958: 312–13). Furious with Bismarck, Napoleon III nearly declared war. In 1868, Napoleon III threatened war again when Bismarck tightened his links to the South German states by creating an all-German 'customs parliament' that was really a *Reichstag*-in-the-making. In 1869, the French emperor threatened war a third time, when King Wilhelm I of Prussia appeared ready to accept the title 'Emperor of Germany' from the newly established North German Confederation. In the midst of this crisis, General Niel recalled a meeting with Napoleon III into which Eugénie intruded, demanding to know when war would be declared (Jarras 1892: 30). She had not long to wait.

Eighteen seventy was a thoroughly bad year for the Bonapartes, so bad that a great war with Prussia commended itself as a possible way out. The year began with a terrible scandal. The emperor's nephew, Pierre Bonaparte, shot and killed a republican journalist who had come to interview him. The journalist's funeral on 7 March was the occasion for tumultuous anti-imperial demonstrations in Paris. Barricades went up, buses were overturned, and great bonfires roared through the night. When Napoleon III's chief of police arrived at the Tuileries at 2 a.m. on 8 March to declare the city under control, he was shocked to meet the emperor himself, awake and in uniform, surrounded by his generals. The emperor had been preparing to ride out to crush the revolution (Waldersee 1922: I, 56). In May 1870, the emperor held the last plebiscite of his reign. Under attack from monarchists and republicans, he asked France to endorse a 'Liberal Empire' that would extend legislative powers to the *Corps Législatif* and broaden press freedom and civil rights. Although Napoleon III had crushed the republic eighteen years earlier with the promise that he would govern as a 'plebiscitary emperor,' he had not actually held a plebiscite since 1852. Predictably, he received a resounding vote of confidence, mainly because French peasants genuinely liked him and considered him a reliable bulwark against urban radicals. Nevertheless, the plebiscite, though stage-managed in the usual way with mayors and prefects getting out the vote, was not entirely successful: 17 per cent of Frenchmen voted 'no'; yet more worrisome, 20 per cent of the army (and 25 per cent of the emperor's own guardsmen) voted 'no'. This was appalling, for a 'no' vote in any Napoleonic plebiscite connoted red republican sympathies, and French soldiers had been given the vote for the first time in 1870 in the hope that they would pad out the emperor's usual majority (Price 1997: 54–8; Waldersee 1922: I, 68).

Stern measures were needed to right the ship of state, and Napoleon III may have clutched at war as his only lever. Although he had just appointed a perfectly able foreign minister in January 1870 – the prudent, watchful Napoleon Daru – Bonaparte impatiently threw him over in May and summoned a more energetic man: the Duc de Gramont. Antoine de Gramont was a notorious thruster, and every newspaper in Paris reported that he had been appointed 'pour faire quelque chose'. Gramont did not disappoint. In July, when the Prussian king's nephew accepted the invitation of the Spanish parliament to ascend the Spanish throne (the Bourbons having died out), Gramont demanded that King Wilhelm I forbid his nephew to accept the crown. The crisis, involving a largely ceremonial crown in a marginal Mediterranean kingdom, was so fatuous that Bismarck, vacationing at Varzin, the vast Pomeranian estate given him by a grateful Prussian public in 1866, did not even bother to return to Berlin. Instead, he sanctioned the king's decision to withdraw Prince Leopold Hohenzollern's candidacy, and got on with his vacation. There the crisis would have ended were it not for Napoleon III's determination to have a war at any price. On 14 July, the French emperor cabled the Prussian king, who was vacationing at the spa of Ems, and increased his demands. In a bid to humiliate Berlin, Napoleon III insisted that Wilhelm I not only withdraw Leopold's candidacy, but pledge to renounce it 'for all time'. Bismarck, who by now had arrived from Varzin (having angrily cancelled plans for a restorative holiday on the Isle of Wight), instructed the king to ignore the note; to underline the insult, he refused to see the French ambassador, who attempted to present Napoleon III's last demand to the Prussian king in person. Louis-Napoleon, who followed the brewing crisis from the telegraph office in his suburban palace at St Cloud, seized upon Bismarck's rebuff as a *casus belli*. On 16 July, France declared war on Prussia.

The French pretext for war was so flimsy that even the bellicose French public, still smarting from the *surprise* of 1866, was sceptical. When Napoleon

III attempted to pitch his declaration of war to parliament in diplomatic terms – arguing that 'France had never permitted a foreign prince to sit on the throne of Spain' – Gambetta reminded the emperor that the Prussians had withdrawn their candidate, effectively removing the *casus belli* (*Journal Officiel de l'Empire Français*, 16 July 1870). No matter, Louis-Napoleon was blind to reason; he gambled that war would make him popular again, and it did. Foreign residents of Paris goggled at the patriotic fury with which the French people celebrated the declaration of war. While Germany's regulars and militi-amen dolefully interrupted their summer leave to rejoin their battalions (everywhere escorted by weeping wives and children), the cities of France blazed with enthusiasm. Crowds of men, women and children surged around the Paris garrison as it marched to the eastern railway stations. As in 1859, the emperor's police pretended not to hear when the mobs, overcome with enthusiasm, roared the *Marseillaise*, the outlawed anthem of the republic (Montaudon 1898: II, 56–9). A Bavarian reserve officer working in Paris when war broke out noted in his diary: 'What I saw defied description. The Tuileries [palace], usually ignored by Parisians, was surrounded by crowds roaring their approval of the emperor and his declaration of war'. The scene on the boulevards was 'indescribable, unforgettable'. Ardent civilians mingled with the troops, pressed flowers and wine on them, and shouted angry slogans: *A Berlin! A bas Bismarck!* (Bayerisches Kriegsarchiv).

To win the war, common sense suggested that Napoleon III had no other option than a rapid invasion of Prussia and the German states. With just 400,000 men against a Prusso-German army that would grow within four weeks to a strength of one million, France needed to drive swiftly across the Rhine, cut North Germany off from Bavaria and the southern states – which would furnish Bismarck with 200,000 additional troops – seize Prussia's prin-cipal rail terminals, and smash in detail whatever Prussian units managed to straggle into the French-occupied Rhineland and North German plain (Messerschmidt, in Förster and Nagler 1997: 272–3). This was an ambitious plan, but one perfectly suited to the reckless character of the French army, which prided itself on its nonchalant deadliness. Accustomed to colonial warfare, which required troops to deploy on short notice without reserves and stores, the French could have invaded Prussia without completing their mobi-lization. While the exacting Prussian corps districts built each of their battalions up to its proper war strength, France's rough-and-ready regiments could have lunged into Prussia without reservists or supply trains; true sons of Napoleon, they would have foraged on German soil for food, drink and shelter. French officers called this marvellous flexibility *le système D* – 'the muddle system' (*on se débrouillera toujours*) – and it was a key facet of France's military reputation: furious and improvised. Though outnumbered by the Prussians in the long run, the French enjoyed even odds in a sprint, and had only to strike quickly into Germany to derail Moltke's war plans and frighten the South Germans into neutrality.

The Franco–Prussian War

Unfortunately, the French found the reality of modern war rather different than the legend they had built themselves over the years. The casual administrative habits that had worked tolerably well in colonial emergencies and against the Austrians proved disastrous in 1870. Napoleon III's hastily contrived war plan called for two French armies to mass at Metz and Strasbourg, the fortified keypoints of Lorraine and Alsace. While the smaller army at Strasbourg (100,000 men) splashed across the Rhine and invaded Baden, cutting South Germany off from the North, the larger army at Metz (200,000) would cross the Saar and occupy the Prussian Rhineland. In theory, Prussian attempts to organize a defence of Germany would be spoilt by these preemptive strikes, which would deliver Moltke's key railheads and march routes into French hands. When the Prussians did belatedly close for battle, the French pincers – one from the Saar basin, the other from Baden – would surround and annihilate them, probably in the vicinity of Frankfurt. In theory, the big French navy (forty-five ironclads and 300 wooden streamships in 1870) would play a key role in the campaign. From forward bases in Denmark (which wanted to avenge the defeat of 1864 and the loss of Schleswig), France's Baltic fleet would sweep along the Prussian coast, pounding it with gunfire, and landing two divisions of marines, who would fan inland, tearing up railways and forcing the Prussian army to detach precious reserves to the littoral. Such was Napoleon III's 'theory of victory'; in practice, the French army and navy delivered none of these things.

The French mobilization was a fiasco. Veterans who had winced at the stumbling deployments to Russia in 1854 and Italy in 1859 were struck dumb by the inefficiency of 1870. On 1 August, when the French mobilization was supposed to be complete, the French navy had not even begun to equip itself. For its part, the army had managed to gather only 100,000 men at Metz. The situation at Strasbourg was even worse: not the promised 100,000 men, but 40,000, scarcely enough to intimidate the small Badenese contingent across the Rhine. The army's reserve force at Châlons was also weak, with just half of its strength of 50,000 present in camp when Napoleon III rather unwisely invaded Prussia on 1 August (*Österreichische Militärische Zeitschrift* 1871b). 'All France follows you with its fervent prayers', he assured his doubting troops. The rest of the emperor's proclamation hinted at the muddle of his plans: '*Whatever may be the road we take beyond our frontiers*, we shall cross the glorious tracks of our fathers' (Howard 1981: 78).

On 2 August, six French divisions took Saarbrücken. It was the first and last time in the war that French troops would fight on German soil. From the 'war and society' perspective, Saarbrücken was a revealing battle, more political than military. The operation, intended to reassure a sceptical public that France was on the attack, was entrusted to the imperial family's favourite general, Charles Frossard, who was being groomed to replace sixty year-old

Marshal Achille Bazaine at the head of the army. Another key personage at Saarbrücken was the crown prince, seventeen year-old *Lou-Lou*, who was rather theatrically provided with a 'baptism of fire' on the Saar. While the Prussian outposts at Saarbrücken obligingly gave ground, Prince Louis rode along the French line, swinging his sabre for the benefit of reporters brought in from Paris for the occasion. For a brief, shining moment, the skirmish at Saarbrücken was more than a military victory; it was a victory for the Bonapartes.

But only for a moment. Even as the Parisians read their illustrated accounts of the 'Victoire de Sarrebruck', Moltke counter-attacked. Untroubled by the French, he had supervised an unprecedentedly rapid deployment. Using five transversal railways, Prussia had deployed sixteen army corps to western Germany in just two weeks. This represented a significant improvement over 1866, when the Prussians had needed a month to mobilize, and had required an average of six to nine days to transport a corps. In 1870, they reduced this average to just three days (*Österreichische Militärische Zeitschrift* 1871a; Deist, in Förster and Nagler 1997: 315–16).

The speed of the Prusso-German deployment changed the strategic situation. Frossard's out-thrust detachment at Saarbrücken found itself encircled by three great German armies: the First Army sweeping down from Trier, the Second Army at Saarbrücken, and the Third Army, lowered like an uppercut, in Baden. Though his invasion of Germany had only just begun, Napoleon III ordered Frossard to pull back to the safety of Metz, France's arsenal and fortified camp in Lorraine. The emperor intended to sidestep Moltke's looming envelopment and then resume the fight on ground of his own choosing. Once again he failed to reckon with the raw speed of Prussian operations. On 6 August Moltke landed his uppercut: the Prusso-Bavarian Third Army swung into Alsace and all but obliterated Marshal Patrice MacMahon's I Corps in brutal fighting around the villages of Fröschwiller and Wörth.

Wörth was a typical battle of the war (see Map 5.1) in that the Prussians vastly outnumbered the French, bringing four entire corps to the field against MacMahon's four divisions. Though the French were entrenched in fine positions, the Prussians prised them out with artillery fire and flanking attacks and drove them into the Vosges, hauling in 9,000 unwounded, thoroughly demoralized prisoners on the way. At Wörth, the French felt the full force of Prussia's superior artillery for the first time. Whereas French shells, designed for the set-piece battles of the past, were time-fused to burst in either a short (1,300 yards) or a long (2,500 yards) zone, Prussian shells were percussion-fused, which meant that German gunners could place devastating fire anywhere at any time simply by putting their guns on target (Strachan 1983: 118; Howard 1981: 99–119). MacMahon's rout at Wörth exposed Napoleon III's flank at Metz. With MacMahon's four divisions out of the way, Moltke could now hit Napoleon III's main army from three directions: north, east and south. After just one week of fighting, the emperor – who had promised to inflict a 'second Jena' on the Prussians – found himself on the brink of just such a fate. Under pressure from Empress Eugénie in Paris, Napoleon III yielded command of the Army of the Rhine to Marshal Bazaine, an unfortunate choice, who was every inch France's Benedek.

Like Ludwig von Benedek in 1866, Achille Bazaine in 1870 was essentially a political choice: a common man for the common people. Born in the atheistic, revolutionary age of Napoleon – hence the pagan name Achille (shrewdly hedged by the unmistakably royalist François) – Bazaine was the rather dimwitted son of a Versailles engineer. Having failed to gain admission to the Ecole Polytechnique in 1830, he had enlisted in the French Foreign Legion as a private soldier and risen through the ranks to general. Like Benedek, he had distinguished himself in the Franco-Austrian War, and had been entrusted with the French expedition to Mexico in 1862. There he had used techniques acquired in Africa to pacify large tracts of Mexico, but was ultimately defeated by the guerrilla war of Benito Juarez. Though personally brave, Bazaine lacked intellect and strategic vision. He was a typical *Algérien* on many counts: stroppy, insubordinate, and most comfortable with small units; like Benedek, he had no idea what to do with an army, which is why Louis-Napoleon's choice of Bazaine to succeed him in 1870 was so odd. Militarily, others were better qualified: Patrice MacMahon, Charles Bourbaki and François Canrobert to name but three. But the emperor's choice placed social and political considerations ahead of military ones. He was pushed this way by Empress Eugénie, who, in a sequence of cables from Paris, demanded that Napoleon III place Bazaine in command 'to reassure the people'.

In this way, the French army was placed in great danger. On 12 August Marshal Bazaine took over the Army of the Rhine. His situation was far from enviable. Deprived of MacMahon's corps, Bazaine had just 180,000 men with him at Metz, against 500,000 Prusso-German troops sweeping in from the east. Still, the French enjoyed certain advantages, including terrain and armament. Metz was a first-class fortress. With outworks on both banks of the Moselle, it was designed to hold and support an army and was supplied with ammunition and food. Even if prised out of Metz, the French had good, defensible ground behind them: first the line of the Meuse, then the Marne, and finally the Loire.

The Chassepot rifle was another French advantage. In a series of defensive battles, the French ought to have been able to decimate the Prussian attackers. Already in the first engagements of the war, the Chassepot had proved its effectiveness by mowing down 16,000 Prussians, more than twice the sum of French dead and wounded. At the battles of Wörth and Spicheren on 6 August, the Prussians had solved the tactical problem posed by the Chassepot's superior range and accuracy by the crudest possible means. Deployed in company columns, they had tried to sprint into range of the French entrenchments and only then divided into 'swarms' to begin the probing, thrusting firefight that was their hallmark. France's long-service regulars had

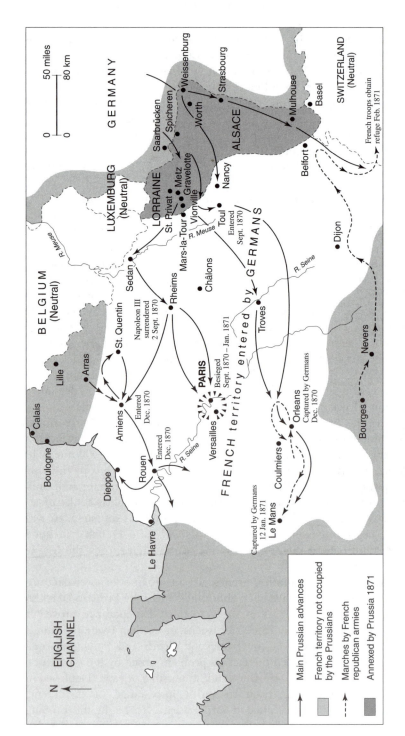

Map 5.1 The Franco–Prussian War, 1870–1

made the most of the opportunity, pouring accurate fire into the Prussian and Bavarian columns from a great distance. After the battle, the Prussians discovered French corpses clutching rifles that were sighted out to 1,500 yards, a tribute not only to the Chassepot's marvellous properties, but to the superior marksmanship of France's veteran soldiers as well (the Prussians were amazed to discover sixty year-old private soldiers in the French ranks: men who had joined during the Bourbon Restoration and re-upped every eight years).

Ultimately, only two things had saved the Prussians, and they were the keys to modern warfare. First, sheer numbers: with more than twice MacMahon's strength at Wörth, the Prussians had simply extended their lines and outflanked the compact French position. Second, artillery: armed with rifled, breech-loading Krupp cannon, the Prussians had pummelled the French entrenchments from long range and disorganized the steady French infantry long enough for German infantry to cross the 'killing ground' of the Chassepot and *mitrailleuse* and march into range of their own antiquated needle rifles. Moltke's 'operations tempo' had been so swift that the French had never found time to counter these improvised tactics. While Napoleon III puzzled over MacMahon's defeat and disappearance at Wörth, Moltke abruptly shifted his attention to Bazaine.

MacMahon's drubbing at Wörth had persuaded Bazaine to withdraw inside the fortifications of Metz. This hedgehog strategy was an unintelligent way to make war, yet one perfectly suited to Bazaine's mediocre talents. Though ordered by Napoleon III to march the Army of the Rhine from Metz to Chalôns with all speed, Bazaine ignored the emperor, settled down in the vicinity of the fortress, and let several critical days pass. These were all that Moltke needed. On 16 August, his Second Army crossed the Moselle below Metz and swung around to the north. In a sharp, bloody clash at Mars-la-Tour (decided again by the Prussian artillery), the Second Army forced Bazaine to yield his last remaining road to the west. Two days later, the decisive battle of the war was fought with reversed fronts – the Prussians with their backs to Paris, the French with Germany behind them – on the line of hills between Gravelotte and St Privat. Concerned above all to maintain contact with the fortress of Metz behind him, Bazaine met Moltke, who came at him in three great columns.

Like Spicheren, Wörth and Mars-la-Tour, Gravelotte was a battle that the French ought to have won. Though outnumbered by the Prussians (200,000 to 160,000), the French held the commanding heights. With each of their seventeen divisions spewing 40,000 rounds a minute from their Chassepots, the French decimated the Prussians: scything down 20,000 men in the course of the day, as many men as the Austrians had lost at Königgrätz. Nevertheless, moulded by the defensive tactics drummed into them since 1866, the French generals steadfastly refused to counter-attack the Prussians, even when they lay in shattered, bloody heaps at their feet. This gave the Prussian artillery time to gallop up, plug the breaches that had opened along the Prussian line, and usher in reinforcements. In this gradual, harrowing way, Moltke's infantry platoons gained the heights above Metz and drove the French down to the fortress. Like Mars-la-Tour, Gravelotte was decided by the Prussian artillery: 70 per cent of French casualties in the two battles were injured by artillery. For the Prussians – faced with France's obsolete bronze guns and defective shells – the ratio was reversed: 70 per cent of Prussian casualties had bullet wounds (Nosinich 1872: 157; Howard 1981: 144–82). Overall, the battle ought to have indicted Prussian tactics, and the very idea of offensives in the age of the rifle. Had the French possessed artillery as advanced as their infantry rifle, they would have annihilated the Prussian army. Instead, due to Bazaine's torpor and the resourcefulness of the Prussian artillery, which managed to rescue most of the stuttering infantry attacks, Gravelotte reinforced the developing 'cult of the offensive' that impelled the suicidal assaults of 1914.

Bazaine neither saw nor heard the battle; he spent most of it in the telegraph office of Plappeville, a brick fort well behind the line at Gravelotte. The marshal's listless conduct in the week before Gravelotte and his apathy during the fight spawned rumours that he had deliberately thrown the battle and sought the confinement of his army at Metz in order to influence the political outcome of the Franco-Prussian War. Bazaine, the rumour-mongers averred, was neither a monarchist nor a republican; he was a would-be dictator, an early version of Pétain, who naively hoped to rescue France from the chaos into which it had plunged under Napoleon III and Eugénie by conserving the Army of the Rhine, negotiating a truce with Bismarck, marching on Paris, and seating himself in power (according to the logic attributed to Bazaine, Bismarck would go along with the plot in order to crush the 'red republican' movement in France and install a trouble-free monarchical government) (G. Andlau 1872: 224–31). Given Bazaine's remarkable dispositions during the battle of Gravelotte, when he repeatedly forbade his generals to counterattack the Prussians and open the road to Paris, and his behaviour in the weeks after Gravelotte, when he missed several chances to break out of Metz, the rumours may very well have been justified (Fay 1889: 258–9; Montaudon 1898: II, 161–3).

After Gravelotte, it was imperative that Bazaine break out of Metz at the first opportunity to join forces with Marshal MacMahon's corps, which, augmented by troops from Paris and the colonies, now numbered 130,000 and had been renamed the Army of Châlons. Had Bazaine joined his Army of the Rhine (150,000 men) to MacMahon's Army of Châlons, the two marshals – reinforced by 450,000 *Gardes Mobiles* slowly arming and training throughout France – would have stood a fair chance of fighting the increasingly overextended Prussians to a standstill. Bogged down in France, ground between the millstones of the regular army, the *Mobiles* and a growing irregular force (the *francs-tireurs*), Bismarck and Moltke would probably have settled for a mild peace, perhaps a large cash indemnity and a share of the French navy, but not Alsace-Lorraine. Yet Bazaine played into Bismarck's hands, so completely as to raise suspicions about his motives. Instead of ripping through the thin Prussian cordon that watched him at Metz, he hunkered down inside the fortress and merely waited. In Paris, the imperial family was dismayed. Bazaine's army – the best equipped, most experienced troops in all of France – was desperately needed to stiffen MacMahon's shoddily equipped green divisions. Yet Bazaine refused to march. Asked after the war why he remained at Metz, he rationalized: 'To my knowledge, it is not the besieged army that ought come to the relief of the free and mobile one' (Bazaine 1883: 163). This rationalization ignored the fact that Bazaine, protected by Metz and in complete control of the Moselle bridges, could rather easily have cut through the Prussian ring and escaped to the west. Although Moltke detached 200,000 men to watch him, they were split between the two banks of the river and spread in a great circle around the French camp and its outlying forts. Bazaine had only to mass his forces in the night, select a vulnerable point, and move at first light. But he did not, and as a result MacMahon's army, marching east from Paris to a rendezvous with Bazaine's that Bazaine had no intention of keeping, was annihilated at Sedan.

The battle of Sedan

To the Prussian general staff, Sedan was the supreme achievement. Unlike Königgrätz four years earlier, Sedan was a *Kesselschlacht* that worked. More than any other event, Sedan accounted for the ebullient optimism with which the Germans would dash off to war in 1914. The battle seemed to prove that defensive firepower could be rolled up by an offensive envelopment. Yet had Moltke and his successors fully appreciated the extent of French tactical and strategic errors in the battle, their faith in the offensive might have dimmed well in advance of 1914, when tens of thousands of Germans would be killed (and hundreds of thousands wounded) trying to emulate Sedan on a larger scale at the Marne and Ypres.

Bazaine's failure to move from Metz shaped the outcome at Sedan more than any other single factor. Indeed, MacMahon would never have ventured as far east as Sedan had he not expected Bazaine to join him there. He set off from Châlons on 22 August only after receiving assurances from Napoleon III that Bazaine was fighting his way toward Paris. One of Bonaparte's officers later testified that MacMahon's fateful march to the east had an ulterior political motive: 'frightened by the spectre of revolution, [the emperor] sought refuge with the army' (Vincennes, *Service Historique de l'Armée de Terre*, Lc1, Paris, 6 March 1903, General Kessler to General Pendezac). With insurgent republicans threatening to topple him in Paris, Napoleon III had no choice but to seek a dramatic victory in the field, no matter how risky the enterprise. It was a *va banque* play; a war that had begun with a sustainable wager now ended with Napoleon III sweeping all of his chips into the pot.

Much against his will, Marshal MacMahon led the march toward Metz. By 27 August, MacMahon knew the worst. Bazaine was not coming and two Prussian armies – the Third and the First (renamed the Meuse Army), comprising 200,000 men – were poised to encircle him. To evade the Prussian pincers, MacMahon swung away to the northwest. He hoped to reach the railway at Mezières and double back to the French capital before the Prussians realized just how exposed he was. Yet the Prussians already knew. One of the lessons they had taken from the Austro-Prussian War was the critical importance of light units and reconnaissance. Whereas Prussian cavalry squadrons had been held back in 1866 – to ride down beaten infantry after the battle – light and heavy regiments alike were sent forward in 1870, to keep in constant contact with the enemy and continuously report his strength and movements to headquarters. The new role for cavalry was elegantly stated by Colmar von der Goltz, one of Prussia's brightest military critics: 'It must encircle the enemy like an elastic band; retire before him when he advances in force, but cling to him and follow him when he retires' (Strachan 1983: 120). Here was another seminal influence on the German *Blitzkrieg* tactics of World War II: real-time intelligence. By 27 August, Moltke knew with certainty that he had the Army of Châlons, reduced to little more than 100,000 men by skirmishing and hard marches, caught halfway between the forts of Paris and Metz. He hurried forward with everything he had to exploit MacMahon's predicament.

Aware that Moltke was upon him, MacMahon dug in at Sedan. It was a decommissioned seventeenth-century fortress set in low country straddling the Meuse. Like Königgrätz, Sedan was all but useless in the nineteenth century. Whereas the hills surrounding Sedan had been beyond the range of artillery in the 1600s, they were veritable gun decks by 1870. Moltke had only to mount his guns along the rim of hills and beat Sedan and its army to dust. He would hardly need his infantry. Marching night and day, the Prussians occupied the commanding heights before the French even detected their approach. These forced marches in the days and hours before Sedan were prodigious efforts, and wholly in keeping with the 'German method of strategy', which prized bold encircling movements over any type of fixed fortification. MacMahon, who had witnessed the German method on a smaller scale at Wörth, belatedly recognized the threat and pushed his men on to the heights around Sedan. All for naught: in the course of 1 September the French were driven off them by the withering fire of Moltke's artillery. This permitted the Prussian infantry to wrestle the Army of Châlons into the cramped space around the ramparts of Sedan, where it was ground up by shell and shrapnel. More than any other battle in the Franco-Prussian War, Sedan was an artillery battle. The casualties on both sides proved this. France lost as many men as it had at Gravelotte; Prussia, preceded everywhere by its steel guns, just half as many (Nosinich 1872: 155–6; Howard 1981: 203–23).

Once apprised of MacMahon's situation on 27 August, the Prussians had made double marches, day and night, to encircle him. Moltke's Third Army – the victor at Wörth – had marched for three days without food in order to pin down MacMahon at Sedan and permit the Crown Prince of Saxony's Meuse Army to outflank the French and close their last remaining escape routes. Had Bazaine exhibited half as much energy as the Prussians, he might have been able to tip the balance at Sedan in favour of MacMahon. Yet while the Prussians marched, the marshal sat. Pressed by his generals, who yearned to break out of Metz and join MacMahon, Bazaine had actually concentrated his army on 30 August and planned a breakout for the next day. What followed was farcical. On 31 August, Bazaine ordered his generals to do nothing until he personally gave the order to attack. The morning crept by, then the afternoon; the Army of the Rhine, armed and provisioned for a great battle, chafed impatiently, not least because the men knew that there was not enough food and drink at Metz to sustain them through a long siege. In the entire course of that pivotal day – which weighed on the outcome at Sedan – Bazaine never left his walled headquarters. The men spent the night under arms and then, on 1 September, the day of Sedan, signalled their disgust by spontaneously falling out and returning to Metz in unorganized bands. Muttering that they had been 'sold out' (*vendu*) by traitorous generals, Bazaine's men refused him their support (*Allgemeine Militär-Zeitung*, 28 April 1892). War and politics had intersected with painful results for the French commandant, who, in possession of a wasting asset, now redoubled his efforts to cut a deal with Bismarck.

The French defeat at Sedan was one of the most shattering defeats of military history. Not only was the Emperor of the French made prisoner, so was his entire army: the 80,000 men who remained in Sedan when the last shot was fired on 1 September. With the emperor's principal armies in captivity, the empress and her ministers had little with which to combat a republican revolution that broke upon Paris on 4 September. The capture of Napoleon III and the overthrow of his government fundamentally altered the nature of the Franco-Prussian War. What had been a limited, negotiable cabinet war between the Bonapartes and the Hohenzollerns became what Léon Gambetta, deputy for Belleville and leader of the newly proclaimed Third Republic, called a 'guerre à outrance', a non-negotiable war for national survival.

The 'republican war': the social dimensions of strategy, 1870–7

Historians distinguish two phases in the Franco-Prussian conflict: an imperial war from July to September 1870, and a republican war from September 1870 until the armistice of January 1871. Militarily, the republican war was of little interest to nineteenth-century soldiers, for it pitted a battle-hardened, professional Prusso-German army against a motley array of newly inducted

French draftees, *Gardes Mobiles* and colonial troops. Predictably, the unseasoned, loosely joined French regiments sought the security of the fortresses that remained in French hands, and the republican war gradually degenerated into a *Festungskrieg*, a 'fortress war' for control of Metz, Strasbourg and Paris. There were mobile operations and savage battles at places like Orleans, Le Mans and Coulmiers in this second phase of the Franco-Prussian War, for the republican government – based on the Loire at Tours with the bulk of its recruits south and east of the river – considered that it had no choice but to try to fight its way back to Paris, where the Prussians were steadily attriting the garrison of 300,000. But these mobile operations had an air of unreality about them. After twice attempting to subvert the new republic with peace feelers to Bismarck, Bazaine surrendered the Army of the Rhine to the Prussians in October, depriving Gambetta of the last professional troops in France. Thereafter, the Prussians crisscrossed the country freely, rarely bothering to secure their flanks or lines of supply against an enemy who rarely attacked. As a contemporary Russian analyst put it: 'After Metz and Sedan, the battles lost all interest, for the weakness of the French gave the Germans full liberty of movement. ... Under these circumstances, *anything* was possible; even the riskiest strokes were easy' (*Österreichische Militärische Zeitschrift* 1874).

Certainly this was an overstatement, but not by much. As at Metz, a relatively small Prussian army managed to blockade Paris – a city of two million with a garrison of 300,000 – for five months. In the crucial battles on the Loire in December, a Prussian corps of 60,000 blocked and obliterated a French army of 200,000 headed for a junction with the Paris garrison. With their best officers in enemy hands, French efforts to move new armies to the Loire broke down completely, with demoralizing effects. Hew Strachan describes an illustrative case:

> At 9.30 a.m. on 7 January 1871, a French battalion arrived to entrain at Bourges. At 9 p.m. the same evening they were ordered to board the train. At 10 p.m. the order was cancelled. At 4 a.m. the following day they finally entrained. At 11 a.m. the first train left. [Four days] passed without moving at all. On 15 January the battalion arrived at Baume. It had travelled 230 miles.
>
> (Strachan 1983: 122)

The defeat of the French Army of the Loire at Orleans and Le Mans dashed once and for all Gambetta's plans to save Paris – the heart of the Republic – and destroy the besieging army there. With no military or diplomatic alternatives, Gambetta and his ministers agreed to an armistice in January and a formal treaty of peace in May (Howard 1981: 371–431). The Prussians extorted a staggering price: the rich provinces of Alsace and Lorraine (which placed the lovely, strategically vital 'blue line of the Vosges' in German, not French hands), and a five-billion-franc indemnity, which amounted to $28 billion, seventy times the reparations demanded of the Austrians in 1866.

Ultimately, what was the chief cause of the French defeat? The question bears directly on the warfare and society theme, for it is difficult to argue that the Prussian victories at Gravelotte and Sedan were in any way decisive. Even after Sedan, the French Republic presided over 800,000 military-aged men, 700,000 of whom were at large in the countryside, well beyond the reach of the Prussian armies at Paris, Metz and Strasbourg. If the French Republic were truly popular – Gambetta and his ministers always insisted that it was – vast armies ought to have formed spontaneously to save the *patrie en danger*. By regular and irregular fighting through the hard winter of 1870–1, the French ought to have been able to exhaust the weary, homesick Prussians – who had made no preparations for a winter campaign – and force them to the peace table. In fact, the opposite occurred. Few French peasants volunteered for the armies of the republic, and it was the exhausted, overextended Prussians who ultimately compelled the French to make peace on calamitous terms.

New research into the war suggests the reasons for the French collapse. For France, a mass mobilization had to be a peasant mobilization, for peasants comprised 75 per cent of the population in 1870. Yet this pool of rural manpower was of little use to the republican regime that ousted the Bonapartes in September 1870. Republicanism was an urban movement. Generally speaking, it was reviled by rural folk, who, from historical experience, equated French republics with disorder, socialism, high taxes and inflation. In the peasant mind, republicans were slackers. The professional politician did not live by the sweat of his brow, nor (according to the peasant) did most of his voters. To the peasant, urban handworkers were rootless, propertyless scum, lacking the status and security conferred by land ownership. Furthermore, the peasant reasoned, since workers had no land, they did not really work. While the peasant toiled around the clock in his fields and vineyards, the urban labourer merely 'punched the clock', checking in and out of a job in which he held no stake in the most transient, irresponsible way. Worst of all was the urban worker's total reliance on the peasant for food. Whereas the peasant could subsist without the implements produced in the cities, the workers needed peasant produce, which widened the gulf between French peasant and worker.

Here, then, was the essential social background to the failed 'republican war' of 1870–1. It had changed little since the peasant-led counter-revolution of 1848–9. The vast legions of the French countryside simply refused to fight wholeheartedly for the Third Republic, which they mistrusted. Although Napoleon III was pretty thoroughly disliked in the cities of France by 1870, he was still popular in the provinces, where he was viewed affectionately: *Pouléon* a reliable strongman who could be counted upon to keep a lid on taxes, the money supply and urban hotheads. Thus, the 'Revolution of 4

September', which launched the Third Republic, was viewed by the French peasant as a catastrophe. Out went *Pouléon*, the resolute friend of the peasant, and in came a government of *bourgeois*, who looked down on the peasant and made no effort to understand his pinched, materialistic world-view. 'There was no one like Napoleon III', peasants wistfully recalled, 'for keeping up hog prices' (Weber 1976: 254–5).

This is just the point made by an excellent new book: Alain Corbin's *Village of Cannibals: Rage and Murder in France, 1870*. Corbin describes a revealing atrocity perpetrated on 16 August 1870 in the southwestern French village of Hautefaye in the Dordogne. On that day, Alain de Monéys, a thirty-two year-old nobleman, walked from his country house to Hautefaye to join in the village fair. That year the *fête* was a somber affair, for it coincided with the French reverse at Mars-la-Tour and followed the bloody defeats at Wörth and Spicheren. Rural France, just informed that mass conscription was about to commence, was prickly and excitable. Louis-Napoleon had beaten the Russians and the Austrians handily, the peasant reasoned; why were the Prussians proving so difficult? To the wary peasant mind, the answer seemed obvious: the emperor was the victim of a Prusso-Republican plot.

In the weeks before and after Gravelotte, French peasants constructed an elaborate conspiracy theory. It went as follows: republicans, aided by landed aristocrats like Alain de Monéys, who welcomed the republic as a means to weaken the peasant smallholder and get at his lands, were conspiring with Bismarck to overthrow the Second Empire. As proof of this, the peasant pointed to mass demonstrations in Paris on 9 August, when a crowd of 20,000 had besieged the French parliament crying *Vive la République!* This act of 'treason' – celebrated by the left, deplored by the right – had come at the very moment when the energies of every able-bodied Frenchman were most desperately needed at the front. No wonder the French peasant set his face against the republic. The atrocity committed in Hautefaye revealed the depth of this hostility.

Alain de Monéys – a quiet, unassuming man – strolled into Hautefaye and was immediately attacked by a crowd of peasants, who tied him to a blacksmith's bench and slowly beat him to death. As the peasants struck Monéys with their boots, fists and tools, they declared that he had to be a 'Prussian' because he had been heard to cry *Vive la République!* (Corbin 1992: 74). The absurdity of this logic revealed the gulf between the French republic and its citizens. Outside of Paris, Gambetta had failed to rally the French people. Stéphane Audoin-Rouzeau's *1870: La France dans la Guerre* arrives at similar conclusions. Although certain that the French did not lack patriotic feeling, Audoin-Rouzeau finds that the most common response to the German invasion of 1870–1 was 'voluntary passivity', an early form of collaboration. Confronted with even small German units, mayors opened their towns, disarmed their national guards, and shooed away insurgents (*francs-tireurs*) in the neighbourhood lest they attract Prussian reprisals. The parallel with 1940 is striking. Audoin-Rouzeau's research also uncovers what he calls a 'crisis of indiscipline' in the armies of the republic. Although tens of thousands of French peasants were conscripted, they fought halfheartedly: rarely attacking, and often shirking at the first opportunity. Audoin-Rouzeau also notes that battle casualties, always a measure of zeal, never attained the levels of the imperial army in the republican army, and that the republicans deserted far more readily (Audoin-Rouzeau 1989: 255; in Förster and Nagler 1997: 393–411). Prussian records of the war also stressed the indiscipline of the French; German troops found that the republican armies (largely *Gardes Mobiles*) were effective only on the defensive, when they were shielded by fortifications or engaged in the defence of their own *pays* (home district) and property. They were certainly not 'attacking troops'; only the regular battalions were good at this, but most of them had been captured at Sedan and Metz in the autumn of 1870. When republican generals did try to attack, they did so with tragic results. Untrained in open-order, small-unit tactics, the armies of the republic lumbered forward in vast, elephantine columns like those last seen in the age of the musket. Lying alongside their guns with well sighted rifles, the Prussians mowed them down. Battles like Beaune-la-Rolande in November and Villiers in December were more like organized slaughters than battles. In both, the Germans inflicted casualties on the panic-stricken French *Mobiles* in a ratio of 10:1.

The Paris Commune

The failure of the new republican government to stop the Prussian advance after Sedan exposed Gambetta to political attacks from right and left. Resistance from the right, outlined above, was, intermittent; it only gradually sapped the energy and spirit of Gambetta's 'government of national defence'. Resistance from the left was volcanic; from the outset, it aimed at the ouster of Gambetta's moderate republic and its replacement with a communist terror state, which, mixing the methods of Robespierre and Marx, would unmask and exterminate 'counter-revolutionary elements'. Needless to say, the revolutionary communism of Paris – where support for the Commune was strongest – served only to further alienate France's rural masses. After the downfall of Napoleon III, peasants not only lost interest in the war; they redefined their enemy. No longer the Prussian, it became the urban *communard*. In seeking the causes of the French defeat in 1870–1, it is essential to grasp this fact: France after September 1870 was embarked on two wars, one with the Prussians, and one with itself: a civil war that pitted the radical cities against the conservative countryside. For Bismarck and the Prussians, this was convenient; it depressed morale inside France, permitting the Germans to pacify the provinces and focus their military efforts on Paris, which fell in January 1871, effectively ending the war.

The Paris Commune – a bloody insurrection that exploded in March

1871, as the Franco-Prussian War wound down – had smouldered throughout the conflict, to the detriment of the French war effort. At bottom, the Commune was a revolutionary attempt to overthrow the liberal republic established after Sedan and replace it with a proletarian dictatorship, which would 'democratize' society by liquidating class enemies, abolishing private property and expropriating the Roman Catholic church. (Besides murdering the Archbishop of Paris and scores of priests, the communards actually issued a warrant for God's arrest and hung Him in effigy [Christiansen 1994: 301–2].) The Commune unmistakably signalled all that was wrong with communism. Though acclaimed in the poor sections of Paris (particularly by women, who were mobilized by the movement), it was fundamentally undemocratic, preferring terror and coercion to the ballot box. Indeed, when the moderate majority of Parisians gave Gambetta's 'bourgeois republic' a landslide vote of confidence in November 1870 (500,000 to 62,000), the jilted communards streamed into the middle-class *arrondissements* and attacked the very government that had just been validated by its people. This early attempt at a Bolshevik coup, which, to the consternation of the French peasant, coincided with the Army of the Loire's desperate fight for survival in the fields around Orleans, was put down by rural troops, who dubbed the Parisian communists *Prussiens de l'intérieur* – 'Prussians of the interior' (Vienna, *Haus- Hof- und Staatsarchiv*, PA IX 96, Paris, 4 November 1870, Hübner to Metternich). It is important to note that the communards launched their bloodiest, most violent insurrection in March 1871, when millions of French voters turned out to reject the communist terror state and return a conserva- tive republic that would make peace with the Prussians, respect private property and restore amicable relations with the Roman Catholic church. Quite characteristically, the communards – who had been isolated from the 'real France' by six months of siege warfare – sought to annul the elections by force and implant socialism in Paris (Becker and Audoin-Rouzeau 1995: 104–9). France's patience with Paris had run out. In May 1871, the French regular army, released from its prison camps by Bismarck, entered Paris and counter-attacked the communists. During 'bloody week', the army, unleashed by the French voter, swept through Paris, killing 17,000 communards and deporting thousands more to the French penal colonies (Gildea 1996: 215–17, 252–3; Christiansen 1994: 366).

Given these internal rifts, is it any wonder that France fell in 1871? Beset by a million-man Prussian army, which very efficiently policed the French provinces, and an enemy within – the communards, who attempted a half-dozen coups against the Third Republic during the siege of Paris – Gambetta had no other option than to conclude an armistice in January 1871 and a formal peace in May. The price was high: Alsace-Lorraine, a ruinous indem- nity, and the pride of the nation; but it seemed accurately to reflect the new balance of power in Europe (Howard 1981: 432–56). Paul Valéry, who witnessed the war, complained that France had been 'methodically conquered by a rational, painstaking, brutal, and expansionist state ... a perfectly oiled and irresistible weapon of political power and economic self-interest' (cited in Pick 1993: 101). The 'German Revolution' of Bismarck and Moltke was complete, Paris eclipsed, Berlin the new 'capital of Europe'.

CHAPTER SIX

New weapons and the 'new imperialism', 1877–1905

Bismarck's wars suggested that Europe had entered a new age. Politically, there seemed little point in heeding international law and treaties. States could now pursue purely selfish interests – what the Italians called *sacro egoismo* – with a reasonable chance of success. Militarily, Bismarck's wars suggested that long wars of attrition were a thing of the past; the future promised what the Prussians called 'wars of annihilation': the short, brutal *Blitzkrieg* that would achieve fast political results at a small cost.

These two related perceptions – that the Germans had egotistically upset the balance of power in 1870–1 and that short wars of conquest were a legitimate means to redress it – encouraged the Russians to launch the last great European war of the nineteenth century: The Russo-Turkish War of 1877–8. What the Russians sought in this war was a vast extension of power and influence in the Balkans and the Middle East to push back Austria-Hungary, undercut British naval superiority in the Mediterranean, and balance Prussia-Germany's territorial gains of 1870–1. After beating the Turks at Plevna in Bulgaria in 1877, the Russian army approached Constantinople and a British fleet sent to protect the Turkish capital. With an Anglo-Russian war in sight – Disraeli insisting that Constantinople was the untouchable 'key to India' – Bismarck, who refused to choose between the Russians and the British, both useful friends, invited the European powers to convene in 1878 (Baumgart 1982: 22). At the Congress of Berlin, Bismarck unveiled a stratagem to soften the resentments that had been building against Germany since its wars of unification. Rather than give back any of Prussia's conquests, he offered the other great powers chunks of the Ottoman Empire. Russia received Bessarabia, Kars and Batum, and was consoled by the extraction of Rumania, Bulgaria, Serbia and Montenegro – all Orthodox states – from Turkey-in-Europe. Austria-Hungary, alarmed by this Russian advance in the Balkans, was compensated with the Turkish provinces of Bosnia and Herzegovina and the Sanjak of Novipazar, a desolate but strategically important corridor separating Serbia and Montenegro. Great Britain took the Turkish island of Cyprus, which would permit the Royal Navy to base troops and warships near the Suez Canal, opened in 1869. France (still agonizing over the loss of Alsace-

Lorraine) was invited to colonize Tunisia. Italy – which considered North Africa its 'fourth coast' and a natural field for expansion (there were far more Italian than French settlers in Tunisia in 1878) – got nothing, a snub that only sharpened Rome's appetite for empire in the years to come (Bosworth 1996: 24–5; Pflanze 1990: II, 430–41).

At the Congress of Berlin, imperial expansion served above all as a safety valve for the unresolved jealousies of Europe. In the short term, Bismarck's gambit worked, in that it relieved pressure on Germany to support the benevolent neutrals (Russia and England) who had boosted Prussia into the German saddle, or compensate the victims (France and Austria). In the long term, however, the push Bismarck gave to imperial expansion had the exact opposite effect intended. Instead of securing Germany, it endangered it, for as the European great powers expanded abroad, German naval, commercial, political and religious groups protested that Germany – Continental Europe's richest, most industrialized state – could not itself neglect overseas colonies, which came to be viewed as the sinews of power. Even Bismarck, who famously objected that Germany's internal problems were so great that colonies 'would be like sable coats worn by Polish noblemen who don't have shirts', was compelled to drop his objections in 1884–5, and consent to the German annexation of Namibia, Cameroon and Tanganyika (Pflanze 1990: III, 114).

Bismarck was impelled in large measure by a new mood called 'social Darwinism': the widespread feeling that the great powers were locked in a struggle for survival and that only the predators would survive. In Britain, Lord Salisbury spoke of the 'dying and living nations', and Herbert Asquith compared the growth of empire to 'the corresponding processes in the growing human body'. In France, Gabriel Hanotaux deemed the acquisition of colonies a sign of 'bodily vigour', failure to acquire a signal of decline (Baumgart 1982: 182). In Germany in 1883 a bestselling book argued that 'the destiny of nations is like that of men; nations rise, they bloom, they decay, and cease to be'. The book assured readers that 'the star of [Germany] had only just risen on the horizon; its full course lies still before it' (Gat 1992: 78–9). Bismarck reluctantly charted this course, justifying colonies to the Reichstag on the grounds that they 'held open a door for German labour, German civilization, and German capital', and shut the door to German rivals (Pflanze 1990: III, 121). Bismarck's push into Africa in the 1880s accelerated the 'Scramble for Africa', a term that refers to the European absorption of 90 per cent of the African continent in the years 1881–1900. By 1900, only Ethiopia, Liberia and the gold and diamond-rich Boer republics in South Africa held out. The Boer War, Britain's rather haphazard attempt to annex the Boer republics and attach South Africa to the Empire, dragged on for three years, from 1899 to 1902. It cost the British Empire as many lives as the Americans would lose in Vietnam many years later, and gave a frightening glimpse of the ways in which warfare had changed since 1870.

In Asia, Russia's attempt to exploit the weakness of China's Ch'ing dynasty and colonize Manchuria and Korea in 1904 provoked a war with the Japanese that signalled Japan's rise to great power status, but also the deadliness of new military technologies that had only been glimpsed in South Africa. The grimmest episodes of the Russo-Japanese War occurred at Port Arthur, a Russian fortress on the Yellow Sea, which saw prolonged trench warfare and the concentrated fire of machineguns and quick-firing, high-explosive artillery for the first time. These new weapons of the *fin-de-siècle* inflicted ghastly casualties on both sides and suggested to some that war had become a form of mass suicide and therefore impossible. Overall, Plevna and Port Arthur bracketed the movement known to historians as the 'new imperialism'. Though far more than a diplomatic phenomenon, imperialism was fundamentally an outgrowth of the 'German Revolution'. And the miscarriage of Bismarck's scheme to allay European fears of German unification by dealing out African and Asian territory merely compounded the military, political, economic and social tensions that would ignite a world war in 1914.

The Russo-Turkish War

The roots of the Russo-Turkish War were visible in 1871, when, as the price of Russian neutrality in the Franco-Prussian War, Tsar Alexander II voided the peace treaties of 1856 by rebuilding the Russian fortifications at Sebastopol and deploying Russian warships in the Black Sea for the first time since the Crimean War. This was more than a reassertion of sovereignty. Alexander II was securing his southern flank against a repetition of the Crimean War, when the British and French navies had steamed through the Dardanelles and attacked Russia's soft underbelly (Jelavich 1991: 156–7; McElwee 1974: 187–8). The tsar was also securing himself against Russia's own 'social Darwinists': Moscow's Pan-Slavs, an influential society of newspapermen, bureaucrats, soldiers and professionals, who agitated for war in 1875–6. The Pan-Slavs feared the growth of German influence in Europe, and demanded Russian expansion into the Balkans to consolidate 'a great Slavic tribe' (Jelavich 1991: 158). The Pan-Slav programme, which aimed to Russianize the Slavic peoples rather than confederate them, neatly fitted Alexander II's own war aims, and he shrewdly adopted it to increase public support for the Russo-Turkish War (Gollwitzer 1969: 45–6). Thus fortified, the tsar used the pretext of Turkish atrocities against the Christian peoples of Bosnia, Herzegovina and Bulgaria to invade the Ottoman Empire in April 1877.

Russia's invasion of Turkey drew heavily on reforms enacted after the Crimean debacle and on lessons learned from the Prussian campaigns of 1866 and 1870 (D. Rich 1998: 65–114). Like Moltke, General Nikolai Obruchev planned a rapid march into enemy territory and a decisive envelopment of the enemy army. Mimicking the Prussian method, he instructed his generals to disregard fortresses and 'secondary operations', seek the main force, and take or threaten the Turkish capital without delay. Overall, Obruchev's plan was unmistakably Prussian; it called for 'great profit at minimum cost' *à la* Bismarck, 'decisive, rapid action' in the Moltkean style, and it relied heavily on deep penetration behind the Turkish lines to take the Turks between two fires: one Russian army cutting its way south from Kishinev to Constantinople; another wheeling in from the west, via Sofia and Plevna, enveloping Turkish resistance to the main army from the flank (D. Rich 1998: 120–7).

Though boldly conceived, the Russian plan was impossibly optimistic; it aimed to surmount the barriers of the Danube River and the Balkan Mountains and reach Constantinople in a matter of *weeks* (Bellamy 1990: 130–2; Menning 1992: 51–3). The Prussians might have pulled this off, but the Russians most certainly would not, for their post-1871, Prussian-inspired military reforms were only half complete. Russia's bronze, muzzle-loading cannon and Krinka rifles were primitive weapons; even the Turks were better armed. Organizationally, the Russians still had no reliable system of conscription to compare with Roon's *Kreise*. They still had no permanent corps. Their reservists, modelled on the German *Landwehr*, were largely untrained; most of them would be trained in battle in 1877 and most would be killed (McElwee 1974: 189–91). In short, whereas Moltke had planned in 1870 to overwhelm France's defensive firepower with a flood of German troops (a million Germans against 400,000 French), the Russians were far too disorganized to take the same precaution. Indeed, Obruchev slammed up against Turkey's mountain strongholds with little more than 200,000 men. This was an insufficient number to replace sick men and malingerers, let alone battle casualties. After some initial successes, the Russian advance, poorly supplied and coordinated, ground to a halt at Plevna.

The three battles of Plevna (July–December 1877) hinted at the problems European armies would face in the First World War. Plevna was a fortified village commanding a horseshoe of hills between Bucharest and Sofia. There the Turks dug in to halt the descent of Obruchev's flanking army on Constantinople. Like the armies of 1914, the Russians initially believed that 'offensive spirit' and cannonades would cut through the Turkish trenches and open the road to the Ottoman capital. This was a foolish misreading of the lessons of 1870–1. The Germans had not beaten the French by 'attacking spirit' and gunfire, but by superior numbers and the flanking attack, which had turned the French out of their rifle pits and into the open field, where they had been easy marks for Moltke's Krupp guns. The Russians sought to imitate this manoeuvre without any of its essential underpinnings. In their three assaults on Plevna in July and September, they advanced in human waves on a narrow front against deeply entrenched Turkish infantry. The Turks, shielded from the worst of the Russian artillery by their excellent trenches, far better than any employed by the French in 1870, scythed the Russians to the ground with rapid fire from their American-made Peabody rifles.

An English officer present at Plevna described the third Russian assault. It is a gripping account that begins in the Russian trenches, where lines of nervous Russian conscripts lie in their white fighting dress, nervously crossing themselves and clutching their rifles until the signal is finally given to attack. Thereafter, a reader could easily mistake the narrative for a First World War vignette. It has all of the familiar characteristics: an invisible enemy, rapid, disorienting fire, confusion and panic in the attack, and heaps of casualties.

> In vain did one look towards Plevna and its defences for any sign of life or activity among the Turks … this great, black, ominous-looking work appeared deserted, nor was any living being to be seen anywhere near it. Although the order to attack had gone forth, the infantry in the ravine, perhaps not understanding to whom it referred, seemed to hang back for a time. A moment or two later, first one, then two, then more officers were seen to spring [out of the trench.] They were rapidly followed by their men, not in any particular formation, but like a swarm of bees, and all of them rushed headlong towards the object of their attack. Silent and dead as the Turkish works had appeared to be, now of a sudden a terrific fire was poured on the attackers from successive lines of shelter trenches. … These trenches had been unobserved and unobservable until this withering fire opened from one trench after another on the advancing Russians, whose losses were terrific. … Coming within a moderate distance of the redoubt, they were suddenly checked by the most murderous fire of infantry and guns, the latter belching out grape and canister without cessation. … The whole of the attacking troops turned and fled. … It is difficult to describe the impression created in one's mind by the frightful slaughter which attended this attack, and one could scarcely believe that the bodies covering the ground were those of killed and wounded human beings.
>
> (Wellesley 1904: 254–6)

Much of the fault for suicidal attacks like this one lay with the Russian generals, who attacked frontally, without turning the Turks out of their position from the flank, as the Prussians had usually done in 1866 and 1870. Nor was the Russian artillery up to the task. One of the war's more important lessons was that properly constructed trenches were invulnerable to flat-trajectoried cannon. In the future, armies would need to procure howitzers, which, with their high angle of fire, could literally drop shells into an enemy trench. Russian artillery officers were the first to discover this; they estimated that six field guns needed to fire non-stop for twenty-four hours to kill a single Turk (Strachan 1983: 119).

In the first clash at Plevna, the Russians lost two thirds of their officers and one third of their troops. (As in 1914, officers fell in disproportionate numbers because of the need to lead from the front in the face of rapid, demoralizing fire.) In both the second and third assaults on Plevna, the Russians lost 25 per cent of their attacking force: 7,000 casualties in the second battle, 18,000 in the third. These were appalling losses; in a typical mid-nineteenth century battle, the rate of dead and wounded had rarely exceeded 10 per cent of effectives engaged. Russian losses at Plevna were many times higher, and ought to have been taken more seriously by European armies (O'Connor 1997). Indeed Bruce Menning's recent study of Plevna points up all of the eerie similiarities between it and the battles of 1914: defective staff work, uncoordinated attacks, stalemated, multi-day offensives, and an overreliance on artillery shells, that more often than not burst harmlessly against the enemy's earthworks (Menning 1992: 60–71). As William McElwee direly concluded his study of the Russo-Turkish War: 'The next great war would not be the greater Sedan of which Schlieffen dreamed in 1900 and which Joffre apprehended in 1914, but Plevna on a continental scale' (J. Fuller 1992: 121; McElwee 1974: 205).

The Russians gave up trying to storm Plevna and besieged it instead; cut off from its supplies, the fortress fell in December, and the Russians passed through the Balkan Mountains and approached Constantinople in January 1878. With Pan-Slav sentiment spreading in Moscow and Sofia, Sultan Abdulhamid prudently signed the Russian-dictated Treaty of San Stefano, which satisfied all of Alexander II's war aims. Armenia and Georgia were attached to the Russian Empire. Bosnia and Herzegovina – the cause of the war – were left in Turkish hands, but given some autonomy, a boon they owed to the Russians. Rumania, Bulgaria, Serbia and Montenegro – the rebellious, largely Christian provinces of the Ottoman Empire that had pinned down a large fraction of the Turkish army in the war – were enlarged and granted their independence, thanks again to the Russians. The most striking feature of the San Stefano treaty was the size of the new Bulgarian state. It extended far beyond the ethnic frontiers of Bulgaria to include Dobrudja, Thrace and Macedonia, lands that included large numbers of Rumanians, Turks, Greeks, Serbs and Albanians. Clearly the tsar intended 'Greater Bulgaria' to serve as a Russian puppet state: a fist raised against Turkey, a foot in the door of the Dardanelles, and a wall against British or Austro-Hungarian expansion into a sphere of influence that the Russians had conquered at a cost of 200,000 casualties and one billion rubles (W. Fuller 1992: 322). The Balkans, in short, were Russia's 'near abroad' of the 1870s, a region neatly delineated by John LeDonne: 'the zones to the Prut forming the inner frontier of the Russian Empire, those south of the river an outer frontier about to succumb to the Russian advance' (LeDonne 1997: 140). While the West European powers pondered overseas expansion, Russia was content to push out its land frontiers, and take up a dominating position in Central Asia, the Balkans and the Middle East.

Alexander II's Pan-Slavic hopes were shortly dashed by the Congress of

Berlin, which Bismarck convened in June 1878 to prevent an Anglo-Austrian war with Russia. Bismarck worried that a great war would cost Germany its 'free hand' in diplomatic affairs by forcing Berlin to choose sides. (There was real cause for worry; indeed the term 'jingoism' dates from 1878, when a bellicose music-hall song swept England with the refrain 'By jingo, the Russians shall not have Constantinople' [Palmer 1992: 154].) Ironically, the Congress of Berlin, which initiated the imperial expansion of the great powers, had exactly the opposite effect on Russia. Poor Alexander II saw most of his gains snatched away. Fearing that Greater Bulgaria would overshadow the new Balkan states and the Turks, the Austrians and the British, seconded by the Germans and the French, combined to whittle Bulgaria down to its ethnic frontiers. Thrace was set aside as an autonomous province of the Ottoman Empire. Macedonia was restored to the Turks outright, depriving the Russians of their most cherished prize: the Mediterranean port of Kevala. Dobrudja was given to the Rumanians. Worst of all, Russia's arch-rival Austria-Hungary thrust into Bosnia, a Turkish province with a large Serbian minority, and placed it under military occupation. Austria also occupied Herzegovina and Novipazar, effectively barring the Serbs from the sea. To Russia – patron of the Orthodox peoples – these were slaps that would sting until 1914. Although still in possession of Bessarabia and a diminished Bulgarian satellite after the Congress of Berlin, the Russians had little else to show for their efforts. They felt humiliated and thereafter assumed a hostile attitude toward the Germans and Austrians. Turkey's retreat from the Balkans – the Ottomans retaining only Macedonia, Thessaly, Epirus and Albania after 1878 – exacerbated the situation (Jelavich 1983: I, 359–60) (Map 6.1). Now the Russians and Austrians were in direct contact, and their constant jockeying in the Balkans brought war closer in the years 1878–1914. This, and Russia's anti-German stance after the Congress of Berlin, explained Bismarck's reluctant decision to conclude the Austro-German Dual Alliance in 1879. It was an anti-Russian instrument that in turn drove St Petersburg to negotiate the Franco-Russian alliance of 1894, effectively polarizing Europe into two heavily armed camps.

The 'new imperialism'

Imperialism, the process by which the European great powers, joined by the Japanese and the Americans, divided up the world in the late nineteenth century, was initially driven by diplomatic considerations. International congresses were held to stake claims and arbitrate disputes in the unindustrialized world, and colonies were distributed with an eye toward maintaining a rough balance between the great powers. Displaying his usual finesse, Bismarck placed himself in the middle of the imperial expansion of the 1870s and 1880s, throwing chunks of Africa to Germany's rivals in the hope that they would forgive the bumps and bruises of German unification and focus their

Map 6.1 The Balkans in 1878

political energies outside of Europe. It was no coincidence that both of the diplomatic summits that led to the partition of Africa were held in the German capital: the Congress of Berlin in 1878 and the Berlin Conference in 1884–5. At the former meeting, Bismarck urged his French colleagues, already in possession of Algeria, to have Tunisia as well: 'The Tunisian pear is ripe and the time has come for you to pluck it' (Mansergh 1949: 44). In 1883, Bismarck helped France acquire Madagascar, which gave the French navy a much-needed coaling station on the sea route to Indochina. Bismarck ('I wish a conciliatory attitude in everything that is not related to Alsace') wanted France to forget the humiliating defeats at Sedan and Metz and focus instead on building an overseas empire to rival that of Great Britain (Baumgart 1982: 149). France was willing; Léon Gambetta, prime minister after the debacle of 1870–1, viewed colonies as the only way to 'make France a great power again' (Kupchan 1994: 192–6).

Bismarck aimed to bury Britain's doubts as well, by tolerating the British army's seizure of the Transvaal in 1877, Egypt in 1882, and Nigeria in 1884–5. When overzealous German explorers offered Bismarck South West Africa (Namibia) in 1883, the German chancellor magnanimously offered it to the British, and took it himself only when London refused to have it (Mansergh 1949: 50). Similar diplomatic considerations governed Bismarck's relations with the Russians. Throughout the 1880s he encouraged Russia to expand eastward: northeast to Siberia and southeast to the Trans-Caspian region, through the Central Asian khanates to the Afghan frontier. In this way, Bismarck hoped that Russia would forget the snub of 1878 and exhaust its considerable energies in Asia rather than Europe (Mansergh 1949: 51–2).

Looked at from Bismarck's perspective, imperialism was little more than a diplomatic chess game (Baumgart 1982: 36–7). Yet had diplomatic considerations really been paramount in the nineteenth-century 'scrambles' for Africa and Asia, there would have been nothing 'new' at all about the imperialism of the *fin-de-siècle*. What made the 'new imperialism' new was the involvement of military, commercial, journalistic and cultural groups in the formation of imperial strategy. In an increasingly industrialized, democratic and literate age, even Bismarck found that he could no longer settle imperial disputes privately and pragmatically. Statesmen like Bismarck were exposed to new pressures, the same ones that would give such a powerful stimulus to war in 1914: business interests, pressure groups and lobbyists, the tabloid press, party politics and shrewd military staffs, who knew how to 'slip the leash' in the general hubbub of late nineteenth-century growth and make vast, unauthorized annexations. France's colonial army – distinct from the metropolitan force – quadrupled in size between 1880 and 1900 and brought much of Africa and Indochina under French protection without any parliamentary direction (Porch 1981: 139–42). Commercial firms were no less enterprising. In 1882, Italy's Rubattino shipping line acquired a small coaling station on the Horn of Africa and asked the Italian government to administer it. One thing led to another and the little protectorate of Assab sprawled the length of the Red Sea coast to become the Italian colonies of Somalia and 'Eritrea', the latter name chosen, like 'Libya', to suggest continuity with the ancient Roman Empire (Bosworth 1996: 98–9). This 'new imperialism' – slapdash, nostalgic, businesslike, militaristic and political – was a volatile cocktail that threatened always to explode the balance of power, wrench control of national strategy from the hands of statesmen, and precipitate a world war.

No one rued this loss of control more than Bismarck. Throughout the 1880s he tried not to take on colonies, arguing that Germany would be wiser to trade African and Asian territory for the friendship of Russia, Britain, France and Italy. But Bismarck – who always greeted colonial enthusiasts with a map of Europe, saying '*this* is my map of Africa' – found himself swept away by the new forces (Baumgart 1982: 152; Bismarck to Eugen Wolf, 1888: 'Your map of Africa is very nice, but my map of Africa is in Europe; here is Russia and here is France, and we are in the centre; that is my map of Africa'). In the first place, there was industrial capitalism. After a decade of rapid growth, European economies slumped in the period 1873–96. It was a peculiar form of depression; while consumption fell off, production actually increased, creating a surplus of goods that needed new markets. The first response of the European states to this downturn was protectionism. In the 1880s and 1890s, all but Britain clapped 'penal tariffs' of 30 and 40 per cent on imported goods to favour local industry (Hobsbawm 1989: 34–40). This strategy failed, and governments, businesses and their workers began looking abroad for salvation, to imagined new markets in Africa and Asia. This 'municipal imperialism', driven by industrial cities with surplus wares to sell, often necessitated the use of European troops, prompting a left-wing Spanish newspaper to condemn European armies as nothing more than 'commercial representatives, who kill and let themselves be killed for the profits of their masters' (Balfour 1997: 2; Vandervort 1998: 31).

'Municipal imperialism' destroyed the tidy 'cartographic imperialism' of 1878, for it made imperialism a vital domestic-political issue by suggesting that a citizen's standard of living hinged on his government's willingness to expand. The population of Europe more than doubled in the nineteenth century, increasing from 200 million in 1800 to 430 million in 1914. Most of the growth was in Russia, Germany and Britain, and it created tremendous pressure for new jobs in towns, and made overseas empires seem a likely place to find them. Colonial societies and patriotic leagues funded by public subscriptions, business interests and national churches stepped up to publicize the issue. These pressure groups were better organized than forerunners like Cobden's Free Traders or the Abolitionists. They made clever use of mass media and modern advertising techniques to capture public opinion, and grandstanded at every opportunity (Gollwitzer 1969: 99–100). Cecil Rhodes, one of Britain's most prominent imperialists, found work for thousands of unemployed Cornish tin miners in the newly discovered gold fields of South

Africa (Hobsbawm 1989: 69). This kind of activity, which won support for colonies from left and right, revealed another facet of the new imperialism: 'social imperialism', the process by which European citizens of all social classes were persuaded (some would say manipulated) to join in the clamour for overseas expansion.

Social imperialism was particularly pronounced in Germany, which, owing to Bismarck's forbearance, found itself mired in the 'long depression' with a much smaller colonial empire than its most serious rivals, England and France. A number of pressure groups formed in the 1880s to shift Bismarck, among them the German Association for Colonization and Export and the German Colonial Society. Both were funded by German banks and industry, and both melded businessmen, government officials, soldiers, and celebrities like the German archaeologist Heinrich von Schliemann. These societies – which had their equivalents in all of the great European states (the Primrose League in Britain, the *Comité de l'Afrique Française* in France, the *Società Nazionale* in Italy) – made generous contributions to biddable parliamentary deputies and newspaper editors, and worked public opinion directly, 'pounding home the thesis that the desperate conditions of German industry and the radicalization of the urban lower classes required colonies to drain off excess goods and people' (Pflanze 1990: III, 115). Some political leaders outdid the pressure groups. Francesco Crispi, Italy's prime minister in the 1880s and 1890s, made no secret of his contempt for parliamentary government, and planned to 'refound' the Kingdom of Italy by conquering a vast African empire that would inflate the prestige of the king and army (Bosworth 1996: 20; Mack Smith 1989: 86–93, 106–13).

Religious groups added a cultural dimension to the economic argument. The Rhine Mission, a league of German evangelists, deplored the rise of atheistic socialism in Germany's industrial zones, and advocated overseas colonies as a place to convert heathens and dump doubting, unemployed Germans as well. Finally, there were the patriotic groups, 'social Darwinists' like the Russian Pan-Slavs or the Pan-German League, founded in 1891 by Germany's most famous explorer and most famous industrialist to exert irresistible pressure for colonial expansion. Moltke had unwittingly given the social Darwinists their cue by pronouncing the successful wars of 1866 and 1870–1 'a link in God's world-design' (Gollwitzer 1969: 178–9). In 1886, a Russian Pan-Slav restated Moltke's thought in sham scientific terms, defining foreign policy as 'the art of pursuing the struggle for existence among social organisms'. Writing of the need for a German navy and world empire in 1898, a German social Darwinist was even more explicit: 'The struggle for life exists among individuals, provinces, parties, and states. [States] wage it either by the use of arms or in the economic field – we cannot help this – therefore we wage it. Those who do not will perish' (Baumgart 1982: 75–6, 86–8). Such men felt the loss of every European emigrant to America in the late nineteenth century, and demanded world empires to catch the outflow and absorb the booming production of 'national labour' (Hobsbawm 1989: 14–15). German patriots also believed themselves to be racing with the British, Americans, French and Russians for control of the world. To sit pat, as Bismarck had done until the 1880s, would invite the 'encirclement' and 'suffo- cation' of Germany (Pflanze 1990: III, 116–17).

It was in this charged enviroment that the European powers nibbled at the fringes of Turkey, Persia and China, swallowed up the entire Indian subconti- nent, laid claim to every atoll in the South Pacific, and annexed eleven million square miles of Africa in the last half of the nineteenth century (Townsend 1941: 4). Bismarck later lamented that he had been 'dragged into the colonial whirl', but so had all the powers (Pflanze 1990: III, 125). European control of the world's land surface increased from 35 per cent in 1800, to 67 per cent in 1878, to 84 per cent in 1914 (Fieldhouse 1973: 3). This relentless expansion forced European states to join the fray or risk losing their place on the ladder of power, for colonies, though they subsequently disappointed, became for a time the very currency of power (Baumgart 1982: 112–35). Consider the following statistics: by 1914, the British Empire measured 13.5 million square miles in extent; this was an area three and a half times the size of Europe, and 140 times the size of the United Kingdom, which, shorn of its colonies, measured just 93,000 square miles. France, enlarged by its forays into Africa and Indochina, presided over a 4.6 million square mile empire that was twenty-four times the size of the *métropole*. Germany, 205,000 square miles in extent, had cobbled together a world empire five times as big: one million square miles of *Deutsches Reich* in Africa and the Pacific. Amid this fierce competition for the sealanes, littorals, markets and resources of the globe, the number of colonial powers doubled in the nineteenth century, from five in 1830 to ten in 1914. They were Great Britain, France, Germany, the United States, Japan, Italy, Belgium, Portugal, Spain and the Netherlands (Baumgart 1982: 7; Johannsen and Kraft 1937). Only Russia, eight million square miles in extent, resisted the trend, but not for long. In 1904 Russia went to war with Japan to acquire colonies in Northeast Asia. The war went badly for the Russians and nearly brought down the Romanovs. Here were early signs of the rancour and insecurity that would cause war in 1914. Fixed by the public eye, scolded by pressure groups, and convinced that territorial expansion was a zero-sum game, none of the European great powers could afford to give way to a rival. It would be political suicide.

The colonial wars

Colonial warfare, as waged in Africa and Asia, confirmed the power and potential of Europe's mid-century military revolution. Small European armies, equipped with breech-loading rifles and early machineguns like the *mitrailleuse* and the Gatling gun, were able to decimate native armies that were many times larger. Small European fleets, armoured and bristling with quick-firing guns, were able to command the world's rivers and littorals and facilitate communications with the imperial capital. All of the European great powers owed their colonial conquests to these military-technological advances, which permitted small expeditionary forces to make vast annexations in every hemisphere.

The military innovations that powered nineteenth-century European expansion were the armoured steamship, breech-loading artillery, the machinegun, the magazine rifle and the telegraph. The impact of the telegraph alone cannot be overstated. When Zulu raiders plundered Lourenço Marques in 1833, Portuguese authorities in the interior of Mozambique did not hear of the incident until a full year had passed. By 1879, all of Portuguese Africa was linked by telegraphs and a submarine cable was laid to Lisbon; news and reactions could pass instantly from the interior to the coast to the capital (Vandervort 1998: 28–9). Other inventions were no less important, for they enabled Europeans to venture off the beaten track: antiseptics, quinine, canned meat, milk powder and margarine (Black 1998: 164–5; Headrick 1981: 64–74). Technological innovation enabled the British to augment the world's biggest empire in the nineteenth century. It facilitated the Russian push into Central Asia and the Far East in the 1860s and permitted the French to take Algeria in the 1840s and add a vast sub-Saharan and Indochinese empire in the 1880s. Americans celebrated their military technology, proudly asserting that it was the lever-action Winchester repeating rifle that 'won the West' from multitudes of outgunned Indians.

A few examples of European military superiority make the point. In 1865, 2,200 Russian infantrymen took Tashkent from an army of 30,000 Uzbeks, completing Russia's annexation of Turkestan. In 1879, eighty-five British riflemen successfully defended Rorke's Drift in South Africa against repeated attacks by 5,000 Zulus. In the Second Afghan War, 7,000 British regulars defeated an Afghan army of 100,000 at Sherpur, securing India's Northwest Frontier. In 1884, a small French naval squadron firing armour-piercing shells sank a large Chinese fleet at Foochow in just thirty minutes, compelling China to abandon its claims to Southeast Asia and recognize French colonial rule in Indochina.

There were occasional lapses. Most Americans know the story of the Little Big Horn in 1876, where General George Armstrong Custer and 200 US cavalrymen were wiped out by 6,000 Sioux Indians. (Chiefly, it would appear, because of bad marksmanship: armed with Springfield carbines, Custer's men spewed 40,000 rounds in the course of the battle, bringing down fewer than 160 Sioux [Strachan 1983: 85].) Most Italians recall the tragedy of Adowa, where 10,000 Italian troops engaged in pushing the Italian colony of Eritrea into neighbouring Abyssinia were set upon and annihilated by 120,000 Ethiopian troops, deferring Italy's dream to control the Horn of Africa until the 1930s. Yet these were the shocking exceptions that proved the rule. The superiority of European warfare made world empires possible, for indigenous armies in the developing world rarely had the means to counter the superior weaponry and tactics deployed by the Europeans, the Americans and, at century's end, the Japanese (Headrick 1981: 108–11).

New weapons

The most spectacular European military invention of the late nineteenth century was Hiram Maxim's machinegun of 1885. The Maxim gun, unlike the *mitrailleuse* or the Gatling gun, was fully automatic and water-cooled. Whereas 'revolver cannons' like the *mitrailleuse* had to be laboriously cranked and left to cool off when their barrels overheated – invariably at the climax of a battle – Maxim's 'machine gun' used the energy generated by its own recoil to eject spent cartridges and load fresh ones from canvas belts of 250 rounds. The Maxim gun also contained a water tank that cooled the barrels while they fired, permitting gunners to fire 600 rounds a minute for sustained periods. Several hundred rounds a minute was a high achievement. Just twenty years earlier, European soldiers had considered that Prussia's rate of fire at Königgrätz – eight-to-ten rounds a minute – constituted a smashing break-through. The Maxim gun raised the stakes in the infantry fight and fundamentally changed it, as the indigenous armies of Africa, Asia and America shortly discovered.

European armies found the Maxim gun particularly devastating when attached to infantry battalions armed with another contrivance of the 1880s: the magazine rifle. Though magazine rifles were as old as the Henry and Winchester repeaters wielded by American cowboys in the 1860s, they were not widely adopted in Europe until the introduction of metal-cased cartridges in the 1870s and the replacement of charcoal gunpowder with smokeless propellants in the 1880s; both developments greatly reduced fouling in the breech and barrel, making repeating rifles a safe bet for the first time (D. Harding 1980: 136–40). The new repeating rifles, spring-loaded from tubular or box magazines, were formidable killing machines: small-calibre brass cartridges fed smoothly into the breech without crushing and jamming like the cardboard or linen tubes of the 1860s. Their smokeless propellant (jellied guncotton or 'cordite', another of Alfred Nobel's inventions) greatly enhanced the effectiveness, stealth and survivability of individual riflemen (Cleator 1967: 150–2). Infantrymen and machinegunners could now fire rapidly without losing sight of their targets in clouds of smoke, and without betraying their position. The smaller calibre of the new bullets also gave them more penetrative power, and enabled men to carry more of them, inflicting greater damage with each shot. In 1866, Austrian and Prussian infantry had carried just sixty rounds of bulky ammunition in their haversacks. This allotment steadily increased with the shift to smaller calibres. By 1877, European infantry campaigned with ninety rounds in their pouches; by 1900 they carried 170, by 1914 more than 200, greatly increasing the effectiveness of land armies. At the battle of Mons in

August 1914, British infantry fired so rapidly – fifteen aimed rounds a minute – that the Germans assumed that they were under attack from machineguns; in fact, it was only the Lee Enfield rifle, cracking away in expert hands (Bloch 1903: xxi).

France's Lebel rifle in 1885 was the first real magazine rifle: one that could be swiftly reloaded from a spring-loaded magazine of eight small-calibre, all-metal, smokeless cartridges. The Lebel spawned knock-offs in every country: the German Mauser (1885), the Austrian Mannlicher (1886), the British Lee Enfield (1899) and the American Springfield (1903) (J. Fuller 1992: 134–5). Armed with magazine rifles, soldiers no longer needed to rummage in their pockets for a cartridge. They needed only to work the bolt of their rifles and lever a fresh round into the breech. The improvement in rate of fire was astounding. In 1870, a French division with Chassepots had been able to fire 40,000 rounds a minute; by 1890, that same division with Lebels was firing 200,000 rounds a minute. With its machineguns, it could do quite a bit more. Clearly, the magazine rifle was a prodigious force multiplier, and it was France's controversial decision to share the multiplier with overseas clients more than any other single factor that accounted for Italy's defeat at Adowa in 1896. Emperor Menelik II (dismissed by Italian King Umberto as 'an African ape') had sensibly purchased 100,000 Lebels and 2,000,000 rounds of ammunition before the battle, which his Ethiopian infantry used to mow down more Italian soldiers in a single day than had died fighting for Italian unification in the years 1859–61 (Vandervort 1998: 158–66; Glover 1980: 200).

Still, Adowa was a lonely exception to a nearly unbroken string of European successes, and such was the pressure for imperial expansion at home that European armies were forced to redeem every setback. Only the collapse of domestic-political support for colonies prevented the Italians from avenging Adowa until the Fascist period (angry opposition deputies shouted 'Viva Menelik!' in the Italian parliament when news of the fiasco reached Rome [Whittam 1977: 136–7]). More efficient imperial powers settled scores instantly. The British expunged their loss to the Zulus at Islandhwana in January 1879 by trouncing them at Ulundi in July. Unlike Menelik's army, the Zulus had not armed themselves with magazine rifles and machineguns; they relied instead on spears and clubs, a poor choice that the British gunners and riflemen fully exploited. A journalist at Ulundi observed that the Royal Artillery's cannon and machineguns 'tore through the Zulus like a harrow through weeds … ravaging their zigzag path through the masses' (Kiernan 1982: 89;Vandervort 1998: 105–12).

And so it usually went (see Map 6.2). When the 50,000 Herero of South West Africa revolted against German rule in 1904, Berlin dispatched 5,000 infantry with thirty guns and twelve machinegun units to drown the rebellion in 'rivers of blood'. The Germans first drove the Herero into the Waterberg – a sandstone cul-de-sac north of Windhoek – and then pulverized them from a great distance with artillery fire. Herero men and women who tried to escape the shrapnel and high explosive barrage were machinegunned or driven into the waterless desert; it was a veritable Sedan, with the difference that French prisoners in 1870 had not been strangled with fencing wire or doused with petrol and burnt alive after the battle (Cocker 1998: 326–34; Vandervort 1998: 196–203). When the French threatened to occupy Sudan in 1898, the British, fearing for Egypt and Suez, hastened to get there first. In one of the most lopsided battles of history, General Horatio Kitchener and 26,000 Anglo-Egyptian troops destroyed a Sudanese army of 50,000 at Omdurman on the Nile. As at Ulundi, the British simply lined up and blazed away at the waves of African infantry, who never even came to grips with their European adversary. The British artillery commenced firing at 3,500 yards; the British infantry, armed for the first time with smokeless magazine rifles, commenced firing at 1,000 yards. The Sudanese, half the men with rifles and the rest with spears and hide shields, panicked and dissolved 450 yards from the British line, no doubt resenting their commander's insistence that the Archangel Gabriel had come to him in the night and ordered that they attack the British 'across an open field'. Omdurman testified as never before to the defensive power of the magazine rifle, and was the first real test of the Maxim machinegun. The British deployed twenty of them, partially accounting for their lavish expenditure of fire: 500,000 bullets and 3,500 shells in the battle. Eleven thousand Sudanese troops were killed, against a trifling British loss of twenty-eight men. The young Winston Churchill, who took part in the battle, characterized it as nothing more than 'a matter of machinery'; the Sudanese dervishes had been beaten by superior technology and training (D. Lewis 1988: 193–202; Dupuy and Dupuy 1997: 928; Black 1998: 186; Vandervort 1998: 166–77).

The Boer War, 1899–1902

Only rampant disease could check the Europeans in Africa and Asia; 71 per cent of Kitchener's casualties in the Omdurman campaign were caused by cholera and typhoid, not enemy action. But as hygiene and 'water discipline' improved, troops learning to filter or boil all drinking water, this last defence of the unindustrialized world began to fall away (Curtin 1998: 194–9). By the turn of the century, only well armed, well disciplined armies stood a chance against the Europeans, and this is what made the Anglo-Boer War of 1899–1902 an object of great interest to European soldiers and pundits. The Boers, or Afrikaners, 'Africa's white tribe', were descended from Dutch dissenters and Huguenot emigrants who had fled Catholic Europe for South Africa in the seventeenth century. The Boers had struggled with Britain since 1815, when the British acquired Cape Town at the Congress of Vienna. As Britain extended its control into Cape Province and neighbouring Natal, effectively severing the Boers from the sea, the Afrikaners made the 'Great Trek', retreating to South Africa's interior provinces of Transvaal and the Orange Free State to found two British-free 'Boer republics'. Peace ensued

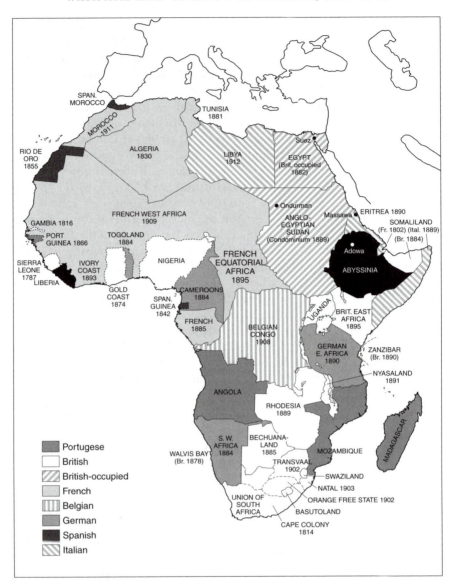

Map 6.2 Imperial expansion in Africa

until the world's deepest crater of diamonds was unearthed at Kimberley in the Orange Free State in 1881. The British, who previously had shown no interest in the arid Boer provinces, promptly demanded a 'border rectification' that would shift Kimberley from the Orange Free State to Cape Province, a British colony. British businessmen, Cecil Rhodes and Alfred Beit in the forefront, arrived to mine the crater and form the spectacularly profitable De Beers Company. The Boers were rudely shouldered aside and compensated with a one-off payment of $400,000, which was less than the Kimberley crater yielded in a day once extraction began in earnest (Twain 1996: 686–7, 699–702). Rhodes – the very embodiment of the 'new imperialism' in that he mixed private and public business – was named Governor of Cape Province, a post that he held in 1886, when the world's biggest gold strike occurred in the other Boer republic, Transvaal. Almost overnight, the little Boer *dorp* of Johannesburg grew into a teeming city of 100,000.

Having secured the riches of the Orange Free State, Rhodes now set to work pulling Transvaal into the British orbit. The stakes were high: gold extraction in Johannesburg's Rand fields rose from $4 million in 1888 to $46 million in 1895. By 1899, the year Britain and the Boers went to war, the Transvaal mines were producing 25 per cent of the world's gold, and Britain was determined to have them (Fieldhouse 1973: 354–8; W. Lewis 1976: 122). 'Stock-jobbing imperialism' was the stock liberal explanation for England's forward policy, but there were profound strategic considerations as well: the Germans had annexed South West Africa (Namibia) in 1884, and had cozied up to the Boer president Paul Kruger in the meantime, dispatching the notorious 'Kruger Telegram' in 1896; the telegram, direct from the German Kaiser, promised the Boers 'friendly assistance' in the event of a war with Britain (I. Smith 1996: 106–8). Fearing that the Germans, who were already enmeshed in Boer mining and railway ventures, might get their hands on the Transvaal first, the British resolved to wrestle Kruger into the British Empire, naively assuming that 'the Boers would turn tail at the first beat of the big drum' (J. Fuller 1992: 139–40; Twain 1996: 671).

Britain's decision to 'beat the big drum' in South Africa reflected an energetic new course in British foreign policy. Joseph Chamberlain, an ardent imperialist, had been Colonial Secretary since 1895. In contrast to many of his predecessors, Chamberlain viewed the Empire, not the British Isles, as the foundation of England's strength. He spoke reverently of 'the greater Britain beyond the seas', and warned repeatedly that England would not 'exist for a single day' if deprived of its prime colonies in America, Africa and Asia. Lamenting that British dependencies had been haphazardly acquired over the centuries as if 'in a fit of absence of mind', Chamberlain insisted on a disciplined reconstruction of the Empire. Colonies would henceforth be selected for their strategic and economic worth, their ability to provide conscripts, naval bases, food and raw materials, and their no less important capacity to absorb British exports and investment capital. South Africa met all of these criteria, and offered the bonus of gold and diamonds, which explained Britain's decision to declare war on the Boers in 1899 (I. Smith 1996: 72–5).

To everyone's surprise, the Boers refused to yield; the British invasion sparked a bloody war that illustrated just how much warfare had evolved in the generation since 1870, and how much more dangerous it had become for combatants and non-combatants alike. On the surface, the Boers ought to have been a pushover. Against the vast armed force of Great Britain and its colonies, the Boers could muster scarcely 1,000 trained soldiers and 40,000 militiamen. But the Boers were quick students. Unlike the British, who were slow to infer the meaning of battles like Omdurman, the Boers immediately grasped the critical lesson of the post-1870 era. Tactical offensives were all but impossible against magazine rifles, machineguns and quick-firing artillery. For this reason, the Boers seldom attacked in the war. If the British wanted to annex the Boer republics, they would have to come and get them, and the Boers would make them pay for every inch of ground in their vast, 430,000 square mile theatre of war.

The price would be high, for the Boers were well armed. Thanks to German aid, the Boers had the latest Krupp cannon, dozens of Maxim machineguns, and 40,000 Mauser rifles. The Mauser was the best rifle that money could buy in the 1890s, as the Spanish had just demonstrated in their war with the United States in 1898. Like Britain's .303 Lee Enfield, the Mauser's magazine held ten smokeless rounds, but whereas the early Lee Enfields had to be loaded with single rounds, Mauser bullets were packaged in clips of five, which permitted the Boers to carry more ammunition and reload more quickly in a hot fight.

The British – hobbled by an inefficient war office and a stingy exchequer that was still trying to cover deficits incurred in Kitchener's long march to Omdurman – moved just 22,000 men to South Africa in 1899 (I. Smith 1996: 337–46). Initially, they fought with Kitchener's Sudan tactics, which derived in large part from Prussian tactics in 1866 and 1870. British companies, dressed in khaki camouflage instead of red tunics, would advance in columns to a point roughly 800 yards from the Boers, then divide into sections. Two sections would sprint forward to 500 yards' range and begin rapid firing to cover the approach of the remaining two sections, which would scramble across the 'fire-zone', using what cover the scrubby veldt provided. This staggered approach was called 'fire and movement' and was intended to suppress Boer defensive fire. Once all sections had closed to within 200 yards of the Boer position, they screwed their bayonets onto their rifles and charged the enemy (Glover 1980: 212–13; McElwee 1974: 213–14). These tactics had worked marvellously against the poorly equipped Sudanese, but they shattered against the Boers, who lay flat or behind cover to avoid the suppressive fire, and pumped astonishingly quick and accurate fire into every British bayonet charge, providing Mark Twain, who toured South Africa during the Boer War, with an irresistible bit of satire: 'The British', Twain wrote, 'stand out in the open to fight Boers who are behind rocks' (Twain 1996: 683–4).

The British army's first days in action against the Boers in December 1899 were disastrous. Advancing to the relief of Kimberley (where the De Beers syndicate anxiously awaited deliverance), a brigade of British Highlanders attempted to drive 8,000 Boer commandos off the rocky ridge at Magersfontein. The Boer Mausers and Maxim guns spewed fire so rapidly that the Highlanders – sensibly deployed in 'skirmish order', with wide intervals between the men – failed to get within 150 yards of their adversary. The Scotsmen reeled back, leaving 948 dead and wounded on the ground (Glover 1980: 216). Four days later, the Boers dealt an even heavier blow. Moving with 21,000 troops to free a large British garrison that had been shut inside the fortress of Ladysmith in Natal, General Redvers Buller attempted to prise 5,000 Boer commandos out of their trenches behind the Tugela river at Colenso. The manoeuvre failed when Buller, like his colleagues at Magersfontein, underestimated the defensive power of the Boer machineguns and the Mauser rifle. A total of 143 British troops were killed and 1,000 more wounded and captured trying to cross the Tugela under withering Boer fire. The Boers lost just six men. No wonder the British called this 'black week'; they had never lost men at this rate in a colonial conflict. The reason was simple: flanking attacks, the most effective reply to defensive firepower, were increasingly difficult in the age of the repeating rifle and the machinegun. The Boers parried every British attempt to turn their flanks, simply by extending their lines. Since one man with a Mauser was equivalent to a six or more with single-shot rifles, a small party of Boers could hold off an entire British brigade for as long as their ammunition held out. At Magersfontein, 5,000 Boers successfully held a frontage of 12,000 yards. The force-to-space ratio was even thinner at Colenso, where 4,500 Boers defended more than eleven miles (20,000 yards) of front. Each British attempt to cut through the Boer lines or sweep around them cracked under the thudding blows of the Mauser rifle and the Maxim machinegun (J. Fuller 1992: 140).

Buller himself was the last casualty of Colenso. He was relieved by Field Marshal Lord Roberts, who arrived in South Africa with Kitchener as his chief of staff, and promptly set about breathing a new spirit into the British army. Roberts sacked eleven generals and a dozen colonels, and adumbrated a British equivalent of Prussian *Auftragstaktik*, writing that 'success in war cannot be expected unless all ranks have been trained in peace to use their wits and … break down the paralysing habit of an unreasonable and mechanical adherence to the letter of orders and to routine' (Glover 1980: 223). The British, in short, were discovering what the Prussians had found in 1866 and 1870: that modern firepower necessitated the division of large units into small ones, and that every soldier needed to be trained to operate individually if armies were to exploit the full potential of precision firearms.

Though sensible and overdue, Roberts' reforms had little impact on the conduct of the war. The Boers grasped the truth of British Colonel C. E. Callwell's maxim that 'tactics favour the regular army while strategy favours the [irregular army]', in this case the Boers, who avoided pitched battles and confined themselves to opportunistic slaughters of isolated or mishandled British formations (Callwell 1996: 85–7). Since the Boers stood no chance against an all-out British effort, they gave ground as the British advanced in powerful columns on the key forts and cities of the interior. Britain cleared and secured the Orange Free State in May 1900, but at the cost of heavy casualties that far exceeded Boer losses at the battles of Spion Kop (2,000 dead and wounded) and Paardeberg (1,300 dead and wounded). With one Boer republic in the bag, the British marched into the other. They took Johannesburg and Pretoria in June, and formally annexed the rest of Transvaal in September. Lord Roberts returned to England, leaving Kitchener in charge of mopping-up operations.

To Kitchener's chagrin, the war dragged on for two more years, until May 1902. Kruger fled into Portuguese Mozambique, and a number of Boer colonels organized a guerrilla war in his absence. Though the struggle seemed futile, the Boer insurgents hoped that the British would tire of defending their long supply lines into Transvaal (750 and 2,000 miles respectively from Durban and Cape Town to Pretoria) and either decamp altogether or make broad economic and political concessions to the Boers. Kitchener, who coordinated the counter-guerrilla operations, was of a different mind altogether. To separate the Boer commandos from the Afrikaner villages that fed and watered them, Kitchener constructed a chain of 8,000 blockhouses extending 3,700 miles across the waist of South Africa. He garrisoned the line with 100,000 troops, who hemmed the Boers in and attacked them with flying columns of British mounted infantry, who successfully adopted the Boer tactics of mobility and surprise. In London, parliament goggled at the mounting cost of the conflict. In 1899, Lord Salisbury's government had predicted that the total cost of the war would not exceed ten million pounds. By 1902, the British had spent twenty-three times that sum (I. Smith 1996: 345–6). To shatter Boer resistance once and for all, Kitchener began systematically to destroy Boer farms, a controversial strategy that the Spanish had just implemented in Cuba, provoking US intervention in the Spanish-American War. Between 1900 and 1902, the British burned thousands of Boer farms and herded their wretched inhabitants into 'concentration camps'. Sixty per cent of the Boer population, 120,000 Afrikaners in all, were 'concentrated' in this way; 28,000 of them perished from cold and illness. This was appalling when one considers that Boer battle deaths in the entire conflict did not exceed 4,000 (Curtin 1998: 215–17). It was a dirty end to a dirty war, one which produced 30,000 British casualties and forced Great Britain to deploy half a million troops to South Africa to beat a Boer army that seldom fielded more than 40,000 men at a time.

Lessons of the Boer War

The Boer War's chief lesson was that machineguns and magazine rifles in skilled hands were terrific force multipliers. Every European army sent observers to South Africa, and they all remarked the difficulty of sending men against fire. The British had nearly always taken the offensive in the war, and had suffered casualties at the rate of ten-to-one. In a European war between great powers, no army could afford casualties on this scale. The well would run dry. How then would armies of the future attack? Jan Bloch, a Polish pacifist who wrote *The Future of War* in 1897, pronounced the tactical offensive all but impossible in the twentieth century. The next great war, Bloch presaged, would be fought from trenches, and crossing the 'fire-zone' between them would be suicidal.

> As for any advance in force, even in the loosest of formations, on a front that is swept by the enemy's fire, that is absolutely out of the question. Flank movements may be attempted, but the increased power which a magazine rifle gives to the defence will render it impossible for such movements to have the success that they formerly had. ... To attack any position successfully, it is estimated that the attacking force ought to outnumber the assailants at least by 8 to 1. It is calculated that 100 men in a trench would be able to put out of action 336 out of the 400 who attacked them, while they were crossing a fire-zone only 300 yards wide.
>
> (Bloch 1903: xxvi–xxvii)

Military men, who would have been put out of their jobs by Bloch's thesis – 'war has become impossible ... it would be national suicide' – were understandably sceptical. General Franz Conrad von Hötzendorf, a leading mind in the Austro-Hungarian army, wrote his own account of the Boer War in 1903 and concluded that war between well armed great powers was in fact still possible if only because 'European conscripts – schoolboys, peasants, mountain folk, workers, artisans, bureaucrats, and shopkeepers – would never shoot as well as the Boers', who were born riders and marksmen. Conrad's other observations were evidence of the overoptimism that continued to prevail in European armies even after the Boer War. The Austrian reasoned that since British casualties at Magersfontein (9 per cent of effectives) and Colenso (5 per cent) were proportionally less than Prussian casualties at Gravelotte (10 per cent) or Russian losses at Plevna (26 per cent), the number of dead and wounded heaped up by the Boer Mausers and Maxims could not have been in and of itself 'decisive' in beating the British, for other armies had endured far worse and won. The British had clearly lost for other reasons: inferior morale, lack of persistence, an undue reliance on 'colonial troops', and so on. Conrad's sigh of relief in *Erscheinungen des Boerenkrieges* is almost audible. War and the infantry attack were still possible; they only had to be undertaken correctly. (Hötzendorf 1903: 6, 14, 58). One wonders how such a keen student of warfare could have been so foolish: the Boers had shredded the British assaults with small numbers of infantry and machinegunners. Larger European armies, even if not sharpshooters like the Boers, would be able to place at least one well armed conscript on every yard of frontage. Simply by laying their rifles across the parapet and blindly firing into 'no man's land' – as the Turks had notoriously done at Plevna – these men would generate carnage on an unprecedented scale, something Conrad himself would witness on the Eastern Front in 1914.

Russia, Japan, and the scramble for China, 1894–1904

Any European army that missed the point of the Boer War had it driven home a second time in the last great war of the 'new imperialist' age: the Russo-Japanese or Manchurian War of 1904–5. Russia's war with Japan was an appropriate climax to an age of imperialism that had begun with Russia's attempt to flood southward into the Balkans and the Middle East, and ended with Russia's shift to 'Eastern strategy', which made expansion into Siberia, Manchuria and Korea key to the survival and standing of Imperial Russia. Though imperial confrontations did not end in 1905 (Germany's bid for Morocco in 1911 nearly triggered a world war), the Manchurian War was the only imperial clash between great powers that escalated to a shooting war in the period 1870–1914. As such, it was the capstone to an age, and a clear pointer to the shape, scale and deadliness of modern warfare.

Prevented from annexing the Balkans in 1878 by what Tsar Alexander II had angrily called 'a European coalition against Russia under the leadership of Prince Bismarck', the Romanov tsars revised their strategy for growth and survival in the 1890s. Nicholas II, Russia's last tsar, who ruled from 1894 to 1917, viewed Manchuria and Korea as Russia's new frontier, Siberia and Mongolia its jumping-off posts. Nicholas was the first Romanov to travel to the Far East. Prodded by his most influential minister, Sergei Witte, he decided that Russia's cultural and economic destiny lay there. With no hope of dominating the rich industrialized powers of the West, Russia would bully the Chinese into accepting Russian mastery (Marks 1991: 4, 138). Witte was a persuasive advocate of this course. He further argued that the only way for Russia to break its industrial and financial dependency on the West European states was to secure its 'economic independence' by colonizing Northeast Asia, just as Britain had based itself on the teeming market of India, and France on Africa. Witte insisted that a Trans-Siberian railway connecting Moscow and Russia's grandly named port on the Pacific, Vladivostock ('Ruler of the East') would accomplish this, by channelling China's trade with Europe through Moscow, and forcing European manufacturers to invest in Russia to be nearer the Chinese market (Marks 1991: 124–6). Witte's scheme had social and political underpinnings: European investments in Russia would create manufacturing jobs, which would alleviate misery and weaken the appeal of communists like Trotsky and Lenin.

To Witte's political rationale the tsar added a racial one. Like the Germans, who pushed into China in the 1890s partly to curb what Kaiser Wilhelm II called 'the yellow peril', Nicholas II feared the burgeoning population of China, which he called an 'inflowing wave' that would one day swamp Holy Russia. 'Eastern strategy' would permit the Romanovs to resettle millions of Slavs in Russia's Far East, where they would bar the Asian approaches to Russia and improve the empire's population density, which Witte and the tsar considered too thick in Europe and too thin in Asia (W. Fuller 1992: 369; Marks 1991: 154–5).

The military-strategic rationale for Russian eastward expansion was this: the British had been carving out trading enclaves and coaling stations on the China coast since the 1840s. By the 1890s, Britain controlled Hong Kong, Canton, Shanghai and much of the Yangtze river valley. Japan joined the scramble for 'concessions' (colonies in all but name) in 1894 by declaring war on the Chinese Empire and seizing Taiwan, the Pescadores, and the right to 'protect' Korea. This in turn persuaded the Germans to seize Kiaochow and the Shantung Peninsula in 1897, which induced the French to lay claim to the southern tracts of Yunnan and Kwangchow near the Vietnamese border, and the Italians Kwangpo near Shanghai. In 1899 the Americans weighed in, demanding that the concession-hunting stop and China be maintained as a sovereign state and a commercial 'Open Door' (Nish 1985: 55–60). Nicholas II, always slow off the blocks, looked on in disbelief. Having invested millions in 'Eastern strategy' (the Trans-Siberian had been completed all the way to Irkutsk by 1898), the tsar was in danger of losing all influence in East Asia. Neither partition nor an Open Door policy suited the tsar's *Vostochniki* ('Easterners'), who sought a continuous Russian land frontier from Kamchatka in the north to Korea in the south (LeDonne 1997: 212–13). One of Nicholas' advisors warned that Vladivostock, the pivot of Russia's intended move east, would shortly be 'threatened with the fate of Sebastopol'. The reference was to the Crimean War, when the British and French had besieged Russia's southern naval station and closed the Black Sea to Russian warships for fifteen years. This time the main threat emanated from the Japanese Empire, which straddled the northern and southern approaches to Vladivostock, cast its shadow over Port Arthur, and threatened to make these Russian terminals on the Pacific 'dead ends'.

Nicholas II – who had a personal financial stake in 'Eastern strategy': 3,200 square miles of prime logging country on the Yalu – concluded that only a quick push into Manchuria and Korea would secure Russian primacy there (W. Fuller 1992: 372–3; LeDonne 1997: 208). To force a break with China, he took an increasingly hard line with the Ch'ings in the 1890s. When Emperor K'ang Yuwei ceded Kiaochow to the Germans in 1897, Nicholas II demanded and got a lease on Port Arthur and the Liaotung Peninsula, the very places the European powers had snatched back from Japan after the Treaty of Shimonoseki. The Chinese emperor's concessions provoked a palace coup in 1898 and the so-called Boxer Rebellion in 1900, when furious Chinese nationalists ('Boxers') attacked the European embassies in Peking. Russia used the pretext of the bloody riots to march 200,000 troops into Manchuria, another violation of Chinese sovereignty. By year's end, Russian troops patrolled Harbin and Mukden; it was a virtual annexation of a province – rich in wheat, coal, and iron – that Japan, to say nothing of China, urgently required for its own development (Nish 1985:89–91; LeDonne 1997:208–15).

Japan threatened war to remove the Russians from Manchuria and North Korea, and Nicholas II happily consented, for all of the reasons cited above, and another. By 1904, Russia seethed with revolutionary activity. Reactionary attempts to popularize the autocratic regime – like the Kishinev Pogrom of 1903, when Russian villagers and Cossacks had been unleashed against the Jews of Bessarabia with ghastly results – had failed to rally the peasants against the revolutionary 'intelligentsia' (Lieven 1993: 132–4). The tsar's government had simply run out of ideas, and was not tempering its autocracy with any degree of efficiency. Russians of all classes wanted reform, and Nicholas II's interior minister, Viacheslav von Plehve, cynically counselled the tsar to trump up 'a victorious little war to stem the revolution' (Figes 1996: 168; Verner 1992: 104–5). Once more, war was manufactured to burn away political and social tensions in a flash of patriotic fervour. It seems never to have occurred to Plehve – who was blown to bits by an assassin's bomb in July 1904 – that war might have the opposite effect in Russia. It might foment revolution rather than deflect it.

The emergence of Japan, 1894–1905

Like most Europeans, the Russians underestimated the Japanese, who had gone through a wrenching political and cultural transformation in the last decades of the nineteenth century. Until 1868, 'Japan' had referred to a feudal patchwork of 250 castle-towns loosely ruled from Tokyo by the Tokugawa shoguns ('great barbarian-suppressing generals'). The shoguns, who had overthrown Japan's Yamato emperors in the thirteenth century, rejected Western influence as 'polluting' and introduced a strict 'seclusion policy' that forbade contact between Japanese and foreigners. Only when powerful American and European fleets – 'black ships of evil mien' – forced open several Japanese ports in the 1850s did Japan's feudal families, the *daimyo*, awaken to the need for modernization. Remarking the size of the Americans and the Europeans and the quality of their technology, the *daimyo* ousted Tokugawa in 1868 and restored the Yamatos. Emperor Meiji, a teenage boy, moved his court from backward-looking Kyoto to modern Tokyo and began a comprehensive prog-ramme of westernization: 'What we must do', the emperor's chief minister wrote, 'is transform our empire and our people, make the empire like the countries of Europe and our peoples like the peoples of Europe'. This in a nutshell was the 'Meiji Restoration'.

Meiji particularly admired the Germans and the English. Japan's reform programme after 1868 was called *fukoku kyohei*: 'a rich country with strong armed forces' (Storry 1979: 14–15). After the French defeat in 1870–1, the Japanese dismissed their French military advisors and replaced them with German ones. Universal conscription was introduced in 1872; a Prussian-style general staff (with total fiscal and political freedom) in 1878 (Ralston 1990: 166–70; J. Thomas 1996: 108–9). In 1885 Major Jakob Meckel, a German general staff officer, arrived to put finishing touches to the Japanese army. Meckel applied the Prussian Kriegsakademie curriculum to the Japanese staff college, rebuilt the field army around German-style permanent corps, and knitted the new units into a rapid mobilization network by urging the construction of single- and double-tracked railways to connect them. While Meckel worked on Meiji's army, a British naval mission took his navy in hand. Thirty-four British officers arrived in Japan in 1873 to teach seamanship and gunnery; they founded a naval war college in 1887 that introduced British and American naval thought, chiefly the Mahanian notion that an island nation has no choice but to command the sea, lest it be isolated and strangled by better armed rivals (Evans and Peattie 1997: 12–13). Overall, the Japanese military melded Anglo-Saxon efficiency with a uniquely Japanese fanaticism, taking as its symbol the cherry blossom, which blossomed briefly in the spring of life and fell while its flower was still perfect (Harries and Harries 1994: 25).

Despite these strides, Japan remained a small, resource-poor island nation. Though Meiji successfully annexed the Kuriles (1875) and Okinawa (1879), this was not enough. With its growing industry and population, Japan wanted an imperial hinterland to grow food and absorb surplus population and production. Here a comparison with social Darwinist, neo-mercantilist European imperialism was almost exact. Japan's version was distinguished only by an especially virulent presumption of racial superiority; a nation that classified millions of its own citizens as 'filthy people' and 'non-persons' could not be expected to treat conquered populations any better (Thomas 1996: 73–5; Iriye 1997: 4–5). Like European imperialism, Japan's overseas expansion was driven as much by industry and pressure groups as by official policy. Early backing for Japan's war with China in 1894 was secured by the 'Turn to the Sun Society', a nationalist lobby that mixed soldiers, politicians and businessmen eager to wrest Korea from its Chinese vassalage and establish the peninsula – rich in coal, ores and lumber – as a Japanese vassal instead. The Japanese declared war in June 1894, and quickly demonstrated that they had absorbed the European art of warfare. On the ground, the Japanese army moved well and used their Krupp guns and Mauser rifles to inflict punishing casualties on the Chinese. European observers were fascinated by the war, for both sides were busy 'Westernizing' their forces. The core of the Chinese army in 1894 – thirteen battalions at Nanking that never made it to the front owing to gross inefficiency – was built on the German model and commanded by German officers and NCOs on loan from Berlin (Ralston 1990: 126–9).

On the sea, the Japanese navy swept to victory as decisively as the army, destroying China's principal fleet at the battle of the Yalu river in September 1894. The battle was a classic mismatch of colonial warfare. The Japanese fleet of eight British-built cruisers was up to date in its weapons and doctrine; the Chinese fleet backward and corrupt. Most of the Chinese ships were twenty year-old German models, poorly gunned and manned. As in the Chinese land army, where generals routinely dismissed troops in order to pocket their wages, corruption flourished in the Chinese navy. It was credibly rumoured that at least one Chinese captain engaged on the Yalu had pawned one of his 12-inch guns to settle a gambling debt. The battle of the Yalu River witnessed an important development in naval tactics; whereas the Chinese fleet rucked up around their two battleships like the Austrians at Lissa – line abreast, wedge formation – the Japanese did what the Italians ought to have done at Lissa; they formed into line ahead and raked the concentrated Chinese fleet with their 6-inch guns. The sight of five Chinese cruisers settling beneath the waves gave lingering proponents of the ram pause; every bows-on Chinese ram stroke had failed, either missing altogether or blown back by the Japanese quick-firers. What damage the Chinese did manage to inflict on the Japanese was with their broadside guns (Evans and Peattie 1997: 38–51; Glover 1980: 181–5). With its navy crippled and its army beaten in Manchuria, China agreed to Japan's terms at the Treaty of Shimonoseki in April 1895. China paid a $150 million indemnity, gave Korea its 'independence' (really Japanese domination), and ceded Taiwan and the Pescadores to Japan. Taiwan was an important acquisition because it positioned Japan to control mainland China's populous Fukien province in the British imperial style (Iriye 1997: 16–18). China also agreed to give the Japanese Port Arthur, the Liaotung Peninsula, and rights to develop a Manchurian railway. Though the European powers combined to deny the Japanese these last concessions – Russia committing the unforgivable sin of appropriating them for itself – the war nevertheless paid a political dividend inside Japan, stirring popular support for the imperial army and its expansionist mission.

> Cheap colored prints stimulated the war fever and embellished the glory of victory. Japanese illustrated books, stretching concertina fashion for seven or eight feet, showed Japan forever winning over her enemy. Every Japanese soldier, sailor, or statesman appeared to be six feet tall, always smartly dressed, while the Chinese, with their queues, were depicted as squat and ugly, and attired in traditional silk robes. In these books, no Japanese soldier ever fell in action, no sailor perished on the seas. Japanese warriors pushed screaming Chinese

over high cliffs and watched as they jumped from the rigging of the ships. The waters were red with Chinese blood, the battlefields piled with Chinese dead. For page after page the Japanese were handsome, tall, and European-looking, whether lopping off Chinese heads, fighting underwater with the aid of flashlights, or on horseback in the snows of Manchuria. ... Hero emulation in the name of the Emperor stirred the [Japanese] people as never before.

(Warner and Warner 1974: 57)

Pushed by public enthusiasm and the acquisitive *zaibatsu* (well connected financial-industrial conglomerates like Mitsui, Mitsubishi and Sumitomo), the line between Japan's official policy and privately funded pressure groups began to blur. In 1901, two of Japan's ranking soldiers backed by Mitsui founded the *Kokuryukai* or 'Black Dragon Society'. Furious with the Russians for stealing the fruits of Japan's victory after 1895, Black Dragon lobbied Emperor Meiji to declare war on Russia, the chief barrier to Japan's imperial ambitions in Asia. The emperor came round; between 1894 and 1900 he increased Japan's military and naval budgets sevenfold, from $16 million in 1894 to $115 million in 1900 (Glover 1980: 184–5). Thanks to Tsar Nicholas II's tactlessness, Japan was even able to pose as the underdog in the contest. Willing to accept Russian domination of Manchuria, the Japanese asked only for a free hand in Korea (Nish 1985: 158–9). Nicholas II, who scorned the 'monkeys' in Tokyo, rejected the deal out of hand. War came in February 1904, when Japanese torpedo boats slipped into the Russian naval station at Port Arthur and launched a sneak attack on the squadron there, crippling three unguarded Russian battleships at a stroke.

The Russo-Japanese War

Japan broke the rules of war because it needed a quick victory to win. At full strength, the Japanese army mustered no more than 700,000 men: 300,000 active duty regulars and 400,000 trained reservists. The 160-ship Japanese navy included just six battleships and eight armoured cruisers. The Russians were quite a bit stronger; their field army counted 4.5 million men, their navy 250 ships, including seventeen modern battleships and ten armoured cruisers (Evans and Peattie 1997: 90–1). Indeed, Japan risked war with the Russian colossus only because it knew that Russia – always menaced by the Germans in Poland, the Austro-Hungarians in the Balkans and communist revolutionaries inside Russia – could never afford to detach more than a fraction of its armed strength to the Far East. Japan's hopes for victory therefore turned on the size of that fraction. Would the Russians send 500,000 men, or a million? Would they reinforce their Pacific fleet with squadrons from the Baltic and the Black Sea, or would they try to beat the Japanese on the cheap?

Regardless of what the Russians decided to do, they would need months

Russians would need months

to reinforce their Manchurian outposts along the 5,500 mile, single-track Trans-Siberian Railway from Moscow to Port Arthur, and as much as a year to drive ships around the Cape of Good Hope to the relief of the embattled squadrons at Port Arthur and Vladivostock. In 1904, only two of Russia's twenty-nine army corps were garrisoned in the Far East (Lieven 1993: 144–5). Japan knew this and planned to strike quickly into Korea and Manchuria with the entire Japanese army and navy, take Port Arthur (thus depriving the Russians of their only ice-free port on the Pacific), destroy Russia's Pacific fleet (seven battleships, nine armoured cruisers and twenty-five destroyers) and then wheel the entire Japanese army into Manchuria to defeat Russia's 100,000 garrison troops there before they could be reinforced from Europe. In their quest for a quick, decisive victory, Japanese strategists counted on political and social problems inside Russia. Diplomats at Japan's embassy and consulates in Russia made secret payments to communist subversives, and correctly predicted that Russian defeats in the Far East would trigger a revolution in St Petersburg, forcing Nicholas II to pull out of Manchuria to defend his throne.

If Japan's best hope was to force the Russians to give battle before the arrival of their supports, Russia's best strategy was to cling to Port Arthur with 40,000 men and pull the rest of the Eastern Army (60,000 men) back to Mukden, where they could await reinforcements from the Trans-Siberian Railway, which could deliver 40,000 men a month to the Manchurian theatre. (Such an approach was all the more advisable in view of the tsar's habit of garrisoning the Far East with the dregs of the Russian army, penal battalions and Cossack hell-raisers, who would be no help in a serious conflict.) After some initial blundering, the Russians wisely slowed the pace of the war. Recognizing that their critical advantage of time was slipping away, the Japanese hastened to capture Port Arthur and push into the Manchurian interior, where General Alexei Kuropatkin was massing the Russian army at Liaoyang (see Map 6.3).

Haste made waste, for the Russian fortifications at Port Arthur had been cleverly sited to maximize the defensive advantage of modern firepower. They consisted of three interlocked, mutually supporting positions: a chain of fortified hills, a ring of concrete forts, and deep trenches around the town itself. Between August and November 1904, the Japanese launched six major assaults on Port Arthur. The results were shocking, even for foreign observers who had been well briefed on the destructive potential of machineguns and magazine rifles. What particularly impressed them was the furious impact of new weapons: the recoilless, quick-firing field gun, the heavy howitzer, and chemically enhanced, high-explosive shells.

Developed by the British, Germans and the French in the 1890s, the first recoilless guns were little different in outward appearance from the German Krupps of 1870; however, a closer look revealed that the gun was mounted on a spring or hydraulic-controlled slide, which absorbed the recoil of the

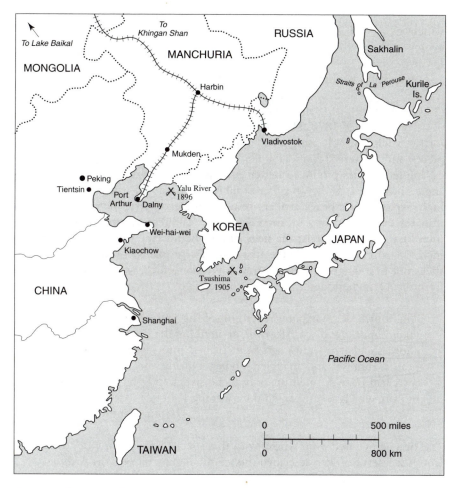

Map 6.3 The Russo-Japanese War, 1904–5

cannon without disturbing the placement of the gun carriage beneath it (D. Harding 1980: 180–3). Artillerymen in the Franco-Prussian War had rarely managed more than three or four rounds per minute, for the lurching gun, which blew backward each time it fired, needed to be run back into place and reaimed after every shot. With recoilless pieces, which slid or sprang back to their original firing position when detonated, gunners could fire 15–30 rounds of explosive shell or shrapnel a minute, their rate of fire further improved by an automatic breech-loading mechanism that ejected the spent shell casing during recoil, leaving the breech open for the rapid insertion of a fresh round (Weller 1966: 81–2). The replacement of charcoal gunpowder with smokeless propellants gave more thrust with less pressure on the gun, and also enabled artillerymen to fire without disclosing their position. Unobstructed by palls of smoke, they could visually register the impact of every round, which made for astonishing accuracy. Enemy artillery foolish enough to deploy in the open could be instantly smashed, and attacking infantry crushed to the ground.

High-explosive shells were another invention of Europe's advancing chemical industry. Filled with newfound bursting charges like 'trinitrotoluene' (TNT), shells of the 1890s inflicted damage out of all proportion to the black powder rounds of 1870. High explosive not only gave more blast (shivering fortress walls and collapsing trenches), it fragmented shell casings into smaller pieces and scattered them at bullet speed across a wide radius. New steel casting techniques produced better guns as well, flat-firing cannon and high-angle howitzers of ever-larger calibre. This combination of chemical high-explosive and heavy artillery resulted in a geometric increase in destruction, for every 100 per cent increase in gun calibre permitted a 700 per cent increase in shell weight. At the siege of Port Arthur, the Japanese deployed 11-inch (28-cm) howitzers for the first time. These giants could lob 550-pound shells out to a range of 10,000 yards. A Russian officer, who endured shelling from the 11-inchers, described the experience:

> The fourth day was but a repetition of the preceding three. Shells … rained upon the place. All cover, or anything that looked as if it might afford shelter, had long ago been turned into heaps of stones, iron, beams, rubbish, and mangled bodies. During the night, shelters of sorts had been scraped up, only to be swept away by the first breath of iron, which accompanied the morning light.
>
> (Connaughton 1988: 200)

The enemy fared even worse; with that special lyricism unique to Japanese troops, a reserve officer described the scrambling assault on Port Arthur:

> The firing … became more and more quick and violent, so that birds could not have found space to fly, or animals places for hiding. Thousands and thousands of shot and shell crossed in the air and made a dull sound in the heavy-laden atmosphere; the whole heaven and earth seemed the scene of the frantic rage of demons, and we could not prophesy when this scene would come to an end. The enemy's artillery fire was very strong; their *time* shells would fly to us in bundles, explode over our heads, and kill and wound our men mercilessly … their spherical shells would hurl up earth and sand before and behind our skirmish line, raising a thick black and white smoke at the spot.
>
> (Sakurai 1907: 96–7)

Under ceaseless shelling like this – shrapnel against troops in the open, high explosive against entrenched positions – the Russians lost 31,000 men at Port Arthur, the Japanese 60,000. The casualties on the Russian side – surprisingly high for a concealed defender – were owed to Japanese experiments with 'indirect fire', a tactic that would become routine in World War I. With a forward-deployed observer, a compass and a range-finder, artillery officers could lob shells into enemy trenches or battery positions without actually seeing them, greatly leveraging the effectiveness of field and fortress artillery. Though the nearly 100,000 men lost at Port Arthur would be regarded as routine carnage in World War I, casualties on this scale were shocking in 1904. General Ian Hamilton, a British observer, recorded what he saw on Hill 203, where Japanese generals spent 12,000 men in the course of their fifth assault in November. Though Hamilton did not know it at the time, he was describing the trench warfare that would consume millions of men between 1914 and 1918:

> First the hill had been sliced into numberless deep gashes, and then these trenches and their dividing walls had been smashed and pounded and crushed into a shapeless jumble of stones; rock splinters and fragments of shells cemented liberally with human flesh and blood. A man's head sticking up out of the earth, or a leg or an arm or a piece of a man's body lying across my path are sights which custom has enabled me to face without blanching. But here the corpses do not so much appear to be escaping from the ground as to be the ground itself. Everywhere there are bodies, or portions of bodies, flattened out and stamped into the surface of the earth as if they formed part of it, and several times in the ascent I was on the point of putting my foot on what seemed to be dust when I recognized by the indistinct outline that it was a human form stretched and twisted and rent to gigantic size by the force of some frightful explosion.
>
> (Connaughton 1988: 201)

The forts of Port Arthur and the ships in the harbour surrendered in January 1905 after a heroic resistance. Strategically, Russia felt the loss keenly. After much dithering, Nicholas II had finally dispatched his Baltic Fleet to the Far East in October. By January it was at Madagascar, and there learned that its final destination was in Japanese hands. The fleet, already exhausted by the first half of its epic 21,000-mile voyage, would now have to make for Vladivostock, a longer trip that would flatten Russian morale, and make opportunities for the fresh, well supplied Japanese navy. Tactically, the siege of Port Arthur seemed to confirm Jan Bloch's dire predictions in *The Future of War*. The battle was World War I in miniature, with helpless infantry platoons clawing their way across shrapnel and machinegun-swept 'fire zones', falling into barbed wire and shell craters, and rarely even coming to grips with their entrenched adversaries. Fire was so thick that Japanese casualties were often written off by surgeons thus: 'whole body honeycombed with gun-wounds'. Small wonder, by 1904 a modern brigade of 3,000 men with artillery was able to spew more shell and rifle fire in a single minute than had Wellington's entire army of 60,000 in the day-long battle of Waterloo in 1815. The impact on the battlefield was dreadful to behold: a Japanese infantryman at Port Arthur was discovered with forty-seven machinegun and rifle rounds in his body, twenty-five in the right arm alone (Sakurai 1907: 152–3). Whereas the worst-hit Prussian units at Gravelotte in 1870 suffered 68 per cent casualties, their Japanese equivalents on Hill 203 lost more than 90 per cent of effectives. Prescient German officers wondered if infantry had not been reduced to the task of offering targets for the artillery and machineguns (Herwig 1997: 48–9, 59–60; Snyder 1984: 79). Bloch had foretold this in 1897, when he tallied the shell stocks of the European powers in peacetime and deemed them sufficient to kill eleven million men (Bloch 1903: 19–20).

After the fall of Port Arthur, the Japanese united all of their disposable troops – 315,000 men with 1,000 guns – and marched off in search of Kuropatkin, who had used the respite afforded by Port Arthur's resistance to pull in reinforcements from the Trans-Siberian Railway and deploy 330,000 men with 1,200 guns in a line of trenches bordering the Manchurian town of Mukden. The battle that followed, from 21 February to 10 March 1905, gave heart to European soldiers depressed by what they had observed at Port Arthur. Japan's Field Marshal Iwao Oyama sought nothing less than a 'second Sedan' at Mukden: a war-ending envelopment of Kuropatkin's army. Since Oyama had fewer men than Kuropatkin, his plan seemed farfetched, yet he nearly pulled it off, in a seductive way which suggested that good soldiering and the latest trench-busting heavy artillery might overcome even the thickest defensive fire.

Although the battle of Mukden dragged on for three weeks, very much in the style of World War I, it was not exactly a stalemate. Rather it was a laborious, blood-soaked manoeuvre, Sedan without the German advantages of terrain and numbers. Oyama threw his wings out as far as was prudent, and tried repeatedly to outflank Kuropatkin's trench line. All the while, Japanese howitzers flattened the Russian trenches with high-explosive shell. After three weeks of this, Kuropatkin's infantry had been reduced to gibbering, nervous wrecks. They called the 11-inch shells brought from Port Arthur 'suitcases', and heard the screaming descent of each one with helpless dread. When Oyama finally turned around the Russian flank, he found the bulk of the Russian army in full retreat, utterly demoralized by the pounding of the Japanese howitzers (Warner and Warner 1974: 504–5; Connaughton 1988: 230–1; Menning 1992: 186–96). In sum, Mukden reassured European soldiers who wanted to believe that the principles and tactics of 1870 were still valid. A closer look revealed the opposite. Mukden was no Sedan, for the Japanese had paid as dearly as the Russians – 53,000 casualties versus 60,000 – and could not replace these men. Indeed, the battle was arguably a Russian win, for Kuropatkin inflicted proportionately heavier losses on the Japanese and then pulled his army away to safety, effectively stalemating the war. Even in victory (such as it was), Oyama had no more cards to play. He could not digest the territorial gains of 1904–5 *and* pursue the Russian army into the vastness of Manchuria. Bloch's prophesy that in future war there 'would be no more victories of genius or military initiative, only of sums' seemed more plausible once the big guns of Mukden had fallen silent and the last Russian troop column had vanished over the horizon, leaving the Japanese army master of nothing more permanent than a pile of corpses (Bloch 1903: 50).

The naval battle of Tsushima, May 1905

Matters worked out differently on the Sea of Japan. There, at Tsushima, the Japanese navy won one of the most decisive naval battles of all time, cementing a victory that had stubbornly eluded them on land. After a gruelling voyage of eight months from its home ports at Libau and Revel, Admiral Zinovy Rozhdestvensky's Baltic Fleet of twelve battleships, nine cruisers and nine destroyers tried to bull its way through the narrow Strait of Tsushima separating Japan and the southern tip of Korea. Rozhdestvensky, bound for Vladivostock, was intercepted by Japan's Admiral Heihachiro Togo, who attacked the Russians on 27 May 1905 with the entire Japanese navy: ten battleships, eighteen cruisers, twenty-one destroyers and sixty torpedo-boats. The short, sharp battle that followed illustrated the great strides taken in ship and gun design since the last great blue water engagement at Lissa in 1866.

By 1905, the bow rams that Austria's Admiral Tegetthoff had used to defeat the Italians in 1866 were relics of the past, for ships had become faster and nimbler, and naval guns had vastly increased their power, range and accuracy. The battleship of 1866, with its relatively feeble broadside guns locked into casemates, had been replaced by the turreted battleship of the 1880s, which could rotate its guns to hit targets on a broad sweep and concentrate fire on a single point. Armour and ammunition had also improved. In the 1880s and 1890s, light steel alloys replaced the heavy iron plates that had threatened to sink warships beneath their inefficient weight as thicknesses were increased to deflect time-fused, armour-piercing ordnance. A battleship that had needed twenty-four inches of wrought iron cladding in 1885 could make do with just six inches of nickel steel in 1896 (Glover 1980: 170–8). This made ships faster and more manoeuvrable. The addition of 12-inch and 8-inch armour-piercing guns doomed the ram forever. Though slow to load (one round every two or three minutes), the 12-inchers could hurl high-explosive shells fitted with armour-piercing chrome caps out to a distance of 7,600 yards. A secondary armament of 8-inch quick-firers could blanket the middle distance with defensive fire. Probably even the Italians of 1866 would have hit their targets with the guns of the 1890s.

Whereas the indecisive naval actions around Port Arthur in 1904 had suggested that big battleships and cruisers could be stymied by cheap, abundant mines and torpedoes, Tsushima restored a sense of purpose to the capital ship. Togo used his armoured cruisers to herd Rozhdestvensky's fleet toward his waiting battleships, which turned majestically across the front of the Baltic Fleet and opened fire with their 12-inchers as the Russians nosed into range at a distance of three and a half nautical miles (7,000 yards). This was Nelson's classic manoeuvre, the 'crossing of the T', and it enabled Togo to concentrate the fire of every ship he had on the Russian lead ships and then work backward through the formation, sinking Rozhdestvensky's warships one by one under tons of high-explosive shell. Russian gunnery was appalling, Japan's formidable. Only three Russian ships made it through the strait to Vladivostock; all of Rozhdestvensky's battleships were sunk, most of his cruisers destroyed, captured or interned in neutral ports. Five thousand Russian seamen were killed and 6,000 more captured. It was a spectacular outcome, and as a consequence it decisively influenced battleship design. Togo had copied British tactics in the battle, alternating salvos from his 12- and 8-inch guns to maintain an uninterrupted fire. Yet Japanese officers (and their British mentors) observed that it was impossible to distinguish the shell splashes of guns of different calibre at extreme ranges, which was the only way to correct fire. Here was the empirical seed of the 'dreadnought revolution' launched in 1906 by the British: the all-big-gun battleship concept. Tsushima gave credence to it. A uniform armament of a single calibre would reduce confusion in battle and devastate the enemy well before he could close to what was called 'decisive range'. That had been the fate of the Russians. Held at arm's length by the thundering Japanese guns, the Russians crews had been rendered harmless, inflicting fewer than 450 casualties on the Japanese in the course of the battle (Evans and Peattie 1997: 116–29).

War and society intersect: the Russian Revolution of 1905

News of Tsushima sparked a revolution in Russia that flared through the cities and into the peasant villages. The Russo-Japanese War revealed Nicholas II to be even more incompetent than most Russians had supposed, and evidence of corruption – the tsar had arguably fought the war to defend personal invest-ments in Korea and Manchuria, his interior minister to 'stem the revolution' – was furiously resented by the Russian people, who lost 400,000 killed and wounded and three billion roubles in the war (W. Fuller 1992: 406). Many Russians rejoiced at the assassination of Plehve in July 1904 and joined demonstrations against the tsar. In the course of 1905, even as war raged in Manchuria, Russian troops had to be called out on 8,000 occasions to suppress riots in the cities, towns and villages of Russia. One such incident was 'Bloody Sunday' in January 1905, when Nicholas's palace guard fired into a crowd of striking industrial workers, killing and wounding hundreds. Leon Trotsky's 'soviets' ('workers councils') rose in protest and were savagely put down. This all-too-visible erosion of imperial authority in the cities encouraged peasants to seize the big rural estates, often murdering their masters, pulping the title deeds, and burning the manor houses in the process (Lieven 1993: 139–41, 149; Verner 1992: 150–4). Increasingly reliant on his army, Nicholas II found it not entirely reliable. An unintended consequence of the 'Prussianization' of the Russian army after 1870 – the adoption of universal conscription – was that the enlisted ranks, once filled with docile peasants, now contained substantial numbers of urban revolutionaries. Even among the peasant troops, discontent reigned; nine tenths of the soldiers engaged in the Far East had no idea what they were fighting for (Lieven 1983: 113; Wellesley 1904: 12–14; Sakurai 1907: 73). Under the strain of a losing war, many units mutinied, as did the Black Sea fleet (famously incited by the battleship *Potemkin*) on 14 June 1905, compelling Nicholas II to make peace with Japan, concede a constitution to his people, and sanction a parliament (the Duma) for the first time.

For Russian communists like Vladimir Lenin and Leon Trotsky, the revolution of 1905 was instructive. In the first place, the Russo-Japanese War suggested that the wars of the future would not be short 'wars of annihilation' like those of 1866 and 1870. On the contrary, with so many men and so much firepower arrayed on either side, future wars between great powers would probably be long struggles of attrition that would exact far higher social and economic costs than this one had done. And if Russia's limited war with Japan had forced Nicholas II to concede a parliament, what might an unlimited, 'world war' against Germany and Austria-Hungary achieve? The shocks of a great war might destroy Imperial Russia and create the right conditions for a communist coup. With a clear grasp of the close connection between war and politics in an increasingly turbulent and democratic age, Lenin assured Maxim Gorky in 1913 that 'a war between Russia and Austria would be a very useful thing for the revolution'. If only, he implored, 'Franz Joseph and Nicky will give us such a treat' (Figes 1996: 249). Lenin, for whom the death of millions meant little where communism was at stake, had not long to wait.

CHAPTER SEVEN

Sea power and popular navalism, 1890–1914

In 1890, Captain Alfred Thayer Mahan, an unremarkable American naval officer on the verge of retirement, published one of the most sensational books of the modern period: *The Influence of Sea Power upon History*. The book transformed Mahan, earning him a transfer from the US Navy's China station to its new war college at Newport, Rhode Island, and establishing him internationally as the leading mind in naval strategy. Mahan's great contribution was this: he analysed control of the sea in *historical* terms – coining the term 'sea power' – and described the process by which little England had carpentered together the world's biggest empire and reserved the strategic keypoints of the globe for the Royal Navy.

Mahan argued that British sea power was principally owed to England's geographical position astride important sea lanes, and its tough and venture-some 'national character'. These happy coincidences facilitated the phenomenal expansion of the British Empire in the modern period. Beginning in 1704 with the conquest of Gibraltar, a rocky bastion on the southern tip of Spain that controlled access to the Mediterranean and physically sliced Britain's arch-foe, the French navy, into two unconnected halves at Brest and Toulon, the British navy had embarked on a patient but dogged campaign to seize choke points around the world: key islands, enclaves and peninsulas like Ceylon, Florida, Mauritius and Minorca. Though Britain could not cling to them all – Minorca was subsequently lost, as was Florida – Mahan stressed that Britain never failed to cover its losses, acquiring Hong Kong, Singapore, Cape Town, Aden, Malta and Suez in the course of the nineteenth century (Mahan 1987: 326–9). By the 1890s, Britain, with its ubiquitous naval bases, refitting yards and coal dumps, most of them linked to London by submarine telegraphs, enjoyed near-absolute control of the world's seaways, and an almost unassailable 'interior position' against newcomers (Map 7.1).

A reader taking up *The Influence of Sea Power* in 1890 would have been struck by Mahan's logic, and depressed to realize that the gulf between Britain and the other powers had only widened with the technological shift from sail to steam power in the 1860s, for Britain, already in possession of the world's cleanest-burning coal, now possessed the best coaling stations as well. At the

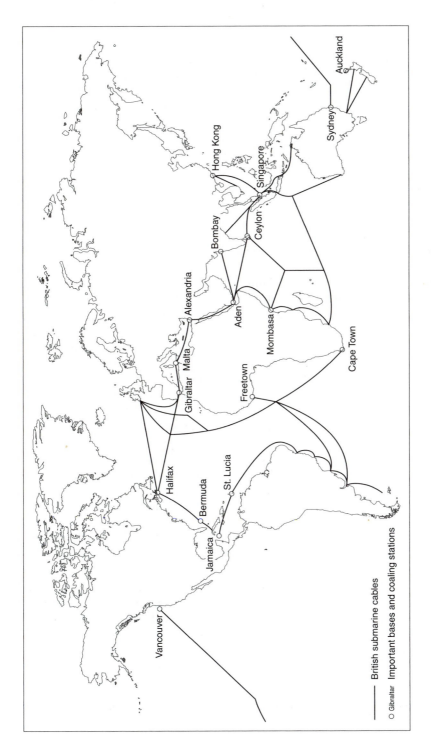

Map 7.1 Naval bases of the British Empire in 1890

British submarine cables

○ Gibraltar   Important bases and coaling stations

end of the nineteenth century, only the British navy enjoyed the luxury of cruising virtually anywhere in the world without fuel constraints, for Britain controlled the Suez Canal – which cut the voyage from London to Bombay in half – and had ports stocked with Welsh coal in every hemisphere.

Few took comfort from Mahan's critics, men like the American historian Brooks Adams or the British geographer Sir Halford Mackinder, who thought Mahan's book misplaced. Mackinder argued that *The Influence of Sea Power* was not only a book about the eighteenth century but that it belonged to the eighteenth century as well: a bygone age when overseas trade and tropical commodities were economically important. At the dawn of the twentieth century, in an age of industrialization, what really mattered were domestic industry and consumption; furthermore, Adams and Mackinder both argued, railways and steam power had opened even the remotest areas to landward exploration and conquest. With such wealth and tools to hand, navies were superfluous. Fortunately for Mahan and the world's navies, the Mackinder critique was largely ignored. Millions read *The Influence of Sea Power* and took its message to heart; the book had run through fifteen printings by 1900, and twenty-four by 1914 (Kennedy 1986: 177–202; Gat 1992: 183–5). Its readers included American congressmen – 'it is to the Ocean that our children must look, as they have once looked to the boundless West' – and the German Kaiser, Wilhelm II, who in his own words, 'devoured' the book and chewed over its worrisome message: that Britain had worked for centuries to hobble adversaries by maintaining an indomitable fleet and a seamless network of naval stations that spanned and controlled the seven seas (LaFeber 1998: 234–5).

In an age of social Darwinism, when territorial expansion seemed the mark of success and one nation's gain was interpreted as another's loss, this British naval dominance came to be viewed as an intolerable provocation. Indeed, the sudden rise of the United States to great power status in the 1890s was owed in large part to Mahan, who encouraged American leaders to build a great navy and challenge Britain's command of the sea. Mahan also left a deep imprint on Germany. Prince Bismarck, ousted by Wilhelm II in 1890, had been content to trade British naval dominance for a free hand in Europe. Britain had accepted the result of the wars of 1866 and 1870–1 in large part because Germany under Bismarck had no maritime ambitions. Wilhelm II, a more ambitious statesman, was not so generous. For the strategic and 'world historical' reasons cited by Mahan, as well as a raft of social and political reasons to be discussed later, Kaiser Wilhelm II decided in 1898 to challenge Great Britain's maritime supremacy. This was the start of the Anglo-German 'Navy Race', which drove Great Britain reluctantly into the Franco-Russian Alliance in 1907 and helped precipitate the First World War.

Early challenges to Britain: France and the *jeune école*

There may never have been a navy race to challenge British supremacy had it not been for the rapid pace of change in battleship design, which regularly rendered old models obsolete and tempted Britain's rivals to think that the Royal Navy could be overhauled by a concentrated spurt of naval construction. France had succumbed to this temptation in the 1870s, when ship and gun designs had fluctuated crazily. While Great Britain wavered between emerging alternatives – muzzle-loading versus breech-loading guns, turrets versus casemates – France determinedly procured 13-inch breech-loaders, mounted them in 'barbettes' (armoured turntables that were lighter and cheaper than fully enclosed turrets), and laid down twenty-two new battleships between 1874 and 1880, nine more than Britain. A navy race was on, not because France alone could threaten the Royal Navy's primacy, but because Britain was historically committed to a 'two-power standard', that is, the ability to defeat the combined navies of any two powers that might coalesce against the British Empire. Since the Italians and the Russians, two potential French allies in an anti-British combination, dramatically boosted their own naval spending in the 1880s, Britain was forced to keep pace, raising expenditures on capital ships from $53 million in 1884 to $76 million in 1890. These outlays effectively staved off the French navy and forced it to consider new ways to challenge Britain at sea (Beeler 1997: 272–6).

Having lost the battleship race, France turned to a 'new school' of naval thinkers, the *jeune école.* The *jeune école* was the brainchild of French Captain Louis Grivel, who instructed French naval officers to renounce 'the whole idea of attaining equality with England in numbers' of warships, an advantage Britain would never concede, and focus instead on wounding Britain economically by commerce raiding, a form of piracy that the French called *guerre de course.* According to this 'new school', France would do well to turn away from expensive, heavily armed battleships, and build fast cruisers and torpedo boats instead. The armoured cruisers would interdict British trade all over the world, and the nimble torpedo boats, armed with self-propelled 'fish torpedoes', would knock out any British battleships foolish enough to approach the French coast. Though Grivel and his principal acolyte in the 1880s, Admiral Théophile Aube, considered themselves Mahanians in spirit (they sought 'command of the great highroad of the sea'), Mahan himself always belittled the *jeune école*, comparing its farflung cruiser patrols to 'policemen on single beats, unable to overcome a massed opponent' (Baer 1994: 23; Kennedy 1986: 182). Mahan's prescriptions were Napoleonic in spirit and always the same: concentrate large numbers of battleships to destroy the enemy's principal fleets and take command of the sea. He criticized the *jeune école* for its meagre appetite: 'It is not the taking of individual ships or convoys that strikes down the power of a nation; it is the possession of that overbearing power on the sea which … closes the byways by which commerce moves to and from the enemy's shores' (Love 1992: I, 371).

Though the hit-and-run warfare of the *jeune école* would have inconvenienced Mahanians by denying them pitched battles at sea and forcing them to divide their fleets to run down fast cruisers, the 'new school' never really materialized. With the exception of England, only France possessed sufficient overseas bases to attempt a *guerre de course* with any hope of success, and even in France traditionalist devotees of the battleship conspired to keep Aube's cruiser force small and unarmoured, posing little threat to British trade anywhere in the world (Beeler 1997: 231–3). As for torpedo boats, though France and Russia combined possessed 165 of them in 1884, causing a minor panic in Britain, which had just nineteen boats and always feared the invention of cheap 'miracle weapons' that might smite the Royal Navy's costly inventory of big ships, the British Admiralty neutralized this threat by introducing the 'destroyer', a light armoured warship specifically designed to patrol the flanks of a battle fleet to destroy incoming torpedo craft (Gat 1992: 202–3).

The rise of the United States

Having failed to oustrip the British in ship construction and tactics, the French quietly desisted, making room for a new competitor and emergent great power: the United States of America. Until the 1880s, the United States had existed apart from Europe, fighting slavery and secessionism in the South and a sequence of wars with Mexico and the Native Americans in the West to round out the new nation's land frontiers and bring the western territories into the union as federal states. Thereafter, the USA, an industrialized nation of 50 million that was demographically younger than Europe, was poised to exploit its resources.

America's resources were immense by any measure. The world's fourth largest economy in 1860, America was the world's largest by 1900, producing goods valued at $13 billion. American railway trackage, which reflected the steady consolidation of the United States as a great power, sextupled in this period, from 35,000 to 193,000 miles. Steel production vaulted from 20,000 tons in 1860 to 10 million tons in 1900; coal extraction from 3 million to 244 million tons. The European powers goggled at this display of wealth and industry. Great Britain, which had produced three times as much coal as the US in 1860, yielded finally to the awesome output of Pennsylvania and Appalachia in 1900. British steel, which had kept pace with American production through the 1880s, began falling behind in the 1890s. By 1900, America produced twice the steel of Britain. Mighty Germany, with its thick-seamed Saxon and Silesian coal pits and its busy mills on the Ruhr and the Saar, did no better by comparison, producing just 60 per cent of America's coal and steel output in 1900. Overall, the US economy amazed onlookers. It climbed through the economically depressed 1890s at an annual clip of nearly 5 per cent; in good times it would potentially do better (Taylor 1987: xxvii–xxxi; Patterson 1989: 20–1).

Sea power was one lever with which America would realize this potential.

In 1890, the same year that he published *The Influence of Sea Power upon History*, Mahan warned Americans that the imminent completion of a canal through Panama, linking the Atlantic and the Pacific oceans, would trigger a scramble for colonies in Latin America and the Caribbean that would draw in the British and the Germans. Mahan warned that the US, twelfth among the world's naval powers, would be defenceless against the onslaught, which would humiliate Washington and furnish America's rivals with naval bases in the western hemisphere and a fast, direct route to the Far East. Here was the ulterior purpose of Mahan's *The Influence of Sea Power*: to convince American statesmen to embrace 'navalism', that is, replace America's 'alphabet of floating washtubs', the old navy, with a modern battle fleet that would shield American interests and project American power in an increasingly competitive world (J. Smith 1994: 50; Baer 1994: 11–12).

Mahan and his followers, men like Assistant Secretary of the Navy Theodore Roosevelt, succeeded in their quest (Shulman 1995: 2). Already in 1883, Congress had agreed to found the Naval War College at Newport to promote the study of maritime strategy and operations. That same year, Congress authorized four armoured cruisers, which laid the foundation of the 'new American navy'. The first battleships followed in 1886, the *Maine* and the *Texas*. Though classified by Congress as 'coastline battleships' to discourage overseas adventures, the American warships were really intended to deter European navies from settling in the vicinity of the Panama Canal, which was begun in 1882. In 1890, Congress voted funds for ten '*Indiana* class' battleships; three were immediately laid down. These 10,000-ton monsters costing $5 million apiece were built entirely of American steel and integrated the latest technologies: full steam power plants capable of 17 knots, double hulls, watertight compartments, 18-inch armour, and three levels of armament: four 13-inch guns in armoured turrets fore and aft, eight quick-firing 8-inch guns in wing turrets, and four 6-inch quick-firers in casemates. The *Indiana* class was intended to challenge the British *Majestic* class, the benchmark among 'first-class' battleships. Congress raised the stakes again in 1892, authorizing the *Iowa* class, an even more powerful design (Love 1992: I, 372–3; J. Smith 1994: 50–2). By 1893, the US Navy had risen from twelfth to fifth place on the ladder of naval strength, and lent its Pacific Squadron to the successful attempt by Sanford Dole, a rich American pineapple planter, to overthrow Hawaii's Queen Liliuokalani and place her islands under US protection (a protectorate that was motivated more by Dole's desire to benefit from federal price supports for American agriculture than by patriotic ideals) (LaFeber 1998: 233–9; Love 1992: I, 376).

With the acquisition of Hawaii, the US Navy set to work building a port and coaling station at Pearl Harbor. Still, Congress and three presidents – Benjamin Harrison, Grover Cleveland and William McKinley – hesitated to step across the Pacific, or anywhere for that matter. Indeed, hesitation would be America's distinguishing mark as a great power until 1941. Given the chance to purchase the Virgin Islands from Denmark in 1867, Congress passed. Offered St Bart's by the Swedes, Congress refused. When the people of Santo Domingo requested American annexation in 1869, Congress turned them down. When the tribal chiefs of Samoa offered basing rights to the US Navy at Pago Pago in 1872, Congress let the offer expire; when the navy grabbed Midway Island for the United States, Congress would not agree to take it. When Dole's planters in Hawaii requested statehood in 1893, Congress balked. Meanwhile, Congress let the American army sink to a strength of just 25,000 men in the 1890s, at a time when the peacetime German army numbered half a million (Cosmas 1994: 45–7). This American diffidence stemmed in large part from the new nation's moral doubts about imperialism, its historical aversion to 'foreign entanglements', and its strict reading of the Monroe Doctrine, which conceded most of the world to the Europeans, reserving only the western hemisphere for the US. It was in this context that Mahan and the American navalists were so important. Mahan 'reversed the traditional American thought of the oceans as a *barrier* against European entanglements', calling them instead 'a great ocean highway; or better, a wide common, over which men pass in all directions' (Musicant 1998: 8–9). By recasting the ocean as a highroad rather than a barrier, as an outlet for expansion rather than a retaining wall, the American navalists helped thrust a doubting republic into the mainstream of world affairs.

Navalism took many forms: political, economic, literary, visual and musical. The US Navy pointedly named its ships after cities and states to win the support of key Congressional delegations and their no less influential local governments. (The *Maine*, for instance, laid down in 1886 and sunk at Havana in 1898, honoured Republican Representative Charles Boutelle of Maine, one of the navy's staunch supporters in Congress.) The economics of ship-building were no less important. With battleships and armoured cruisers costing $3–5 million apiece, an Iowa congressman correctly judged the US Navy 'a great national industry ... [that] afforded work to large sections of the people'. Governors and congressmen competed to build ships or ship parts in their states, lucrative industries that won broad support for the navy in the years after 1890 (LaFeber 1998: 233–4, Shulman 1995: 128–31).

The navy's cultural influence was no less compelling. *Youth's Companion*, the most popular boy's monthly in America, radically changed its content in the late 1880s. Prodded by contributors like Admiral Stephen Luce, who wrote a typical piece in 1889 titled 'Just the boy that's worked for the Navy', *Youth's Companion* increasingly used the US Navy as a vehicle for heroic tales of travel and adventure. News magazines also increased their navy-related content in the period 1889–97, from zero to 3 per cent of articles in *Harper's*, and from 5 to 8 per cent of articles in the *North American Review*. And whereas past coverage had focused only on shipwrecks or procurement scandals, the new journalism exalted the navy, advocated investment in a battlefleet, and extolled the discipline and manliness of American sailors. Daily newspapers were quick to discover that the navy, always on station in some exotic place, piqued reader interest. Papers like Joseph Pulitzer's *New York World* enthusiastically supported US naval construction and issued dire warnings about the growth of foreign navies. A typical Pulitzer headline deplored 'The Partition of Africa by the Nations of Europe among Themselves', disclosing, among other alarming titbits, that Britain and France had each annexed more than 2.5 million square miles of African territory with a combined population of 61 million in the years since 1882. The figures were neatly manipulated to approximate the size and population of the United States in the 1890s. Another entry posed a rhetorical question of more than a little interest to New Yorkers: 'Could a foreign warship lie in the outer harbor and bombard New York?'. The scaremongering answer followed: a list of twenty-seven foreign battleships whose guns could lob shells into the streets of Manhattan from Coney Island (Shulman 1995: 46–50).

This was 'popular navalism' in its purest form: a direct, jolting appeal to the masses by naval, political, business and cultural elites. It could be as subtle as John Philip Sousa's Marine Corps Band, which was the model for hundreds of college and high school bands in the 1880s and 1890s, all of which thumped their way across the squares and football fields of America to the strains of *Semper Fidelis* and other naval hymns. Or popular navalism could be spectacular, like the massed naval review in New York Harbor during the 1892 celebrations of Columbus' discovery of America, or the 348-foot-long full-scale model of the battleship *Illinois* that the US Navy plunked down in the centre of Chicago in 1893 (Shulman 1995: 54–7).

The drift of all this was power: Mahan's Darwinist presumption that America needed to adopt a more assertive foreign policy in the face of European and Japanese expansion or perish. Theodore Roosevelt, Assistant Secretary of the Navy in the 1890s and US President from 1901 to 1909, was himself a naval historian and an outspoken social Darwinist. 'Cowardice in a race, as in an individual, is the unpardonable sin', he declaimed in 1897. That same year, he gave a speech at the Naval War College that developed this critique of America: the new nation was simply too rich, too materialistic and too self-absorbed.

> A rich nation that is slothful, timid, or unwieldy is an easy prey for any people which still retains ... the soldierly virtues. All the great masterful races have been fighting races, and the minute that a race loses the hard fighting virtues, then, no matter what else it may retain, no matter how skilled in commerce and finance, in science or art, it has lost its right to stand as the equal of the best.
>
> (Brands 1997: 317)

Mahan, Roosevelt and leading Republicans saw clearly that the United States faced serious challenges to its new status as a great power in the 1890s.

In the western hemisphere, Great Britain routinely flouted the Monroe Doctrine, first attempting to push the frontier of British Guyana into neighbouring Venezuela's gold-rich Orinoco Basin, then seizing Nicaragua's customs house in 1895 to cover unpaid debts. These were snubs, designed as much to put America in its place as to secure economic advantage. Indeed, during the Venezuelan boundary crisis the British had actually contemplated marine landings in New York and New England with 100,000 troops to punish American intransigence. Against such a force, backed by the Royal Navy, the Americans would have had little defence (Love 1992, I, 380). On the other side of the globe, Japan, Russia, Britain, France and Germany exerted increasing pressure on China's Ch'ing dynasty, making a mockery of America's 'Open Door' policy, which aimed to stop the partition of China before it reached African proportions. Like the British, the Germans drafted plans for amphibious attacks on America's east coast and Caribbean holdings to discourage American interference (Lambi 1984: 129–30; Schoonover 1998: 118–24; Cosmas 1994: 32–3). Clearly, the United States needed a more forceful policy, and poor, backward Spain, which still clung to a handful of colonies in the Caribbean and the Pacific, would be the proving ground.

The Spanish–American War, 1898

America's war with Spain in 1898 might never have happened were it not for the swirling interplay of war and domestic politics, both in the United States and Spain. The US President in 1898 was William McKinley, an inveterately cautious Ohio Republican, who, in Theodore Roosevelt's devastating judgement, had 'no more backbone than a chocolate éclair'. Roosevelt's judgement was too harsh; an older man, McKinley had fought in the Civil War and witnessed war's horrors; moreover, having just fended off a presidential challenge from the populist William Jennings Bryan, McKinley felt constrained to solve America's economic problems before embarking on foreign expansion (Bradford 1993: 216; Musicant 1998: 97; J. Smith 1994: 37). Those who knew McKinley considered it unthinkable that he would declare war on anyone at century's end, but the president was pushed that way by the outbreak of revolution in the Spanish colony of Cuba, which lay just ninety miles off the coast of Florida. Having made up their minds to 'reconcentrate' Madrid's dwindling power in Peninsular Spain and the few colonies that remained to it as a prelude to extensive modernization, the Spanish repressed the Cuban revolt with unexpected savagery. The poor Cubans, who had long since given up on Spain and begun forging links with the nearby US, were caught in the jaws of this 'reconcentration'. Anticipating British practice in the Boer War, 120,000 Spanish troops and an army of labourers ran a line of blockhouses across the waist of Cuba to stop the flow of guerrillas and facilitate pacification. Based in the fortified *trocha*, the Spanish army killed, jailed or starved an estimated 500,000 Cubans between 1895 and 1898 (Cosmas 1994: 72; J. Smith 1994:

11–13). It was a veritable holocaust for the little island; indeed the scale and brutality of the Spanish war effort, which partly explained the American decision to enter the war, revealed Madrid's determination to keep its prime colonies. Even Spanish liberals vowed to 'fight to the last peseta, the last drop of blood', sanctioning a fivefold expansion of the Spanish army between 1895 and 1897, and embarking 214,000 soldiers for the threatened colonies (Balfour 1997: 11). Most of the new recruits were undisciplined conscripts, rudely yanked from their provincial backwaters and shipped off to Cuba, and their inevitable excesses when confronted with a hostile population drove still more refugees onto the shores of Key West and Miami.

Yet Madrid fought on, heedless of American protests. Spain viewed the colonies, Cuba in particular, as indispensable and non-negotiable. 'Spain without Cuba', *La Epoca* rather tactlessly opined in 1897, 'would be as little valued among the nations of Europe as Portugal'. When the US threatened to intervene to rescue the Cubans, the Spanish prime minister vowed to keep them out, contriving a remarkable analogy in the process: 'Cuba is Spain's Alsace-Lorraine; the honour of the country is at stake' (Balfour 1997: 6–7; J. Smith 1994: 9–10). Besides emotional appeal, Spain's empire offered substantial economic incentives. Cuba produced a third of the world's sugar through much of the nineteenth century, and Spanish tariffs made all of the colonies – parts of Morocco, the Canary Islands, Cuba, Puerto Rico, the Philippines, and the Mariana, Pelew and Caroline Islands – profitable dumping grounds for Peninsular Spain's otherwise uncompetitive goods: Castilian wheat and leather, Andalusian wine, Catalan textiles, and the costly services of the banks, ports and shippers who handled the one-sided trade. Like all 'new imperialisms', Spain's empire also served a critical domestic-political function. Removed from power by the Restoration of 1876, the Spanish *burguesía* found solace in a captive overseas market that made them rich, but also dangerously dependent on colonies that were one of the only markets for their overpriced products (Balfour 1997: 2–3).

Although Spanish military action in the Caribbean – a flagrant breach of the Monroe Doctrine – made it difficult for McKinley to sit pat, the main push for war in 1898 came not from Madrid, but from well heeled American pressure groups like the Cuban League (whose membership included leading US politicians and bankers), Cuban-American sugar planters (who stood to lose $50 million if the fighting continued) and the popular press in America, the so-called 'yellow journals' (LaFeber 1998: 377–8; Cosmas 1994: 63). The yellow journals, printed on cheap yellow-bleached paper and priced at a penny to capture the mass market, had their equivalents in every industrialized nation. In America they were William Randolph Hearst's *Journal* and Joseph Pulitzer's *World*. Both Hearst and Pulitzer understood that war no less than navies made sensational copy and they clamoured for it in February 1898 when the US battleship *Maine* sank in the roads at Havana. No one knew what really sank *Maine*; the US Navy blamed the accident on a Spanish mine; Spanish investigators charged that *Maine*'s own boilers had exploded, sending the warship and all hands to the bottom. Whatever the cause of the tragedy, it ought to have been resolved by diplomacy, a fact that President McKinley fully appreciated. Yet diplomatic parleys yielded at once to a popular frenzy unleashed in large part by Hearst and Pulitzer.

Hearst, who gained 250,000 paid subscribers during the Spanish-American War, grandly offered a $50,000 reward 'for the conviction of the criminals who sent 258 American sailors to their death'. His *New York Journal* headline on 17 February was a fabrication: 'The Warship *Maine* was Split in Two by an Enemy's Secret Infernal Machine'. Pulitzer's *World* would not be outdone: 'The *Maine* Explosion Was Caused by a Bomb – Suspicion of a Torpedo' (Musicant 1998: 144; J. Smith 1994: 40–1). On 18 February, Hearst demanded an immediate declaration of war: 'Remember the *Maine*! To Hell with Spain!' Hearst's gallantry derived in large part from Spain's isolation. Though the Spanish queen was Austrian Emperor Franz Joseph's niece, Madrid's efforts to join the Triple Alliance in 1887 had failed; neither the Germans, the Austro-Hungarians nor the Italians wanted to be made liable for Spain's sprawling empire. And whereas Spain would almost certainly have benefited from British support in years gone by (if only to pique the Americans), Germany's decision to build a high seas fleet in 1897 instantly convinced London of the need to get along with the United States (Balfour 1997: 6–7). With the Spanish so isolated, the US ran little risk by provoking them, a perception that only compounded the war fever. In Chicago in February, the *Tribune* scolded Congress ('our national debating society') for delaying military action, and confidently assured its readers that the Spanish were 'exulting over the *Maine* disaster'. In Indianapolis, the *Journal* insisted that 'Spain be driven off this hemisphere for the same reason that a community assumes the right to suppress a nuisance' (Wilkerson 1932: 106). War fever rippled across the nation. In March, Hearst's *Journal* ran a popular cartoon of 'Uncle Sam', chained and tethered, being whipped by a cruel 'Spanish Don'. (Spanish cartoons showed a ragged Uncle Sam stepping across the strait from Florida to Cuba, a bottle of rum in one hand, a box of dynamite in the other.) Hearst himself escorted five key Congressmen on his yacht to Cuba to observe conditions there. They returned – full of wine, rum and cigars – spoiling for a fight. Even mild-mannered university professors were carried away. When Congress voted a $50 million military appropriation in March, E. Benjamin Andrews, president of Brown University, assured the nation that 'war is a good medicine' (Wilkerson 1932: 110–11; J. Smith 1994: 41–2, 45). The public outcry, part genuine and part contrived, drove McKinley toward a conflict that he would have liked to avoid.

While McKinley wavered, the US Navy planned. Three options for what the navy delicately called a 'special problem' – war with Spain – had already been elaborated at the start of the Cuban Revolution. The first option, a naval attack on Spain itself, was rejected as too ambitious and too likely to entail intervention by a European power. The second option, an attack on Spain's Pacific colonies of Guam and the Philippines, recommended itself as a means to secure bases in the Far East and pressure Spain to accept terms. A third option, overwhelming land and sea attacks on the Spanish colonies of Cuba and Puerto Rico, was most appealing because the two islands were close to the US and far from Spain, and because they nestled in the vicinity of the Panama Canal and the Mississippi delta, America's chief strategic concerns. Moreover, US Naval Intelligence noted that a war to 'liberate Cuba' from Spanish rule would be more palatable to the average American than a war of imperial expansion, and would garner broad public support (J. Smith 1994: 54–7; Musicant 1998: 100).

Ultimately, the Americans chose the second and third options, sending their Asiatic Squadron (five armoured cruisers) against the Spanish Philippines and dispatching their Atlantic fleet (five battleships and two armoured cruisers) and an infantry corps of 17,000 men to the island of Cuba. The first clash of the war occurred in the waters of Manila Bay, where Commodore George Dewey's Asiatic Squadron suffered just eight casualties, sinking four Spanish cruisers and silencing Spain's powerful shore batteries at Cavite. Like the sea battles of the Yalu and Tsushima, Manila Bay demonstrated the effectiveness of modern, well handled naval guns. With his ships in line ahead, Dewey passed and repassed Admiral Patricio Montojo's Pacific fleet, which, to Dewey's amazement, never left its moorings. With the Spanish conveniently anchored up, the Americans poured in salvos of 8- and 6-inch shell from a range of 5,500 yards. Using electric rangefinders to locate their targets, the American squadron first wrecked the Spanish flagship, then raked high explosive across the rest of the Spanish fleet. Montojo's crews were awed by the systematic destruction of their admiral's flagship. Within minutes the *Reina Cristina* was reduced to a smoking hulk, its steering gear shot away, its masts, rigging and signal flags brought down, and its magazines, bridge and wardroom obliterated (Trask 1981: 100–1). One by one the rest of the Spanish warships subsided beneath the waves; those ships not sunk by Dewey's guns scuttled themselves. Technology alone did not account for the American victory, for the Spanish ships were nearly as well equipped as the American ones. It was American training and seamanship that made the difference. Whereas American shooting was rapid and well aimed, Spain's gunners scored no hits, neither from their ships nor their shore batteries at Cavite (Musicant 1998: 217–23). As in land warfare, war at sea required continual practice to wring advantage from improving technologies.

The battle of Manila Bay was the first of two peripheral operations designed by the Americans to exert indirect pressure on Spain and force it out of Asia and the Caribbean. Once Dewey had eliminated Spain's Pacific fleet and secured the excellent harbour at Subic Bay – for which Congress gave him a $10,000 jewelled sword from Tiffany's – the US Navy was able to move 10,000 troops from San Francisco to the Pacific theatre. They debarked in July and took Manila in August after joining forces with local anti-Spanish guerrillas under Emilio Aguinaldo, who mistook the Americans for liberators. By the time Aguinaldo realized his mistake, the United States had seated itself as the new colonial power in the Philippines, forcing Aguinaldo back into the bush, where he continued the liberation struggle without success until 1902.

America's second operation involved a full-scale land and sea assault on the islands of Cuba and Puerto Rico. This ought to have been a difficult operation, for Spain had 230,000 troops in Cuba: ten times the American force. And yet much of the Spanish army was dispersed in counter-guerrilla operations against an estimated 40,000 Cuban rebels. Of the troops available for war with the Americans, one third was prostrate with yellow fever. This left a force of little more than 40,000 for field operations, most of whom were described by a British observer as 'boys of 15 or 16 who have never held a rifle till this moment, and now are almost ignorant which end it fires' (Cosmas 1994: 70, 74). In this the Americans were very fortunate. So inefficient was their own military organization that they managed to transport fewer than one fifth of the 200,000 men called up overseas. In Cuba, they would need every available combatant (Koistinen 1997: 86).

McKinley entrusted the Cuban invasion to Admiral William Sampson's Atlantic Fleet and General William Shafter's Army V Corps. Though there were heroic episodes in the Spanish-American War – Dewey's bold push into Manila Bay, the 'Rough Riders' attack up San Juan Hill – little went according to plan in the badly mismanaged conflict. Spanish execution was everywhere characterized by indolence and carelessness, American operations by bureaucratic rigidity and chronic disorganization. Admiral Sampson failed to intercept Spain's principal fleet as it zigzagged across the Atlantic scrounging everywhere for coal before arriving safely in Cuba, immensely complicating the US Army's war plans. Instead of enjoying command of the sea, which would have permitted the army to coordinate ground operations with naval bombardments and move troop transports freely into Cuba and Puerto Rico, the army was forced throughout the war to fight without the benefit of naval fire and keep one eye peeled over its shoulder for the approach of the Spanish fleet, which held Sampson's five battleships in check at Santiago de Cuba.

On land, the chief lesson of the war was tactical. Armed with the .45 calibre Springfield, a thunderingly obsolete single-shot rifle that belched charcoal rather than smokeless ammunition, American infantry often resorted to bayonet charges to root the better armed Spanish troops from their positions. These American attempts to take Spanish trenches and barricades by storm were punished with heavy, avoidable casualties. Equipped with Mauser repeaters and dug in behind tangles of barbed wire – 'not single lines of wire, but pieces running perpendicularly, diagonally, horizontally, and in every other direction', an American veteran recalled – the Spanish took full advantage of the 'offensive spirit' that imbued the American army after twenty years of

Indian warfare. President McKinley himself demanded a swift, war-winning offensive before the American corps was even in place on Cuba, and one of his generals wildly proclaimed that 'the charge is the safest form of attack'. Since the Spanish Mauser could fire five times more quickly than the American Springfield, he may have been right, though for the wrong reasons. At all events, this can-do Yankee mentality (which would infuse American operations against the Germans in 1918 with no less tragic results) in part explained the heavy American casualties on San Juan Hill, where 1,600 Americans fell. Fire from the Spanish Mausers was so thick that the Americans supposed that they were fighting 12,000 men; in fact, there were just 600 Spanish troops on the height (Cosmas 1994: 217–18). Despite the losses on the hills above Santiago, where some American units lost 25 per cent or more of their effectives to Spanish fire, Lieutenant Colonel Theodore Roosevelt, ever the bloodthirsty Darwinist, insisted that 'it could not be wrong to go forward' on the modern battlefield. There was a moral imperative to do so (Jamieson 1994: 141; Cosmas 1994: 214).

Down the chain of command, at the company and platoon level, less cele-brated American officers drew more sensible conclusions from the war. American artillerymen remarked the need for a European-style system of indirect fire that would enable concealed batteries well behind the lines to bombard the enemy with the aid of forward observers. Actual practice in the Spanish-American War recalled the Civil War of the 1860s: gunners pushed their pieces into the skirmish line to deliver direct fire at close range, only to be blown back by Mauser fire and bursts of shrapnel (Cosmas 1994: 214–15). American infantry officers witnessed the dreadful efficacy of the Gatling gun wherever it was deployed. On San Juan Hill, Roosevelt's stumbling, Mauser-ravaged attack was rescued by the last-minute insertion of a battery of Gatlings, which drove the Spaniards from their hilltop positions. An American captain recalled that the mere appearance of machineguns 'greatly demoral-ized the enemy, some of whom could be seen running from their places'. No wonder: one of Teddy Roosevelt's Rough Riders described what he saw atop San Juan Hill after the Gatlings had done their work:

> When we arrived at the Spanish trenches … we saw the work of the Gatling guns. Most of the Spaniards had been shot through the head – some two or three times. So help me God, they looked like kids about twelve years old. Hundreds of them were lying there dead. It was a pitiful sight. All of us boys felt ashamed of ourselves.
>
> (Balfour 1997: 41)

Tactically, American infantrymen used their bayonets for little besides mashing coffee beans. With their high rate of fire, Spain's Mauser rifles shredded bayonet charges from a great distance. There was the additional problem posed by smokeless gunpowder. American units, dashing forward with the bayonet, often failed to locate even large Spanish troop formations, which emitted no puffs of smoke. In Cuba and the Philippines, American officers further remarked the disorienting effect of smokeless shells and bullets; troops wheeled confusedly in circles, mistaking the burst of a shell or the sound of a bullet flicking past for the crack of the gun itself (Jamieson 1994: 134). American junior officers also noted something that would become even more apparent in the Boer and Manchurian Wars. With so much fire and confusion on the battlefield, command and control continually devolved to smaller units, even to private soldiers. On Cuba, American officers noted that bravery and individual initiative were essential attributes in modern war, for quick-firing artillery, machineguns, and magazine rifles instantly disintegrated large troop formations, forcing them to scatter in search of cover. The Spanish were bad small-unit fighters, in large part because their best officers had refused to come over from Spain to join the fighting, even when promised accelerated promotion for doing so. Of Spanish officers in Cuba and the Philippines, 80 per cent were reservists, more concerned to return safely to their civilian occupations than to die a hero's death; many of the rest were teenage cadets commissioned after a few months' study. Whereas discipline in Spanish units tended to wilt under fire (not least because the men were rarely paid), American commanders approvingly noted the 'well-regulated conduct' of their men, even in small units (Jamieson 1994: 137–8; Balfour 1997: 12). In future war, which would be characterized by unimaginable casualties and suffering, this moral capacity for self-discipline and self-sacrifice would make or break armies.

The US Army's capture of the hills above Santiago sealed the fate of Spain's Caribbean fleet, which comprised four armoured cruisers and three destroyers. Unaware that the American army was succumbing to yellow fever, malaria and dysentery as precipitately as its Spanish adversary, Admiral Pascual Cervera feared that the Americans would shortly mount guns on the heights and take his warships between two fires: Shafter's from land, Sampson's from the sea. Cervera thus made a break for freedom and, like Montojo's fleet at Manila Bay, felt the full weight of Sampson's guns. Against four American battleships, Cervera's cruisers had no chance, meeting with blistering salvos as they attempted to gain the open sea. Turning away from the American fire, they ran aground, one after the other. Cervera's flagship was the first run aground; the admiral jumped overboard and swam ashore, where he arrived dripping and half-naked. It was an inglorious end to a modern navy that had been constructed at great cost to the Spanish taxpayer. Two thousand Spanish sailors were killed or wounded in the action, compared with US losses of just three men. Like the action at Manila, the battle of Santiago Bay emphasized the importance of naval gunfire and lent credence to the evolving concept of the 'all big gun battleship' or dreadnought. The run from Santiago also confirmed the futility of Lissa-style ram tactics; Cervera's flagship had attempted to ram a hole in the American line only to be riddled with shells, set afire and driven aground (J. Smith 1994: 146–50).

'Everything is broken in this unhappy country', Madrid's *El Correo* commented after the war. 'There is no government, no electorate, no political parties; no army, no navy; all is fiction, all decadence, all ruins' (Balfour 1997: v). Indeed, with its principal fleets destroyed, its treasury empty, its monarchy in danger and its long sea coast wide open to American attack, Spain had little choice but to sue for peace in August 1898. The 'Disaster of 1898' – *El Desastre* – rocked Spanish society, and forced an abrupt capitulation. When news of Santiago's fall reached London, Lord Salisbury classified Spain a 'dying nation', a reference that would sting for years to come. On the American side, war had the opposite effect, refreshing American politics and making the United States a great power fit to range itself against the Europeans, all at a cost of $250 million and fewer than 2,000 dead and wounded. Militarily, the US began to creep into the mainstream of world affairs. Showered with $30 million of extraordinary funding during the conflict, the US Navy added ships and missions all over the globe. The US Army, which had drawn most of its troops from National Guard units in 1898, won approval to increase its peacetime strength to 65,000 men after the war, a diminutive force by European standards, but progress nonetheless. In 1900, General Shafter could boast with some justification that 'we are getting used to war now and have the necessary appliances and means to do with' (Koistinen 1997: 86–8; Cosmas 1994: 100–1, 106, 305–6). This was certainly the perception in Europe. Count Agenor Goluchowski, Austria-Hungary's foreign minister at the turn-of-the-century, deplored the American breakthrough and spoke of the need for the European nations to 'fight shoulder to shoulder against this common danger' (LaFeber 1998: 377–8). It was a strangely far-seeing comment by a notoriously myopic statesman, and the Germans were first into the breach, helping themselves to the Spanish Carolines, Marianas and Pelews to limit American gains in the Pacific (Balfour 1997: 46–8). Vague about his ultimate intentions throughout the conflict ('no accurate map of nations engaged in war can be traced until after the war is over'), McKinley moved swiftly to annex Puerto Rico, Guam and the Philippines, and to take Cuba under American protection once Spain was beaten (Cosmas 1994: 110). Though the Americans called this 'benevolent assimilation' rather than imperialism, it amounted to the same thing (J. Smith 1994: 222–4). The US would tolerate no more European interference in the Americas and the Caribbean, and McKinley annexed the Philippines to give the US a voice in the Far East as well. After the last shots were fired on Cuba and Luzon, the US peremptorily demanded that the European powers end their concession-hunting in China – home to one fourth of the human race – and work to uphold free trade and the territorial integrity of the Chinese Empire instead. These demands were contained in John Hay's 'Open Door notes' of 1899–1900. Though initially backed by little real force (Hay himself conceding that America's brave talk was little more than 'flap-doodle'), they symbolized a new American commitment to world affairs (LaFeber 1998: 380–3; Bartlett 1994: 37).

'Fleet policy' and the Anglo-German navy race, 1898–1912

America's decision to fight Spain and appropriate its colonies was in large part a response to the ongoing European carve-up of the world. Americans resented the spread of British influence in Africa and Asia, and were alarmed by the aggressive overseas expansion of Kaiser Wilhelm II, who had ascended the German throne in 1888 at the age of twenty-nine. Whereas Wilhelm II's father, guided by Bismarck, had rather cautiously unified the German states and deliberately eschewed colonies to avoid provoking a 'revenge coalition' against Germany, Wilhelm II had no such scruples. He represented a generational shift in German attitudes, and came to power at a moment when the German Empire was bursting clear of the Long Depression that had dogged Europe since the 1870s. The German population was soaring; it climbed from 41 million in 1871 to 60 million in 1890 to 70 million by 1914; German industrial production (100 million tons of coal, 13 million tons of steel per annum in the 1890s) was rocketing past British levels for the first time in history; German laboratories and universities were producing more commercial and industrial patents than any other country, and leading the 'second industrial revolution' in chemicals, electrical equipment and transport. For Wilhelm II, who wished to step out of Bismarck's shadow and make Germany a *Weltmacht* or 'world power' like the British Empire, Germany's demographic and economic expansion provided the justification for what he called *Weltpolitik* – 'world policy'.

Weltpolitik was founded on the social Darwinist belief that Germany had either to expand or stagnate. Wilhelm II's naval secretary warned the Kaiser throughout the 1890s that overseas colonies were 'a question of survival'. If Germany did not seize them, it would 'sink back to the status of a poor farming country' (Herwig 1987: 35; Gat 1992: 79). Fearing that Britain and France would complete the carve-up of the globe, taking the best pieces for themselves and leaving Germany the 'scraps', Wilhelm II became an aggressive imperialist. In 1896 he dispatched the 'Kruger Telegram' to the Boer republics in South Africa. The telegram offered encouragement to the Boers in their colonial struggle with the British, and hinted at a plan to extend German influence from South West Africa, across the Zambesi to the gold and diamond fields of the Transvaal and Kimberley (Lambi 1984: 113–14; Lowe 1994: 103–6). In 1897, Wilhelm II took things a step further, dispatching troops and warships to seize the Chinese port of Kiaochow and the surrounding Shantung Peninsula; the Kaiser boasted that 'the German Empire has at long last set foot firmly in Asia' (Lowe 1994: 115). Though aimed primarily at the Japanese, Kiaochow also challenged the British, who conducted 70 per cent of China's trade, a flourishing business that accounted for nearly 20 per cent of Britain's commercial revenues (LaFeber 1998: 316). The Kruger Telegram and Kiaochow – real crises in their time – heralded a new German style in foreign affairs, an uncompromising determination, in Wilhelm II's phrase, to 'conquer for ourselves a place in the sun'. For this, a powerful German navy was needed, not the derisory little coastguard that had hugged Germany's Baltic ports and estuaries since the 1860s, but a 'High Seas Fleet' able to range itself against the Royal Navy and open communications to Germany's new colonies in Africa and the Pacific. In a speech at Hamburg in 1901, Wilhelm II reflected on Germany's new imperial responsibilities and pledged to build a great navy:

> Despite the fact that we do not have the navy we should have, we have conquered for ourselves a place in the sun. It will now be my task to see to it that this place in the sun shall remain our undisputed possession, in order that the sun's rays may fall promptly upon our activity and trade in foreign parts, that our industry and agriculture may develop within the state and our sailing sports upon the water, for [Germany's] future lies upon the water.
>
> (Hart 1920: I, 95)

The Kaiser was an avid reader of Mahan (he placed the German edition of Mahan's classic in the wardroom of every German warship), and considered sea power the essential lever for making Germany a world power. Though Germany lagged far behind Britain in total warships in the 1890s, Wilhelm II's navy secretary Admiral Alfred von Tirpitz conceived a 'risk theory' that gave the Kaiser hope. Working from the assumption that constant improvements in metallurgy, chemical explosives and guns regularly rendered navies (like any other technology) obsolete, Tirpitz reckoned that even from a standing start, the German navy could overtake the British within a generation by building three battleships and two cruisers a year beginning in 1898, yielding a fleet of sixty state-of-the-art battleships and forty cruisers by 1918. Tirpitz further reckoned that the British, weighed down with global commitments, would have to build ninety battleships and nearly as many cruisers in the same period just to keep pace. And even with ninety battleships, Tirpitz felt certain that the British would not dare challenge a German navy of sixty ships, for the risk would be too great. If the Royal Navy incurred heavy losses against the Germans, it would have nothing left to defend its home waters and colonial possessions against a German counter-attack, or French, Japanese, Russian or American incursions. And whereas the German fleet would be densely concentrated in the North Sea – like a 'sharp knife, held gleaming and ready only a few inches away from [England's] jugular vein', in Paul Kennedy's suggestive phrase – the British navy would be scattered from Bermuda to Hong Kong. Would any British statesman risk offending the Germans under such conditions? This in a nutshell was Tirpitz's 'risk theory' (*Risikogedanke*), which formed the basis of German hopes in their navy race with the British (Berghahn 1993: 49–52; Kennedy 1986: 214–16).

By threatening the British with a 2:3 ratio, Tirpitz aimed to compel London to assent peaceably to a German overseas empire. Tirpitz and the Kaiser assumed that rather than run the risk of a naval war with the Germans, the British would invite them into a 'global balance of power system', in which the British would actively support German colonial aspirations (Berghahn 1993: 52). Though clearly a strategic initiative, as the above sketch makes clear, the German High Seas Fleet was also intended as a tool of national and social integration. In Germany more than any other power, *Flottenpolitik* ('fleet policy') was conceived by political and military leaders as a means to rally public opinion behind an increasingly unpopular government, and to shift attention from a looming class war. The clear danger of this stratagem was that armaments used in this way – for domestic-political ends – had a dangerous knock-on effect in the wider world. Powers like Great Britain naturally took the increase in German naval construction for a strategic threat rather than an internal political gambit, and ratcheted up their own production, accelerating the arms race that helped plunge Europe into war in 1914.

'Fleet policy', as conceived by Wilhelm II and Admiral Tirpitz, seemed a good way to square the vicious circle of German politics in the 1890s. Since unification in 1871, German society and the German political system had been all but throttled by class, political, regional and religious antagonisms. An 'empire state' featuring an all-powerful Kaiser and Reich chancellor had been created by Bismarck to direct German affairs. Though Bismarck had also created a regionally appointed federal council (*Bundesrat*) and a popularly elected parliament (*Reichstag*) to give the appearance of constitutional monarchy, the two legislatures were not really checks on the power of the crown. Bundesrat voting was always stacked in favour of Prussia, and the Reichstag, though popularly elected, lacked the power to replace an imperial chancellor who did not represent the popular interest. Only the German Kaiser (who was also King of Prussia) enjoyed this prerogative, which explained the ease with which Wilhelm II gravitated toward 'personal rule' after Bismarck's resignation in 1890, ruling first through a pair of nobodies, then directly through the man he called 'my Bismarck': Prince Bernhard von Bülow (Wehler 1991: 52–4, 64).

And yet the Kaiser's ability to appoint pliable ministers in no way altered the severe social and political problems afflicting Germany in the 1890s. As Germany industrialized, its urban population grew to 30 million (50 per cent of Germans in 1900), and its 'blue collar' working class increased from one fifth of the population in 1870 to one third in 1907. Whereas conservative German peasants had outnumbered radical workers 2:1 in 1871, the ratio was reversed by 1914 (Herwig 1987: 2). It was no wonder that Wilhelm II's Reichstag, in contrast to his father's, filled rapidly with reform Liberals and anti-monarchical, anti-capitalist Social Democrats. Social Democrats were elected in ever greater numbers by an ever more numerous working class. In the 1880s they doubled their share of the vote in elections (from 10 to 20 per cent) and more than doubled their seats, from eleven to twenty-four, over-coming official persecution and gerrymandering aimed at containing the spread of socialism. By 1896, the Social Democrats had fifty-six seats in the Reichstag, the liberal parties one hundred. By 1912 the Social Democrats would have 110 seats (Sperber, in Barclay and Weitz 1998: 184–5). Clearly, the 'reds' ought to have contended for the Reich's highest offices, but were shut out by Wilhelm II's personal rule, which reserved the Reich ministries for loyal monarchists (Wehler 1991: 78–80). Relations between the Kaiser and his workers worsened in the 1890s. He trod warily into international crises, complaining in 1894 that he 'dared not dispatch a single soldier from German soil' so long as the threat of 'red revolution' loomed at home. 'First gun down the socialists', he stormed to his army chiefs in 1897, 'then behead them and render them harmless, if need be by a bloodbath, and *then* war outside our borders' (Herwig 1994: 162; Berghahn 1993: 28). The problem, however, was that even the service chiefs had begun to doubt the loyalty of German troops in the event of a German revolution. Universal conscription in a rapidly urbanizing society had so diluted the German army's hard core of peasant conscripts and NCOs that it was difficult to say what the army might do in the event of an imperial coup or an urban insurrection. For whom would it fight? It was a vexing question that never ceased to worry the Kaiser and his entourage (Kitchen 1968: 154–86).

Given the rigidity of the German political system and its inability to reform without shaking the unshakable prerogatives of the Prussian crown and nobility, the Kaiser, guided by Bülow and Tirpitz, conceived a large German navy as a possible solution to Berlin's political problems, what Volker Berghahn has called 'an instrument of distraction and social integration' (Berghahn 1993: 42). The instrument would work as follows: starting in 1898, the German navy would begin building three battleships and two armoured cruisers a year. Shipbuilding at this rate would have a pump-priming effect on the German economy as factories geared up to produce armour plate, guns, turbine engines, electrical supplies and naval stores (Krupp Steel alone would double its workforce between 1904 and 1909, and would be selling 12 per cent of production to the *Kriegsmarine* by 1912 [Bartlett 1994: 59; Herwig 1994: 31, 67]). New jobs would be created and wages would rise, as builders and suppliers added workers to forge and assemble components and man expanded shipyards at Wilhelmshaven, Kiel, Danzig, Hamburg, Bremen and Stettin. Since Tirpitz and the Kaiser insisted on the automatic replacement of German warships every twenty years (to guard against wear and obsolescence, but also to keep the economy ticking along), it could reasonably be assumed that better employment and wages would trickle continuously through German society. This in turn would enable Germany's working classes to pay more for their food and drink, which they shortly would have to do, for the price of Conservative support for the navy was an agricultural tariff that reserved the German market for high-priced German produce, shutting out cheap Russian and American grain. As Tirpitz saw it, German workers would gladly pay the higher cost of living once settled in their new jobs, and reform-minded German burghers would turn away from liberal politics and take to beating their breasts and lining their pockets instead, as a result of political pressure from groups like the German Navy League and the economic jolt provided by lavish public spending (it helped that the German navy, in pointed contrast to the army, would be a middle-class service, with most of its offices taken not by Junkers but by bourgeois aspirants). Overall, Tirpitz pledged that the fleet would 'offer a strong palliative against educated and uneducated Social Democrats' (Herwig 1994: 35). Jobs in naval yards and supporting industries would square the circle of German politics by luring 'red workers' into a grand coalition with agrarians and industrialists.

To Tirpitz's material incentives, Bülow added psychological ones. The Kaiser's chief minister aimed to use the navy as a bully pulpit to whip up national feeling and solidarity. Fleet policy, he argued in 1898, is a 'policy that mobilizes the best patriotic forces … a policy that appeals to the highest national emotions'. Such a 'national policy under the not firm leadership of a purposeful and gallant government', Bülow suggested, was the optimal way to fight the German socialists: 'We must unswervingly wrestle for the souls of our workers; [we] must try to regain the sympathies of the Social Democrat workers for the state and the monarchy [and] to keep the non-Socialist workers away from Social Democracy'. Mixing a patriotic vision with tangible incentives would, in Bülow's words, 'pull [the worker] away from the ensnarements of the socialists and accustom him to the monarchical order' (Berghahn 1993: 43–4). In sum, Germany's fleet, though indubitably a strategic asset, was also an exercise in social imperialism on a titanic scale.

And yet Tirpitz's grand design to refound the Reich on a solid economic foundation, in which happy workers would mingle with prosperous Junkers and industrialists, was based on two overoptimistic assumptions. First, it assumed that Britain would resist the temptation to 'Copenhagen' or preemptively destroy the German fleet in the twenty years needed to cross the 'danger zone' from zero ships to sixty. Second, it assumed that Britain would not tap extra sources of income simply to outbuild or technologically outstrip the Germans in order to prevent Tirpitz gaining the leverage needed to implement his 'risk theory'. Although the British never punished the first assumption, they stood ready to at all times. In 1905, a senior Admiralty official warned the Germans that 'the Royal Navy would get its blow in first, before the other side even had time to read in the papers that war had been declared' (Herwig 1994: 37). As for the second assumption, Tirpitz found that naval mastery was one area in which the British – scorned by the Germans as a penny-pinching 'nation of shopkeepers' – were prepared to spend lavishly. Faced with the German navy bills of 1898, 1900 and 1908, which aimed to force 'a new division of the globe', Britain resolved not only to match

German construction, but to keep well ahead of it (Steiner 1977: 48–59; Herwig 1994: 19). Thus began the Anglo-German Navy Race, which eventually drowned Bülow's hopes of a great internal-political coalition or *Sammlung* in a sea of red ink, bankrupted Germany's central government, starved the German army of needed funds for expansion and modernization, and drove Great Britain into the arms of the Franco-Russian alliance, which, with the adherence of Britain, became the Triple Entente in 1907 (Bond 1986: 54–5).

Although the Anglo-German Navy Race was most intense in the years between 1907 and 1914, it commenced with Tirpitz's Navy Bill of 1898. Noting the upsurge in German building and braggadocio ('I am the *arbiter mundi*', and 'The trident belongs in [my] fist', were typical Wilhelmine boasts of the 1890s), the British Admiralty vowed to stay ahead of the Germans. One British official warned that 'the Germans aim to push us into the water and steal our clothes' (Berghahn 1993: 61; Herwig 1994: 18). To prevent this, the Royal Navy began returning ships to home waters, a controversial step that involved stripping overseas stations like Singapore and Malta of their naval protection to beef up the Home Fleet. In 1903, Britain created a North Sea fleet to keep Tirpitz's growing navy under observation, and based it at Rosyth on the east coast of Scotland (Kennedy 1986: 214–18; Joll 1992: 51). Had the Germans any doubts about British mettle, these were conclusively dispelled in 1904, when sixty-three year-old Sir John 'Jackie' Fisher, an anti-German hawk, was named First Sea Lord. To focus on the German threat, Fisher recalled the bulk of the Royal Navy to England; by 1909, 75 per cent of Britain's battleships swung at anchor in Dover or Rosyth. To match German technological improvements, Fisher scrapped 154 battleships and cruisers and poured the savings into new construction. Although Fisher's 'shake-up' was hotly debated – he was accused of abandoning the Empire – he did put crushing pressure on Tirpitz and the wobbly German political system by outbuilding the Germans 'two keels to one', and by launching a revolutionary new class of battleship in 1906: HMS *Dreadnought* (Kennedy 1976: 216–18; Marder 1961–70: I, 39–41).

Dreadnought was the world's first turbine-driven, all-big-gun battleship. It carried no secondary armament, only ten 12-inch guns, which gave it a broadside twice as powerful as that of any battleship afloat. *Dreadnought* truly feared nothing, because its centrally controlled, electronically targeted guns could fire 1,500-pound armour-piercing shells from well beyond the range of pre-dreadnought battleships and rather easily put them out of commission. Even more worrisome from the German perspective was the speed of *Dreadnought*. 'Speed is armour' was a Fisher aphorism, and at a time when few battleships could make 18 knots, *Dreadnought*'s 70,000-horsepower turbines whisked her along at 21 knots, usually without a breakdown. Eight years into their hugely expensive naval construction programme, the Germans were plunged into obsolescence (Sumida 1989: 112, 256–7; Hough 1983: 10).

Fisher's 'dreadnought revolution' upped the ante in the Anglo-German

Navy Race to a level that Tirpitz – already under fire from the German army, which wanted a slice of his budget – would not be able to sustain forever. Albert Ballin, director of the Hamburg-America Line, stated the obvious in 1908: 'We just cannot *afford* a race in dreadnoughts against the much wealthier British' (Berghahn 1993: 90; Herwig 1994: 61). The British, with their big overseas investment portfolios, were not only richer than the Germans, but they had less need of an army, and could therefore focus spending on the fleet. The Germans were not so fortunate. To pay for the 'dreadnought leap', the Kaiser was forced to tag a 35 per cent *Novelle* (supplementary appropriation) onto Tirpitz's already exorbitant naval estimates for 1906, increasing German naval spending from one fifth to one quarter of the defence budget and doubling capital ship construction costs. The army cried foul, as did a growing number of Reichstag deputies worried about further reductions in Reich services and subsidies, yet Tirpitz and the Kaiser ploughed ahead. British spending on dreadnoughts and 'battle cruisers' – all-big-gun armoured cruisers – would necessitate a second *Novelle* in 1908, a third in 1911 and a fourth in 1912. Tirpitz needed money for ever larger fleets of 'capital ships' (dreadnoughts and battle cruisers), but also for crews, repair, maintenance, and the excavation of the Kiel Canal connecting the Baltic and the North Sea (Stevenson 1996: 101; Herwig 1994: 58–9). Politically, the 'dreadnought leap' dealt a death blow to Reich Chancellor Bülow. Even had he been a Bismarck, Bülow would have had difficulty wriggling out from under the crushing weight of Tirpitz's naval estimates (300 million marks a year by 1907) which added nearly two billion marks to the German national debt between 1897 and 1914 (Herwig 1994: 61). In 1907 the chancellor wrote Tirpitz a letter suggesting that naval expenditures at this dizzying level no longer served a tranquilizing political function: 'When will you finally be sufficiently advanced with your fleet so that the unbearable political situation can be relieved?' (Herwig 1994: 62). Tirpitz's budgets and *Novellen* were 'crowding out' essential spending in other areas, alienating virtually every German political constituency, to say nothing of foreign powers. Yet given British counter-measures (Fisher planned to build no less than eight dreadnoughts in 1909, twice the German rate) Tirpitz could not relent, and Bülow's bloc or *Sammlung* collapsed in 1909, due largely to public exasperation with the 'Tirpitz fleet'. The politically influential German army, which had been starved of funds since 1898 to feed the navy, angrily turned its back on the chancellor, and German conservatives, who had formed the backbone of the 'Bülow bloc', deserted it when they realized the degree to which Germany's economy was being mortgaged to the big naval contractors and its security to the navy, which would be a questionable asset at best in the event of a French or Russian land invasion (Berghahn 1993: 90–6).

Through all of this turmoil, Tirpitz remained sanguine. He saw clearly that dreadnoughts offered Germany a splendid new opportunity. If HMS *Dreadnought* really did render all previous battleships obsolete, then Fisher had done something quite foolish. In his rush to embrace new technology, Fisher – who scrapped seventeen older battleships to make room in the Admiralty budget for *Dreadnought* – had thrown away Britain's superiority in pre-dreadnought battleships and cruisers, and had levelled the playing field in the Anglo-German Navy Race, giving the Germans their best chance ever to catch up (Herwig 1994: 49, 54). Hence the *Novellen*: Tirpitz believed that a last great effort on the part of the German taxpayer would bridge the battleship gap and establish the soundness of the 'risk theory'. The role of the press and political pressure groups like the German Navy League was a fascinating aspect of this contest. In Britain and Germany, popular newspapers and lobbyists made it difficult for the governments to approach one another calmly. The British Naval Board's prediction in 1909 that Germany might have the capacity to put seventeen dreadnoughts to sea by 1912 to Britain's eighteen ignited a 'navy scare' featuring recriminatory speeches, angry demonstrations and a vogue for 'invasion literature', bestselling novels like *The Riddle of the Sands*, *Britain at Bay* and *The Invasion of 1910*. Most of the novels described a German 'bolt from the blue' across the North Sea to the unguarded British Isles. Saki's effort, *When William Came: A Story of London under the Hohenzollerns* (1913) described a defeated Britain 'incorporated within the Hohenzollern Empire ... as a Reichsland, a sort of Alsace-Lorraine washed by the North Sea instead of the Rhine' (Ferguson 1998: 2–3, 13–15; Marder 1961–70: I, 180–1; Herwig 1994: 51). Under the influence of literature like this and Fisher's dire warnings that the Germans could build eight dreadnoughts a year, the British people, previously content to build four dreadnoughts per annum, took up the cry 'we want eight and we won't wait'. Winston Churchill, Fisher's successor in 1911, drily noted the impact of public opinion: 'The Admiralty had demanded six ships; the economists offered four; and we finally compromised on eight' (Morris 1984: 178; Bartlett 1994: 61; Hough 1983: 15).

In Germany, Bülow, his successor Theobald von Bethmann Hollweg, and the Kaiser laboured under similar restrictions. Bülow, a suave aristocrat, had always lamented the rise of 'beer-hall politics' in Germany, by which he meant grassroots pressure from beer-swilling nationalists of the lower and middle classes. Such men, long disdained or ignored by the Prussian old guard, flexed their muscles after 1898, organizing into politically influential pressure groups like the Pan-German and Navy Leagues and the Colonial Society, and pushing Kaiser Wilhelm II to adopt a more assertive tone in his dealings with rival powers. The Navy League, with a million members and rich subsidies from German heavy industry, was the most powerful German pressure group, and it tended to manipulate the Kaiser, rather than the other way round (Ferguson 1998: 16–20; Eley 1980). Half-hearted attempts by Tirpitz or Bülow to woo political partners or appease foreign powers by slowing the pace of naval construction, ignited indignant rallies and press campaigns overseen by the Navy League. By 1900 'popular navalism' was deeply entrenched in Germany. Tirpitz had created a special news bureau to manipulate the press, had converted the navy's dull professional journal into a glossy popular magazine, and had founded a naval newspaper, *Die Flotte*, which attracted 750,000 paid subscribers. The Kaiser, who indulged a passion for naval uniforms and yachting, and unfailingly dressed his children in sailor suits, organized naval rallies all over Germany, and sent his most charismatic officers into the Reichstag to lobby for even bigger naval budgets. As many as 270 German scholars, including luminaries like Max Weber, Hans Delbrück and Hermann Oncken, signed on as 'fleet professors', touring Germany to lecture on the importance of sea power (Herwig 1994: 39–41).

Pressured by these new cultural and political forces, the British and German governments raced to build dreadnoughts and faster, even better armed 'super dreadnoughts' in the years before 1914. The Second Hague Peace Conference (the first in 1899 had accomplished little more than a ban on dum-dum bullets and poison gas) convened to discuss disarmament at the Hague in 1907, got nowhere, most of the powers seeming to share Tsar Nicholas II's view that 'disarmament was an idea just of Jews, Socialists, and hysterical women' (Stevenson 1996: 109). In fact, the Germans were the principal obstacle to disarmament, for they rightly suspected that a British-proposed freeze on dreadnought construction was intended merely to perpetuate German naval inferiority. With the Russian fleet rusting on the floor of the Pacific, the British could afford a smaller navy, and needed only to persuade the Germans to stop building. Tirpitz, with the Navy League breathing fire down his neck, could not give way. Between 1908 and 1912 he laid down four keels a year, and built Germany's first 'super dreadnoughts'; they were longer than two football pitches laid end-to-end, 2,000 tons heavier than the dreadnoughts, and capable of racing along at 22 knots (Herwig 1994: 65–8; Sumida 1989: 190). When pressed by the British to slow down, Tirpitz exploded: 'You, the colossus, come and ask Germany, the pygmy, to disarm. From the point of view of the public it is laughable and Machiavellian, and we shall never agree to anything of the sort' (Stevenson 1996: 108). In fact, the Kaiser was willing to slow down, but only on condition that the British break with France and Russia and give the Germans 'freedom of movement' on the Continent (Marder 1961–70: I, 177). As the British could not agree to such a barefaced bid for hegemony, the naval race continued.

By 1911 the Germans had nine dreadnoughts to Britain's fifteen. British alarmists, who had direly predicted seventeen German dreadnoughts by this date, had plainly overestimated German capacity. So too had the Kaiser. In July 1911, Wilhelm II attempted to use his growing navy to prise apart the Triple Entente. He searched for a lever – a place disputed by the French and the British and of no value to the Russians – and found Morocco. Far from Russia's Balkan and Asian spheres of interest, and wedged between French Algeria and British Gibraltar, Morocco seemed the perfect place to test the

Anglo-French alliance. Certain that the British would not back French claims to North Africa, the Kaiser's foreign secretary, Alfred Kiderlen-Wächter, countered France's military occupation of Fez in May 1911 by sending a German cruiser to lay claim to Agadir in July. Kiderlen wanted compensation in Morocco or Central Africa, and a complete reshuffling of colonies worldwide to Germany's advantage (Herrmann 1996: 148–9; Keiger 1983: 34–5).

This Second Moroccan Crisis was Germany's second attempt to pressure the French and British into a redistribution of their colonies. The German-instigated First Moroccan Crisis in 1905 had fallen flat (the French stunning the Germans by actually arming for war) and Tirpitz knew all along that this second attempt would also fail, for the Germans, having let their army run down to build a navy, had neither the military nor the naval strength to fight a war with the British, French and Russians in 1911. Indeed, so certain was Tirpitz of defeat that his Naval Office declined to contribute more than a single gunboat to the operation (rather than the four cruisers sought by Kiderlen) and speculated throughout on the 'tremendous indignation' that failure in Morocco would arouse in Germany (Lambi 1984: 316–21; Berghahn 1993: 112). The navy's rather unpatriotic gamble paid off; in July 1911 Britain's Liberal government lined up solidly beside the French, forcing the Germans to accept a humiliatingly small strip of the French Congo in return for France's outright annexation of Morocco. With uncharacteristic humour, Germany's colonial secretary grumbled that the ceded territory was 'partly almost worthless, partly completely worthless' (Steiner 1977: 70–8; Joll 1992: 136). As Tirpitz had foreseen, the Second Moroccan Crisis gave a fresh impetus to the Anglo-German Navy Race. Angered by Britain's intransigence, the Reichstag voted the third *Novelle* in 1911 to equip a fleet of twenty-five battleships and eight battlecruisers by 1913. Even Germany's Social Democrats succumbed to war fever, resolving at their party congress in September 1911 not to obstruct the mobilization of the German armed forces if the crisis with Britain and France came to a head (Stevenson 1996: 193). Ultimately, the Moroccan Crisis did not trigger a general war, but only because Wilhelm II discovered in the midst of the crisis what his general staff had been telling him for years: that the Kaiser's single-minded focus on sea power had left the German army in a vulnerable position *vis-à-vis* the combined, growing armies of England, France and Russia. The Moroccan Crisis would therefore force a reorientation in German armaments policy; priority would be shifted from the navy to the army.

What made this German *Rüstungswende* (armaments reorientation) so explosive was the fact that the Germans in no way relented in their navy race with the British as they began to race with the French and Russians on land. In March 1912, the British offered the Germans a 'naval holiday', a suspension of new construction that would permit both powers to ratchet down expenditures and balance their budgets. Wilhelm II declined; indeed he characterized the British offer as yet another 'perfidious' attempt to deny the

Germans their rightful place in the sun, and authorized a fourth *Novelle*. But was the protection of German interests the Kaiser's sole motive, or was the 1912–14 burst of German shipbuilding the last gasp of 'fleet policy'? Probably both: 1912 was a thoroughly bad year for Wilhelm II. In Reichstag elections, the Social Democrats broke through at last, becoming Germany's largest political party with 110 seats. The mines and factories of the Ruhr were closed by strikes, and reopened only when army troops were brought in to break the picket lines. All of this discord prompted renewed talk in the Kaiser's entourage of a *Staatsstreich* or coup against the Reichstag, and seems to have persuaded Wilhelm II that war was as good a means as any to release the social and political pressure building in Germany. Whatever the exact mix of motives, the Kaiser did nothing to ease tensions with England as his domestic predicament worsened. Together with Tirpitz, he decided to forge ahead at all costs to complete the battle fleet of his dreams: three squadrons of eight dreadnoughts and twelve battle cruisers, sixty capital ships in all. It was an unattainable dream; by 1913, poor, straitened Germany would be spending 90 per cent of its national income on defence (Bond 1986: 80).

Finances were never Tirpitz's chief concern; hence the irrepressible navy secretary reckoned that even allowing for British counter-measures, German construction would yield a 95:61 ratio by 1920, favourable enough odds to jettison the 'risk theory' and embrace a new one that envisioned German *victory* on the high seas (Stevenson 1996: 197). German hopes (and British fears) were pinned on the qualitative excellence of the German dreadnoughts. Last into the dreadnought race, the Germans had carefully examined early British models (like HMS *Dreadnought*) and improved them in some respects. The German battleships built before 1914 were described by one historian as 'the most difficult-to-sink warships in naval history'. Squatter and wider than the British dreadnoughts, the German battleships had more underwater protection than their British rivals and honeycomb subdivision (13–20 watertight compartments) inside the hull. And because Tirpitz's *Kriegsmarine* was based principally in home waters, the ships could be more heavily armoured than British ones, which needed fuel efficiency to cruise between distant stations. Thus a typical German dreadnought carried 13¾ inches of armour, a British dreadnought just 12. Though the British ships were faster and better armed, the Germans looked to be bridging this gap as well, fitting their second- and third generation dreadnoughts with diesel engines and testing massive 20-inch guns in 1914 (Hough 1983: 46–7; Herwig 1994: 58–67).

So even with one-third fewer ships than the British, the Germans would be a fearsome adversary, particularly in view of England's global commitments. With this in mind, the British abandoned their traditional policies of 'splendid isolation' and 'business as usual' after 1900. To contain Tirpitz's High Seas Fleet in future crises, the British joined forces with the French, a development that would have been anathema to both parties under normal circumstances. Henceforth the Royal Navy would patrol the North Sea and the English Channel, the French the Mediterranean. Tirpitz's 'risk theory' had always been founded on the assumption that the British would not strip the Empire of naval protection to defend England. In the event, the British did just that, grimly reducing their global presence after 1900 to defend home waters, and placing greater emphasis on a land army to aid the French and the Belgians (French 1986: 13–14; Kennedy 1976: 229). Ironically, the 'Tirpitz fleet', which had been conceived in part to make Germany more *bündnisfähig* or 'alliance worthy' by endowing the Reich with a naval weapon, had in fact made Germany more isolated, driving once-friendly powers like England and the US into outright hostility, and increasing rather than decreasing Germany's reliance on its one stalwart ally: weak, volatile Austria–Hungary. As the Second Moroccan Crisis wound down, Winston Churchill confided Britain's heightened state of alert *vis-à-vis* Germany to his diary: 'So now the Admiralty wireless whispers through the ether to the tall masts of ships, and captains pace their decks absorbed in thought' (Stevenson 1996: 186). A world war was in sight.

CHAPTER EIGHT

War plans and armaments: the deadly spiral, 1911–14

Germany's diplomatic defeat in the Second Moroccan Crisis galled the Kaiser's military entourage, who increasingly viewed war as the only means to win respect in Europe and a global empire. In October 1911, General Friedrich von Bernhardi published *Germany and the Next War*, a sensational call to arms by a respected military figure, that scolded the Kaiser for relenting in Morocco and insisted that Germany had a duty not only to defend itself and Austria-Hungary, but to 'struggle for the sovereignty of the world' (Bernhardi 1914: 78–9). Bernhardi contrasted Italy's bold declaration of war on the Ottoman Empire in 1911 and its seizure of Libya with Germany's timid conduct in Morocco, first going to the brink of war, then backing down. Germans, Bernhardi argued, needed to behave more like Italians: in the reckless spirit of *sacro egoismo*. Tirpitz quite agreed; he wrote the Kaiser a secret memorandum in April 1912 rather shockingly titled: 'Bringing about the outbreak of war'. In it, the navy secretary posed a blunt question: 'Should Germany speed up [the outbreak of war] or attempt to delay it?' Several months later, Field Marshal Colmar von der Goltz met with Reich Chancellor Bethmann Hollweg to discuss prospects for a great army bill Bethmann was preparing to submit to the Reichstag. The bill was immense: it requested 188 million marks of supplementary spending, and was intended to make good the neglect of the German army since the 1890s (Herrmann 1996: 171). This level of military spending, on top of Tirpitz's latest *Novelle*, was certain to raise cries of protest in the Reichstag and in foreign capitals. With this in mind, Bethmann Hollweg told von der Goltz: 'If we make such large demands, *then we must firmly intend to strike soon*'. The field marshal agreed: 'Yes, of course, then we would be pursuing *a proper policy*'. Both men spoke reverently of Bismarck on this occasion, characterizing Bismarck's nineteenth-century wars with Austria and France as 'preventive wars', and suggesting that a new round was needed 'for the benefit of the fatherland' (Wilson and John Röhl, in Wilson 1995: 40–3; Tunstall 1993: 118–19).

The Schlieffen Plan

Germany's eagerness to wage war stemmed from the offensive nature of German war planning. Although the Prussian belief in the efficacy of preventive, annihilating wars dated at least from the reign of Frederick the Great, Moltke and Bismarck had engraved the reflex on Prusso-German military thinking (Rothenberg, in Paret 1986: 296–7). Faced with Austrian and French opposition to Prussian expansion in Germany in the 1860s, Moltke and Bismarck had gruffly eliminated the obstacles, crushing the Austrians in 1866 and the French in 1870–1. In both instances, diplomacy had been quickly, intentionally used up and replaced with war. Indeed, Prussia's delegate to the German Confederation in Frankfurt had still been arguing Prussia's case for federal reform in June 1866 when the Prussian army smashed down the frontier posts of Holstein, Hanover and Saxony and began the invasion of Austria and its German allies. In 1870, Bismarck needled Napoleon III until the French emperor frustratedly declared war on Prussia, justifying a swingeing Prusso-German invasion of France. In both cases, 1866 and 1870, war had sliced cleanly through political knots. The Austrians, deeply enmeshed in the German states, offering scads of legal, historical, and procedural objections to every Prussian attempt to streamline the German Confederation, had been roughly removed from Germany at the battle of Königgrätz. The French, wedged like a chisel into Germany's western borderlands, had been smashed at the battles of Gravelotte and Sedan and driven from Alsace-Lorraine. Although the French recovery from defeat was to proceed more quickly than anyone had anticipated, France had been conclusively removed as a factor in German national life, and the new German Reich was proclaimed in Louis XIV's palace at Versailles to underline the point.

The history of 1866 and 1870 profoundly influenced the subsequent generations of German statesmen and general staff officers. As Germany's foreign relations worsened in the 1890s – England alienated by 'fleet policy'; Russia by punitive tariffs and Wilhelm II's Slavophobic rantings; France by the loss of Alsace-Lorraine and Germany's bullying 'world policy' – Moltke's successors on the general staff crafted a military plan to escape what they perceived as the steady 'encirclement' (*Einkreisung*) of Germany. This was the so-called Schlieffen Plan, fashioned by General Alfred von Schlieffen in the years between 1894 and 1905. Ironically, Bismarck and Moltke would almost certainly have disavowed the plan had they lived to see it take shape. Bismarck had always held the Prussian army on a short leash, fighting for *limited* objectives in Austria and France, and striving throughout to neutralize interested powers like Britain and Russia. Moltke, who owed his victories in 1866 and 1870 in large part to Germany's early adoption of universal conscription, which had made war with Austria feasible and literally drowned the small French army in German manpower, saw clearly that this crucial advantage was lost forever after 1871, when all European armies, including the French and

Russians, adopted compulsory military service. As a result, Moltke had become cautious in the years after the Franco-Prussian War, arguing, like Bismarck, that Germany's task was henceforth defensive: to maintain the German borders of 1871. Indeed, Moltke would spend the last years before his death in 1888 arguing for a defensive strategy that would fit with Bismarck's own defensive 'politics of national consolidation' (*Konsolidierungs-politik*). Unfortunately, such prudence was not for Schlieffen and a younger generation of German officers, who viewed Germany's *fin-de-siècle* troubles as merely an evolved, higher-stakes version of the difficulties faced by Moltke and Bismarck in the 1860s. Like Moltke then, Schlieffen in 1900 saw offensive war planning as Germany's best hope for survival in a world that was indifferent or hostile to German interests.

The Kaiser appointed fifty-eight year-old Alfred von Schlieffen Chief of the German General Staff in 1891. Schlieffen's great misfortune was to assume the staff post at the very moment when republican France and imperial Russia were burying their ideological differences and forging a military alliance aimed at the Germans. Whereas Moltke had faced such a prospect certain that defensive German spoiling attacks – brutally augmented by modern firepower – would gradually wear down even a Franco-Russian combination, Schlieffen was not so sure. He made a study of European armies in 1892 and concluded that the French and Russians together outnumbered the Germans by a ratio of 2:1 (Bucholz 1991: 154). To Schlieffen and the Kaiser, it seemed foolhardy to give the French and Russians time to develop this numerical advantage. Since the Russians were notoriously slow to mobilize (Schlieffen's report approvingly noted 'the almost railwayless vastness of Russia'), Schlieffen proposed settling any serious dispute with the French or the Russians by the following method: the massed German army would invade and crush France within six weeks and then redeploy to Russia, where, assisted by the Austro-Hungarians, it would smash the slow-moving Russian army at the very moment that it was completing its mobilization, roughly ten weeks from the invasion of France. To sceptics in Vienna who objected that the Russians might overrun Austria-Hungary before the arrival of the German army from France, Schlieffen confidently replied that 'the fate of Austria will be decided not on the Bug but on the Seine' (Stone, in Kennedy 1979: 224; Snyder 1984: 115–17). He meant that the rapid elimination of the French army would isolate the Russians, and permit the Germans and Austro-Hungarians to destroy them at their leisure.

Schlieffen's inspiration was unusual. In 1900, as he wrestled with the problem of how simultaneously to fight the French and Russians and overcome a two-to-one disadvantage in troop strength, he read Hans Delbrück's *History of the Art of War* and was struck by Delbrück's account of the battle of Cannae in 216 BC. Cannae was the greatest feat of ancient arms; with just 25,000 men, Hannibal had annihilated an army of 50,000 Roman legionaries. Hannibal had accomplished this by wheeling his Carthaginians around the flanks of the Roman legions to hit them in the rear, where they were thinly defended and easily panicked. The Carthaginians killed 48,000 legionaries in the course of the battle, effectively disarming the Romans. Since Schlieffen too was outnumbered on the order of two-to-one, he took Cannae as a kind of model for a war with France and Russia. Hannibal had succeeded because he had skirted the Roman front and struck instead 'along the entire depth and extension of the hostile formation', pushing chaos and panic into the Roman legions from the flank before rolling them up from behind (Bucholz 1991: 156–7). Schlieffen proposed to apply the same basic principle to a war with the French. A German army invading France would not tiptoe up to the excellent French fortifications around Verdun and Belfort and obligingly deploy itself for a siege, rather it would hook through Belgium and Luxembourg, brush past the foremost French armies and fortifications, turn into their rear and pulverize them from behind. Liddell Hart aptly characterized Schlieffen's plan as 'a revolving door' (Liddell Hart 1964: 68–9). The German army would revolve through neutral Belgium and Luxembourg to bypass France's eastern forts, pivot west of Paris, and then circle in behind the French army, crushing it against the Jura and the Swiss border.

Although some questioned the violation of Belgian neutrality on the grounds that it would draw England into the war, Schlieffen retorted that 'a German army that seeks to wheel around Verdun must not shrink from violating the neutrality of Belgium as well as that of Luxembourg' (Stone, in Kennedy 1979: 224). If the British dispatched an expeditionary force to defend Belgium or disengage the French, so much the better. The British army would either be knocked into the sea or scooped up and driven with the French and the Belgians towards France's eastern border to be destroyed by the massed German army at their rear, and a smaller German force that would seal Schlieffen's 'pocket' in Alsace-Lorraine (Herwig 1997: 46–7; Turner, in Kennedy 1979: 204–5). The most striking feature of the Schlieffen Plan was its confident disregard of political complications (like the attitude of England, Belgium or Holland), and the ease with which Germany's civilian decision-makers were persuaded to accept it. The Kaiser backed the plan from the start, as did his chief ministers. In 1900 Schlieffen discussed his plan with government officials for the first time. Friedrich von Holstein, the German foreign ministry's elder statesman, spoke for his colleagues when he said: 'If the Chief of the Great General Staff, and particularly a strategic authority such as Schlieffen, thought such a measure to be necessary, *then it would be the duty of diplomacy to adjust itself and prepare for it in every possible way*' (Bucholz 1991: 177; Turner, in Kennedy 1979: 206–7; Joll 1992: 100–1).

In the years after 1900, Schlieffen carefully plotted the Cannae-like encirclement of the French. At first, he planned merely to deploy the bulk of the German army against the French. Then, in 1904–5, something extraordinary happened; Russia, France's key ally, was flattened by the Manchurian War. With its navy destroyed, its army gutted and its peoples convulsed by the

Revolution of 1905, Russia was rendered all but useless to the French for several years. This permitted Schlieffen to take his slowly maturing plan to its logical conclusion: in 1905, he stripped Germany's eastern defences to mass the entire German army – nearly two million men – against a French army that would have been hard-pressed to muster 800,000 combat troops. A recent study of European war plans and armaments indicates that had the First Moroccan Crisis in 1905 ended in war, the Germans would probably have won it. Untroubled by the Russians, they would have enjoyed unbeatable odds against France (Herrmann 1996: 45–51).

War did not come in 1905, and the Kaiser, never comfortable with elder statesmen and soldiers, asked for Schlieffen's resignation at year's end. Schlieffen continued to develop his plan in retirement, and died in 1912 at the age of eighty, imploring the officers gathered at his bedside to 'keep the right wing strong', that is, to concentrate the entire German army in the West, and pivot heavily through Belgium to annihilate the British and take the French in flank and rear before turning against the Russians. Schlieffen was succeeded by Field Marshal Helmuth von Moltke, the nephew of the 'Elder Moltke', as Germans now reverently called the great one. Though handsome, charming, glib and personally brave, the 'Younger Moltke' was a poor strategist. Indeed, he seems to have been chosen by the Kaiser principally for his martial looks. To Bülow, Moltke frankly confessed: 'I lack the power of rapid decision; I am too reflective, too scrupulous, or, if you like, conscientious for such a post. I lack the capacity for risking all on a single throw' (Turner, in Kennedy 1979: 210). Moltke was also hampered by the war plan inherited from Schlieffen. The plan was freighted with the political irritants described above, and was militarily feasible only if the Russians remained down and out. As the Russians recovered in the years after 1905, the Schlieffen Plan appeared increasingly unworkable to Moltke. Financed by the French, who had a powerful interest in Russia's military recovery, the Russian army not only reformed its weapons and tactics, it embarked on a railway construction programme to accelerate mobilization and scupper all of the hopeful assumptions behind the Schlieffen Plan.

Pressed in east and west, Moltke and his hard-working chief of operations, Colonel Erich Ludendorff, began making adjustments, small ones at first, and then fundamental changes. Whereas Schlieffen had implored his successors in 1911 to 'throw the whole of Germany against one enemy … the Anglo-French', Moltke and Ludendorff detached four entire corps to the Russian front, and would send two additional ones in 1914. At the same time, they effectively threw Schlieffen's 'revolving door' into reverse by weakening the 'right hook' through Belgium in order to strengthen the units defending Alsace-Lorraine. This ran counter to the spirit of the Schlieffen Plan, which had aimed to pull the French into Alsace-Lorraine so that the massive 'right hook' could push into their rear with decisive, shattering impact. By deploying an additional fourteen divisions to defend Germany's western border,

Moltke made it likely that French attacks in Alsace and Lorraine would *not* succeed; indeed they would probably be driven backward into the path of the German right wing descending through Belgium, the exact opposite of what Schlieffen had intended (Turner, in Kennedy 1979: 211–12). Had Schlieffen lived to see the battle of the Marne in September 1914, he would have shed tears at Moltke's revision of his plan, which stranded Germany between two stools: too weak in the West to win decisively, too weak in the East to defend Germany's frontiers and brace Germany's Austro-Hungarian ally against the Russian steamroller. And yet the plan remained: a dangerous provocation and an ever-present harbinger of German aggression.

What made the Schlieffen Plan so provocative was its hair-trigger quality and its militaristic willingness to overrun neutral states like Belgium. Since tremendous speed was required to beat the French and Russians in quick succession, the plan could tolerate no diplomatic tergiversations, and utterly depended upon a violation of Belgian neutrality that would connect up the dense German railways on the lower Rhine with the rail net of northeastern France. (Hence the Kaiser's rather shocking demand of the King of the Belgians in 1904 that he promptly deliver the Belgian forts and railways into German hands in the event of a Franco-German War [Bucholz 1991: 176; Turner, in Kennedy 1979: 206–7].) If a crisis threatened war, the Schlieffen Plan had to be implemented at once, or the advantages of speed and surprise would be lost, giving the French time to 'refuse' or pull back their threatened flank, the British time to dig in, and the Russians time to crawl across their 'vast, railwayless space' to the German and Austrian frontiers. Indeed, speed was so essential that Ludendorff told Moltke in 1912 that 'the Kaiser would not even be asked in case of war'. War would simply be declared by the German general staff (Herwig 1987: 24). Finally, Schlieffen's decision, upheld by Moltke, to sweep through Belgium despite its neutrality, virtually guaranteed the intervention of England in a Continental war. Given the power of the Royal Navy and its uncompromising determination to keep Belgium's ports out of German hands, this was a reckless decision; Schlieffen would not live to see its consequences, but his successors would: a blockade of the German ports, famine, and revolution in the streets of Germany.

Austro-Hungarian war plans

The pandemonium that swallowed the Austro-Hungarian mobilization in 1914 – comically described in Jaroslav Hasek's *The Good Soldier Svejk* – tends to make one think in retrospect that the Austro-Hungarians were a relatively harmless, comic opera power. Quite the contrary: until 1897, the Germans and Austrians planned for war together, linking the Schlieffen Plan to an Austrian offensive in the East that would stun the Russians and prevent them coming to France's aid. Unfortunately, joint Austro-German planning petered out after 1900, mainly due to German mistrust of the Austro-Hungarian general staff, which by the 1890s had been penetrated by Russian spies (Tunstall 1993: 50). Nevertheless, the Germans and Austrians remained military allies, and the Austro-Hungarian army possessed forty-eight infantry divisions. It was reasonably well equipped, and commanded by the wildest general in Europe: Franz Conrad von Hötzendorf.

Conrad – fifty-four years old in 1906 when he became Chief of the Austro-Hungarian General Staff – was a deadly serious soldier whose career in the Habsburg army had been moulded by the Great Disaster of 1866. Indeed, Conrad's life might best be interpreted as an angry reaction to the strategic fumbling and defensive hesitancy that had characterized Benedek's command in the Austro-Prussian War. The ambitious little *Wiener*, with his bristling moustaches, flashing blue eyes and wizened mask, devoted his life to bringing order and decision to the notoriously inefficient Austro-Hungarian army, a quest that ended tragically in 1914. Lamenting that Austria spent most of its energy negatively, i.e. repressing rebellious nationalities, Conrad argued for a more positive programme. With the examples of Cavour and Bismarck in mind, he wrote that 'a strong state must have positive goals; it must be internally unified and externally focused' (Hötzendorf 1903: 101; 1921–3: I, 39–43). Indeed, to Conrad the chief lesson of the Bismarck wars was that armies needed political goals in peacetime and clear military objectives in wartime. Just as Bismarck and Moltke had successively targeted the Danes, the Austrians and the French to achieve the aim of German unification in the 1860s, Conrad targeted the Russians, Serbs and Italians as the main threats to Austria-Hungary's survival as a multinational empire, and planned to destroy them in war (Rauchensteiner 1994: 20).

Conrad's determination to 'refound' the Austro-Hungarian Empire through victorious wars with Russia and Serbia was the basis of 'War Case R+B', drafted during the First Balkan War in 1912 and refined in the months before July 1914. On paper, Conrad's war plan was a marvellously elastic instrument designed to wring maximal advantage from Austria-Hungary's relatively small army, which, numbering just forty-eight divisions, was little more than one-third the size of the Russian army. The Conrad plan sliced the Habsburg army into three pieces: *Minimalgruppe Balkan*, *A Staffel* and *B-Staffel*, and set each of them a different task. In the event of a war with both Russia and Serbia (the most likely scenario) the nine infantry divisions of *Minimalgruppe Balkan* would thrust across the Danube and the Drina, take Belgrade, and erase Serbia as a threat to Austro-Hungarian primacy in the Balkans. Meanwhile, the twenty-seven infantry divisions of *A-Staffel* would combine with at least twelve German divisions in Poland and Ukraine to attack the Russians and unhinge their mobilization. Once the conquests of France and Serbia were complete, Russia could be beaten and partitioned at a more leisurely pace by the combined German and Austrian armies (Tunstall 1993: 138). The ten infantry divisions of *B-Staffel* were a floating reserve to be deployed against Russia, Serbia or Italy as circumstances dictated (Herwig

1997: 52–3). The fact that Italy was technically an Austrian ally until 1915 reassured no one in Vienna. Though the Italians always took care to remain on good terms with the Germans, they secretly concluded a non-aggression pact with the Russians in 1909, and actively planned for war with the Austro-Hungarians, building dreadnoughts faster than the Austrians to contest the Adriatic, and reconfiguring their fortresses and railways to facilitate battles for Trentino, Gorizia and Trieste, three Austrian provinces dubiously claimed by the Italians since 1861 (Bosworth 1983: 55–8). Only Italy's costly decision to declare war on the Ottoman Empire and annex Libya in 1911–12 moderated the Italian threat to Austria. The Libyan War pinned down 100,000 Italian troops, cost 500 million lire, and stalled King Vittorio Emanuele III's plans to expand and modernize his armed forces on the eve of World War I (J. Gooch 1989: 136–7, 145; Stevenson 1996: 226–9; Rauchensteiner 1994: 48–9).

Still, the extreme difficulty of Conrad von Hötzendorf's strategic situation, and the complexity of his war plan – one army moving south, another east, a third floating in between – all but forced the Austrians to choose the moment for war, for they not only had to move in three directions at once, but they also had to finish with Serbia quickly in order to mass their entire army on the eastern front against the Russians and prepare for the eventuality of an Italian attack. Conrad was more sanguine than most, predicting that he could beat Serbia *and* have twenty-seven divisions on the Russian front by 'M+15' (fifteen days after the start of mobilization) and the bulk of the army there by M+25. To accomplish this, speed would be essential, a blinkered haste that would leave no room for diplomacy in a crisis. To make his plans work, Conrad would need to seize upon a crisis and spring swiftly into action. Conrad was willing, perhaps too willing: in 1909 he begged the Austrian emperor to exploit the havoc wrought by an earthquake in Sicily to invade Italy; and in 1911 he seized upon Rome's bungled invasion of Libya as the best chance ever for a preemptive strike across the Alps, gross indiscretions that resulted in his temporary removal from the general staff on the eve of the Balkan Wars. In Berlin, the Younger Moltke lamented these 'Austro-Hungarian follies', by which he meant the likelihood that Vienna, not Berlin, would choose the moment for the next war and launch it not for a vital German interest, but a peripheral Austrian one (Tunstall 1993: 120).

French, British and Russian war plans

French war plans were the handiwork of General Joseph Joffre, an offensive-minded strategist appointed Chief of the French General Staff in July 1911 during the Second Moroccan Crisis (King 1951: 11–14). Fifty-nine year-old Joffre – the portly son of a Pyrenéan barrel-maker – had first experienced combat forty years earlier during the Franco-Prussian War. Like Ferdinand Foch and Louis Grandmaison, the French army's apostles of the 'offensive spirit' between 1870 and 1914, Joffre inferred a rather too simple lesson from

Moltke's rapid encirclement of Bazaine and MacMahon in 1870: defensive operations and tactics were to be avoided at all costs. They demoralized the men and handed the initiative to the enemy. From this inference it was natural to conclude that only headlong offensives into enemy territory held the promise of victory. The real danger of this post-Sedan mentality was its psychological dimension. Joffre's field service regulations for 1913 declared that 'the offensive alone leads to positive results. ... *Battles are above all moral struggles*'. Naturally, attacks were intended to seize the initiative from the enemy, but Joffre – a republican and a freemason – was also tapping into a French political phenomenon called the 'new nationalism', which had reversed the old party lines on the issue of war in the 1890s. Ever since the Dreyfus Affair, which had scandalized the French right, it had been the French left, the Radical Republicans, who had most aggressively espoused a revanchist foreign policy to beat the Germans and reclaim Alsace-Lorraine. Joffre's tactics suited them, for the *offensive à outrance* seemed to conform better to the French national character (furious and proud), and, with officers leading and falling from the front, it was more republican in spirit (Becker and Audoin-Rouzeau 1995: 250–5; Gat 1992: 164–6; Snyder 1984: 70–5, 96–8).

The French 'cult of the offensive' was also cheap; Radical deputies and the generals like Joffre who indulged them convinced themselves that 'moral force' would somehow suffice to overcome the German army's numerical and material superiority, which was on the order of two-to-one in 1913 (Travers 1987: 254). Clearly, there was much dishonesty in the French tactics; Joffre, far too practical a man to be fooled by the high-flown rhetoric of his theorists, knew that the storm tactics were flawed but kept at them to please his political bosses. Real insights, like those of Colonel Philippe Pétain at the Ecole de Guerre, who stressed the inevitable preponderance of defensive fire on the twentieth-century battlefield, were stolidly ignored (Porch 1981: 217–19, 246–7; Travers 1987: 254). Needless to say, this foolhardy insistence on the offensive at all costs further destabilized a political situation that was already tilting toward war under the great weight of the Schlieffen Plan.

The basis of French war planning was tactical, and stemmed from the opposite conclusions drawn from the Franco Prussian War by French and German military thinkers. Whereas the Germans studied their heavy casualties at battles like Spicheren and Gravelotte, and concluded that massed battalions of infantry and bayonet charges no longer had a place on the modern, fire-intensive battlefield, the French viewed the German victories *despite* heavy casualties as proof that fire was not the decisive element in modern war; morale was. The most famous exponent of this romantic view was Colonel Charles Ardant du Picq, who was killed in action at Metz in 1870. Ardant du Picq's *Battle Studies*, based on a questionnaire circulated to French troops in 1868 and the author's own observations in the war of 1870, was published posthumously in 1880. Although the book is more balanced and sensible than is generally believed, it suggested to the casual reader that 'moral action' could outweigh 'destructive action' on the modern battlefield, that a foe relying too much on 'superiority of material' could be swept away by one's own essentially psychological 'determination to get to close quarters' (Howard, in Paret 1986: 515; Gat 1992: 31–2). This was a suicidal recommendation at the end of the nineteenth century, when clip-loaded rifles, machineguns and high explosive had made battlefields geometrically more dangerous than in 1870. It also made a virtue of the attack, impelling the French army to deploy most of its strength on the German border for an eventual reconquest of Alsace-Lorraine and a lunge at Berlin.

In 1912 Joffre began drafting Plan XVII, the war plan that France would execute with self-mutilating results in 1914. Whereas Plan XVI had strung the French army along defensive positions from the Channel coast to the Swiss frontier, Plan XVII positioned nearly 80 per cent of the French army near Alsace-Lorraine for a prompt attack into Germany. It was Ardant du Picq's *offensive à outrance* on a grand scale, and it ignored the likely impact of German defensive firepower (Williamson, in Kennedy 1979: 145). In 1911, France's war minister, General Adolphe Messimy, would have puzzled anyone who had studied the results of the Boer and Russo-Japanese Wars when he observed that 'neither numbers nor miraculous machines will determine victory; this will go to soldiers with … superior physical and moral endurance and superior offensive spirit'. Captain Georges Gilbert, who did study the Boer War, insisted that it was not the Mausers and the Maxim guns of the Boers that had done in the British, rather the superior morale of the Boer guerrillas, and the correspondingly low morale of the British colonial troops. Gilbert was the bright French theorist who also postulated that the spirit of 'the offensive automatically doubles the energy of the attacking troops' (Snyder 1984: 64–5). General Ferdinand Foch, future generalissimo of the Entente armies in World War I, shared the views of Gilbert, Messimy and Joffre, confronting French cadets at St Cyr before the war with the following equation: 'victory = will' (Herwig 1997: 65–7).

What exactly were the French generals thinking? Tim Travers perhaps comes closest to reading their minds by suggesting that they – and their imitators in Britain – did not really believe that superior morale was invincible; rather, having witnessed the devastation wrought by modern weapons, they needed to find a way to prod their men into the 'fire-swept zone'. These generals – Joffre and Foch in France, Haig and Robertson in Britain – cleverly substituted what Travers calls the 'psychological battlefield' for the real one, and hoped that their men would not notice the difference until they were well forward (Travers 1987: 66–72). Whatever the rationale, the fact remains that Plan XVII was bad strategy. It transported the bulk of the French army far away from the main German blow in Belgium, and set it the almost impossible task of wresting the wooded, heavily fortified hills of Alsace-Lorraine from two entire German armies. Perhaps the only argument in Plan XVII's favour was that the French, unlike the Germans, did not have to defend themselves on two fronts. They could throw everything they had across the Rhine, which, after passage of the French service law of 1913, was a substantial sum of men and material, some 700,000 troops. Overall, Joffre's unaccountable optimism in 1914 must have alarmed the Germans. He made light of the Schlieffen Plan (obtained by French military intelligence in 1903–4) and spoke confidently of a brusque 'four-week offensive' through Alsace-Lorraine and central Germany. The fact that Joffre's planning had no clear objectives must have made it all the more alarming to the Germans, who would not have credited such folly, and, with less than 10 per cent of their army holding the line in Alsace-Lorraine, would have sought anxiously for the reasons behind Joffre's frothy overconfidence (Herwig 1997: 67; Snyder 1984: 81–2).

Since French resources and manpower were inadequate both to invade Germany and defend France, Joffre relied heavily on the Russians and the British to disengage him in the event of war. In annual staff talks with the Russians beginning in 1912, the French exacted a Russian pledge to invade East Prussia with 800,000 men within twenty-three days of the French mobilization, a lag that would be reduced to fifteen days by 1914 (Stevenson 1996: 161). Joffre understood that only large-scale Russian assistance could draw off Germany's vast reserves and give Plan XVII a hope of success, and the Russians were willing. After the debacle of 1904–5 in Manchuria, Tsar Nicholas II had reorganized his army on a territorial basis, increased its peacetime strength to 1.4 million men, and concentrated twenty-seven of his thirty-seven army corps in European Russia (Menning 1992: 222–7). Guided by General Vladimir Sukhomlinov, Russian war minister from 1909–15, the tsar even came to share Joffre's enthusiasm for the offensive. Indeed, the Russian army celebrated the 1912 centenary of Napoleon's repulse at Moscow by deploring the defensive scorched-earth strategy adopted in 1812, and exalting the *sokrushenie* instead: the short war of annihilation *à la* Napoleon or Moltke. And the Russians really did want to annihilate the Germans and the Austrians. A French officer in St Petersburg noted that Russian military men hated Austria-Hungary to an extent 'as to totally take away judgement', Germany nearly as much (Lieven 1993: 116–17).

With these resentments in mind, the Russians finalized 'Plan 19' in May 1912. This Russian war plan promised attacks on the Germans with three armies and the Austrians with four by M+15: fifteen days after the commencement of French mobilization. Schlieffen had assured the Kaiser that the Russians would need forty days to transport armies to the front. For the Russians, M+15 was a blistering pace, a fact noted by the Germans, who worriedly looked on as Russia rearmed and constructed double- and quadruple-tracked railways to the German and Austro-Hungarian frontiers in the years between 1910 and 1914. This feverish Russian activity, instigated and subsidized by the French, effectively concealed much vacillation in the Russian high command – between fortifications and railways, between the

Austrian and German fronts, between field artillery and fortress guns – compounding German fears of encirclement in the months before the Great War (Stone 1975: 33–6; Menning 1992: 243–8, 270–1).

In the West, Joffre relied heavily on the British Expeditionary Force (BEF), which promised to land six divisions in Belgium and France upon the outbreak of war and build to a strength of 300,000 by M+40. Although Britain historically preferred a 'strategy of limited liability' in Europe, this preference began to change when Sir Henry Wilson became Director of Military Operations at the War Office in August 1910. In contrast to his predecessors, who had distanced themselves from *revanchard* generals in Paris, Wilson was for fast, effective cooperation with the French, insisting that Britain mobilize with the French and pitch in on Joffre's left flank against any German push through Holland, Belgium or Luxembourg. For Wilson (nicknamed 'dooble-vay' by critics less enamoured of the French), aid to France was much more than a defensive plan. His tenure at the War Office coincided with the publication of Sir Julian Corbett's influential *Principles of Maritime Strategy* (1911), which turned Mahan's prescriptions on their head. Whereas Mahan had insisted that navies put to sea to fight navies, Corbett, citing the Peninsular Campaign against Napoleon, the Crimean War and the Russo-Japanese War, argued that navies were best employed fighting armies, that is, in joint operations to land troops on a hostile shore or an unguarded flank and keep them well supplied with food, ammunition and supports (Corbett 1988; Gat 1992: 218–19). Wilson at the War Office and Churchill at the Admiralty were both 'Corbettians'; like Sir Julian, they viewed the British army and navy as 'the blade and hilt of one weapon', and resolved early on to use the Home Fleet to rush troops to the Continent to deal a decisive blow on the German flank in Flanders, Artois or Picardy (Philpott 1996: 3–7; J. Gooch 1974: 289–90; Williamson 1969: 302–5).

In this gradual way, the war plans of the Entente powers assumed a character as menacing as those of Germany and Austria-Hungary. Indeed, at the height of the Second Moroccan Crisis in 1911, when Sir Henry Wilson left London to make a bicycle tour of the Franco-Belgian frontier, the Belgians considered *him* far more likely to violate their neutrality than Moltke, and angrily told him so (Williamson 1969: 179–80; in Kennedy 1979: 142–3). The fact was, in a crisis leading to mobilization, time for the Entente would become as critical a commodity as it was for the Central Powers, dashing the chances for last-minute diplomacy in July 1914.

The European arms race, 1911–14

In *The Arming of Europe and the Making of the First World War*, David Herrmann argues that it was 'European perceptions of a changing balance of military power' more than any other single factor that caused war in 1914 (Herrmann 1996: 4–5). Though World War I had many long- and short-term causes, it was the nerve-wracking race after 1911 to expand strategic railways, create new infantry divisions, and add batteries of machineguns and artillery that strained relations between the Triple Entente and the Central Powers to breaking point. Herrmann's argument is substantiated by the findings of British historian David Stevenson in his recent book *Armaments and the Coming of War: Europe 1904–14*. Stevenson describes a 'great acceleration' in European armaments after the Second Moroccan Crisis, a transition to 'medium-term preparedness' after the 1912–13 Balkan Wars, and a deliberate resort to war in 1914 (Stevenson 1996: 231).

The starting gun in this land armaments race was the German Army Law of May 1912. Unable or unwilling to restrain Tirpitz and the Navy League, who cashed in their losing hand at Agadir with record naval appropriations in 1912, the Kaiser and his ministers decided that the German army had to be vastly augmented along with the navy. Why? Because the Germans considered war with the Entente 'inevitable'. The growing 'Tirpitz fleet' was ruining relations with England at the same time as successive crises with France and Russia over colonial and Balkan issues were making a two-front land war probable. In December 1911, Moltke lamented that 'the political grouping of Europe today will make an isolated war between France and Germany … impossible'. Even more lamentable was the fact that the Schlieffen Plan no longer seemed practicable. The Russians had come a long way since 1905, and could now mobilize and deploy large numbers of troops faster than in Schlieffen's day (Hermann 1996: 169). Yet rather than slow naval construction or appease the French and the Russians, the Kaiser decided to arm for war on all fronts (Herrmann 1996: 165–6).

As always in Wilhelmine Germany, politics and armaments were interconnected. Wilhelm II was driven to rearm partly by a new political pressure group, the German Army League (*Deutscher Wehrverein*), which warned Germans to prepare for a *Krieg ums Dasein* – a 'war for survival' – against the encroaching British, French and Russians. The Army League accused Germans of 'going soft' and 'rotting' like overripe fruit amid their *fin-de-siècle* prosperity. In newspaper columns and beer-soaked rallies, the Army Leaguers enjoined their fellow citizens to prepare for war to rejuvenate the Reich and secure its interests (Coetzee 1990: 52, 100–2; Ferguson 1998: 18–20). But the blustering of the *Wehrverein* and warmongers like Bernhardi was not really needed to make a bigger army, for military expansion was genuinely popular with agrarians and industrialists, and with millions of German voters, who saw profit, prestige and security in a bigger, more forceful army. (Of course the army bill was also *unpopular* with masses of German Social Democrats, which is why Volker Berghahn speaks of 'the complete internal paralysis' of Germany in 1912. Armaments construction and the log-rolling it entailed had become a kind of substitute for democratic politics (Berghahn 1993: 135, 140ff; Asprey 1991: 67–8).) Overall, however, the chief motive for the army bill was strategic. The Kaiser and his entourage projected continued growth and improvement in the French and Russian armed forces, and wished to prepare hurriedly for war, so as to be able to fight on advantageous terms before 1916, when the Russian army was expected to be fully modernized (Herrmann 1996: 161–8).

The Second Moroccan Crisis had revealed grave weaknesses in the German army. While the *Kriegsmarine* had creamed off most of the Reich's defence appropriations after 1898, the German army had quietly gone to seed, or so it seemed. After attending German autumn manoeuvres in October 1911, Lieutenant-Colonel Charles Repington, military correspondent of *The Times* in London, had published a stinging critique: 'The German Army, apart from its numbers, confidence ... and organization, does not present any signs of superiority over the best foreign models, and in some ways does not rise above the level of the second rate' (Herrmann 1996: 164). What made the German army 'second rate' in 1911 was a shortage of artillery, machineguns and technical units, and – Repington's praise for German 'numbers' notwithstanding – the annual underuse of German manpower. Whereas the French wrung an army nearly as large as Germany's from a much smaller population by conscripting 1.2 per cent of their adult males every year and foreclosing every conceivable exemption from military service, the Germans drafted less than 1 per cent of their men, leaving the Reich without the pool of trained reserves that it would need in a great war with the Entente.

Austria-Hungary's predicament added urgency to the army issue in Germany. Legislative infighting between the Austrian and Hungarian halves of the Dual Monarchy established in 1867 had reduced Austria-Hungary's peacetime army to little more than 300,000 men by 1911, all but striking Germany's key ally from the list of great powers. Austria's impotence was embarrassingly exhibited in the course of the two Balkan Wars in 1912–13, when Serbia joined with its neighbours to drive the Turks out of the Balkans, vastly increasing Belgrade's territory and population. Austria-Hungary, which ought to have intervened to confine the Serbs to their 'ethnic frontiers' and keep them out of Macedonia and Albania, sat on its hands throughout the crisis (Bled 1992: 292–4). The extent of Austria's decline was suggested by the fact that Russia's decision to retain a single class of army recruits through the Balkan crisis of 1912–13 – when an Austro-Serbian war was anticipated by everyone but the Austrians – effectively increased the Russian army by 350,000 men, more men in a single class in other words than were contained in the entire Austro-Hungarian army. Considering that the peacetime Russian army was comprised of four 350,000-man classes, the Germans were quite right to question Austria's staying power (Gat 1992: 92–3; Stevenson 1996: 237).

To improve prospects for the Central Powers, the German Reichstag passed a massive army bill in 1912 that aimed to accomplish in a single year what had previously been budgeted for five. It increased the annual conscription of German men, creating two new army corps from scratch, and increasing the peacetime strength of the German army from 515,000 to 544,000 men. Recognizing that more infantry required more artillery, the Germans increased the strength of the field artillery from 592 batteries to 633. The Army Law also provided a machinegun company for every infantry regiment, and paid for much needed technical units: telegraph and railway companies, searchlight units, bicycle troops, more Zeppelins, and the army's first fixed-wing aircraft for aerial reconnaissance and attack (Stevenson 1996: 246–7; Herrmann 1996: 168). To foreign observers, the salient feature of the German increases was their offensive emphasis. Budgeted funds were spent almost exclusively on combat units, which were forward deployed on Germany's frontiers. Indeed, the German war minister proudly asserted that 'the entire present bill is directed toward raising the army's striking power'. This was unusual; most armies – the Italians, the Russians and the Austro-Hungarians to name three – still routinely squandered large fractions of their military budgets on fortifications and bureaucracy. The German Army Law of 1912 was keyed entirely to restoring a healthy respect for German arms, and facilitating offensive warfare (Stevenson 1996: 210–11).

And yet the Germans believed themselves to be merely rebalancing their forces and preparing to defend the Reich against an encircling alliance. Recent scholarship suggests that the 1911–14 European arms race was pushed along as much by the Russians and the French as the Germans. Indeed, some found the French positively eager for war in 1912. Buoyed up by the outcome of the Second Moroccan Crisis and alarmed by Germany's intention to rebuild its land forces, the French saw 1912 – when the German army was still relatively small and Austria-Hungary was diverted by Serbia's advance in the Balkans – as their own optimal moment for war. In September 1912, French military intelligence actually recommended war to President Raymond Poincaré on the grounds that with Austria's strength deployed against the Serbs, the Germans would be forced to transport large numbers of troops to the Russian front and therefore fight the French 'in a state of considerable numerical inferiority'. There was a cynical edge to French calculations. The French general staff wanted a war before Russia could finish its modernization and free itself from financial, technical and military dependence on Paris (Keiger 1983: 98–100; Herrmann 1996: 174–8; Stevenson 1996: 240–1). Thus the French blew on the Balkan embers, trying to fan them into a general conflagration involving Austria, Germany and Russia. In a speech at Nantes in October 1912, Poincaré declared that France would not shrink from a war with Germany, a provocative statement for the time. In December, Joffre's deputy, General Noel de Castelnau, baldly stated that he wanted war, and France's civilian war minister, Alexandre Millerand, assured the Russians that France would back them if the Austro-Serbian conflict escalated beyond control.

While the Balkan crisis wore on, the French army used the autumn and winter of 1912–13 to carry out 'trial mobilizations' (*essais de mobilisation*) on the German border. Combat units were reinforced with reservists; extra machineguns were distributed; fortresses were provisioned; bridges and railways were placed under military guard; and – the crowning indignity – German rail cars in France were requisitioned to convey French troops and guns to the eastern border. In August 1913, the French National Assembly passed the 1.1 billion franc Three-Year Law. A remarkable achievement by a parliament previously noted for its anti-militarism, the *Loi des Trois Ans* extended compulsory military service from two years to three, effectively increasing the French army by one third. Given the gulf between the stagnant French (forty million) and rising German (seventy million) populations, this was the only way for the French army to grow, and grow it did, from a peacetime strength of 545,000 in 1913 to 735,000 the following spring (Keiger 1997: 152–4; Stevenson 1996: 302–3).

Overall, the Germans would quite reasonably have assumed in 1912–13 that the French were doing their utmost to precipitate a 'war of revenge' for Alsace-Lorraine and the lost glories of 1870. Indeed, Paris seems to have been deterred from this project only by Russia's hesitation. Though pressured by the Austrians, who carried out trial mobilizations of their own in Galicia in 1912–13 and delivered 50,000 Mannlicher rifles and fifty million cartridges to the Bulgars in the hope that they would turn them against Serbia, the Russians chose not to react. When pressed by the French to do *something*, the Russian command replied that they dared not, for 'a mere trifle would suffice to set the entire machine in motion'. Here was the mechanistic view of armaments that would escalate the July Crisis of 1914 to a general war: the nagging fear that wars could be decided instantly by superior prewar planning, organization and armament. Though unwilling to go to war in 1912, the Russian general staff reassured the French that all 'was well prepared, it would suffice to press a button to set [a war] in motion' (Herrmann 1996: 194–5; Stevenson 1996: 240–6).

And yet all was not well prepared in Russia, which explained the tsar's refusal to sanction a war in 1912–13. Like Wilhelm II, Tsar Nicholas II was an avid sailor and Mahanian, who had let his army run down in the years since the Russo-Japanese War. Committed to rebuilding the navy lost at Port Arthur and Tsushima, Nicholas had poured most of Russia's defence appropriations into shipbuilding after 1905. In 1909, he had authorized a ten-year 750 million rouble naval construction programme to build three great fleets from scratch: one in the Baltic, another in the Black Sea, and a third in the Pacific at Vladivostock (Gatrell 1994: 134–6, 300–4). While the Russian navy revived, the army slumbered, a state of affairs that changed only because the Balkan Wars made a clash with Austria-Hungary probable, because French demands for a more rapid Russian mobilization schedule could not be ignored forever, and because the German Army Bill of 1912 could not go unanswered.

Russia's answer was the Great Army Programme of 1913, a 1.5 billion rouble spending spree to expand and modernize the Russian army on the eve of a war with Germany and Austria-Hungary that Nicholas II now regarded as inevitable. Indeed, Russian memoir literature describes frantic last-minute preparations in 1913 for an 'unavoidable' war with Germany and Austria in 1914. The conscript class was called early; horses were quickly broken and trained; ammunition was stockpiled, and food and fodder were laid in for a summer campaign (Littauer 1993: 105–28). The most costly and menacing aspect of the Great Programme was its 40 per cent increase in the troop strength of the Russian army; 500,000 troops were added to the peacetime strength in a single year. Of this half million, 300,000 joined the infantry, which raised its strength to 123 divisions; 126,000 went to the artillery, which Sukhomlinov vowed to raise to German levels. By 1917, the Great Programme would procure 8,400 guns, mainly the 12- and 15-centimetre pieces needed to pulverize fortifications, trenches and gun emplacements. Interestingly, Tsar Nicholas II compared Russia's army expansion to Britain's naval race with Germany. Nicholas informed the British ambassador in St Petersburg that just as Britain had to maintain a 16:10 ratio with the Germans at sea, Russia had to uphold the same ratio on land (Gatrell 1994: 132–4; Stone 1975: 35; Stevenson 1996: 318, 332–3; Lieven 1983: 111).

And yet all the men and guns in the world would accomplish nothing if the Russians could not get them to the fighting front. To cross from Russia to Germany in 1913 was still a palpable experience; single-track railways and tumbledown stations bloomed on the German side of the frontier into double- and quadruple-tracked lines that skimmed through gleaming stations equipped with a dozen platforms and sidings. Roads changed from glistering dirt tracks to paved highways flanked by shade trees (right up to 1914 Russian infantrymen morosely joked that 'in Russia, the hard roads are made of sand'). It was this dearth of modern infrastructure that made Russian mobilizations so laughably slow. Indeed, the Schlieffen Plan was premised upon this dearth and the delay that it would entail. Though a number of Russian officers grasped the military necessity of expanding the empire's roads, railways and river ferries and 'welding them into a single strategic framework', the tsar had single-mindedly poured money into the navy until 1913 (Gatrell 1994: 132). What funds were spent on the army after 1905 had gone on fortresses, a ribbon of modern forts in Poland and Ukraine that would undoubtedly slow German and Austrian invasions, but would not get the Russian army to the frontier in time to save the French or the Serbs. All of this changed abruptly in 1913, when a syndicate of French banks, prodded by the French govern-ment, presented the Russian army with sufficient funds to double- and quadruple-track some 3,000 miles of single-track railway connecting the Russian interior with the German and Austro-Hungarian borders. Though the additional lines had little commercial viability, they were swiftly built. Not only would they shorten the time needed for a Russian army to strike west-ward, but they provided tens of thousands of new industrial and construction jobs at a critical moment in the troubled reign of Nicholas II. Whereas

Russia's rural society had always turned a cold shoulder to the tsar's navy, they embraced the army and railway buildups with enthusiasm. Indeed the free-spending army programmes, which contributed heavily to a 30 per cent increase in Russian jobs between 1908 and 1913, have prompted one historian to judge them 'the last argument of tsarism' (Stevenson 1996: 323–4; Gatrell 1994: 174–7, 303–4).

The potent combination of the Great Army Programme and the Franco-Russian Railway Agreement induced the Russians to revise their war plan a final time. In 1913–14, the Russian General Staff introduced Plan 20, which further shortened deployment times against the Germans and the Austrians, and planned rapid offensives into East Prussia and Galicia to devastate Germany's eastern districts and put the Habsburg army to rout (Snyder 1984: 183–8). Naturally, these developments struck fear into the Germans and the Austrians. As recently as 1910, only the Germans had possessed truly offensive war plans. By late 1913 France and Russia had them as well, and were every bit as determined as the Germans to seize the initiative in the next war by attacking at once. No wonder Moltke and Ludendorff revised the Schlieffen Plan in 1913–14; there seemed little point in it anymore (W. Fuller 1992: 442–5; Stevenson 1996: 302, 321). Schlieffen's hedge against 'encirclement' – Russia's elemental backwardness – was steadily falling away. Russian railways, troop strengths and firepower were all on the rise, making the tsar's 'steamroller' more formidable than ever.

If the Germans felt threatened by Russia's Great Army Programme and Plan 20, one can imagine the fright of Conrad and the Austrians. With half the population of Russia and a small, neglected army, the Austro-Hungarians awoke in 1914 to a radically altered situation on their eastern border. To their amazement, the Austrians found that the Russians now had nine, mostly double-tracked railways running to their concentration areas along the Austro-Hungarian border. These Russian lines were capable of moving 260 trains a day. The Austrians found themselves with just seven lines, five of them single-tracked; at best, the Austrians might move 153 trains a day. This was how generals thought in 1913–14. It was scientific, and it represented a great change from the devil-may-care approach of the last wars: the Austrians in 1866, the French in 1870 and the Russians in 1904. And it was just this sort of thinking that forced Conrad to reconsider his offensive plans in the months before World War I. Apprised of Russia's improving readiness and rail capacity, he pulled the entire Austro-Hungarian army back from the frontier in early 1914, essentially ceding Galicia – Austria's easternmost province – to the Russians (Stevenson 1996: 356).

The throes of Austria-Hungary, 1912–14

What ailed Austria-Hungary? How could such a big empire, the second largest country in Europe after Russia, fledge such a paltry army? The answer was political. As late as 1866 the Austrians had still been reckoned the 'gendarme of Europe'; they had thought nothing of fighting the Prussians and the Italians at the same time in 1866 because their army was large and well equipped: bigger than Prussia's, equal to France's, and second only to Russia's armed horde. As previously discussed, this state of affairs began to change in 1867, when Emperor Franz Joseph reformed his empire in a great constitutional *Ausgleich* or Compromise, splitting Austria into two pieces: German-controlled, largely Slavic 'Austria' in the west, Magyar-controlled, largely Slavic and Rumanian 'Hungary' in the east. Austria officially became Austria-Hungary, a transformation that wrought wrenching, debilitating changes (Bled 1992: 275–9; Sked 1989: 187–97).

The rationale for the *Ausgleich* was that it would help solve Austria's nationality problems by appeasing the Magyars – the most restive nationality of all – and buying their complicity. Since Austria-Hungary was a largely Slavic empire, Emperor Franz Joseph needed help repressing vibrant nation-alities like the Czechs and the Croats, who preferred home rule or independence to continued membership in the Austrian Empire. He turned to the Hungarians – a non-Slavic people – to assist him in this mission. Like the Germans of Austria, the Magyars of Hungary were a minority: ethnic islets in a sea of Slavic and Rumanian peoples. In 1867, Austria's new prime minister had assured his Hungarian colleague with a wink: 'you manage your hordes and we'll manage ours'. In this rather cynical spirit, Franz Joseph had conceded the Hungarians home rule in 1867, and permitted them to harass their non-Hungarian peoples with a malicious vim that is nowhere better described than in R. W. Seton-Watson's *Racial Problems in Hungary*, which reads as unnervingly today as it did upon publication in 1908 (Stone 1999: 226–30, 239–40; Bled 1992: 289–91).

Franz Joseph even authorized the Magyars to raise their own army: the Hungarian-speaking *honvéd*. Technically the *honvéd* was just a national guard; the Hungarians were still obliged to supply regular regiments to a joint Austro-Hungarian army whose language of command would be German. Yet Franz Joseph failed to stipulate the proportion of Hungarian troops who would serve in the two armies, which enabled the autonomous Hungarian parliament to shift ever larger classes of recruits to the *honvéd* in the decades after 1867. Efforts by the joint Austro-Hungarian war ministry in Vienna to redirect Hungarian conscripts to the regular army were invariably defeated in Budapest. Since Austro-Hungarian defence budgets had to be approved by both parliaments – the Austrian Reichsrat in Vienna and the Hungarian Diet in Budapest – the Magyars acquired the habit from the 1880s of vetoing army bills that would have expanded and modernized the Austro-Hungarian army. From the Magyar perspective, the joint or *k.u.k.* army was an abomination; by forcing recruits to learn German, it 'de-nationalized' Hungarian recruits and provided the Habsburg emperor with a ready force of German-drilled 'mamelukes' with which to wipe out Hungarian home rule. Hence the

Hungarian parliament routinely pared Austro-Hungarian military budgets. In 1900, the joint army received a trifling budget of 439 million crowns. This represented just 35 per cent of Britain's defence expenditures, 40 per cent of Russia's, 41 per cent of Germany's and 45 per cent of France's.

The Habsburg army withered away after 1900. One of the biggest armies in Europe in 1866, it was one of the smallest by 1914. It counted just 355,000 men, and possessed woefully inadequate quantities of machineguns, field artillery and shells. Whereas one man in sixty-five was a soldier in France in 1913–14, the ratio was 1:132 in Austria-Hungary. And whereas the French and German armies had one artillery piece for every 195 men, the ratio in Austria was 1:338, considerably worse even than Italy's ratio of 1:295; this was worrisome in the new age of 'artillery battles' glimpsed at Sedan, Port Arthur and Mukden (Anon 1902: 31). Austria's predicament was exacerbated by Emperor Franz Joseph's decision to begin constructing a dozen dreadnoughts in 1906. Besides the expense, the new battleships and cruisers would have to be manned from Austria-Hungary's stagnant pool of military recruits. Since the Hungarians refused politically to increase the annual conscription of eighteen year-olds, the Austro-Hungarian war ministry was forced to divert thousands of needed recruits and serving regulars to the navy, further depressing the quality and quantity of the army's conscriptions in the years before 1914 (Stone 1999: 238–9; Stevenson 1996: 85–6).

The two Balkan Wars in 1912–13 revealed Austria-Hungary's military backwardness as never before. In the first place, it was immensely humiliating for the Austrians to look on while the Balkan states joined to quell 'disorders' in the Ottoman Empire, a policing function that had been exercised by the Habsburgs since the 1700s. 'Disorders' aplenty were supplied by Serbian and Montenegrin irregulars, and the First Balkan War (October 1912–May 1913) began (Macfie 1998: 71–2). Ignoring threats from Vienna, Serbian and Montenegrin troops wrested the Albanian port of Shkodër from the Turks, giving landlocked Serbia an outlet to the sea (and Russia a potential port on the Adriatic). In the Second Balkan War (June–July 1913), Serbia doubled its land mass by attacking its erstwhile Bulgarian ally, annexing much of Macedonia and a large swath of Albania, and then pushing across the formerly Austrian Sanjak of Novipazar. Serbia's seizure of the Sanjak, and its thrust across Kosovo to the Albanian port of Durrës, were calculated to prick the Austrians and expose their weakness. They did just that; the Austrians would never have a better chance than 1912–13 to smash the Serbs, but they simply could not. The *k.u.k.* army, with most of its strength on leave or in reserve, could not be rapidly mobilized, and when the Austro-Hungarian General Staff did order five corps to mobilize (three in Galicia, two in Bosnia), the measure neither deterred the Serbs nor demonstrated Austro-Hungarian resolve. The Hungarian parliament refused to back Habsburg intervention in the Balkans, judging it 'Austrian imperialism', as opposed to Austro-Hungarian, while the Austrian parliament failed to endorse intervention because of a month-long filibuster organized by Croatian, Czech, Slovenian and Ukrainian deputies who sympathized with the Serbian government more than their own. Even Austria's Germans were cool; like the Frenchmen who wearily asked in 1939 whether it made sense to 'die for Danzig', Austria's German press wondered in 1912 if one ought really 'fight a war for the corridor to Durrës'. At his wits' end, Emperor Franz Joseph finally procured the $25 million needed for the partial mobilization of his army, not from his own parliaments but from New York's Kuhn, Loeb & Co., a Wall Street investment bank (*Neue Freie Presse* [Vienna] 13 December 1912).

Once underway, Austria's partial mobilization went no better than the pre-mobilization measures. Many recruits reported to their regiments singing Serbian anthems. In Slovenia and Dalmatia, angry crowds smashed the windows of German shops and declared their support for Belgrade in the crisis. In Austria's Czech provinces, the parents and friends of army recruits and reservists turned out in mass demonstrations to prevent the young men entraining for the front. While the Serbs overran Macedonia and Albania with 200,000 troops, the Austro-Hungarians deployed fewer than 12,000 men to Bosnia, hardly a credible deterrent (Stevenson 1996: 254). It did not help that Austria-Hungary's general staff chief resigned at the peak of the crisis, as did the Austro-Hungarian war minister General Moritz von Auffenberg, who stood accused of insider trading on the shares of firms to which he planned to award army contracts. No sooner were replacements named than Vienna was wracked by the biggest spy scandal in its history: the Redl Affair. To everyone's dismay in Vienna and Berlin, it was revealed that forty-seven year-old Colonel Alfred Redl, head of the Austro-Hungarian army's counter-intelligence unit, had been selling German and Austrian war plans to the Russians since 1905, when he had begun a homosexual affair with a Russian officer (*Neue Freie Presse* [Vienna] 10–14 December 1912; Williamson 1991: 145–6; Asprey 1959).

After the debacle of 1912–13 – as much spiritual as military – Austria-Hungary seemed to totter on the brink. The Austro-Hungarian general staff took stock of Serbia's annexations in the two Balkan Wars and projected that they would furnish Belgrade with the men and resources to double the strength of the Serbian army from 200,000 to 400,000 men. General Blasius von Schemua, the general staff chief removed in December 1912 to make room for Conrad von Hötzendorf's return, glumly acknowledged that the Austro-Hungarians, whose own army numbered less than 400,000 men, would be unable to fight both the Russians and an augmented Serbian army: 'our forces will no longer be sufficient for both' (Herrmann 1996: 178). Kaiser Wilhelm II recognized this, and promptly set to work rebuilding the Turkish army 'to get hold of every musket in the Balkans that is prepared to go off *for* Austria *against* the Slavs' (Macfie 1998: 103). Pressed to the wall by so many threats, Vienna would take a hard line with the Serbs in July 1914, and the Germans would back them unconditionally, precipitating the First

World War. After failing to contain the Serbs in 1912–13, the Austrians felt constrained to hit them in 1914 before they could digest their territorial gains. Moreover, the Serbs constituted a permanent threat to the integrity of the Habsburg Monarchy. Serbia considered itself the 'Prussia of the Balkans', and planned to evict Austria from southeastern Europe as effectively as Prussia had evicted the Habsburgs from Germany in 1866. The support for Serbia throughout Austria-Hungary in 1912–13 meant that no quarter could be given in this political-psychological struggle. Austria would fight to reduce Serbia to an innocuous rump; Serbia would fight to drag in Russia and destroy Austria-Hungary forever (Stevenson 1996: 233–7).

Even the Hungarians could not fault this awful logic; with millions of Croats, Serbs, Rumanians and Slovaks yearning for release from Magyar oppression, the Hungarians knew that they needed to pump new life into the Dual Monarchy to avoid going under themselves. Thus the Hungarians tardily and grudgingly voted funds for a bigger army in 1912–13, increasing the 125,000-man annual contingent to 180,000 in 1913. Yet the simultaneous reduction in the term of military service from three years to two all but nullified the increases. Instead of having three classes of 125,000 men, the Austrian army would have two of 180,000. It was a peculiarly Austro-Hungarian solution to a life-threatening problem. As for strategic railways and artillery, these key weapons were utterly neglected; the Hungarians refused to pay for railways that might benefit Austria economically, and disingenuously maintained that the heavy howitzers and mortars needed for the field army were not needed (Stevenson 1996: 142–5, 279–80). Despondent, Archduke Franz Ferdinand, the Austro-Hungarian army inspector and heir to the throne, demanded that 'the Monarchy awake from its lethargy and proceed forcefully. Should it not do so, its role is played out' (Stevenson 1996: 259).

If the Austro-Hungarians were worried by Serbia's rise, the Germans were positively terrified. Having lost the Turks as a militarily effective ally in the fighting of 1912–13, they could not contemplate a world without Austria-Hungary. In it, they would be friendless and isolated: girded in the east by Russia, in the south by Italy, Serbia and a league of Slavic states, in the west by France, and on the high seas by England (Stevenson 1996: 285–6). There seemed only one way out: fight a great war as quickly as possible to save Austria-Hungary, destroy Serbia and defeat France and Russia before their military expansions were complete. Berlin's certainty that Austria was on the ropes and that Germany was heading into 'a struggle for existence' (the Kaiser's phrase) explains the extraordinary *Kriegsrat* or 'war council' convened by Wilhelm II in Potsdam in December 1912 after the Serbian occupation of Durrës and the Russian winter mobilization. At the *Kriegsrat*, the Kaiser suggested that Austria use the pretext of the First Balkan War to take a hard line with the Serbs and provoke a war with Russia, which would in turn force the French and British to back the Russians, and enable the Germans to smash them all in a well timed sequence of ground campaigns. The Kaiser had met with the Austro-Hungarian military attaché before the meeting, and confidently assured him that 'Germany's sword lay loose in the scabbard; you can count on us' (Stevenson 1996: 251–2).

As it chanced, war did not come in 1912–13. Moltke found that he needed time to 'prepare public opinion' (to say nothing of the army), and Tirpitz asked for more months to build submarine pens, widen the Kiel Canal for dreadnoughts, and take delivery of torpedo boats and aircraft. Yet the Germans assumed that a great war was coming and that they would control the time and place of its outbreak. In 1913, the Kaiser supplemented the Army Law of 1912 with a mammoth 400 million mark Army Act, a legislative feat that was greatly facilitated by centenary celebrations of the Wars of Liberation against Napoleon all over Germany. Amid the patriotic clamour, the German army increased its peacetime strength again, from 544,000 to 890,000 men (Gat 1992: 95; Stevenson 1996: 290–1). This dramatic increase reflected two realities. First, Austria-Hungary's decline: more German troops were needed because the Austrians would not hold for long against either the Russians or the Serbs. Second, the French and Russian military expansions: more men were needed to give the Schlieffen Plan a hope of success (Stevenson 1996: 286–98, 302).

Though pessimistic in the long run, the Germans perceived opportunity in the short term, specifically in the year 1914. France's Three Year Law would increase the peacetime, fully trained French army from 545,000 men in 1913 to 690,000 in 1914 to 730,000 in 1916. Initially this growing army would be inadequately supported by artillery. The French parliament had refused funds for field howitzers in 1913, and it would take months for the French army to recover what heavy guns it did have from the French navy, which used them in peacetime as shore batteries. The few long guns and mortars the French army had succeeded in getting through parliament would not be delivered until 1915 (Stevenson 1996: 314).

As for the Russians, their Great Programme would need years to take full effect. Tsar Nicholas II did not approve the army's spending priorities until November 1913, and when he did, he did not 'front-load' expenditures in the German style, but staggered them over several years so as not to alarm liberals in the Duma. This meant that most of the new infantry, artillery and aviation units paid for by the Great Programme would not be operational until 1917. Moreover, some of the strategic railways and river crossings funded by the Franco-Russian Railway Agreement of 1913 would not be finished until 1918 (Bucholz 1991: 306–7; Herrmann 1996: 197–208; Stevenson 1996: 322–3). In May 1914, General Georg von Waldersee, Moltke's right-hand man, took stock of Germany's adversaries and declared that although they themselves were not ready for war, Germany was ready. The Reich had rapidly spent the army budgets of 1912–13, and was momentarily, fleetingly stronger than any other power in Europe. Waldersee was determined to exploit this fleeting advantage, and suggested that war be declared at once.

Germany has no reason to expect to be attacked in the near future; on the other hand, it not only has no reason whatever to avoid a conflict, but also, more than that, the chances of achieving a speedy victory in a major European war are today still very favourable for Germany and the Triple Alliance. Soon, however, this will no longer be the case.

Like everyone on the German general staff, Waldersee worried that the Austro-Hungarians would waver in a crisis, and therefore noted the usefulness of the repeated flare-ups with Serbia. They would force the Austrians into the breach, whereupon the Germans could wade in to widen the war and settle accounts with the British, French and Russians. In this, the Austro-Hungarians would be brutally sacrificed to slow the advance of the Russian army and buy time for the Germans to win in the West. Moltke met with Conrad in May 1914 and insisted that a war with Serbia and Russia be constructed at once, for 'to wait any longer meant a diminishing of our chances'. While Moltke lectured Conrad, Waldersee dined with the Kaiser's foreign secretary, Gottlieb von Jagow, and instructed him to 'conduct policy *with the aim of provoking a war in the near future*' (Röhl, in Wilson 1995: 40–6; Herwig 1997: 20–1; Ferguson 1998: 16–20). From the German perspective, all that was needed was a crisis that would embroil the Austro-Hungarians. This was the larger significance of the pistol shots that killed Austrian Archduke Franz Ferdinand and his wife in the streets of Sarajevo in June 1914. The assassination of the Habsburg heir to the throne was a provocation from which the Austrians could not shrink, nor even the Hungarians. The subsequent Austro-Hungarian mobilization against the Serbs drew in the Russians, which was all the excuse needed by the Germans to commence their long-sought 'struggle for the sovereignty of the world'.

CHAPTER NINE

The outbreak of World War I in 1914

In June 1914, Austrian Archduke Franz Ferdinand, Emperor Franz Joseph's nephew and heir to the throne, toured Austria's newly annexed provinces of Bosnia and Herzegovina for the first time. The archducal tour was intended to annoy Serbia, which was itself a constant annoyance to Austria, still refusing to recognize Austria-Hungary's annexation of Bosnia-Herzegovina and brazenly insulting the Habsburg Monarchy at every turn. 'A gaudy bird made of borrowed feathers' and 'the state without a nation' were stock Serbian epithets for Austria-Hungary, effrontery that gnawed at the grizzled old emperor and his generals (HHSA n.d.) To remind the Serbs who was boss in the Balkans, Franz Joseph ordered Franz Ferdinand to cap his Bosnian tour with military manoeuvres on the Serbian border. It was hoped that the stern presence of the archduke and the racket generated by 60,000 well armed Austro-Hungarian troops would leave the Serbs in no doubt as to Austria-Hungary's fortitude.

For the Serbs, none of this would do. Franz Ferdinand had been a pea in their shoe for years; his 'trialist' plan to refashion the Austro-Hungarian Dual Monarchy into a Triple Monarchy that would extend the Croats the same privileges enjoyed by the Germans and Magyars represented a truly inspired attack on Serbia's appeal to the Slavs of the Habsburg Monarchy. More recently, the Serbs blamed Franz Ferdinand for their failure to secure the Albanian port of Skhodër in the First Balkan War. The archduke had worked with the Germans to deny them the port, and had been one of the principal architects of the new state of Albania, which effectively landlocked Serbia.

After leading Austro-Hungarian manoeuvres in the last week of June, Franz Ferdinand departed for Vienna. To annoy the Serbs one last time, he stopped on the way at Sarajevo – the largely Muslim capital of Bosnia rather puzzlingly claimed by Belgrade – on 28 June, Serbia's national day. The decision to tour Sarajevo was fateful; anticipating it, a half dozen Bosnian Serbs, trained and armed by rogue officers in Belgrade, placed themselves with Serbian-issue hand grenades and Browning pistols along the route of the archduke's motorcade (Dedijer 1966: 285–323). Two would-be assassins struck as the archduke's car wheeled through the city centre; both attempts – one a grenade, the other a pistol shot from thirty feet – missed their target, and the archduke drove on. When Franz Ferdinand learned that the errant grenade had wounded passengers in the car behind him, he gave orders for the entire motorcade to make an unscheduled detour to the Sarajevo hospital to visit the victims. Unfortunately, the archduke's driver, a Bosnian chauffeur pressed into service at the last minute by the Austro-Hungarian Motor Club, spoke no German and misunderstood his orders; he sped past the turning for the hospital, braked suddenly, and then slowly began to reverse. Gavrilo Princip – the third assassin – could not believe his luck. Archduke Franz Ferdinand and Archduchess Sophie were momentarily stalled an arm's length away. Princip stepped through the crowd, drew his pistol and fired twice: the first bullet killed the archduke; the second bullet bored into Sophie's stomach, killing her slowly over the course of several agonizing hours (Jerabek 1992: 82–8; Bled 1992: 303–5).

Reaction in Austria-Hungary to the assassination was predictable. The murder of Sophie in addition to her husband, which orphaned three small children, goaded even the anti-Austrian peoples into joining the outcry against 'Dog Serbia'. Street demonstrations insisted that Belgrade be punished and took up the cry *Serbien muss sterbien*, a play on words that meant 'Serbia must die'. Counter-demonstrations washed through Serbia and Montenegro. In Cetinje, the Montenegrin capital, a crowd tried to storm the Austrian legation and was dispersed only when King Nikola himself appeared to beat the rioters back with his cane. Austrian diplomats in Serbia pleaded for war; Wilhelm Storck, the Austrian *chargé d'affaires* in Belgrade, begged Vienna to 'destroy Serbia before it becomes a military factor in the European sense', meaning before it organized its newly conquered provinces and absorbed deliveries of the latest French artillery, machineguns and rifles (HHSA 1914; Bridge 1990: 335–6). The Habsburg army also pushed for war in the crisis – Conrad and war minister Alexander Krobatin in Vienna, General Oskar Potiorek in Sarajevo – and had a hand in the tough wording of an ultimatum that was delivered to the Serbs nearly a month after the assassination on 23 July. The Austrians demanded that Serbia cease agitating against the Habsburg Monarchy and sought unrestricted access to Serbian government offices to determine whether Princip and his associates had links to Belgrade. Although the Serbs accepted some points of the ultimatum, agreeing to stop the spread of Serbian propaganda in Bosnia, for example, they would not give the Austrians access to their ministries and archives, and therefore could not comply entirely with the ultimatum. For the Austrians, this was all the excuse needed to sever diplomatic relations on 25 July and declare war on the 28th (Williamson 1991: 190–205; Bridge 1990: 341–2). Only the Magyars held back, wringing their hands as usual about the dangers of Austrian expansion at Hungarian expense, but the cold-blooded murder of the heir to the throne and his wife made it impossible even for Budapest to erect obstacles in the path of war.

The Austrians were not the only ones spoiling for a fight in July 1914. So too were the Germans. Indeed one of the more interesting aspects of the July Crisis was what it revealed about the proclivities of the European states. Whereas the British and French governments went to war with extreme reluctance, the Russians with mixed feelings, and the Italians not at all, the Austrians and Germans chose the moment for war and deliberately forced its outbreak. The reason why has already been explored: Austria-Hungary needed a dramatic win over Serbia to fortify its rule in East Central Europe; Germany considered 1914 its last chance to break through a ring of strengthening enemies to create the vast sea and land empire that would secure the future of the *Kaiserreich*. Added to this motive was the realization that the German and Austro-Hungarian armies had grown as much as their peoples, parliaments and resources would permit. The Entente powers, just beginning to expand in earnest and augmented by burgeoning Serbian and Rumanian armies and potentially the Italians as well, still had plenty of room to grow. Indeed the Russians, French and British – with an aggregate population of 260 million against 120 million Germans and Austro-Hungarians – had already overtaken the Central Powers in armed strength by 1914; the formal adhesion of the Belgians and the Serbs to the Entente only widened the gap, giving the Entente powers fifty-eight corps (sixty-three if the Rumanians were included, seventy-two with the Italians) to the fifty-four corps of Germany and Austria-Hungary. Three and a half million German and Austro-Hungarian troops found themselves ringed by 5.4 million Russian, French, British, Belgian and Serbian soldiers. It was enough to give anyone pause, even a daredevil like Conrad, who grimly noted the shifting odds in July 1914: 'In 1908–9 [war with the Entente] would have been a foregone conclusion; in 1912 it would have been a game with decent chances; *now* we play *va banque*' (Herrmann 1996: 217–21; Herwig 1997: 62).

In this risky game, the Germans believed that they held two trumps, which explained their willingness to wage war despite the tilting balance of military power. Although the question of German 'war guilt' has been hotly debated by 'revisionists' and 'antirevisionists' – the former seeking to exculpate the Germans, the latter to fix blame on them – the fact is that the Germans encouraged the Austrians in the early stages of the crisis and did nothing to stop the slide to war in the last week of July (Langdon 1991; Stevenson 1997: 5–9). Instead they hastened to play their two trumps; the first was the superior preparedness of the German army, an advantage that did not extend to the shoddily equipped, understrength Austro-Hungarians. The second trump was the Schlieffen Plan, which held out the hope of a quick, decisive victory. Nearly all historians now agree that the German general staff did not *force* the civilian leadership to declare war; rather German generals and statesmen agreed that the Schlieffen Plan had to be triggered without delay to avoid squandering its advantages (Trachtenberg 1991: 90–4; Stevenson 1997: 28–32). This amounted to a reckless militarization of policy that severely limited the options of Germany's adversaries. The problem with Germany, an English contemporary exploded, was that it was such a 'carefully built, smooth-running machine … that any fool could drive it' (Pick 1993: 138). Britain simply could not afford to spot the Germans a head-start; this was unquestionably the French and Russian view as well. The Russians began to mobilize on 29 July; on 31 July, Joffre warned his government that each day of delay in calling reservists would entail the loss of 12–15 miles of French territory (Bucholz 1991: 310–11).

In terms of preparedness, the Germans had learned well the lessons of the Manchurian and Balkan Wars. In Manchuria, the Russians had fired 87,000 artillery shells a month, a breathtaking rate of fire for the time. By 1912, the Bulgarian artillery operating against the Turks in the First Balkan War was firing 254,000 rounds a month. The trend was clear; even men in trenches were not safe from high-explosive blast, and men in the open were 'dead men walking', for the blast radius of a single shrapnel round in 1914 was 25×150 yards (Zabecki 1994: 9). These sobering facts tended to promote artillery over infantry as 'queen of the battlefield'. With this in mind, the Germans attached 144 field guns and light howitzers to each of their infantry corps; this was more than the French (120) or the Russians (108), and the advantage was far greater than the numbers alone suggest, for each German corps deployed eighteen 105mm howitzers – the best light field howitzer in Europe – and sixteen 150mm heavy field howitzers as well. In 1914, only the Germans augmented their corps artillery with the heavy guns that the Entente armies (and the Austrians) were still scrambling to produce. When war broke out, the Germans had seven times as many heavy guns as the French, and they knew how to use them (Zabecki 1994: 11). France, focused on morale and infantry tactics, clearly did not; in 1913 a French general exclaimed:

> Ask 100 officers picked at random 'what is heavy artillery? What is it used for? How is it used? Whom does it support? Where is it positioned?' The odds are 100–1 that you will get no answer or that the same questions will be asked of you.
>
> (Porch 1981: 236; Travers 1987: 255)

Indeed, the French army did not order its first batch of heavy howitzers until late 1913; they would not be delivered until the Great War was already underway and going badly. Part of the explanation for this was the French army's near total reliance on the 75mm field gun, a remarkable light cannon introduced in 1897; its ultra-modern axial recoil system permitted a rate of fire of 20–30 rounds per minute. The French wrongly assumed that the 75's relatively light charge would be offset by its mobility and its ability to saturate objectives with fire (it is well to remember that the Russians had made the same mistake in 1877, attacking the Plevna trenches with flat-trajectoried cannon that proved all but useless). The rest of the explanation for France's neglect of heavy artillery lay in the 'cult of the offensive'. French officers did not want to be encumbered with heavy guns as they dashed forward; many rejected machineguns, with their bulky ammunition boxes and plodding mule trains, for the same reason (Travers 1987: 255; Herrmann 1996: 19–20).

The Germans had thought the matter out considerably more intelligently. Eager to take the offensive but leery of defensive fire, the Germans after 1906 made artillery the 'skeleton of battle'; in a war of movement, massive concentrations of German guns would gouge open channels down which their infantry would advance in relative safety. These were the first 'combined arms' tactics; to make them work, the German artillery practised infantry support, counter-battery fire, and artillery registration beyond the visual, using aircraft and telephone-linked forward observers. If their 105mm and 150mm guns proved inadequate, German armies held 21cm howitzers in reserve, and 42cm railway guns. In the early struggles of the Great War, the German guns were unbeatable, which explained the monstrous casualties suffered by the French, British and Russian field armies; Germany's superior artillery, as well as the impetuous tactics of the Entente armies, also accounted for Niall Ferguson's discovery that the Germans were able to inflict 'maximum slaughter at minimum expense', spending just $11,345 to kill an enemy soldier whereas the French, British and Russians needed $36,485 to do the job (Ferguson 1998: 336–8). Even when the French and British took delivery of their big guns, they used them poorly, pounding the German lines with week-long bombardments and then sending the infantry 'over the top' without fire support, a failing that was not remedied until 1918. In East and West, the German artillery took a more nuanced approach, preparing assaults but also disengaging infantry with precise, observed fire, a practice that came to be called 'fire and manoeuvre'. The Germans were also well ahead in the technical equipment and companies of engineers that were needed to move armies swiftly and dig them in for a firefight. The German army had 202 engineer companies in 1914, the Russians 168, the French ninety-five, the British only twelve (Herwig 1997: 59; Herrmann 1996: 221; Hughes 1999).

The Schlieffen Plan was considered so valuable that the Germans rudely bundled the Austrians into war in 1914 so as to be able to implement it. Though the Austro-Hungarians did want a war with Serbia to avenge the murder of Franz Ferdinand and secure primacy in the Balkans, they did not want a war with the Russians, still less the world, but allowed themselves to be pushed into one by the Germans, who needed Austrian spoiling attacks in Galicia to delay the Russian onslaught (Fellner, in Wilson 1995: 16–21). The Kaiser too was pushed. When he paused to consider British offers to negotiate on 1 August, Moltke protested that even a day's delay to parley with the British or French would surrender all the advantages of the Schlieffen Plan (Bucholz 1991: 311–12; Goerlitz 1995: 155–6; Fischer 1967: 74–5). It was of course significant that Moltke characterized the British offer to confer as 'interference'. He wanted war at once and bullied Conrad – who belatedly protested that Austria-Hungary was not ready for one – into an immediate invasion of Serbia to prevent a diplomatic solution (Joll 1992: 17–18; Fischer 1967: 85; Liddell Hart 1964: 31–2; Stevenson 1996: 406).

Moltke was in a great hurry because the Schlieffen Plan's strength was the underlying mobility and war-readiness of the German army. Such was Russia's fear of the German juggernaut that the tsar felt that he had no choice but to order full mobilization on 29 July, the day after the Austrian declaration of war on Serbia, lugubriously noting that the decision would 'send thousands and thousands of men to their deaths' (Stevenson 1997: 23; Lieven 1993: 202). Though German apologists subsequently sought to pin blame for the war on the Russians, the Germans knew full well that the Russians had to begin full mobilization at once to stand a chance against the better organized Germans. Though well financed, Russian railways were poorly built, limiting the speed and flow of troop trains along them. Moreover, the Russian tradition of mixing Poles and Asians into ethnic Russian regiments to limit linguistic and national problems further slowed mobilization (Lieven 1983: 149–51). The Germans knew all this yet hastened to break with the Russians; after inventing an 'aerial attack' on Nuremberg by dastardly French aviators, they broke with the French as well (Keiger, in Wilson 1995: 140; Keiger 1983: 162; Stevenson 1996: 405–6). By this convoluted process, the German army was finally unleashed.

The speed and breadth of the German mobilization stunned onlookers, even Germans accustomed to efficiency. A clerk in Frankfurt noted in his diary that 'in a few hours, nearly all the men one knows have disappeared from civilian life' (Sulzbach 1981: 22). Not coincidentally, the declaration of war also solved Germany's 'socialist question' for a time. In the Reichstag, the 'internationalist' Social Democrats put their country first and voted war credits; several socialist deputies even volunteered for service in the Kaiser's army. More importantly, the proletarian rank-and-file renounced wage demands and strikes for the duration of the war and trooped off to the front with the same wild enthusiasm as everyone else in Germany (Joll 1992: 211–12). In August 1914, the German General Staff assembled these men, four million in all, and deployed them to the frontiers. It was a breathtaking feat. In just 300 hours – during which fifty-four-car German trains packed with troops, guns, horses and supplies rolled across Germany at ten-minute intervals – Moltke had 200,000 men on the Russian frontier and 1.8 million men along the borders of Belgium and France (neutral Luxembourg had been overrun by German troops on 1 August, the first day of mobilization) (Asprey 1991: 51–2; Herwig 1997: 75). On 4 August the Germans struck into Belgium. Determined to seize the Belgian railways intact and get to France, the Germans dealt ruthlessly with all civilian interference. The Germans burned the marvellous city of Louvain to punish alleged partisan attacks; thereafter they were called 'Huns'. When German soldiers repairing the bridge at Dinant were fired upon, they rounded up 612 civilians and shot them as reprisals; the youngest reprisal was a newborn baby clutched in the arms of its mother (Gilbert 1994: 42). It was a chilling replay of Germany's harsh conduct in France in 1870–1.

On 20 August the Germans swarmed into France on every available road and railway (Map 9.1). As Schlieffen had planned, the entire operation was executed with stunning speed and precision. The French, having committed the bulk of their army to Lorraine in line with Plan XVII, were nearly crushed by the sudden German descent on their flank and rear. While sixty-two French divisions lunged into Alsace and Lorraine, eighty-seven German divisions rolled over the six divisions of the British Expeditionary Force (BEF) at Mons and Le Cateau. The BEF had rushed to France without howitzers, hand grenades or radio equipment, and were brushed aside. Observing a German artillery barrage for the first time in the Sambre valley, a British officer described his feelings with remarkable innocence, as if he had never heard of Port Arthur or the Balkan Wars: 'A chill of horror came over us. … Hitherto it had been war as we had conceived it, hard blows, straight dealing, but now for the first time we felt as if some horrible Thing, utterly merciless, was advancing to grip us' (Winter 1991: 34–5; Gilbert 1994: 51–2). The 'Thing' was high explosive, which the well armed Germans rained on the British, Belgian and French front lines and rear areas. Though the British had noted the usefulness of heavy artillery in the Boer War, endowing every division in 1914 with as many heavy guns as light ones, they failed to move more than a handful of heavy guns to France in time for the German invasion (Zabecki 1994: 11). Consequently, the Germans were able to pitch shells into the British lines with impunity; the British 13-pounders, with just half the range of the German 105mm howitzers (5,900 versus 11,670 yards), often failed even to reach the German lines. On the retreat from Mons, where hundreds of British troops were ground into 'unidentified remains' by the German long guns, the men 'stumbled along more like ghosts than living soldiers'; these were the first victims of a new medical condition: 'shell-shock' (Showalter, in Strachan 1998: 40–5; Gilbert 1994: 55–61; Herwig 1997: 70–1; D. Harding 1980: 182–5).

The first battles of the First World War disclosed the folly of France's 'offensive spirit' and the wisdom of Germany's more balanced approach. As the German right wing wheeled through Belgium and northern France, the German left wing gave ground in Alsace-Lorraine, drawing the bulk of Joffre's forces into firestorms at Mulhouse and Morhange. Belatedly realizing that he was being encircled, Joffre detached an army to block the German descent through Luxembourg; it too was chewed up, producing more casualties. Indeed, the German army turning through Luxembourg and Champagne was only the nearest of five parallel German armies wheeling in behind the French. Were it not for the fighting retreat of the Belgians and the quick arrival of the British, the French would have been enveloped. As it was, they suffered gruesome casualties in these frontier battles; charging ahead

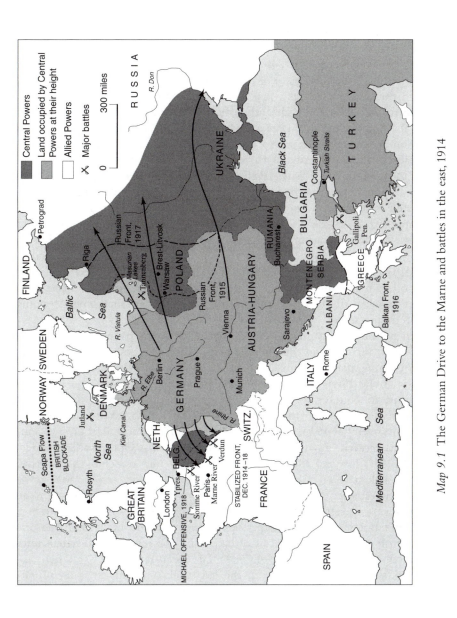

Map 9.1 The German Drive to the Marne and battles in the east, 1914

shoulder-to-shoulder with fixed bayonets in blue tunics and red trousers behind brass bands and regimental flags, the French lost 300,000 men in the opening days of the war, a quarter of their total strength. The French guns were little help; envisioning a short war, the war ministry had provided each French 75 with just 1,300 rounds of ammunition, about forty-three minutes of uninterrupted fire (Zabecki 1994: 10). 'Astonishing changes in the practice of war', was Foch's comment on the slaughter (Gilbert 1994: 47). It was a pity that he and his colleagues had not noted the changes earlier.

With the unflappable calm that was his hallmark, Joffre recast Plan XVII, reacting to the Schlieffen Plan with a marvellous improvisation that has been called 'the Schlieffen Plan in reverse'. Leaving his First and Second Armies at Nancy and Verdun with orders to 'hold at any price', he concentrated all available reserves in the vicinity of Paris and wheeled the French Third, Fourth and Fifth Armies as well as the BEF backward to the Marne River. That was all the respite they needed, for the German advance shortly broke down. Exhausted by its long sweep through Belgium, Moltke's First Army – which was supposed to engulf the British army and 'brush the Channel with its sleeve' before circling around Paris – turned eastward prematurely to shorten its long march and close a thirty-mile gap between itself and the German Second Army on its flank. As it turned back to the East, the German First Army offered its flank to the French and British behind the Marne, who counter-attacked the Germans in the first two weeks of September, stopping them in their tracks.

Both sides now began a 'race to the sea', each trying to make the Channel coast first to turn around the enemy's flank. What they found in these battles was something that had already been demonstrated at Magersfontein and Colenso in the Boer War. Defensive fire permitted armies to spread themselves thin to counter flanking attacks. Even lightly guarded flanks could defend themselves, as the Germans discovered at Ypres. There in October–November 1914, thin lines of British infantry and their French reinforcements mowed down waves of attacking Germans. 'Open warfare' ended, and both sides lowered themselves disconsolately into trenches; the war had become a stalemate.

'Schlieffen's notes do not help any further, and so Moltke's wits come to an end', a German general scathingly observed (Liddell Hart 1964: 97–8). In fact, Schlieffen's notes had long since stopped helping. The master's march and ammunition tables were years out of date, with the result that German units consumed supplies and munitions at a far faster rate than Schlieffen had predicted, slowing their advance in the last week of August to a crawl. The collapse of the Schlieffen Plan meant the collapse of Germany's hopes in the war. The Kaiser had pinned everything on victory in France and Belgium by the fortieth day of mobilization. The reverse at the Marne and the ensuing stalemate gave the British time to clamp a naval blockade on the German coast, and the Russians a free hand in the East (Tucker 1998: 28–37; Herwig 1997: 99–105; Snyder 1984: 150–3).

Fighting in the East revealed the deficiencies that the Russian and Austro-Hungarian armies had struggled to correct in the months before August 1914. Though the Russians had made great strides in their railways and organization, Plan 20 – the 'hasty attack strategy' – came to grief in the face of German counter-measures. In the first weeks of the war, 173,000 German troops amply supplied with artillery and shells knifed between two Russian armies with a combined strength of 485,000 and defeated them separately: the first at Tannenberg (where the Germans inflicted 142,000 casualties on the Russians) and the second in a sequence of running battles past the Masurian Lakes, the dazed Russians 'running faster than the Germans could chase them' (Tucker 1998: 39–44; Herwig 1997: 83–7). As in the West, these early German triumphs were owed to superior preparedness. The Russian army in 1914 was only beginning to procure modern instruments of war and communication. The artillery was still deficient – and rendered even more so by the German capture of 500 Russian guns at Tannenberg – and Russian communications were sketchy. The 150,000-man Russian Second Army beaten at Tannenberg possessed just twenty-five telephones, ten automobiles, and four motorcycles. Most of its forty-two aircraft were grounded with mechanical problems, which meant that reconnaissance and communications were generally carried out by men on horseback. Even where modern technology was in place, the Russians often thwarted it with bureaucratic routine. Thus, for example, telegraph communications between Second Army's corps and headquarters had to be addressed to the Warsaw post office, where they were collected, decoded and then dispatched in automobiles all the way back to East Prussia, a journey of 100 miles. Faced with obstacles like this, General Alexander Samsonov, the luckless Russian commander at Tannenberg, rode into a wood and shot himself as night fell on 30 August (Showalter 1991: 216–18; Stone 1975: 51, 63; Steinberg, in Coetzee and Coetzee 1995: 276–98).

Further down the Eastern Front (see Map 9.1), things went better for the Russians, chiefly due to the blundering of the Austro-Hungarians. Having initially decided to concentrate against the Serbs, Conrad was forced quite predictably to turn the bulk of his army against the Russians. The problem was the three-part mobilization plan adopted in 1912–13: *A-Staffel* with twenty-seven divisions destined for Russia, *B-Staffel* with eleven divisions, and *Minimalgruppe Balkan* with nine divisions for Serbia. In theory, *B-Staffel* was a floating reserve, not a Balkan army, but Conrad's hatred of the Serbs contravened all reason in the heat of the July Crisis, and in August the four corps of *B-Staffel* thus entrained for Bosnia and Croatia instead of Galicia. The Russians meanwhile wrung full advantage from their French-financed railways and deployed in Poland and Ukraine in half the time needed by the Austrians, forcing even Conrad to rethink the wisdom of a 'Serbia first' strategy. Having already committed *B-Staffel* to the Balkan Front, Conrad tried to turn it around and send it to Galicia. This was easier said than done. In fact, Austrian railway officials found that they had no option but to deliver the eleven divisions of *B-Staffel* to the Balkans, get them off their trains, load them into new ones, and then put them on their way to the Russian front. It was a maddeningly time-consuming process, and it sapped the morale of tens of thousands of Austro-Hungarian troops. While the men of *B-Staffel* sweated in their boxcars, the men of *A-Staffel* limped along the dusty Galician roads to the Russian border. As their trains had been withdrawn to reroute *B-Staffel*, these men were ordered to make foot marches of twenty miles a day just to reach the front (Herwig 1997: 52–6; Stone 1975: 70–80). Doubts as to the acumen of their leaders swelled in their minds like the blisters on their feet, a process that only accelerated in the days to come.

Though numerically weaker than the Russians, Conrad hoped to exploit the confusion that split the Russian army into two unconnected halves: three armies in East Prussia against the Germans, and four in Poland and Ukraine against the Austrians. The problem was that even these odds did not favour Conrad, who faced seventy-two Russian divisions with just thirty-seven of his own. Initially Conrad fared well; the Austro-Hungarians won two battles on their left flank in late August, but spread themselves so thin in the process that the Russians – whose divisions contained more men and machineguns than the Austrians and two to three times the number of light and heavy artillery pieces – had little difficulty counter-attacking the exposed Austrian right flank in the first week of September. In bloody battles at Lemberg (Lvov), Przemsyl and Tarnów in which the Austrians ran at the Russians in battalion masses not unlike those of 1866, Conrad lost 300 guns and more than a third of the Austro-Hungarian army: 100,000 dead, 220,000 wounded, and 100,000 prisoners, many of whom ran joyfully into captivity. Things went no better on the Serbian front, where the Austrians lost an additional 227,000 troops and 180 guns in difficult conditions. This was attrition that the Austro-Hungarian army, which had strained every fibre to raise its strength to one million, simply could not afford; indeed, virtually all of the trained cadres of the Habsburg army were wiped out in 1914; for Emperor Franz Joseph, these defeats were political no less than military. Every reverse in Serbia and Poland was accompanied by massive defections, as Austria-Hungary's Slavic regiments (the bulk of the army) exhibited a distressing tendency to surrender rather than fight (Showalter, in Strachan 1998: 48–50; Wawro, in Cecil and Liddle 1996: 399–412). As summer turned to autumn, the Austro-Hungarian government had little choice but to cede its war effort to the Germans, who agreed to reinforce Conrad's beaten army in exchange for control of its movements. It was a bad start to a war engineered in large part to save and invigorate the Habsburg Monarchy (Herwig 1997: 89–95; Stone 1975: 84–90; Tucker 1998: 44–9; Bridge 1990: 346–7).

Autumn turned to winter, and few Europeans celebrated the new year. A war that was supposed to be over 'before the leaves fell' looked set to drag on indefinitely. Although the Germans shifted much of their army to the Eastern Front in 1915 to rescue the Austro-Hungarians and defend Germany's eastern provinces, they were still able to shatter British and French offensives on the Western Front. The reason for this and the ensuing years of trench warfare was the preponderance of defensive fire that had already been well established in the Russo-Japanese War. Norman Stone has correctly characterized the armies of the First World War as 'twentieth century delivery systems with nineteenth century warheads' (Stone 1975: 50). Revolutions in agriculture, transport and communications permitted the conscription and deployment of unprecedent-edly large armies – four million Germans mobilized in 1914, and nearly as many French and Russians – but once these vast assemblies marched off from their railheads they became immediately bogged down. Though the British army would have 56,000 trucks by 1918, it had none in 1914, nor did any of the other armies. Without trucks or tracked vehicles, the armies moved on foot and relied on horse transport, which consumed so much fodder that many convoys carried little besides the hay and oats needed to feed the draught animals (pound for pound, horses eat ten times more weight than men, a dismaying discovery for Great War logisticians).

With so much carrying capacity dedicated to fragrant heaps of fodder, the resupply of ammunition in adequate quantities inevitably became a problem, as the Germans discovered during their swing through Belgium and France in August 1914. Whereas German infantrymen had fired an average of fifty-six rifle rounds in the entire Franco-Prussian War, their grandchildren fired six times as many rounds in the first month of the Great War alone. The German artillery was at least as spendthrift; whereas their predecessors in 1870–1 had fired 199 shells per gun in the seven-month war, the 1914 class of gunners ran through 1,000 shells per gun in just six weeks. Unfortunately, Stone's 'nine-teenth century warhead' was simply unable to cope with ammunition expenditure on this scale; it needed trucks, tractors and light railways, things that would not be procured until late in the war. Finally, without armoured vehicles or tactical air support, the armies found that there was no easy way to dislodge adversaries from entrenched, fortified positions. As the Boers had shown in the Boer War, rapid-firing weapons permitted a thin force-to-space ratio; it became difficult to outflank adversaries because they could keep extending their threatened flank with quick-firers and small parties of riflemen and machinegunners (Tucker 1998: 11–16). And as every old soldier knows, every flank attack ends as a frontal attack on the exposed flank. In the nine-teenth century, such attacks usually carried; in the Great War they never did: the volume of fire from modern artillery, machineguns and rifles was too much.

German efforts later in the war to use 'infiltration tactics' to penetrate the Entente trenches invariably went 'a trench too far', exposing the onrushing German flanks to enfilading fire and forcing them back to their original lines.

The British and French preferred 'bite and hold' operations, taking a section of the German line with horrendous casualties and forcing the Germans to take it back at the cost of heavy casualties of their own. The lines would shift minutely, and thousands more corpses would sink into the mud (Griffith 1994: 29–38). Only when the Americans joined the war in 1917, conferring an unbeatable material superiority on the Entente, did the lines begin to move, powered everywhere by artillery. The French had gone to war in 1914 with a stockpile of five million artillery shells; by 1916 they were firing this many rounds at the Germans every month; by 1918, they were firing ten million shells a month at the Germans (Zabecki 1994: 8). The Germans wilted under the barrage; starved of food and material by the British blockade, German morale broke, as did the German army's ability to resist. The Germans had no steel left over for tank construction, and routinely absorbed twenty British, French or American shells for every one they were able to send back in 1918 (anyone who wonders how this felt must read Ernst Jünger's *Storm of Steel*, which leaves even the armchair soldier with a reverberating din between the ears). Still, to the end the Germans made the Entente pay dearly for every inch of ground; they used steel and cement to fabricate an early version of the Maginot Line, and kept fighting to the last (Travers, in Strachan 1998:288–90). On the Southwestern Front, it was the same overwhelming superiority of material and the attendant collapse of Austro-Hungarian morale that doomed the Habsburg army, not the manoeuvring of the Italians. Indeed the Italians, beset with their own problems, did not even bother attacking the Austro-Hungarians for a full year from October 1917 until October 1918; they simply left the Austrians in their trenches to rot from cold, hunger, fatigue, demoralization and nationalist propaganda (Wawro, in Cecil and Liddle 1996: 406–10). A war that had begun with dreams on all sides of a glorious 'second Sedan' ended squalidly in a wasteland of corpses and muck.

In closing, it is useful to reflect on how Europe arrived at this pathetic juncture. Carnot, Napoleon and the other captains of the French Revolution had coined the ideas and vocabulary of modern war, grouping their conscript armies in mobile all-arms divisions and using speed and surprise to rout the unreformed old-regime armies of Britain, Austria, Russia and Prussia. As the Napoleonic Wars lengthened, France's adversaries gradually absorbed the French methods – the general staff, conscription, corps and divisions, the battery system, shock tactics – and turned the tide. After 1815, European armies retained French organization and tactics, but attempted to reduce the size of armies to spare the state the expense of their upkeep. Little Prussia shattered this comfortable arrangement in the 1860s by reintroducing universal conscription, which briefly gave Europe's smallest great power its biggest army. The Prussians bestowed unprecedented speed and mobility on this large army by linking it to an extensive network of railways and telegraphs. The aim was Clausewitzian: to find the enemy main force and annihilate it in battle; this would open all doors. In 1866, the Prussians rolled over the Austrians, in 1870–1 the French. In both wars, Prussia used speed and forethought to overtake and envelop relatively small professional armies that still moved and fought at an eighteenth-century tempo, relying largely on horse-drawn supplies and foot marches. In both wars the Prussians used superior firepower to overcome their enemy: the needle rifle in 1866, the breech-loading Krupp cannon in 1870–1. This was the 'Prussian military revolution': a smooth, mass mobilization, a rapid deployment, and a tooth-jarring knockout-blow: Königgrätz in 1866, Sedan in 1870.

After 1870, every European army adopted the Prussian formula. They introduced conscription, expanded their railways and telegraphs, procured magazine rifles, machineguns and quick-firing artillery, set their general staffs the task of planning *offensive* wars in painstaking detail, and assigned a recklessly bowdlerized version of Clausewitz to their war colleges: 'Go for your man', General William 'Wully' Robertson lectured British cadets at Camberley in 1910. 'You can win only by the offensive. That is obvious to everybody' (Woodward 1998: 2–5, 10). Forgetting that the Napoleonic 'revolution in military affairs' had lost its punch once every other army in Europe adopted it, these generals went to war in 1914 labouring under the 'short war illusion'; they were somehow convinced that their planning, armaments and tactics would defeat the enemy, even though the enemy possessed virtually the same technologies and doctrines that they did. The bloody battles of 1914 shattered this particular illusion; the ensuing four years of industrialized slaughter obliterated any that remained.

Bibliography

Addington, Larry H. (1984) *The Patterns of War since the Eighteenth Century*, Bloomington: Indiana University Press.

Allen, Louis (1971) *Japan*, New York: American Heritage.

Andlau, Gaston (1872) *Metz: Campagne et Négociations*, Paris: Dumaine.

Andlau, Joseph (1869) 'Die Generalstäbe', *Österreichische Militärische Zeitschrift*, vol. 10: 155–6, 486–98.

Anon ['einem Österreicher'] (1902) *Die Militarismus in Österreich-Ungarn*, Vienna: Seidel.

Arno, Wolf Scheider von (n.d.) 'Die Österreichisch-Ungarisch Generalstab', 8 vols, Vienna, Kriegsarchiv, unpublished manuscript, vol.VI, 32–3.

Apfelknab, Egbert (1984) *Waffenrock und Schnürschuh*, Vienna: Österreichischer Bundesverlag.

Asprey, Robert B. (1959) *The Panther's Feast*, New York, Carroll & Graf.

—— (1991) *The German High Command at War*, New York: Morrow.

Audoin-Rouzeau, Stéphane (1989) *1870: La France dans la Guerre*, Paris: Armand Colin.

Baer, George (1994) *One Hundred Years of Sea Power*, Stanford: Stanford University Press.

Balfour, Sebastian (1997) *The End of the Spanish Empire, 1898–1923*, Oxford: Clarendon Press.

Barclay, David E. and Weitz, Eric D. (1998) *Between Reform and Revolution: German Socialism and Communism from 1840 to 1990*, New York: Berghahn.

Barnhart, Michael A. (1995) *Japan and the World since 1868*, London: Edward Arnold.

Bartlett, C. J. (1994) *The Global Conflict: The International Rivalry of the Great Powers, 1880–1990*, London: Longman.

Barzini, Luigi (1986) *Memoirs of Mistresses*, New York: St Martin's Press.

Baumgart, Winfried (1982) *Imperialism: The Idea and Reality of British and French Colonial Expansion, 1880–1914*, Oxford: Oxford University Press.

Bayerisches Kriegsarchiv, HS 888, Munich, LW Lt. Joseph Danziger, 'Kriegstagebuch, 1870–71'.

Bazaine, F. A. (1883) *Episodes de la Guerre de 1870*, Madrid: Gaspar.

Beck, Hermann (1995) *The Origins of the Authoritarian Welfare State in Prussia*, Ann Arbor: University of Michigan Press.

226

Becker, Jean-Jacques and Audoin-Rouzeau, Stéphane (1995) *La France, La Nation, La Guerre: 1850–1920*, Paris: Sedes.

Beeler, John F. (1997) *British Naval Policy in the Gladstone-Disraeli Era, 1866–1880*, Stanford: Stanford University Press.

Bellamy, Christopher (1990) *The Evolution of Modern Land Warfare*, London: Routledge.

Beller, Steven (1966) *Francis Joseph*, London: Longman.

Bentley, Nicolas (ed.) (1996) *Russell's Despatches from the Crimea, 1854–56*, London: Andre Deutsch.

Berghahn, Volker R. (1982) *Militarism: The History of an International Debate, 1861–1979*, New York: St Martin's Press.

—— (1993) *Germany and the Approach of War in 1914*, 2nd edn, New York: St Martin's Press.

—— (1997) *Sarajewo, 28. Juni 1914: Der Untergang des alten Europa*, Munich: DTV.

Bernhardi, Friedrich (1914) [1912] *Germany and the Next War*, New York: Eron.

—— (1920) *The War of the Future*, London: Hutchinson.

Bertaud, Jean-Paul (1988) [1979] *The Army of the French Revolution*, trans. R. R. Palmer, Princeton: Princeton University Press.

Best, Geoffrey (1982) *War and Society in Revolutionary Europe, 1770–1870*, New York: St Martin's Press.

Beveridge, Albert (1904) *The Russian Advance*, New York: Harper.

Bierman, John (1988) *Napoleon III and his Carnival Empire*, New York: St Martin's Press.

Black, Jeremy (1994) *European Warfare, 1660–1815*, New Haven: Yale University Press.

—— (1998) *War and the World*, New Haven: Yale University Press.

Blanchon, Georges (1918) *The New Warfare*, Edinburgh: Turnbull and Spears.

Blanning, T. C. W. (1986) *The Origins of the French Revolutionary Wars*, London: Longman.

—— (1996) *The French Revolutionary Wars, 1787–1802*, London: Edward Arnold.

Bled, Jean-Paul (1992) [1987] *Franz Joseph*, trans. Teresa Bridgeman, Oxford: Blackwell.

Bloch, I. S. (1903) [1897] *The Future of War*, Boston: Ginn.

Bond, Brian (1986) *War and Society in Europe, 1870–1970*, Oxford: Oxford University Press.

Bosworth, Richard (1983) *Italy and the Approach of the First World War*, London: Macmillan.

—— (1996) *Italy and the Wider World: 1860–1960*. London: Routledge.

Bourne, Kenneth (1970) *The Foreign Policy of Victorian England, 1830–1902*, Oxford: Clarendon Press.

Bouvier, Jean, Girault, René, and Thobie, Jacques (1986) *L'Impérialisme à la Française*, Paris: Editions Découverte.

Bradford, James C. (ed.) (1993) *Crucible of Empire*, Annapolis: Naval Institute Press.

Brands, H. W. (1997) *T. R.: The Last Romantic*, New York: Basic Books.

Brandt, Harm-Hinrich (1978) *Der Österreichische Neoabsolutismus: Staatsfinanzen und Politik, 1848–60*, Göttingen: Vandenhoeck & Ruprecht.

Bridge, F. R. (1990) *The Habsburg Monarchy among the Great Powers, 1815–1918*, New York: Berg.

Brogan, D. W. (1989) [1957] *The French Nation: From Napoleon to Pétain, 1814–1940*, London: Cassell.

Browning, Oscar (1903) *Wars of the Century and the Development of Military Science*, London and Philadelphia: Linscott.

Bucholz, Arden (1991) *Moltke, Schlieffen and Prussian War Planning*, New York: Berg.

Bury, J. P. T. (1989) *France 1814–1940*, 5th edn, London: Methuen.

Cahm, Eric (1996) *The Dreyfus Affair in French Society and Politics*, London: Longman.

Callwell, Col. Charles Edward (1996) [1906] *Small Wars: Their Principles and Practice*, 3rd edn, Lincoln NE: University of Nebraska Press.

Carr, William (1991) *The Origins of the Wars of German Unification*, London: Longman.

Carroll, E. Malcolm (1996) *Germany and the Great Powers, 1866–1914: A Study in Public Opinion and Foreign Policy*, Hamden: Archon.

Carsten, F. L. (1989) *A History of the Prussian Junkers*, Aldershot: Scolar.

Case, Lynn M. (1972) [1954] *French Opinion on War and Diplomacy during the Second Empire*, New York: Octagon Books.

Cecil, Hugh and Liddle, Peter (eds.) (1996) *Facing Armageddon*, London: Leo Cooper.

Chaliand, Gérard (1994) *The Art of War in World History: From Antiquity to the Nuclear Age*, Berkeley: University of California Press.

Chandler, David G. (1966) *The Campaigns of Napoleon*, New York: Macmillan.

Christiansen, Rupert (1994) *Paris Babylon: The Story of the Paris Commune*, New York: Viking.

Clark, Alan (1991) [1961] *The Donkeys*, London: Pimlico.

Clark, Martin (1984) *Modern Italy, 1871–1982*, vol. 7 of *The Longman History of Italy*, London, Longman.

Clausewitz, General Carl von (1960) [1832] *Principles of War*, ed. Hans W. Gatzke, Harrisburg: Stackpole.

—— (1976) [1832] *On War*, ed. Michael Howard and Peter Paret, Princeton: Princeton University Press.

—— (1995) [1843] *The Campaign of 1812 in Russia*, New York: Da Capo.

Cleator, P. E. (1967) *Weapons of War*, New York: Crowell.

Clemente, Steven E. (1992) *For King and Kaiser! The Making of the Prussian Army Officer, 1860–1914*, Westport: Greenwood.

Cobb, Richard (1987) *The People's Armies*, New Haven: Yale University Press.

Cocker, Mark (1998) *Rivers of Blood, Rivers of Gold*, London: Jonathan Cape.

Coetzee, Frans and Coetzee, Marilyn Shevin (eds) (1995) *Authority, Identity, and the Social History of the Great War*, Providence: Berghahn.

Coetzee, Marilyn Shevin (1990) *The German Army League: Popular Nationalism in Wilhelmine Germany*, New York: Oxford University Press.

Collingham, H. A. C. (1988) *The July Monarchy: A Political History of France, 1830–1848*, London: Longman.

Connaughton, R. M. (1988) *The War of the Rising Sun and the Tumbling Bear*, London: Routledge.

Connelly, Owen (1965) *Napoleon's Satellite Kingdoms*, New York: Free Press.

—— (1987) *Blundering to Glory: Napoleon's Military Campaigns*, Washington: Scholarly Resources.

Coppa, Frank (1992) *The Origins of the Italian Wars of Independence*, London: Longman.

Corbett, Julian S. (1988) [1911] *Some Principles of Maritime Strategy*, Annapolis: Naval Institute Press.

Corbin, Alain (1992) *The Village of Cannibals*, trans. Arthur Goldhammer, Cambridge MA: Harvard University Press.

Corvisier, André and Childs, John (eds) (1994) *A Dictionary of Military History*, revised edn, Oxford: Blackwell.

Cosmas, Graham A. (1994) *An Army for Empire: The US Army in the Spanish-American War*, College Station: Texas A&M University Press.

Cox, Gary P. (1994) *The Halt in the Mud: French Strategic Planning from Waterloo to Sedan*, Boulder: Westview.

Craig, Gordon A. (1955) *The Politics of the Prussian Army, 1640–1945*, Oxford: Clarendon Press.

—— (1964) *The Battle of Königgrätz*, Philadelphia: Lippincott.

Curtin, Philip D. (1998) *Disease and Empire: The Health of European Troops in the Conquest of Africa*, Cambridge: Cambridge University Press.

Curtiss, John Shelton (1979) *Russia's Crimean War*, Durham NC: Duke University Press.

Dawson, W. H. (1926) *Richard Cobden and Foreign Policy*, London: George Allen & Unwin.

Déak, István (1992) *Beyond Nationalism: A Social and Political History of the Habsburg Officer Corps, 1848–1918*, Oxford: Oxford University Press.

Dedijer, Vladimir (1966) *The Road to Sarajevo*, New York: Simon & Schuster.

Di Scala, Spencer M. (1998) *Italy: From Revolution to Republic, 1700 to the Present*, Boulder: Westview.

Dixon, Norman (1994) [1976] *On the Psychology of Military Incompetence*, London: Pimlico.

Donia, Robert J. (1981) *Islam under the Double Eagle: The Muslims of Bosnia and Hercegovina, 1878–1914*, Boulder: East European Monographs.

Duffy, Christopher (1986) *The Military Life of Frederick the Great*, New York: Atheneum.

Dumas, Samuel and Vedel-Petersen, K. O. (1923) *Losses of Life Caused by War*, Oxford: Clarendon Press.

Dupuy, R. Ernest and Dupuy, Trevor (1997) *The Harper Encylopedia of Military History, from 3500 BC to the Present*, 4th edn, New York: Harper Collins.

Eley, Geoff (1980) *Reshaping the German Right*, New Haven: Yale University Press.

Ellis, Geoffrey (1997) *Napoleon*, London: Longman.

Ellis, John (1993) [1976] *The Social History of the Machine Gun*, London: Pimlico.

Elting, John R. (1988) *Swords Around a Throne: Napoleon's Grande Armée*, New York: Free Press.

Epstein, Robert M. (1994) *Napoleon's Last Victory and the Emergence of Modern War*, Lawrence: University Press of Kansas.

Esdaile, Charles J. (1995) *The Wars of Napoleon*, London: Longman.

Evans, David C. and Peattie, Mark R. (1997) *Kaigun*, Annapolis: Naval Institute Press.

Evans, R. J. W. and Strandmann, Hartmut Pogge von (1990) *The Coming of the First World War*, Oxford: Clarendon Press.

Falls, Cyril (1961) *The Art of War: From the Age of Napoleon to the Present Day*, Oxford: Oxford University Press.

—— (1961) *A Hundred Years of War*, 2nd edn, London: Duckworth.

Fay, Charles (1889) *Journal d'un officier de l'Armée du Rhin*, Paris: Berger-Levrault.

Fay, Sidney B. (1966) *The Origins of the World War*, 2 vols, 2nd edn, New York: Free Press.

Ferguson, Niall (1988) *The Pity of War*, London: Penguin.

Ferri-Pisani, Col, (1868) 'Urteile über den Preussischen Feldzug 1866', *Österreichische Militärische Zeitschrift*, vol. 9: 188–9.

Fieldhouse, D. K. (1966) *The Colonial Empires*, New York: Delacorte.

—— (1973) *Economics and Empire, 1830–1914*, Ithaca: Cornell University Press.

Figes, Orlando (1996) *A People's Tragedy: The Russian Revolution, 1891–1924*: New York: Penguin.

Finley, Milton (1994) *The Most Monstrous of Wars: The Napoleonic Guerrilla War in Southern Italy, 1806–11*, Columbia: University of South Carolina Press.

Fischer, Fritz (1967) *Germany's Aims in the First World War*, orig. 1961, New York: Norton.

—— (1974) *World Power or Decline: the Controversy over Germany's Aims in the First World War*: New York: Norton.

Förster, Stig and Nagler, Jörg (1997) *On the Road to Total War: the American Civil War and the German Wars of Unification, 1861–71*, Cambridge: Cambridge University Press.

French, David (1986) *British Strategy and War Aims, 1914–16*, London: Allen & Unwin.

Fuller, J. F. C. (1992) (1961) *The Conduct of War, 1789–1961*, New York: Da Capo.

Fuller, William C. Jr (1992) *Strategy and Power in Russia, 1660–1914*, New York: Free Press.

Gall, Lothar (1986) *Bismarck: The White Revolutionary*, trans. J. A. Underwood, 2 vols, London: Allen & Unwin.

Gat, Azar (1992) *The Development of Military Thought: The Nineteenth Century*, Oxford: Clarendon Press.

Gates, David (1986) *The Spanish Ulcer: A History of the Peninsular War*, London: Allen & Unwin.

Gatrell, Peter (1994) *Government, Industry and Rearmament in Russia, 1900–1914*, Cambridge: Cambridge University Press.

Gibbs, Peter (1963) *The Battle of the Alma*, Philadelphia: Lippincott.

Gilbert, Martin (1994) *The First World War*, New York: Henry Holt.

Gildea, Robert (1996) *Barricades and Borders: Europe 1800–1914*, 2nd edn, Oxford: Oxford University Press.

Glover, Michael (1980) *Warfare from Waterloo to Mons*, London: Cassell.

Goerlitz, Walter (1995) [1952] *History of the German General Staff, 1657–1945*, New York: Barnes & Noble.

Goldfrank, David M. (1994) *The Origins of the Crimean War*, London: Longman.

Gollwitzer, Heinz (1969) *Europe in the Age of Imperialism, 1880–1914*, London: Thames and Hudson.

Gooch, Brison (1959) *The New Bonapartist Generals of the Crimean War: Distrust and Decision Making in the Anglo-French Alliance*, The Hague: Martinus Nijhoff.

Gooch, John (1974) *The Plans of War: The General Staff and British Military Strategy, c. 1900–1916*, New York: Wiley.

—— (1989) *Army, State and Society in Italy, 1870–1915*, New York: St Martin's Press.

Greene, Jack and Massignani, Alessandro (1998) *Ironclads at War*, Conshohocken: Combined.

Greer, Donald (1935) *The Incidence of the Terror during the French Revolution: A Statistical Interpretation*, Cambridge, MA: Harvard University Press.

Griffith, Paddy (1994) *Battle Tactics of the Western Front*, New Haven: Yale University Press.

—— (1998) *The Art of War of Revolutionary France, 1789–1802*, London: Greenhill.

Gudmundsson, Bruce I. (1989) *Stormtroop Tactics*, Westport: Praeger.

Hall, Major John R. (1909) *The Bourbon Restoration*, London: Alston Rivers.

Hamerow, Theodore (1972) *The Social Foundations of German Unification, 1858–71*, Princeton: Princeton University Press.

Hamley, Edward Bruce (1878) *The Operations of War*, 4th edn, London: Blackwood.

Harding, David (ed.) (1980) *Weapons: An International Encyclopedia from 5000 BC to 2000 AD*, New York: St Martin's Press.

Harding, Richard (1999) *Seapower and Naval Warfare, 1650–1830*, Annapolis: Naval Institute Press.

Harries, Meirion and Harries, Susie (1994) *Soldiers of the Sun*, New York: Random House.

Hart, Albert (ed.) (1920) *Harper's Pictorial Library of the World War*, 12 vols, New York: Harper, I, 95.

Hayes, Carlyon J. H. (1941) *A Generation of Materialism, 1871–1900*, New York: Harper & Row.

Headrick, Daniel R. (1981) *The Tools of Empire*, New York: Oxford University Press.

Hearder, Harry (1983) *Italy in the Age of the Risorgimento, 1790–1870*, vol. 6 of *The Longman History of Italy*, London: Longman.

Herrmann, David G. (1996) *The Arming of Europe and the Making of the First World War*, Princeton: Princeton University Press.

Herwig, Holger H. (1987) *'Luxury' Fleet: The Imperial German Navy, 1888–1918*, revised edn, Atlantic Highlands: Ashfield.

—— (1994) *Hammer or Anvil?* Lexington: D. C. Heath.

—— (1997) *The First World War: Germany and Austria-Hungary, 1914–18*, London: Edward Arnold.

HHSA (Haus-Hof-und Staatsarchiv) (n.d.) Vienna, PA I, 810, Int. LXX/1, 'Berichte-Presse'.

—— PA I, 810, Int. LXX/1, Belgrade, 1 July 1914, Storck to Berchtold.

Hobsbawm, E. J. (1985a) [1968] *Industry and Empire*, London: Pelican.

—— (1985b) [1975] *The Age of Capital, 1848–75*, London: Abacus.

—— (1987) [1962] *The Age of Revolution, 1789–1848*, London: Abacus.

—— (1989) [1987] *The Age of Empire, 1875–1914*, New York: Vintage.

—— (1990) *Nations and Nationalism since 1780*, Cambridge: Cambridge University Press.

—— (1996) [1994] *The Age of Extremes: A History of the World, 1914–1991*, New York: Vintage.

Horne, Alistair (1996) *How Far from Austerlitz? Napoleon 1805–1815*, New York: St Martin's Press.

Hötzendorf, Franz Conrad von (1903) *Infanteristische Fragen und die Erscheinungen des Boerenkrieges*, Vienna: Seidel.

—— (1921–3) *Aus meiner Dienstzeit, 1906–18*, 4 vols, Vienna: Rikola.

Hough, Richard (1983) *The Great War at Sea, 1914–18*, Oxford: Oxford University Press.

Howard, Michael (1976) *War in European History*, Oxford: Oxford University Press.

—— (1981) [1961] *The Franco-Prussian War*, London: Methuen.

Howard, Michael (ed.) (1966) *The Theory and Practice of War*, New York: Praeger.

Hughes, Daniel J. (1999) 'Tactics and command in the Prusso-German army, 1870–1914': unpublished manuscript.

Hull, Isabel V. (1982) *The Entourage of Kaiser Wilhelm II*, Cambridge: Cambridge University Press.

Imprimerie Nationale (1870) *Papiers et Correspondance de la Famille Impériale*, Paris, Imprimerie Nationale, vol. 8: 52, Paris, 20 July 1866, Magne to Napoleon III.

Iriye, Akira (1997) *Japan and the Wider World*, London: Longman.

Jamieson, Perry D. (1994) *Crossing the Deadly Ground: United States Army Tactics, 1865–1899*, Tuscaloosa: University of Alabama Press.

Jarras, Louis (1892) *Souvenirs*, Paris: Plon.

Jelavich, Barbara (1983) *History of the Balkans*, 2 vols, Cambridge: Cambridge University Press.

—— (1991) *Russia's Balkan Entanglements, 1806–1914*, Cambridge: Cambridge University Press.

Jenkins, T. A. (1994) *The Liberal Ascendancy, 1830–1886*, New York: St Martin's Press.

Jerabek, Rudolf (1992) *Potiorek*, Graz: Verlag Styria.

Johannsen, Gustav and Kraft, H. H. (1937) *Germany's Colonial Problem*, London: Butterworth.

Johnson, Paul (1991) *The Birth of the Modern: World Society, 1815–30*, New York: Harper Collins.

Joll, James (1992) *The Origins of the First World War*, 2nd edn, London: Longman.

Jomini, Baron Antoine-Henri (1965) [1838] *Summary of the Art of War*, Harrisburg: Stackpole.

Kagan, Donald (1995) *On the Origins of War and the Preservation of Peace*, New York: Doubleday.

Kaiser, David (1990) *Politics and War*, Cambridge MA: Harvard University Press.

Keegan, John (1993) *A History of Warfare*, New York: Knopf.

Keiger, John F. V. (1983) *France and the Origins of the First World War*, London: Macmillan.

—— (1997) *Raymond Poincaré*, Cambridge: Cambridge University Press.

Kemp, P. K. (1969) *History of the Royal Navy*, New York: Putnam.

Kennedy, Paul M. (1976) *The Rise and Fall of British Naval Mastery*, New York: Scribner.

—— (1979) *The War Plans of the Great Powers, 1880–1914*, London: Unwin Hyman.

—— (1985) [1981] *The Realities Behind Diplomacy: Background Influences on British External Policy, 1865–1980*, London: Fontana.

—— (1987) [1981] *The Rise of the Anglo-German Anglo-German Antagonism, 1860–1914*, London: Ashfield Press.

—— (1988) *The Rise and Fall of the Great Powers: Economic Change and Military Conflict from 1500 to 2000*, London: Unwin Hyman.

Kiernan, Victor G. (1982) *European Empires from Conquest to Collapse, 1815–1960*, London: Fontana.

King, Jere Clemens (1951) *Generals and Politicians*, Berkeley: University of California Press.

Kitchen, Martin (1968) *The German Officer Corps, 1890–1914*, Oxford: Clarendon Press.

—— (1975) *A Military History of Germany: From the Eighteenth Century to the Present Day*, Bloomington: Indiana University Press.

Koch, H. W. (1978) *A History of Prussia*, New York: Dorset.

Koch, Klaus (1984) *Franz Graf Crenneville*, Vienna: Bundesverlag.

Kohut, Thomas A. (1991) *Wilhelm II and the Germans*, New York: Oxford University Press.

Koistinen, Paul A. C. (1997) *Mobilizing for Modern War*, Lawrence: University Press of Kansas.

Kolb, Eberhard (ed.) (1987) *Europa vor dem Krieg von 1870*, Munich: Oldenbourg.

Kupchan, Charles A (1994) *The Vulnerability of Empire*, Ithaca: Cornell University Press.

LaFeber, Walter (1998) [1963] *The New Empire*, Ithaca: Cornell University Press.

Lambert, Andrew (1990) *The Crimean War*, Manchester: Manchester University Press.

Lambi, Ivo (1984) *The Navy and German Power Politics, 1862–1914*, Boston: Allen & Unwin.

Langdon, John W. (1991) *July 1914: The Long Debate 1918–1990*, New York: Berg.

Langer, William L. (1969) *Political and Social Upheaval, 1832–52*, New York: Harper.

LeDonne, John P. (1997) *The Russian Empire and the World, 1700–1917*, Oxford: Oxford University Press.

Lewis, David L. (1988) *The Race to Fashoda*, New York: Weidenfeld and Nicolson.

Lewis, William Roger (ed.) (1976) *Imperialism: The Robinson and Gallagher Controversy*, New York: Franklin Watts.

Liddell Hart, B. H. (1964) [1930] *The Real War, 1914–18*, Boston: Little, Brown.

—— (1967) *Strategy*, 2nd edn, London: Meridian.

Lieven, D. C. B. (1983) *Russia and the Origins of the First World War*, New York: St Martin's Press.

—— (1993) *Nicholas II: Twilight of the Empire*, New York: St Martin's Press.

Lincoln, Bruce (1978) *Nicholas I*, Bloomington: Indiana University Press.

Littauer, Vladimir (1993) [1965] *Russian Hussar*, Shippensburg: White Mane.

Love, Robert (1992) *History of the US Navy*, 2 vols, Harrisburg: Stackpole.

Lowe, John (1994) *The Great Powers, Imperialism, and the German Problem, 1865–1925*, London: Routledge.

Luvaas, Jay (1959) *The Military Legacy of the Civil War*, Chicago: University of Chicago Press.

Lyons, Martyn (1995) *Napoleon Bonaparte and the Legacy of the French Revolution*, New York: St Martin's Press: 1995.

McElwee, William (1974) *The Art of War from Waterloo to Mons*, Bloomington: Indiana University Press.

Macfie, A. L. (1998) *The End of the Ottoman Empire, 1908–23*, London: Longman.

McGuffie, T. H. (ed.) (1966) *Rank and File: The Common Soldier at Peace and War, 1642–1914*. New York: St Martin's Press.

Mack Smith, Denis (1989) *Italy and its Monarchy*, New Haven: Yale University Press.

McMillan, James F. (1991) *Napoleon III*, London: Longman.

McNeill, William H. (1982) *The Pursuit of Power: Technology, Armed Force, and Society since AD 1000*, Chicago: University of Chicago Press.

McPherson, James M. (1988) *Battle Cry of Freedom: The Civil War Era*, Oxford: Oxford University Press.

MacRory, Patrick (1966) *Signal Catastrophe: The Story of the Disastrous Retreat from Kabul, 1842*, London: Hodder & Stoughton.

Mahan, A. T. (1898–1902) *The Influence of Sea Power upon the French Revolution and Empire, 1793–1812*, 2 vols, Boston: Little, Brown.

—— (1899) *Lessons of the War with Spain*, Boston: Little, Brown.

—— (1900) *The Problem of Asia*, Boston: Little, Brown.

—— (1987) [1890] *The Influence of Sea Power upon History, 1660–1783*, New York: Dover.

Malozemoff, Andrew (1958) *Russian Far Eastern Policy, 1881–1904*, Berkeley: University of California Press.

Mansergh, Nicholas (1949) *The Coming of the First World War: A Study in the European Balance, 1878–1914*, London: Longmans Green.

Marder, Arthur J. (1961–70) *From the Dreadnought to Scapa Flow*, 5 vols, Oxford: Oxford University Press.

Marks, Steven G. (1991) *Road to Power: The Trans-Siberian Railroad and the Colonization of Asian Russia, 1850–1917*, Ithaca: Cornell University Press.

Marx, Karl (1969) [1852] *The Eighteenth Brumaire of Louis Bonaparte*, New York: International Publishers.

Massie, Robert K. (1991) *Dreadnought*, New York: Random House.

Mayer, Arno J. (1981) *The Persistence of the Old Regime: Europe to the Great War*, New York: Pantheon.

Menning, Bruce W. (1992) *Bayonets before Bullets: The Imperial Russian Army, 1861–1914*, Bloomington: Indiana University Press.

Mercer, General Cavalié (1985) [1870] *Journal of the Waterloo Campaign*, London: Greenhill Books.

Miller, Steven (ed.) (1985) *Military Strategy and the Origins of the First World War*, Princeton: Princeton University Press.

Mitchell, Allan (1979) *Bismarck and the French Nation, 1848–1890*, New York: Pegasus.

Moltke, Helmuth von (1988) [1892] *The Franco-German War of 1870–71*, New York: Howard Fertig.

Mommsen, Wolfgang J. (1980) *Theories of Imperialism*, New York: Random House.

Moncure, John (1993) *Forging the King's Sword: Military Education between Tradition and Modernization – The Case of the Royal Prussian Cadet Corps, 1871–1918*, New York: Peter Lang.

Montaudon, Jean-Baptiste (1898) *Souvenirs Militaires*, 2 vols, Paris: Delagrave.

Morgan, H. Wayne (1965) *America's Road to Empire*, New York: Wiley.

Morris, A. J. M. (1984) *The Scaremongers*, London: Routledge.

Mosse, W. E. (1958) *The European Powers and the German Question, 1848–71*, Cambridge: Cambridge University Press.

Muir, Rory (1996) *Britain and the Defeat of Napoleon, 1807–15*, New Haven: Yale University Press.

—— (1998) *Tactics and the Experience of Battle in the Age of Napoleon*, New Haven: Yale University Press.

Musicant, Ivan (1998) *Empire by Default: The Spanish-American War and the Dawn of the American Century*, New York: Henry Holt.

Musil, Lt Col (1868) 'Über die Mitrailleuse und den Einfluss der verbesserten Feuerwaffen auf das Heerwesen', *Österreichische Militärische Zeitschrift*, vol. 9: 98.

Myerly, Scott Hughes (1996) *British Military Spectacle: From the Napoleonic Wars through the Crimea*, Cambridge MA: Harvard University Press.

Nicolson, Harold (1974) [1946] *The Congress of Vienna: A Study in Allied Unity, 1812–22*, New York: Harvest.

Nish, Ian (1985) *The Origins of the Russo-Japanese War*, London: Longman.

Nofi, Albert A. (1993) *The Waterloo Campaign, June 1815*, Mechanicsburg: Combined.

Nosinich, Johann (1872) 'Der Krieg 1870–71', *Österreichische Militärische Zeitschrift*, vol. 13: 155–6.

—— 'Der Krieg 1870–71', *Österreichische Militärische Zeitschrift*, vol. 13: 157.

Notestein, Wallace (ed.) (1918) *Conquest and Kultur: Aims of the Germans in Their Own Words*, Washington: Committee on Public Information.

O'Connor, Maureen P. (1997) 'The vision of soldiers: Britain, France, Germany and the United States observe the Russo-Turkish War', *War in History*, vol. 4: 264–95.

Offner, John L. (1992) *An Unwanted War*, Chapel Hill: University of North Carolina Press.

Österreichische Militärische Zeitschrift (1868) 'Urteile über den Preussischen Feldzug 1866', vol. 9: 188–9.

—— (1869) 'Die Süddeutsche Heere', vol. 10: 161.

—— (1871a) 'Die Eisenbahnen im Deutsch-Französischen Kriege, 1870', vol. 12: 191–4.

—— (1871b) 'Der Krieg von 1870–71', vol. 12: 239–41.

—— (1874) 'General Heinrich Antonowitsch Leer über den Krieg 1870–71', vol. 15: 41–3.

Palmer, Alan (1992) *The Decline and Fall of the Ottoman Empire*, London: Campbell Thompson.

—— (1994) [1987] *The Crimean War*, New York: Dorset.

Palmer, R. R. (1971) *The World of the French Revolution*, New York: Harper.

Paret, Peter (ed.) (1986) *Makers of Modern Strategy: From Machiavelli to the Nuclear Age*, Princeton: Princeton University Press.

Parker, Geoffrey (1988) *The Military Revolution: Military Innovation and the Rise of the West, 1500–1800*, Cambridge: Cambridge University Press.

Parker, Geoffrey (ed.) (1995) *Warfare: The Triumph of the West*, Cambridge: Cambridge University Press.

Patterson, James T. (1989) *America in the 20th Century*, New York: Harcourt Brace.

Pemsel, Helmut (1975) *A History of War at Sea*, Annapolis: Naval Institute Press.

Pflanze, Otto (1990) *Bismarck and the Development of Germany*, 3 vols, Princeton: Princeton University Press.

Philpott, William James (1996) *Anglo-French Relations and Strategy on the Western Front, 1914–18*, New York: St Martin's Press.

Pick, Daniel (1993) *War Machine*, New Haven: Yale University Press.

Pinkney, David H. (1986) *Decisive Years in France, 1840–47*, Princeton: Princeton University Press.

Porch, Douglas (1974) *Army and Revolution: France, 1815–48*, London: Routledge.

—— (1981) *The March to the Marne: The French Army, 1871–1914*, Cambridge: Cambridge University Press.

—— (1991) *The French Foreign Legion*, New York: Harper Collins.

Price, Roger (1989) *The Revolutions of 1848*, Atlantic Highlands: Humanities Press International.

—— (1997) *Napoleon III and the Second Empire*, London: Routledge.

Ralston, David B. (1990) *Importing the European Army*, Chicago: University of Chicago Press.

Rauchensteiner, Manfried (1994) *Der Tod des Doppeladlers*, Graz: Verlag Styria.

Rémond, René (1969) [1954] *The Right Wing in France: From 1815 to de Gaulle*, trans. James Laux, Philadelphia: University of Pennsylvania Press.

Riall, Lucy (1994) *The Italian Risorgimento: State, Society and National Unification*, London: Routledge.

Rich, David A. (1998) *The Tsar's Colonels*, Cambridge, MA: Harvard University Press.

Rich, Norman (1977) *The Age of Nationalism and Reform, 1850–1890*, New York: Norton.

—— (1985) *Why the Crimean War? A Cautionary Tale*, Hanover, CT: University Press of New England.

Roosevelt, Theodore (1937) *Colonial Policies of the United States*, New York: Doubleday.

Ropp, Theodore (1959) *War in the Modern World*, Durham, NC: Duke University Press.

Ross, Steven T. (1979) *Quest for Victory: French Military Strategy 1792–1799*, South Brunswick: A. S. Barnes.

Rothenberg, Gunther E. (1976) *The Army of Francis Joseph*, West Lafayette: Purdue University Press.

—— (1978) *The Art of Warfare in the Age of Napoleon*, Bloomington: Indiana University Press.

—— (1982) *Napoleon's Great Adversaries: The Archduke Charles and the Austrian Army, 1792–1814*, Bloomington: Indiana University Press.

Sakurai, Tadayoshi (1907) *Human Bullets*, Boston: Houghton Mifflin.

Sauvigny, Guillaume de Bertier de (1966) *The Bourbon Restoration*, trans. Lynn M. Case, Philadelphia: University of Pennsylvania Press.

Schmedes, Ernst (1871) 'Die Taktik der Preussen', *Österreichische Militärische Zeitschrift*, vol. 12: 194–6.

Schmidt-Brentano, Antonio (1975) *Die Armee in Österreich: Militär, Staat und Gesellschaft, 1848–67*, Boppard: Harald Boldt.

Schom, Alan (1992) *One Hundred Days*, New York: Oxford University Press.

Schoonover, Thomas (1998) *Germany in Central America*, Tuscaloosa: University of Alabama Press.

Schroeder, Paul W. (1994) *The Transformation of European Politics, 1763–1848*, Oxford: Clarendon Press.

Seton-Watson, R. W. (1917) *The Rise of Nationality in the Balkans*, London: Constable.

Sheehan, James J. (1989) *German History, 1770–1866*, Oxford: Oxford University Press.

Showalter, Dennis E. (1975) *Railroads and Rifles*, Hamden: Archon.

—— (1991) *Tannenberg*, Hamden: Archon.

—— (1996) *The Wars of Frederick the Great*, London: Longman.

Shulman, Mark R. (1995) *Navalism and the Emergence of American Sea Power, 1882–1893*, Annapolis: Naval Institute Press.

Sked, Alan (1979) *The Survival of the Habsburg Empire: Radetzky, the Imperial Army and the Class War, 1848*, London: Longman.

—— (1989) *The Decline and Fall of the Habsburg Empire, 1815–1918*, London: Longman.

Smith, Iain R. (1996) *The Origins of the South African War, 1899–1902*, London: Longman.

Smith, Joseph (1994) *The Spanish-American War: Conflict in the Caribbean and the Pacific, 1895–1902*, London: Longman.

Snyder, Jack (1984) *The Ideology of the Offensive*, Ithaca: Cornell University Press.

—— (1991) *Myths of Empire: Domestic Politics and International Ambition*, Ithaca: Cornell University Press.

Sondhaus, Lawrence (1989) *The Habsburg Empire and the Sea*, W. Lafayette, Purdue.

Stargardt, Nicholas (1994) *The German Idea of Militarism: Radical and Socialist Critics, 1866–1914*, Cambridge: Cambridge University Press.

Steiner, Zara (1977) *Britain and the Origins of the First World War*, New York: St Martin's Press.

Stern, Fritz (1979) [1977] *Gold and Iron*, New York: Vintage.

Stevenson, David (1982) *French War Aims against Germany, 1914–19*, Oxford: Clarendon Press.

—— (1996) *Armaments and the Coming of War: Europe, 1904–14*, Oxford: Clarendon Press.

—— (1997) *The Outbreak of the First World War*, New York: St Martin's Press.

Stone, Norman (1975) *The Eastern Front, 1914–17*, London: Hodder & Stoughton.

—— (1999) *Europe Transformed, 1878–1919*, 2nd edn, Oxford: Blackwell.

Storry, Richard (1979) *Japan and the Decline of the West in Asia, 1894–1943*, New York: St Martin's Press.

Strachan, Hew (1983) *European Armies and the Conduct of War*, London: George Allen & Unwin.

—— (1984) *Wellington's Legacy: The Reform of the British Army, 1830–54*, Manchester: Manchester University Press.

—— (1985) *From Waterloo to Balaclava: Tactics, Technology, and the British Army, 1815–54.* Cambridge: Cambridge University Press.

Strachan, Hew (ed.) (1998) *The First World War*, Oxford: Oxford University Press.

Sulzbach, Herbert (1981) *With the German Guns*, Hamden: Archon.

Sumida, John Tetsuro (1989) *In Defence of Naval Supremacy: Finance, Technology and British Naval Policy, 1889–1914*, London: Routledge.

Taylor, A. J. P. (1946) *The Course of German History*, New York: Capricorn.

—— (1967) *Germany's First Bid for Colonies, 1884–85*, Hamden: Archon.

—— (1969) *War by Time-Table: How the First World War Began*, London: Macdonald.

—— (1987) [1954] *The Struggle for Mastery in Europe, 1848–1918* Oxford, Oxford University Press.

—— (1988) [1948] *The Habsburg Monarchy, 1809–1918*, London: Pelican.

Thomas, Hugh (1997) *The Slave Trade*, New York: Simon & Schuster.

Thomas, J. E. (1996) *Modern Japan*, London: Longman.

Tolstoy, Leo (n.d.) [1855], *Sebastopol*, London: Greening's.

Tone, John Lawrence (1994) *The Fatal Knot*, Chapel Hill: University of North Carolina Press.

Townsend, Mary Evelyn (1941) *European Colonial Expansion since 1871*, Philadelphia: Lippincott.

Trachtenberg, Marc (1991) *History and Strategy*, Princeton: Princeton University Press.

Trask, David F. (1981) *The War with Spain in 1898*, New York: Macmillan.

Travers, Tim (1987) *The Killing Ground*, London: Routledge.

Truesdell, Matthew (1997) *Spectacular Politics: Louis-Napoleon Bonaparte and the* Fête Impériale, *1849–1870*, Oxford: Oxford University Press.

Tucker, Spencer C. (1998) *The Great War, 1914–18*, London: UCL Press.

Tunstall, Graydon A. (1993) *Planning for War against Russia and Serbia*, Boulder: Social Science Monographs.

Turner, Gordon B. (ed.) (1956) *A History of Military Affairs since the Eighteenth Century*, New York: Harcourt Brace.

Twain, Mark (1996) *Following the Equator and Anti-imperialist Essays*, Oxford: Oxford University Press.

Van Creveld, Martin (1985) *Command in War*, Cambridge, MA: Harvard University Press.

—— (1989) *Technology and War: From 2000 BC to the Present*, New York: Free Press.

Vandam, Albert (1897) *Undercurrents of the Second Empire*, London: Heinemann.

Vandervort, Bruce (1998) *Wars of Imperial Conquest in Africa, 1830–1914*, London: UCL Press.

Verner, Andrew (1992) *The Crisis of Russian Autocracy*, Princeton: Princeton University Press.

Vigny, Alfred de (1964) [1835] *The Military Condition*, trans. Marguerite Barnett, Oxford: Oxford University Press.

Waldersee, Alfred Graf von (1922) *Denkwürdigkeiten*, 3 vols, Stuttgart: Verlagsanstalt.

Walter, Jakob (1991) *The Diary of a Napoleonic Foot Soldier*, New York: Doubleday.

Warner, Denis and Warner, Peggy (1974) *The Tide at Sunrise*, New York: Charterhouse.

Wawro, Geoffrey (1992) 'The Austro-Prussian War: politics, strategy and war in the Habsburg monarchy, 1859–66', Ph.D. dissertation, Yale University, 716.

—— (1995a) 'An "Army of Pigs": the technical, social, and political bases of Austrian shock tactics, 1859–1866', *The Journal of Military History*, vol. 59: 407–34.

—— (1995b) 'The Habsburg *Flucht nach Vorne* in 1866: domestic political origins of the Austro-Prussian War', *The International History Review*, vol. 17: 221–48.

—— (1996a) *The Austro-Prussian War: Austria's War with Prussia and Italy in 1866*, Cambridge: Cambridge University Press.

—— (1996b) 'Austria versus the Risorgimento: a new look at Austria's Italian strategy in the 1860s', *European History Quarterly*, vol. 26: 7–29.

—— (1996c) 'Inside the whale: the tangled finances of the Austrian Army, 1848–1866', *War in History*, vol. 3: 42–65.

Weber, Eugen (1976) *Peasants into Frenchmen*, Stanford: Stanford University Press.

Wehler, Hans-Ulrich (1991) [1973] *The German Empire, 1871–1918*, New York: Berg.

Weigley, Russell F. (1984) [1967] *History of the United States Army*, Bloomington: Indiana University Press.

Weller, Jac (1966) *Weapons and Tactics*, New York: St Martin's Press.

Wellesley, F. A. (1904) *With the Russians in Peace and War*, London: Nash.

White, Jonathan R. (1996) *The Prussian Army, 1640–1871*, Lanham: University Press of America.

Whittam, John (1977) *The Politics of the Italian Army, 1861–1918*, Hamden: Archon.

Wilkerson, Marcus (1932) *Public Opinion and the Spanish-American War*, New York: Russell & Russell.

Willems, Emilio (1986) *A Way of Life and Death: Three Centuries of Prussian-German Militarism – an Anthropological Approach*, Nashville: Vanderbilt University Press.

Williamson, Samuel R. (1969) *The Politics of Grand Strategy: Britain and France prepare for War, 1904–14*, Cambridge, MA: Harvard University Press.

—— (1991) *Austria-Hungary and the Origins of the First World War*, New York: St Martin's Press.

Wilson, Keith (ed.) (1995) *Decisions for War, 1914*, New York: St Martin's Press.

Winter, Denis (1991) *Haig's Command*, New York: Viking.

Wohl, Robert (1979) *The Generation of 1914*, Cambridge, MA: Harvard University Press.

Woodward, David R. (1998) *Field Marshal Sir William Robertson*, Westport: Praeger.

Woolf, Stuart (1979) *A History of Italy, 1700–1860*, London: Routledge.

Wright, Harrison M. (1976) *The 'New Imperialism': Analysis of Late-19th Century Expansion*, 2nd edn, Lexington: D. C. Heath.

Zabecki, David T. (1994) *Steel Wind*, Westport: Praeger.

Zeldin, Theodore (1970) *Conflicts in French Society*, London: Allen & Unwin.

Zorzi, Alvise (1985) *Venezia Austriaca, 1798–1866*, Rome: Laterza.

Index